GUARANTEE

This book belongs to:

_____

_____

Price $13.50

It is GUARANTEED right in price. edition, condition and course *through the first two weeks of the quarter. Guarantee void if this slip is altered or removed.*

DuBOIS BOOK STORE
TRY US FIRST FOR ANY BOOK
332 S. Lincoln, Kent, 673-4730
Yours for lower cost of higher education

PROGRAMMING ASSEMBLER LANGUAGE

PROGRAMMING ASSEMBLER LANGUAGE

Peter Abel

British Columbia Institute of Technology

RESTON PUBLISHING COMPANY, INC.
Reston, Virginia
A Prentice-Hall Company

Library of Congress Cataloging in Publication Data

Abel, Peter
   Programming assembler language.

   Includes index.
   1. Assembler language (Computer program language)
2. IBM 360 (Computer)—Programming.   3. IBM 370
(Computer)—Programming.   I. Title.
QA76.73.A8A23   001.6'424   79-255
ISBN 0-8359-5658-X

© 1979 by
Reston Publishing Company, Inc.
A Prentice-Hall Company
Reston, Virginia 22090

10   9   8   7   6   5   4   3   2   1

Printed in the United States of America.

CONTENTS

PART II   BASIC ASSEMBLER CODING

APPENDICES

PREFACE

Assembler language is the fundamental "low-level" language of the IBM 360 and 370 computers. As such, it is directly translatable into machine language; thus, one Assembler instruction typically generates one machine code instruction. "High-level" languages like COBOL and PL/I are easier to learn. Why then an emphasis on learning Assembler language? An understanding of Assembler language can help the programmer in a number of ways:

— A knowledge of Assembler can facilitate learning of any other language, including "high-level" languages and other assembly languages. And with a background in Assembler, the user can more clearly understand what the computer is doing.
— A knowledge of Assembler can help the programmer become more efficient. High-level languages like COBOL and PL/I can be deceptive, and appear to execute in some mysterious fashion. A programmer familiar with Assembler can code high-level languages with an understanding of what machine code they generate, and what is the more efficient technique. For example, why in COBOL does the use of COMPUTATIONAL, COMPUTATIONAL-3, and SYNC have considerable effect on the program's efficiency? What is the significance in PL/I of Decimal Fixed, Aligned, and Defined? With knowledge of Assembler, a programmer can examine the generated code to determine more efficient ways to write certain routines.
— Although most high-level languages provide extensive debugging aids, there are times when the programmer needs to delve into the generated machine code or examine storage dumps.
— Programs written in Assembler may be considerably more efficient in storage space and execute-time, a useful consideration if such programs are run frequently.
— Some advanced areas, such as technical support and telecommunications, require an extensive knowledge of Assembler.

Although the material in this text has been used successfully as an introduction to programming, most educational institutes would not teach Assembler as an introductory language. Generally, the concepts of logic and programming style are easier to learn when there is less need for concern with rigorous rules and field sizes. The text does not, however, assume that the reader has had much, if any, programming experience. The approach of the text is to introduce simple processing using card input and printer output, first with character data only, and then with simple decimal arithmetic, all by Chapter 4. In this way, packed (decimal) data and editing are introduced early, and the user is soon writing quite realistic programs.

The book should provide both a practical guide for the Assembler student and also may act subsequently as a useful reference. These two objectives are accomplished by:

1. A step-by-step progression of material, from simple processing through to complex. There are many practical examples of complete and partial programs to illustrate concepts as they are introduced.
2. Chapters organized by logical topics, such as character data, packed, binary, input/output. The user can concentrate on mastering one programming area at a time, and most related material is contained in its own chapter.

The complexities of base/displacement addressing and file definition are delayed through use of several simple macros, similar to those used in many colleges. The text drops these macros by Chapters 6 and 7, where the technical material is covered in detail. Appendix E provides a listing of the macros for those who want to catalogue them on their own system.

The two major IBM operating systems are DOS and OS. The text covers the differences between them, giving examples for both.

It is possible to proceed through the text by several routes. Chapters 0 through 3 are fundamental, and the normal steps would be to continue sequentially with decimal arithmetic in Chapters 4 and 5. It is recommended next to cover the important material in Chapter 6 on base/displacement addressing and the instruction format, and then the elements of input/output in Chapter 7. By this point the user should be capable of coding some quite advanced programs. Chapter 8 on Programming Strategy could be covered in part or total, perhaps the sooner the better to get the user into subroutine logic. Following Chapter 8, the chapters need not all be covered sequentially. The following diagram indicates related chapters in boxes that may be taken in any sequence following Chapters 6 and 7:

Chapters 9, 10, and 11 develop related material on processing binary data. Chapter 12 on Magnetic Tape introduces basic material required for an understanding of Disk Storage in Chapter 13. To complete Chapter 14 (Macro Writing) would require some familiarity with the material in Chapter 9. Anyone interested in linking separately assembled programs could attempt Chapter 15 directly after Chapter 7, perhaps referencing Chapter 9 for some basic binary operations. Chapter 16 on Operating Systems is presented for general useful information, although not entirely related to Assembler programming as such.

Among the users of earlier versions of this text, many have worked ahead of the course, experimenting with binary operations, macro writing, and subprogram linkage. Such motivation is certainly commendable and should be encouraged.

The IBM manuals concerned with the material in this text require a bookshelf about five feet wide. Readers should not expect, therefore, that this or any other single book will provide all there is to know about the Assembler language and related topics. Eventually the IBM manuals have to be referenced for current detailed information. The following IBM manuals or their equivalent are especially recommended:

IBM FORM	TITLE
GA22-7000	IBM System/370 Principles of Operation. (370 system organization, machine instructions, input/output.)
GC33-4010	OS/VS-DOS/VS-VM/370 Assembler Language. (Assembler statements and macros.)
GC33-5373	DOS/VS Supervisor and Input/Output Macros.
GC28-6646	OS Supervisor Services and Macro Instructions.
GC26-3746	OS Data Management Services Guide.
GC26-3794	OS Data Management Macro Instructions.

Other useful manuals include those on Job Control, disk file organization, tape labels, disk labels, and the operating system.

Peter Abel

ACKNOWLEDGMENT

The author is grateful for the assistance from all those who contributed typing, reviews, and suggestions, and to IBM for permission to reproduce some of their copyrighted materials. The following materials are printed with permission, and with modifications from publications copyrighted in 1966, 1970, 1972, 1973, and 1974 by International Business Machines Corporation as IBM form numbers GA22-7000, GX20-1850 and GC20-1649: Figures 2-2, 13-2, 16-3, Appendix A, and Appendix C.

PART I

INTRODUCTION TO THE COMPUTER AND THE ASSEMBLER

CHAPTER 0

BASIC COMPUTER CONCEPTS

INTRODUCTION

This chapter discusses computer concepts and systems in general terms, then introduces basic technical detail concerned specifically with the 360 and 370 computers. The three main areas are general computer systems, binary number system, and 360/370 organization.

The first generation of computers was introduced in the early 1950s. These computers were characterized by many vacuum tubes and relatively slow processing speed. The second generation, introduced in 1957–1958, used transistorized circuitry that permitted smaller size, higher speed storage, and lower costs. Finally, the third generation computers, introduced in the early 1960s, replaced the transistorized computers with integrated circuits. These computers featured higher speeds, greater storage capacity, and more facilities.

IBM introduced System/360, a third generation computer, in 1964 to replace and to improve upon a variety of then existing IBM computers. Some had been specialized for business applications, others for scientific purposes. The 360 provided a single computer designed to serve effectively in both fields. The 360 (and computers of other manufacturers) provided many other advantages over the second generation computers. First, its performance was considerably faster. Second, it had a greater size and capacity for performing more functions. These characteristics enabled the computer to handle larger and more complex applications. Finally, the 360 had the ability to expand. IBM adopted a building block concept to enable the user to increase the size of computer storage without always requiring a different computer. Similarly, because the programming languages were standardized for 360 models, little reprogramming was required when transferring to a larger system.

An important feature of the 360 (and of many other computers) was its supervisor capability. It contained a *control program* that permitted error recovery, storing of programs and data on disk storage or magnetic tape for subsequent processing, continuous job processing with limited operator intervention, and multiprogramming (concurrent processing of several data processing jobs).

In 1970 IBM introduced System/370 with significant improvement in computing performance over the 360. Although the 370 has some additional instructions and capabilities, it was designed for compatibility with the 360, with the same languages and control programs. This text covers differences where applicable.

In 1977, the 370 was further extended into a more complex processor system: the 3031, 3032, and 3033. In 1979, IBM announced the 4300 series. Through all the various improvements, the basic Assembler language remains the same.

THE COMPUTER SYSTEM

Although computers have evolved radically since the 1940s, and although there are many manufacturers and models, their basic structure remains the same. Figure 0-1 illustrates the four main components: input/output, storage, arithmetic/logic, and control. Arithmetic/logic and control together form what is called the *Central Processing Unit (CPU)*.

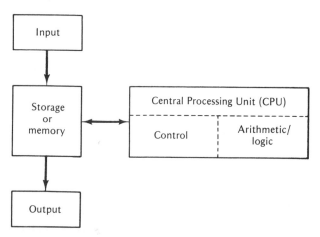

FIGURE 0-1   Basic computer components.

INPUT/OUTPUT.   The computer must be able to access new data. The computer "reads" data into its storage from such input devices as card readers and magnetic tape. Also, because the computer must communicate its results to the user, it "writes" data from storage onto such devices as printers and tape.

STORAGE, OR MEMORY.   We write a program using computer instructions to solve a specific problem. The program consists of *instructions* (such as read, add, and compare) and *data* (numbers used in calculations, and areas to develop answers and to read input data). The·instructions and data area may be on punched cards which are read (loaded) into the computer storage. This program in storage is the *stored program* that reads input data, makes calculations, and writes output according to the program instructions. Another program loaded in storage can replace the previous program to work on a different problem and data. Figure 0-2 depicts a layout of instructions and data areas.

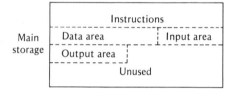

Areas may be anywhere in storage, in any sequence.

FIGURE 0-2   Simplified map of main storage.

The size of storage varies considerably by computer model, from as little as a few thousand storage positions to millions. Storage size in an installation depends generally on the volume of data and the complexity of the problems. Each storage location is numbered, the first position being zero, the second number one, etc. An instruction may require only a few locations. An area for data may require from one position to hundreds.

Here is a simple example using an imaginary computer. We are to add the number '005' to '125'. Assume the '005' is in locations 1338, 1339, and 1340, and that the '125' is in locations 1263, 1264, and 1265:

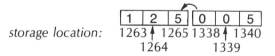

storage location: 1263 ↑ 1265 1338 ↑ 1340
                            1264   1339

Assume that an add operation is the letter 'A'. The instruction to add the *contents* of locations 1338-1340 to the *contents* of locations 1263-1265 could be:
$\boxed{A \mid 1 \quad 2 \quad 6 \quad 3 \mid 1 \quad 3 \quad 3 \quad 8}$. (The 360/370 work similarly to this.) Locations 1263-1265 now contain '130'. Locations 1338-1340 still contain '005', unchanged by the add operation. This instruction would itself require nine storage locations consisting of three parts. A is the *operation,* telling the computer what function

to perform; '1263' and '1338' are respectively *operand-1* and *operand-2* that specify which storage positions to process.

CENTRAL PROCESSING UNIT.

ARITHMETIC/LOGIC.   In order to solve problems, the computer must be able to perform arithmetic and make decisions.

ARITHMETIC.   Computers add and subtract, and most can multiply and divide. With these basic functions, the computer can be programmed to perform, for example, square roots, trigonometric functions, and calculus.

LOGIC.   A program generally must make tests and comparisons. For example, does a divisor have a zero value? If so, then a division cannot be performed. Is a value negative? If so, we cannot calculate its square root. Similarly, we may have to check if a value is greater than, less than, or equal to another. The ability to make such decisions is the computer logic.

CONTROL.   The computer requires a component to control its actions. The control device that performs this function does the following:

— Causes the computer to execute each instruction in the stored program, step-by-step. Typically, each instruction is stored and executed one after another, such as "Read", "Add", "Move", "Print".
— Involves control of the input/output devices.
— Handles the transfer of data between storage positions.
— Handles the transfer of data between storage and arithmetic/logic.

The time required to transfer data is known as *access time*. Access time is measured in thousandths of a second, millionths (microseconds), or even billionths (nanoseconds). The number and type of input/output devices, the size of storage, the type and complexity of arithmetic/logic circuitry, and the access time vary considerably by computer model.

INPUT/OUTPUT DEVICES

There are many types of input/output devices, of various capacities and speeds. This section discusses the two basic common ones, the card reader and the printer. Later chapters cover magnetic tape and disk storage devices.

THE PUNCHED CARD.   A common source of input data is the punched card. The card represents data by means of small rectangular holes punched by a keypunch machine. The holes in the card, when read by a card reader, are translated into electrical impulses and transferred into storage.

The punched card normally has 80 vertical *columns* (numbered columns 1 through 80) for storing data. (Other systems may use different card sizes.) Each column represents one character of data by means of the punched holes in any of its twelve horizontal *rows*. The rows are numbered as in Figure 0-3. Digits 0 through 9 are punched as a single hole, from row 0 through row 9. Alphabetic and special characters are punched with multiple holes: the 0–9 *numeric* rows and the *zone* rows, 10, 11 and 12. (Note that the numeric row 0 is the same as zone row 10.) For example, the letter A in column 16 consists of zone 12 and numeric 1.

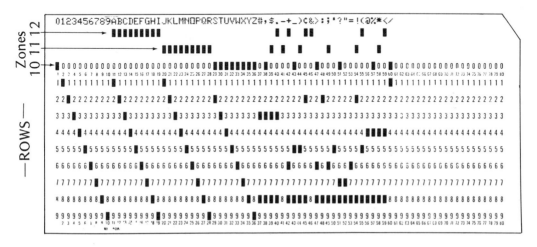

FIGURE 0-3 Punched cards featuring keypunch codes.

A *field* is one or more related columns. A *record* consists of one or more fields. The card itself is a record of data, and may be subdivided into fields. Some fields contain *alphabetic* data, such as customer name. Other fields contain *numeric* data, such as an invoice amount. (A field such as address may contain *alphameric* data, mixed alphabetic and numeric.) Not all card columns need be defined or punched. Fields may contain subfields: a date field could contain subfields month, day, and year.

A minus sign indicates that a field has a negative value. In data processing, the minus sign is usually an 11-zone punch over the units position of the amount field. For example, if an amount field in columns 63–67 is minus, we punch an 11-zone in column 67.

The punched card serves two main purposes:

1. To record *programs*.
2. To record *data*. Information for data processing is supplied to the keypunch department on *source documents*. Examples are customer payments, sales, and employee hours worked. These data are punched according to a predesigned card format. The cards are then submitted as input to the computer department for processing.

A group of records (card, tape, or disk) that contains related information is called a *file,* or *data set.*

THE PRINTER.   There are many different types of printers, but all have certain common features. They print at speeds ranging from a few hundred to several thousand lines per minute. Many can print 60 or more different characters, including the numbers 0 through 9, letters A through Z, and various characters such as $, #, *, and +. Typical printers print 10 characters to the inch, and 120, 132, or 160 characters on a line.

The paper used for printing is called *continuous forms.* The forms are perforated horizontally so that each sheet may be separated after printing. Manufacturers supply the forms in various widths, such as 11" and 15", and lengths such as 8½". This length at six lines per inch permits up to 60 lines of print per page. It is available in single-part, or, with carbon inserts, two or more parts. The forms may be pre-printed according to the user's design (e.g., customer bills), or they may contain only horizontal lines or bars (*"stock tab"* forms or *"continuous printout"*).

BINARY NUMBER SYSTEM

Binary numbers provide the basic numbering system of computers. Whereas a decimal (base 10) number has ten digits, a binary (base 2) number has two: 0 and 1. For both decimal and binary, the position of the digit determines the value. Consider the decimal number 1111:

$$\text{decimal } 1111$$
$$= (1 \times 10^3) + (1 \times 10^2) + (1 \times 10^1) + (1 \times 10^0)$$
$$= \quad 1000 \quad + \quad 100 \quad + \quad 10 \quad + \quad 1$$

Whereas a decimal number uses the base of ten, a binary number uses the base of two. Consider the same number, 1111, this time expressed as binary:

$$\text{binary } 1111$$
$$= \text{decimal } (1 \times 2^3) + (1 \times 2^2) + (1 \times 2^1) + (1 \times 2^0)$$
$$= \qquad\qquad 8 \quad + \quad 4 \quad + \quad 2 \quad + \quad 1 \quad = 15 \text{ (or } 2^4 - 1)$$

As another example, the value of the decimal number 1010 is determined as:

$$\text{decimal } 1010$$
$$= (1 \times 10^3) + (0 \times 10^2) + (1 \times 10^1) + (0 \times 10^0)$$
$$= \quad 1000 \quad + \quad 0 \quad + \quad 10 \quad + \quad 0$$

A decimal digit zero as shown has no value, nor has a binary digit zero. The number 1010 expressed in binary is:

binary 1010

$= $ decimal $(1\times2^3) + (0\times2^2) + (1\times2^1) + (0\times2^0)$

$=$ 8   +   0   +   2   +   0 $= 10$ (decimal)

Through the use of digits 0 and 1, binary numbers can represent any decimal value. For example, the binary number 101101 equals:

$$2^5 + 0^4 + 2^3 + 2^2 + 0^1 + 2^0$$

$$= \text{decimal } 32 + 0 + 8 + 4 + 0 + 1 = 45$$

A binary value may also have a *binary point,* equivalent to the decimal point. We calculate a binary number with a point such as 101.1101 as:

$$2^2 + 0^1 + 2^0 + 2^{-1} + 2^{-2} + 0^{-3} + 2^{-4}$$

$$= 4 + 0 + 1 + \frac{1}{2^1} + \frac{1}{2^2} + \frac{0}{2^3} + \frac{1}{2^4}$$

$$= 4 + 1 + \frac{1}{2} + \frac{1}{4} + 0 + \frac{1}{16}$$

$$= 5 + .5 + .25 + .0625$$

$$= 5.8125$$

Later chapters cover binary representation and binary arithmetic in detail.

BITS AND BYTES

In computer terminology, a binary digit is called for short a *"bit".* A storage location consists of a specified number of bits, and can be related to binary digits, since a computer bit can be OFF (zero) or ON (one). The number of bits in a storage location varies by computer (the 360 and 370 use nine bits). Assume a storage position that contains five bits. Four bits represent data and the other is a *parity bit:*

In the diagram, each bit is indicated by a '0', with the binary value of the bit above it. Each bit can contain the value 0 or 1, so if the bit numbered 1 on the right is ON, the contents of the byte are 00001, and the value is 1. If only bit 2 (second from the right) is ON, the contents are 00010, and the value is 2. Both bits 1 and 2 ON (00011) represent 3, and combinations of ON bits provide values 1 through 9. All bits OFF means zero.

The bit on the left is the parity bit. The typical storage location must have "odd parity"; the number of bits ON must always be an odd number. For example, the value in a location is 7; bits 4, 2, and 1 are ON. Because this is an odd number of bits, the computer sets the parity bit OFF:

P	8	4	2	1
0	0	1	1	1

value = 7, odd parity

Assume that the value in a location is 9: bits 8 and 1 are ON. To force odd parity, the computer sets the parity bit ON:

P	8	4	2	1
1	1	0	0	1

value = 9, parity bit ON for odd parity

Setting bits ON and OFF is entirely an automatic process over which we have no control. When processing the contents of a location, the computer automatically checks the parity. If the parity is not odd, the computer circuitry may require servicing; the computer signals a warning to the operator and may stop processing.

On the 360/370, the configuration in a storage location (a "byte") is eight data bits and one parity bit. A hardware malfunction such as losing odd parity causes a "machine interrupt", as explained in Chapter 16.

S/360 AND S/370 ORGANIZATION

As Figure 0-1 illustrated, the computer system consists of the following units: the Central Processing Unit (CPU), which contains the arithmetic/logic unit and the control section, input and output devices and facilities, and Main Storage or Memory. In addition, the 360 and 370 have a special unit called *general purpose registers* that serve such purposes as arithmetic and addressing. Most 360s and all 370s have as well *floating-point registers* that perform floating-point arithmetic. Another feature, *Program Status Word (PSW)*, controls the sequence of instructions executed by the program and records the current status of the program. The next sections briefly describe the CPU, Input/Output, Storage, the general registers, and the PSW.

THE CENTRAL PROCESSING UNIT (CPU).   The CPU is the control center of the 360/370 computer system. It consists of two sections: control and arithmetic/logic, and provides facilities for the following features:

1. Addressing of main storage locations.
2. Accessing data from storage and storing data in storage.
3. Arithmetic and logical processing of data.
   — Arithmetic operations (add, subtract, multiply, and divide) can be performed on data in three different formats: ordinary decimal (packed), fixed-point binary, and floating-point. This text covers each format.
   — Logic operations include comparing, testing, translating of characters, and editing (sign and punctuation control).
4. Executing instructions in main storage in the required sequence.
5. Initiating communications between main storage and the input/output (I/O) devices.

INPUT AND OUTPUT (I/O) DEVICES.   There are various models of each input/output device, providing different capabilities and I/O speeds. Disk and magnetic tape supply external data storage of practically unlimited capacity. Among the I/O devices that most 360 and 370 models may use are:

DEVICE	INPUT	OUTPUT	TYPICAL USES
Direct Access Storage Devices (Disk & Drum)	X	X	Large external storage of data.
Magnetic Ink Character Readers (MICR)	X		Processing checks in banks.
Magnetic Tape	X	X	Large external storage of data.
Manual Controls (console typewriter)	X	X	Communication between the computer operating system and the human operator.
Optical Readers	X		Reading bills printed by a computer, and cash register tapes.
Printers		X	Printing reports, programs, and diagnostic messages.
Punched Card Devices	X	X	Reading and punching the common punched card.
Visual Display Terminals	X	X	Used to enter data into the computer from a remote location, and to make inquiries.

MAIN STORAGE.   Each 1,024 storage positions is called 1K. Addressable storage varies from a minimum of 8,192 (8K) locations to a maximum of 16,777,216 (16,384K).

BITS.   Storage on the 360 is composed of ring-shaped magnetized ferrite cores, each of which is a bit. The cores may be magnitized clockwise as ON and assigned the value one, or magnetized counterclockwise as OFF and assigned the value zero. Combinations of bits represent the various digits and characters used in computer processing. 370 data is stored in small "chips" called *monolithic* circuits.

BYTES.   The basic building block of main storage is the *byte, which represents a single storage location.* Each byte consists of nine bits. Eight bits represent data. The ninth is the parity bit to ensure odd parity, and is not a programming consideration. The eight data bits are "split" into two portions of four bits (half-bytes), a *zone* and a *numeric* portion:

	Byte	The value represented in a byte varies from zero

Byte

½-byte ½-byte

bits: `0 0 0 0 0 0 0 0`

value: `8 4 2 1 8 4 2 1`

portion: zone   numeric

The value represented in a byte varies from zero (all bits OFF, 0000 0000) through 255 (all bits ON, 1111 1111). The CPU normally executes a program by accessing bytes or groups of bytes.

Bytes serve different purposes and may represent:

1. *Instructions.* A 360/370 instruction is always 2, 4, or 6 bytes, depending on the type of instruction. Every instruction begins on an even-numbered storage location.
2. *Data.* Although some instructions can access bits or half-bytes, we consider the byte the smallest data length. We may define data so that it is represented in bytes in various formats:

Character Format. A character field (such as the letters A through Z, the numbers 1 through 9, and special characters as $ or * or &) requires one byte for each character. The eight bits in a byte can represent 256 (2^8) possible characters. For example, the ON bits 1100 0001 represent the letter A. The character code is called the *"extended binary-coded-decimal-interchange code" (EBCDIC).*

Decimal, or Packed, Format. For ordinary decimal arithmetic, the digits 0 through 9 are *"packed"* two digits per byte. For example, the digits 4 and 7 appear in a byte as the bits 0100 0111. Whereas a character '1' requires a full byte (11110001), a packed digit '1' uses a half-byte (0001).

Binary Format. For binary arithmetic, addressing, and special features, each bit represents a binary 0 or 1. The binary value 01000111 equals the decimal value 71.

Floating-Point Format. Used to represent extremely small or large values.

GENERAL PURPOSE REGISTERS.   The 360 and 370 have 16 general purpose registers (GPR's), numbered 0 through 15. Instead of being part of main storage, they are special circuitry. Each register consists of 32 bits. The two main uses of registers are:

1. Addressing storage positions, by means of "base displacement addressing." Every reference to a location in main storage is by means of a "base address" in a register and a "displacement" from that address.
2. Performing binary arithmetic in the registers, done at extremely high speed.

PROGRAM STATUS WORD (PSW).   The Program Status Word (PSW) is a 64-bit hardware feature in the control section of the CPU. The PSW contains the current status of the computer and controls the sequence of instructions being executed.

One PSW feature important to the programmer is the 2-bit *"condition code"* that indicates the result of an arithmetic test (minus/zero/plus) or a logical comparison (low/equal/high). Another field, the 24-bit *"instruction address"* contains the address of the next instruction to be executed.

OPERATING SYSTEMS AND THE SUPERVISOR

Computer manufacturers supply various programs (software) to support the computer system. These programs include language translators such as Assembler, COBOL, and PL/I, and "utility" programs to facilitate disk and tape processing. Except for the smallest models, the 360 and 370 are supplied with a set of related programs called an *"operating system"* to provide for preparation and execution of the user's programs and to minimize operator intervention. The two major IBM operating systems are Disk Operating System (DOS) for medium-sized users, and Operating System (OS) for large users. The operating system programs are stored on disk (or tape), and the heart of the operating system, the *Supervisor,* is at all times stored in the lower part of the computer's main storage, as indicated in Figure 0-4.

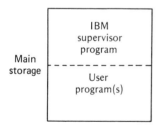

FIGURE 0-4   Supervisor and user programs.

Among the functions of the Supervisor are:

— Determine the sequence in which programs will be executed.
— "Loading" a program into main storage prior to its execution.
— Generally control and coordinate the various programs being executed.
— Handle all input/output operations.
— Provide error message and error recovery where possible.

Both the programmer and the computer operator can request the Supervisor to perform certain actions. For example, if we want the system to "assemble" a program, we can enter a *job control statement* such as //EXEC ASSEMBLY that tells the Supervisor to arrange for the assembling of the program following.

PROGRAM INTERRUPTION.   The Program Status Word contains bits that record the status of the program. Among these conditions are bits to record "program interrupts." An interrupt occurs when our program asks the Supervisor to perform some special task, such as input/output. Basically, our program is "interrupted," and control is passed to the Supervisor program. An interrupt also occurs, for example, when a serious processing error occurs—such as invalid data in an arithmetic operation. The Supervisor may have to "flush" the interrupted program and resume processing with the next job.

HEXADECIMAL REPRESENTATION

A hexadecimal numbering system uses base-16. Hexadecimal (or hex) numbers are 0 through 9 and A through F, for the decimal values 0-15. *We use hexadecimal numbers to represent the contents of storage.* Hexadecimal is only a representation of storage—at no time does the computer actually work in base-16 as such. One hex digit depicts four bits of a byte, and two hex digits represent all eight bits in a byte. Figure 0-5 lists the equivalent decimal, binary, and hexadecimal numbers.

Decimal	Binary	Hexadecimal	Decimal	Binary	Hexadecimal
0	0000	0	8	1000	8
1	0001	1	9	1001	9
2	0010	2	10	1010	A
3	0011	3	11	1011	B
4	0100	4	12	1100	C
5	0101	5	13	1101	D
6	0110	6	14	1110	E
7	0111	7	15	1111	F

FIGURE 0-5   Decimal, binary, and hex representation.

Two hex digits can represent the contents of any storage location, regardless of the data format that it contains. For example, a byte contains the character 'A'. The binary representation of A in main storage is 1100 0001, and the hex representation of this is 'C1', or as commonly notated, X'C1'. Thus, if an input record contains an 'A' in a certain position, when read into storage, it appears in a byte as 1100 0001, and we can represent its contents as either character A or as hex 'C1'.

Since there are 256 possible bit configurations in a byte, there is no way to represent each possibility as a single character (there are only about 60 different print characters). Assume that a byte contains the packed digits 4 and 5. The binary representation of the byte's contents is 0100 0101. There is no single character that can represent this 8-bit code, but we can represent it with two hex digits as X'45'.

A byte used for binary data could contain 0101 1011 (which equals decimal value 91). The hexadecimal representation is X'5B'. In this way, hex format can represent all 360/370 formats, such as character, packed, and binary, one hex digit for each half-byte (four bits). The computer Supervisor and the Assembler both use hex extensively to represent the contents of storage, although only the programmer knows that the specific contents of bytes and fields are in a particular format. Among the uses of hexadecimal format are:

1. The Assembler converts source code to object code. It prints the locations of instructions and their object code entirely in hex format.
2. To facilitate tracing program errors, we can instruct the Supervisor to print a "*storage dump*". The dump prints the contents of storage, two hex digits per byte.
3. Some special purpose characters, for example, control the printer carriage (spacing lines, skipping to a new page), and "edit" data fields with punctuation and sign (as $1,250.00CR). Many of these special characters are bit configurations that cannot be printed. We can represent them, however, in our Assembler program with hex numbers.

Since the Supervisor and the Assembler print storage addresses in hex, a knowledge of hexadecimal arithmetic is quite useful (and so would be 16 fingers for doing it). Note how X'F' overflows when we add 1:

DECIMAL VALUE		HEX VALUE
15	=	F
+ 1		+ 1
16	=	10

Thus, X'10' equals the decimal value 16. Also, note that X'5' + X'5' = X'A', and X'8' + X'8' = X'10'. The following examples illustrate more hex addition:

X'21'	X'385'	X'412A'	X'53A6'
+ 15	+ 385	+ 94	+ 92A
X'36'	X'70A'	X'41BE'	X'5CDO'

Appendix A provides conversion of hexadecimal numbers to decimal, and decimal to hex, a useful reference. Understanding hex notation is extremely important in Assembler programming, and you are urged to grasp it fully.

Now complete the remaining problems in this chapter.

PROBLEMS

0-1. What are the basic components of a digital computer? What is the function of each one?

0-2. Distinguish between instructions and data.

0-3. What holes are punched in a card for the letters READ?

0-4. Define the following: (a) Stored program; (b) Access time; (c) Field; (d) Record; (e) File, or data set; (f) Alphameric data.

0-5. What is the decimal value of binary (a) 1110; (b) 11001; (c) 101101?

0-6. What is a "bit"? What is a bit's relationship to a "byte"?

0-7. The left four bits of a byte are the_____portion; the right four bits are the_____portion. The ninth bit is called_____; what is its purpose?

0-8. What are the two main purposes of the general registers?

0-9. What is the purpose of an "operating system"?

0-10. Where is the Supervisor stored? What are its main functions?

0-11. What is a "program interrupt"?

0-12. What action does the system take when a serious processing error occurs?

0-13. What is the purpose of hexadecimal representation?

0-14. Give the hexadecimal representation for the following binary values: (a) 1110; (b) 0101 1101; (c) 1011 0011; (d) 1111 0010 1100 1110.

0-15. Convert the following decimal values to hexadecimal (refer to Appendix A): (a) 10; (b) 16; (c) 24; (d) 32; (e) 275; (f) 2048; (g) 4096.

0-16. Convert the following hex values to decimal: (a) F; (b) 10; (c) 2D; (d) 4F; (e) 80; (f) 800; (g) 1000.

0-17. Add the following hex values: (a) 24 + 6; (b) 3A +7; (c) AAA + 555; (d) FFF + 1; (e) 437B + 2A4B.

CHAPTER 1

THE ASSEMBLER

The previous chapter examined the computer organization and its "hardware" features. This chapter covers the Assembler program, a "software" feature, and the requirements for coding and assembling a program in Basic Assembler Language. This text recommends standard coding practices, such as naming conventions for fields and files, in order to make computer programs more comprehensible and more easily maintained.

LANGUAGES

The 360/370 come equipped with a set of executable machine instructions similar for all models. Instructions include the ability to read input data, move data in storage, add and subtract the contents of storage locations, compare, and print data records.

MACHINE LANGUAGE. The 360/370 execute only instructions that are in machine language. The Supervisor must enter or "load" these instructions into main storage where they become the "stored program". Each storage location (*byte*) has a unique numeric address; the "operands" of the machine language instructions refer-ence the addresses of storage locations by their number. On the earliest computers, programmers coded at this basic level. On the 360/370 and most other current computers, however, coding in machine language is far too complex.

SYMBOLIC LANGUAGE.   Because of the complexity of machine language, pro-grammers code in "symbolic languages". These are special languages the manufac-turers design to facilitate program coding. An earlier example showed a hypothetical machine instruction A 1263 1338 that adds the contents of storage locations 1338–1340 to those of 1263–1265. Such an instruction could be coded in a symbolic language like Assembler as ADD ACCUM,AMOUNT. We then use a *translator program* such as Assembler, COBOL, PL/I or FORTRAN to translate the operation (ADD) into a machine code instruction and the symbolic addresses to machine language addresses.

THE ASSEMBLER

Basic Assembler Language (BAL) with which this text deals is the fundamental 360/370 language. It is reasonably standardized for all models. Although we code pro-grams in symbolic Assembler language, the computer cannot execute such instruc-tions. The Assembler translator program is required to "assemble" or translate the symbolic language into computer machine language.

PROGRAMMING STEPS.   The following explains the steps in programming, from coding through assembling and testing.

CODING.   We code the *source program* in symbolic language on special Assem-bler coding sheets. The program consists of Assembler instructions and data areas.

KEYING.   These sheets are then keyed onto punched cards, or onto disk via a terminal.

ASSEMBLY.   We ask the Supervisor (through a job control statement) to *assemble* the source program, and the Supervisor loads the Assembler program from disk into main storage. The Assembler program then reads our source program as data into the computer. The Assembler program performs the following:

— Accounts for the amount of storage required for each instruction and each data area, and assigns storage locations to them in the sequence in which they are coded.
— Supplies messages for programming errors, such as the invalid use of an instruc-tion and spelling errors.
— Includes any required routines that are written in Assembler language and are catalogued on disk.

— Prints the original symbolic coding and the translated machine language on a printed form. This print-out is necessary to "debug" the program and to make subsequent changes.

— Writes the machine language *object* program onto an output device such as a card punch, disk, or tape, for use when the program is to be executed.

The Assembler uses a *location counter* to account for the length of each data field and instruction. If the Assembler has just assigned a 4-byte instruction starting at location 10,024, the location counter now contains 10,028, the starting address of the next instruction. The Assembler always assigns the address to the leftmost byte of a data area or constant.

ERROR CHECKING.   We correct any errors that the Assembler signals, reassemble the program and execute it using test data. The Assembler cannot recognize errors in our program logic—these errors we must find through testing and "debugging".

ADDRESSING.   The first storage location is numbered zero, with subsequent bytes numbered consecutively. Therefore, a size of 16,384 has addresses numbered zero through 16,383. (Note that 1K = 1024 bytes.) Addressing is done by means of the rightmost 24 bits of a register. These 24 bits provide a capacity of 2^{24} or 16,777,216 addressable bytes of storage. Machine language uses a two-address system for addressing. It consists of:

1. A *base register* (any available general purpose register). The base register contains the beginning address of an area in storage used by the program, and provides a reference point for the next 4096 bytes. The program requires one base register for each 4096 bytes used.

2. A *displacement,* or the number of bytes from zero to 4095, from the first byte of the area to which the base register points.

At this point, it is not necessary to understand base/displacement addressing, and a full discussion will be given in a later chapter.

When we code an Assembler program, we do not know, or need to know, where in storage our instructions and addresses will be. We code in symbolic language, assigning names to the various instructions and data fields. For example, an instruction may have the name A10READ, and an accumulator to count the number of pages printed may be called PAGECTR. The name we give refers only to a single storage location, the leftmost byte of the field. For example, the contents of PAGECTR may be three bytes long, and the Assembler assigns it to locations 10516, 10517, and 10518. A reference to PAGECTR is to a three-byte field *beginning in location 10516:*

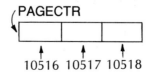

RELATIVE ADDRESSING.   We may reference a storage position relative to a symbolic address. For example, we define an area of 80 bytes called CARDIN for reading and storing 80-column cards. The name CARDIN refers to the first byte of the area. We may reference the second byte as CARDIN+1, the third byte as CARDIN+2, and the 80th as CARDIN+79:

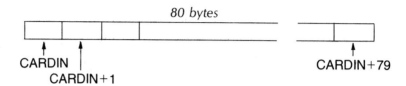

Any location in main storage can be referenced by similar relative addressing.

INSTRUCTION FORMAT.   The Assembler translates our symbolic instructions into machine-language object instructions, with correct format and length. The Assembler aligns the first byte of every instruction on an even-numbered storage location. When the computer executes a machine-language instruction, it accesses the operation-code from storage, and recognizes from the operation-code the format and the length of the instruction. There are five basic instruction formats, with instruction lengths of two, four, and six bytes. The *operation code* (such as Add, Subtract, Move) in machine-language is always the first byte, therefore providing for 256 possible op-codes. (The 370 has a sixth type, called S-format, that has a two-byte operation code.) The instruction usually contains one or more *operands*. Typically, an operand is a reference to a storage location or a register. Data may be transferred between registers, between registers and storage, or between storage locations.

The five main instruction formats are RR (Register-to-Register), RX (Register-to-Indexed Storage), RS (Register-to-Storage), SI (Storage Immediate), and SS (Storage-to-Storage), as shown in Figure 1-1. The 370 has a special sixth one called S-format.

Length in bytes	Format	Typical use
2	RR Register-to-Register	Data movement between registers.
4	RX Register-to-Indexed Storage	Data movement between a register and storage.
4	RS Register-to-Storage	Data movement between a register and storage.
4	SI Storage Immediate	Data movement from one-byte constant in the instruction to storage.
6	SS Storage-to-Storage	Data movement between two areas in storage.

FIGURE 1-1   Assembler instruction formats.

For example, an RR format instruction, AR, can be used to add the contents of register-8 to register-6. It is coded in Assembler language as:

$$\overset{\text{operation code}}{\nearrow}\text{AR}\quad\overset{\text{operand-1}}{\underset{}{6,8}}\overset{}{\searrow}\text{operand-2}$$

The machine language code for AR is X'1A'. The Assembler translates the symbolic instruction to two bytes of object code, in hexadecimal as 1A68. The object code for operands that reference storage.is more complex because the Assembler converts their addresses to base/displacement format, explained in Chapter 6.

MACRO INSTRUCTIONS.   Assembler is a *"low-level"* language—that is, close to machine-language level. The Assembler translates one symbolic instruction into one machine-language instruction. But there is provision for *macro instructions,* specially written instructions that the Assembler recognizes. Depending on its requirements, *the macro causes the Assembler to generate one or more machine-language instructions.* IBM supplies macros to facilitate Supervisor and input/output operations, for example, CALL, GET, RETURN. In contrast to the low-level Assembler language are *"high-level"* languages such as COBOL, FORTRAN, and PL/I which we code entirely with macro instructions.

THE ASSEMBLER CODING SHEET

Figure 1-2 depicts the IBM Assembler coding sheet, Form GX09-0010, used for the coding of Assembler programs. The coding on the form is strictly illustrative, and is not intended to be understandable at this time. The space at the top of the form for the program name, programmer name, date, and page number should be completed on each page. There are 80 columns for punching onto the standard 80-column card.

Some characters that are written alike may be key-punched incorrectly. Although there is no universal standard, the following conventions may be used to distinguish among certain easily confused characters:

— Code the digit zero as 0, and the letter O as Ø (some use the opposite convention).
— Code the digit one and the letter I clearly.
— Code the letter Z as Z̵ to distinguish it from the digit 2.
— There is often confusion between the digit 5 and the letter S, between the left parenthesis ('(') and the letter C, and between the letters U and V.
— Where not otherwise clear, indicate a blank position by ƀ.

The Assembler accepts coding that is "free-form"; that is, although the form has predefined columns for Name, Operation, and Operand, we do not have to code these fields in the defined columns. However, there is little need to vary from the

IBM System/360 Assembler Coding Form

PROGRAM: Assembler List Program
PROGRAMMER: Waldo Pflug
DATE June 21, 19xx
PUNCHING INSTRUCTIONS — GRAPHIC / PUNCH

Name	Operation	Operand	Comments	Identification-Sequence
	TITLE	'EXAMPLE ASSEMBLER PROGRAM TO LIST CARDS'		LIST0000
	EJECT			LIST0002
	PRINT	ON,NODATA,NOGEN		LIST0006
	ISEQ	73,80		LIST0010
	SPACE			LIST0020
*		INITIALIZATION		LIST0040
**		------------		LIST0060
PROG02	INIT		INITIALIZE	LIST0070
	OPEN	CARD,PRINTER		LIST0090
	SPACE			LIST0100
	PUTPR	PRINTER,PRHEAD,SK1	SKIP TO NEW PAGE	LIST0110
	PUTPR	PRINTER,PRHEAD,WSP1	PRINT HEADING	LIST0160
	SPACE			LIST0170
*		READ & PRINT ROUTINE		LIST0180
**		--------------------		LIST0200
A10READ	GET	CARD,CARDIN	READ A CARD	LIST1010
	MVC	PRINT+10(80),CARDIN	MOVE CARD CONTENTS TO PRINT	LIST1020
	PUTPR	PRINTER,PRINT,WSP1	& PRINT	
	B	A10READ	BRANCH TO READ NEXT CARD	
	SPACE			
*		END-OF-FILE ROUTINE		
**		-------------------		

FIGURE 1-2   Assembler coding sheet.

22

defined columns, and there is a need for standardized, legible programs. The examples in this text use only the defined columns.

CODING FORMAT.   There are three types of coding statements:

1. *Instructions,* such as add and compare, that provide the program logic for execution.
2. *Declaratives,* such as accumulators and constants, used by instructions.
3. *Comments,* used as documentation to make the program clearer. They do not become part of the machine-language code.

The fields on the coding sheet are described as follows:

COLUMN

1–8 NAME. We assign a name to each instruction and declarative that we intend to reference in the program. In Figure 1-2, for example, A10READ is the name of an instruction. The rules governing the name (or label) are:

— The name that defines the address of an instruction or declarative must be unique in the program—defined only once.

— The name may be one to eight characters long. The first character must be a letter A through Z (and $, #, or @, although these are not recommended). Remaining characters may be letters or digits, as A10READ. The name may not contain any blank characters.

— There must be at least one blank position between the name and the next field, Operation.

If column 1 is *blank,* the Assembler assumes that the instruction or declarative has no name; Figure 1-2 shows many such unnamed instructions. If column 1 contains an asterisk (*), the Assembler assumes that the entire line is a *comment*—see Figure 1-2.

10–14 OPERATION. This is the symbolic (mnemonic) operation code for an instruction, declarative or macro. The Assembler must be able to recognize it. Figure 1-2 shows operations such as TITLE and PRINT. There must be at least one blank position between Operation and the next field, Operand.

16–71 OPERAND. The operand identifies data on which the operation is to act. Depending on the operation, there may be none, one, or more operands. A comma separates each operand, with no blank spaces either within operands or between them; the Assembler assumes that a blank ends the operands. In the following, Name is A20ADD, Operation is AP (add), and Operand is ACCUM,FIVE.

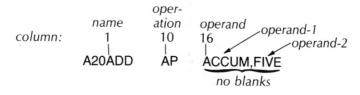

Comments may be indicated for an entire line by an asterisk in column 1. They may also appear on a line following an instruction, with at least one blank between the operand and the comment. The coding in Figure 1-2 aligns comments beginning in column 41 for readability and to facilitate keypunching. For example:

```
column:   10    16                    comments
          |     |                     |
          MP    HOURS,RATE    CALCULATE WAGE
```

COLUMN

72 CONTINUATION. Operands and comments may not continue past column 71. If more columns are required, then we must do the following:

— Code *any* character in column 72. This text uses a plus (+) sign.
— Continue coding the statement on the next line beginning in column 16. The first statement in Figure 1-2, TITLE, illustrates continuation. Depending on the Assembler version, one or more continuations are permitted.

73–80 IDENTIFICATION SEQUENCE. We may optionally use this field to identify the program—a recommended practice. A useful identification sequence is as follows. Columns 73–76 contain the program identification, such as P023 for Payroll program 023. Columns 77–80 contain a card sequence number. If the sequence numbers are consecutive, then we cannot insert additional instructions between them. Therefore, a good practice is to number the sequence in intervals of ten, such as 0010, 0020, 0030. Major program sections may begin with a value such as 1000 or 2000.

We may force the Assembler to check the sequence of card columns 73–80 by coding an Assembler card with the instruction ISEQ (Input Sequence Checking), discussed in the section Assembler Instruction Statements.

ASSEMBLER INSTRUCTION STATEMENTS

The Assembler translates instructions such as AP (Add) or MVC (Move) into machine-language executable code. Others, such as DC, LTORG, START, and TITLE, the Assembler recognizes as requests to perform certain operations during assembly. The Assembler acts on them during the assembly and generates no executable code.

NAME	OPERATION	OPERAND
[symbol]	TITLE	1–100 characters, within apostrophes
omit	EJECT	blank
omit	SPACE	blank or a number
omit	PRINT	one, two, or three operands
omit	ISEQ	blank, or 2 digits of the form, *l, r*
omit	END	blank or a symbol

TITLE. The purpose of TITLE is to identify the assembly listing and the object card deck (if any). See Figure 1-2 for an example. The name field may be omitted. If it is present, the Assembler punches the first four characters into columns 73–76 of the object program card deck, if any.

The operand field is enclosed in apostrophes to denote the start and end of the title. It contains any descriptive title that we want printed at the top of each page of the Assembler listing (see the top line of Figure 1-4). The maximum length is 100 characters. But, if the title exceeds 56 characters, we must code a continuation character in column 72, and continue the title on the next line in column 16. An apostrophe or ampersand used in the operand must be coded as *two* apostrophes or ampersands. The Assembler stores and prints only one. Example: TITLE 'JEAN && SAM''S PROGRAM'.

EJECT. After printing a full page, the Assembler automatically ejects to the top of the next page. However, we may want to eject the page before it is fully printed, for example, to print the declaratives or the start of a new major routine. We code EJECT, causing the Assembler to start a new page for the listing.

SPACE. The SPACE instruction tells the Assembler to space one or more blank lines on the listing. We code the number of lines to be spaced in the operand. If we leave the operand blank, the Assembler assumes a space of one line:

Column	10	16	
	SPACE		Space 1 line
	SPACE	1	Space 1 line
	SPACE	2	Space 2 lines
	SPACE	3	Space 3 lines

Note: The Assembler acts on EJECT and SPACE but does not print them. It does, however, increment the statement (STMT) number on the listing; see, for example, missing statement number 73 in Figure 1-4.

PRINT. This instruction controls the general format of the program listing. It contains any or all of the following three operands, in any sequence. The common requirement is PRINT ON,NOGEN,NODATA.

ON   Print the program listing from this point on.
OFF   Do not print the listing.

GEN   Print all statements generated by macro instructions.
NOGEN   Suppress statements generated by macros. In Figure 2-1, OPEN is a macro; its generated code is seldom of value, so we normally suppress it.

DATA   Print the full hexadecimal contents of constants (on the left side of the listing, under OBJECT CODE).

NODATA   Print only the leftmost 8 bytes, or 16 hex digits. We normally code NODATA because the full hex printed contents of constants are of little value.

ISEQ.   This instruction causes the Assembler to sequence-check the input source cards. The operands *l* and *r* specify the leftmost and rightmost card columns of the field being checked. The field is normally the "Identification Sequence" between columns 73 and 80, and the instruction is coded as ISEQ 73,80, as shown in the example coding. Since each card checked must contain a higher sequence value than the previous one, low, equal, or blank fields cause error messages. ISEQ with a blank operand will terminate sequence-checking.

END.   The END instruction must be the last statement of the program. It causes termination of the program's assembly. We may code the operand with a symbolic address, such as END PROG02. The operand PROG02 in this case designates an address in the program to which control is to transfer when the program is loaded for execution. Thus, the address is that of the program's normal first executable instruction.

Remember that these instructions simply tell the Assembler how to handle the program, and generate no machine code. This section provides the most commonly required information. The Assembler manual contains more detail on these instructions. Later chapters cover other instructions, such as EQU, LTORG, ORG, and USING.

THE ASSEMBLER CARD

Figure 1-3 shows the IBM Assembler card (one of the cards punched from the coding sheet in Figure 1-2). The cards are punched column for column, one card for each line. Since the operators who punch the cards are normally unfamiliar with Assembler language, we must code clearly and neatly. Unclear printing causes many programming errors.

CODING CONVENTIONS

This text uses certain clear and meaningful conventions to define the names of fields and instructions.

DECLARATIVE NAMES.   A declarative is a nonexecutable instruction that defines constants, counters, input/output areas, etc. There are two types:

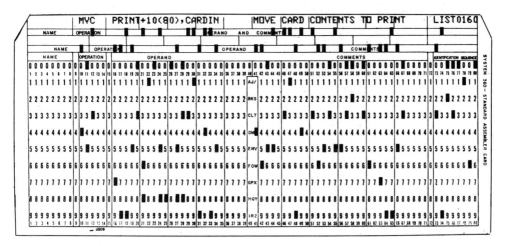

FIGURE 1-3   The Assembler card.

DEFINE STORAGE, DS.   DS defines an area of storage within the program, such as an input/output area. When the program first executes, the contents of a DS are unpredictable, and could contain any "garbage." The instruction CARDIN DS CL80 defines a field called CARDIN, character format, length 80 bytes. Each time a record reads into this area, it erases the previous contents of CARDIN.

DEFINE CONSTANT, DC.   DC defines an area containing a constant value. The instruction HEADING DC C'FORD MOTORS' defines a field called HEADING containing a character constant used for a report heading. In this case, the contents of HEADING are intended never to change during the program's execution.

In both cases, CARDIN and HEADING, the name references the leftmost byte of the defined field. A DS or DC, however, need not have a name.

Declarative names should be unique and descriptive. Since a name (or label) can be up to eight characters long, it is more meaningful to use, for example, the name EXPENSE rather than EXP. Also, it is often useful to identify a packed field with a suffix PK, such as AMOUNTPK, and a binary field with BIN, as AMTBIN. We may give input/output areas descriptive labels as CARDIN for a card input area, and PRINT for a print area. (The *declarative* PRINT in Figure 1-4 is the name of a 133-byte field. It should not be confused with the assembler *instruction* PRINT. This symbol PRINT illustrates how we can use the same name for both an operation and a declarative; the Assembler can tell from the use of the symbol whether it references a declarative or an instruction.)

ADDRESS NAMES.   We give an instruction a name if it is referenced elsewhere in the program. The example in Figure 1-4 reads and prints card records. In order to repeat

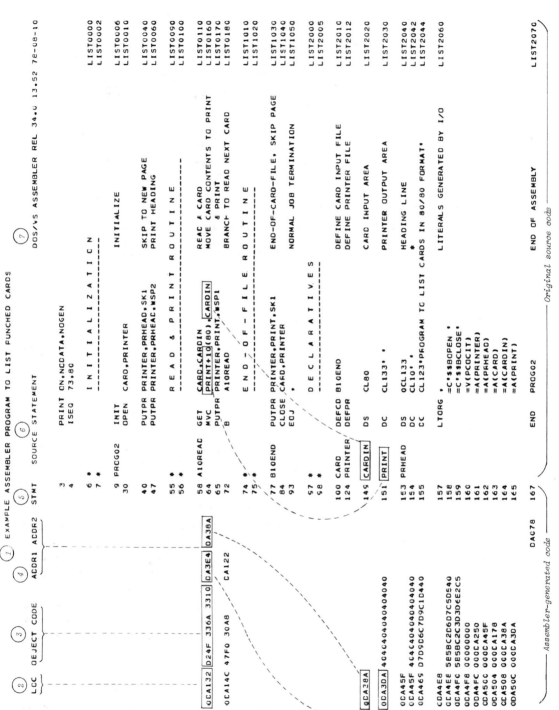

FIGURE 1-4 Sample Assembler program to read and list records.

28

the read operation, we "branch back" to read the next record of the read (GET CARD,CARDIN). In order to reference the GET, we must give it a name—in this case A10READ. The program uses the instruction B A10READ to branch to A10READ, the address of the GET instruction.

This text uses a convention that requires that the first character of an address label be an alphabetic letter, A through Z. The next two or three characters are digits, for example, A10, D35, P200. In the first main logical section of the program, the labels begin with A. Address labels, where required, are numbered within this section starting with A10, then increasing by intervals of ten, such as A20, A30, etc. This practice facilitates the following:

— All labels are sequential, and therefore easy to locate.
— Because all labels are clearly in sequence, there is less chance of using duplicate labels in the program.
— We can easily insert additional labels where required, such as A12 and A15.

The next main logical section and all others begin with a letter higher than the previous, such as B, E, G, and X. Each section uses digits starting with 10 and increasing by intervals of 10. The first label of a logical section and all other labels to which we branch from outside the section are given descriptive suffixes, such as A10READ and X10EOF. An examination of the sample programs throughout this text should make clear the advantages of such coding conventions.

THE ASSEMBLED PROGRAM LISTING

Figure 1-4 provides a sample Assembler program that reads cards and lists them in "80/80" format (the 80 card columns are printed column-for-column in 80 print positions). This section briefly describes the assembled program listing. Some of the detail may not be clear until after Chapter 3:

1. The first line lists the contents of the TITLE card (if any) at the top of each page. The Assembler prints the page number to the right.

The second line is described next:

2. LOC, for Assembler Location Counter, is the assembled location or address of the first (leftmost) byte of the object code instruction or declarative, *in hexadecimal format.* The first address shown is X'0DA132', which is the address of the leftmost byte of the instruction on that line. (The Supervisor occupies the lower part of main storage, and this program occupies a following area.)
3. OBJECT CODE lists the hexadecimal object code instruction, or the contents of a constant, as assembled. The column shows the actual contents of storage. In the listing, the first executable instruction is the INIT statement. Because INIT is a macro, and we coded PRINT NOGEN earlier, the Assembler has suppressed

printing INIT's generated code. The first object code listed is for statement 64, D24F 336A 3310. The first byte, D2, is the machine-language code for the symbolic operation MVC (Move Character). The D2 is stored in location X'0DA132'. The second byte, 4F, gives the hexadecimal length of operand-1, and the other four bytes are the machine code operands. The actual machine operand addresses consist of a "base register" and a "displacement". This section merely describes the purpose of these columns—do not expect to understand the assembled object code at this time!

4. ADDR1 ADDR2 shows the "effective" addresses of operand-1 and operand-2. These addresses do not appear in main storage as part of the machine code; *the Assembler prints them only as a convenience to the programmer.* The first line printed shows DA3E4 DA38A, which refers to the actual storage locations of operand-1 and operand-2 of the MVC instruction (PRINT+10 and CARDIN respectively).

5. STMT means Statement Number. The Assembler counts each statement in the program and prints the assigned statement number in this column. The first instruction, TITLE, and the second, EJECT, are not listed. The first statement number in this example is 3 for the PRINT ON instruction. Certain other statements are also not printed. Statement 57, for example, is the instruction SPACE, which the Assembler counts but does not print. Similarly, because we coded PRINT NOGEN, the printing of instructions generated by macros (such as GET) is suppressed. (The instruction PRINT GEN will force the Assembler to list generated macro-code.)

6. SOURCE STATEMENT lists our original source code from Assembler cards, exactly as coded.

7. DOS/VS ASSEMBLER REL shows the "release" and "version" number, which varies by computer system.

The *declaratives* are coded in an area separate from the instructions. The declarative CARDIN, for example, begins here in location (LOC) X'0DA38A'. The contents of DC's (but not DS's) are shown in hexadecimal format under OBJECT CODE. Since PRINT NODATA was specified, the Assembler lists only the first eight bytes (16 hex digits) of DC contents, as shown by statement 151. Note that the object code contents of PRINT show eight hexadecimal 40's, the 360/370 blank character. Coding PRINT DATA would cause the Assembler to print the entire hex constant, resulting in more printed lines of little value to the programmer.

ASSEMBLER DIAGNOSTIC MESSAGES

Figure 1-5 provides the assembled program listing, similar to the previous example, with a random assortment of coding errors. Immediately following the program is a list of any errors that the Assembler has identified, along with the statement number and explanation. (The code numbers under ERROR NO. can help locate further explanations in the IBM Assembler manual, although this is seldom necessary.)

```
LOC   OBJECT CODE      ADDR1 ADDR2  STMT   SOURCE STATEMENT

                                     3                PRINT ON,NODATA,NOGEN

                                     5 *                   I N I T I A L I Z A T I O N

                                     7 PROG2B   INIT                       INITIALIZE
                                    28          OPEN  CARD,PRTR

                                    38          PUTPR PRINTER,PRHEAD,SK1   SKIP TO NEW PAGE
                                    45          PUTPR PRINTER,PRHEAD,WSP2  PRINT HEADING

                                    53 ***                 R E A D  &  P R I N T  R O U T I N E

                                    55 A10READ  GET   CARD,CARDIN          READ RECORD
                                    61          MCV   PRINT+10(80),CARDIN  MOVE TO PRINT
             *** ERROR ***
                                    62          PUTPR PRINTER,PRINT,WSP1      & PRINT
0CA146 0000 0000                    69          B     A20READ             GET NEXT RECORD
             *** ERROR ***

                                    71 ***                 E N D - O F - F I L E  R O U T I N E

                                    73 B10END   PUTPR PRINTER,PRINT,SK1   SKIP PAGE
                                    80          CLOSE CARD,PRINTER
                                    89          EOJ   .                   END OF JOB

                                    93 ***                 D E C L A R A T I V E S

                                    95 CARD     DEFCD B10END              DEFINE READER
                                   119 PRINTER  DEFPR                     DEFINE PRINTER

                                   144 CARDIN   DC    CL80                INPUT AREA
             *** ERROR ***
0CA38A 4040404040404040            146 PRINT    DC    CL133' '            PRINT AREA

0DA40F                             148 PRHEAD   DS    0CL133              HEADING LINE
0CA40F 4040404040404040            149          DC    CL10' '                 *
0DA419 D7D9D6C7D9C1D440            150          DC    CL123'PROGRAM TO LIST CARDS'
                                   151          SAPCE
             *** ERROR ***
0DA498                             152          LTORG .                  LITERALS
0DA498 5B5BC2D6D7C5D540            153                =C'$$BOPEN '
0DA4A0 5B5BC2C3D3D6E2C5            154                =C'$$BCLOSE'
0DA4A8 00000000                    155                =V(PCOCIT)
0DA4AC 000CA250                    156                =A(PRINTER)
0CA4B0 000DA40F                    157                =A(PRHEAD)
0DA4B4 000DA178                    158                =A(CARD)
0CA4B8 00000000                    159                =A(CARDIN)
             *** ERROR ***
0DA4BC 000CA38A                    160                =A(PRINT)

                                   162          END   PROG02             END OF ASSEMBLY
             *** ERROR ***
```

DIAGNOSTICS AND STATISTICS

```
STMNT  ERROR NO.   MESSAGE

   35   IPK156      SYMBOL 'PRTR' UNDEFINED
   61   IPK097      UNDEFINED OP CODE 'MCV', OR MACRO NOT FOUND
   69   IPK156      SYMBOL 'A20READ' UNDEFINED
  144   IPK128      CONSTANT FIELD MISSING OR PRECEDED BY INVALID FIELD, ' '
  151   IPK097      UNDEFINED OP CODE 'SAPCE', OR MACRO NOT FOUND
  159   IPK156      SYMBOL 'CARDIN' UNDEFINED
  162   IPK144      INVALID END OPERAND
  162   IPK149      SYMBOL 'PROG02' NOT PREVIOUSLY DEFINED
```

FIGURE 1-5 Assembled program with error diagnostics.

Check this section immediately on receiving the assembled program listing. The Assembler denotes some, but not all, errors to the left of the invalid statement with *** ERROR ***. Before reading the following explanation, try to locate the cause of each error message.

Statement 35, indicating that PRTR is undefined, refers to the OPEN statement. The use of PRINT NOGEN has caused the statements generated by macros not to print. The printer device is defined in statement 119 as PRINTER.

Statement 61 spells the instruction MVC as MCV; the Assembler generates no object code, because it does not know if the operation is supposed to be a macro or normal instruction.

Statement 69 indicates B A20READ instead of A10READ. Statement 144 should either be a DS or should define a constant for the DC. Statement 151 is supposed to be a SPACE instruction.

Statement 159 is in the literal pool that the Assembler generates, caused by the fact that the GET instruction references CARDIN. This is a common case of one error (144) causing another. Correcting 144 will cause 159 to disappear.

Statement 162 should be coded as END PROG2B, one error which caused the Assembler to generate two messages.

If the computer attempts to execute this program, it will quickly "bomb out." Be sure to correct all error diagnostics before reassembling and executing.

PROBLEMS

1-1. What steps are required to assemble a program? Where is the assembled program stored?

1-2. How does the Assembler account for the address of each instruction and declarative?

1-3. Indicate which instruction formats are used to move data (a) between registers; (b) between storage locations; (c) between registers and storage.

1-4. Explain (a) machine language instruction; (b) symbolic instruction; (c) macro instruction.

1-5. Comment on the validity of the following Assembler program names (labels): (a) W25; (b) START-UP; (c) READDEVICE; (d) $AMT; (e) TOT AMT; (f) *TO-TAL; (g) 25CENTS.

1-6. On the coding sheet, what does an asterisk in column 1 indicate? What would it indicate in column 72?

1-7. How can we cause the generated code for a macro to print on the Assembler listing?

1-8. What statement causes the assembled program listing to space 3 lines?

1-9. How may the Assembler check the sequence of a deck of program source cards?

1-10. Does the EJECT statement cause the printer to skip to the top of a page during an assembly, during program execution, or both?

1-11. What statement terminates assembly of a program?

1-12. Refer to the IBM Assembler manual. Define in your own words (a) Self-defining terms; (b) Absolute and relocatable expressions.

1-13. This chapter describes an address labelling system used in this text. What are the advantages of such a system?

1-14. What is a declarative? How do DS and DC differ?

1-15. Distinguish between "source program" and "object program."

1-16. On the assembled program listing, what is meant by (a) LOC; (b) OBJECT CODE; (c) ADDR1 and ADDR2; (d) STMT?

CHAPTER 2

PROGRAM EXECUTION

Chapter 1 covered the requirements for coding an Assembler program. This chapter covers the basic instructions for executing an Assembler language program: initialization, the defining of files, and the input/output macros. We also examine the input of a data record and its format in main storage. Now that we are close to coding a program, we also examine the conventional analytical tool for program design, the flowchart. The next chapter provides enough information so that we can write programs that use character data.

PROGRAM EXECUTION STATEMENTS

An Assembler program requires certain special coding for program execution. It is necessary initially to "load base registers" for addressing, to define the input and output files, to activate these files, and to provide for termination of program execution and for termination of the assembly. This section describes the simple macros used for these complex functions. It is desirable for the beginning programmer to write a program as soon as possible; thus, this text uses four macros that have been specially written for introducing Assembler programming, INIT, DEFCD, DEFPR and

PUTPR. They handle some complex coding and enable the beginner to get started quickly. All other macros used in this text are standard IBM macros.

INITIALIZATION.   The first statements in an Assembler program vary somewhat by Assembler version and requirements of the computer installation. The INIT macro sets the Assembler location counter and "loads base registers." Chapter 6 covers the precise Assembler initialization requirements.

NAME	OPERATION	OPERAND
Programname	INIT	blank

DEFINING CARD & PRINTER FILES.   This text begins with the simplest, basic input/output: punched cards and the printer. The names of the card and printer files used in the program must be defined. This definition is handled by two special macros, DEFCD (Define Card) and DEFPR (Define Printer) that generate some complex Assembler code. (The standard IBM macros, DTFCD and DTFPR (or DCB), are covered in Chapter 7.) Other macros such as OPEN and GET reference these files by the defined names.

cardfile	DEFCD	end-of-file address
printfile	DEFPR	blank

DEFCD defines the card reader file with any valid unique name. Under DOS, the last card of our input data must be a job control card containing /* in columns 1–2. As each data card is read, the system checks the first two positions. If they contain /*, the system directs the program to our end-of-file address. In the case of the DEFCD macro, we enter this address in the operand field (with any unique name). Typically the name begins a routine that may print final totals and terminate the program execution. Under OS, the /* job card is optional.

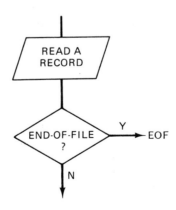

DEFPR defines the name of the printer file with any unique name. The printer is an output file and has no associated "end-of-file".

OPENING AND CLOSING FILES.   Most programming languages require the programmer to code statements that "activate" (OPEN) the files at the start of the program and "deactivate" (CLOSE) them at the end. The normal function of OPEN is to make the file available to the program (it may be damaged or in use by another program). At the end of the program execution, CLOSE releases the file for use by other programs. For both macros, the operands are the card and printer file names defined by DEFCD and DEFPR. (Under many large systems, the programmer may omit the OPEN and CLOSE of card and printer files.)

Under Disk Operating System (DOS), OPEN and CLOSE are coded as:

	OPEN	cardfile,printfile
	CLOSE	cardfile,printfile

Under Operating System (OS), we code OPEN and CLOSE with the operands in brackets. Also OPEN must specify if the file is INPUT or OUTPUT; CLOSE may omit the references.

	OPEN	(cardfile,(INPUT),printfile(OUTPUT))
	CLOSE	(cardfile,,printfile)

↑extra comma denotes omission of (INPUT)

For either DOS or OS, we may open or close one or more files with one statement.

READING INPUT RECORDS.   The GET macro reads input records. There are two operands: Operand-1 designates the card file name defined by DEFCD (or by the IBM macro DCB or DTFCD); Operand-2 is the name of an 80-byte input area in main storage.

	GET	cardfile,cardarea

GET causes the card device to read a record and store its contents in the input area, erasing the previous contents of the area. The card input area may have any unique name. Prior to storing in the input area, the macro checks the record; if it is the end-of-file card (/*), the program branches to the end-of-file address defined in the DEFCD macro. An example:

```
              OPEN    READER              Open input file
              GET     READER,INAREA       Read record into INAREA
              .
              .
              .
D10END        CLOSE   READER              End-of-file, CLOSE READER
              .
              .
              .
READER        DEFCD   D10END              Define cardfile as READER
INAREA        DS      CL80                Define 80-byte input area
```

PRINTING LINES.   Printing lines during program execution requires special treatment, because we may want to space on the page without printing, or print and space one or more lines. To simplify the requirements involved in spacing the print forms, in the early chapters this text uses a special macro, PUTPR. (Do not confuse this printing during execute-time with the SPACE or PRINT statements that control the printing of the program listing during assembly-time.)

	PUTPR	printfile,printarea,print-command

For PUTPR, operand-1 is the name of the printer file defined by DEFPR (or by the IBM macros DCB or DTFPR). Operand-2 is the name of the print area where we have stored data that is to be printed. The print area may have any unique name, and there may be more than one print area. Operand-3 specifies the forms control:

WSP0	Write, no space	SK1	Skip to new page
WSP1	Write, space 1 line	SP1	Space 1 line
WSP2	Write, space 2 lines	SP2	Space 2 lines
WSP3	Write, space 3 lines	SP3	Space 3 lines

For example, PUTPR PRINTER,PRINT,WSP1 causes the program to print the contents of an area, PRINT, and to space to the next line on the page. WSP0 may be used occasionally for underlining important information. SK1, SP1, SP2, and SP3 simply move the printer; nothing prints on the page, regardless of the contents of the print area. PUTPR uses the first byte of the print area to insert a special forms control character; any character that we may have already stored there will be erased. If the print area is defined as PRINT DS CL133, then PRINT+0 is the position that the control character uses. The remaining positions, PRINT+1 through PRINT+132, are available for storing our printable data. (The standard IBM macro, PUT, requires the programmer to define and insert the control character, as discussed in Chapter 7.)

> *Note:* PUTPR does not clear the print area. Because unwanted data may still be in the area from the previous print operation, it is usually desirable to clear the print area to blanks after printing so that the next printing does not contain "garbage". Also, if the print area is a DS, then it may contain

garbage from some previous program. It is useful to define the print area as a DC, as PRINT DC CL133' ', to initialize the print area to blanks.

TERMINATING EXECUTION.   After closing the files, we terminate program execution under DOS with the EOJ macro, which causes a return to the Supervisor program. Under OS, termination involves the RETURN macro.

	EOJ CANCEL	blank , or ALL	(normal termination) (abnormal termination)

More advanced programs are written to check if the input record contains invalid data, and we may want to cancel the run if the input is invalid. The CANCEL macro also terminates processing, but as well it "flushes" any remaining input records. The beginning programmer may want to delay using CANCEL until becoming more advanced. Under OS, the macro equivalent to CANCEL is ABEND.

END OF ASSEMBLY.   EOJ and CANCEL are concerned with terminating the program's *execution,* and may be coded in any logical place within the program. To terminate program *assembly,* the last statement in the program must be END, which tells the Assembler that there are no more statements.

The operand of the END instruction stipulates the address of the first executable statement in the program. Through most of this text, this address will be the program name, as:

PROG07	INIT . . END	Start of program
		PROG07 End of program

The END instruction is not a macro and generates no executable code; it does, however, provide the starting address for the Supervisor to begin execution of the program.

Figure 2-1 combines the preceding Assembler macros and declaratives into a skeleton program, the overall logic required for many programming problems. The only instruction not covered is B A10READ which causes the executing program to go to ("branch" to) the instruction labeled A10READ.

CONDITION CODE

Computers must have logic: the ability to compare the contents of one field to that of another, and to check if a value is positive, negative, or zero. On the 360/370,

```
1 (NAME) 10    16 (OPERANDS)           41 (COMMENTS)

*                 I N I T I A L I Z A T I O N
PROGEX   INIT                         INITIALIZE
         OPEN   CARD,PRINTER          ACTIVATE FILES

*                 M A I N   P R O C E S S I N G
A1OREAD  GET    CARD,CARDIN           READ AN INPUT RECORD
            •
            •     (PERFORM VARIOUS CALCULATIONS,
            •       SET UP PRINT AREA FOR PRINTING)
            •
         PUTPR  PRINTER,PRINT,WSP1    PRINT OUTPUT RECORD
         B      A1OREAD               GO TO READ NEXT RECORD

*                 E N D - O F - F I L E
B1OEND      •
            •     (PRINT FINAL TOTALS IF REQUIRED)
            •
         CLOSE  CARD,PRINTER          DE-ACTIVATE FILES
         EOJ                          TERMINATE RUN

*                 D E C L A R A T I V E S
CARD     DEFCD  B1OEND                DEFINE CARD FILE & EOF ADDRESS
PRINTER  DEFPR                        DEFINE PRINTER FILE
CARDIN   DS     CL80                  CARD INPUT AREA
PRINT    DC     CL133' '              PRINT AREA
         END    PROGEX
```

FIGURE 2-1   Program outline.

comparing or checking fields sets the *condition code,* two bits in the Program Status Word (PSW). Many compare and arithmetic instructions set the condition code according to the results of the operation:

RESULTS OF THE OPERATION	CONDITION CODE SETTING
Equal or zero	0
Low or minus	1
High or plus	2
Arithmetic overflow	3 (arithmetic field is too small for the calculated answer)

The purpose of the condition code is to facilitate the computer logic. Certain operations set the condition code. Subsequently we can use other instructions that can test what condition was set. In this way, we can change the flow of the program logic.

As an example, a file of Accounts Receivable records must be read into the computer in sequence by Customer. The program *sequence-checks* the file by comparing the Customer number on the input record just read against the Customer number on the record that was previously read and processed. The possibilities are as follows:

NEW CUSTOMER NUMBER READ	CONDITION CODE SET	DECISION
Equal	0	Same Customer as previous
Low	1	Out-of-sequence error
High	2	Next Customer

Similarly, the program may check an amount field to determine whether its contents are zero (0), negative (1), or positive (2).

INPUT DATA

The card constitutes a record of data, such as a Customer Balance record. The record is divided into fields of data, as customer number, name, and balance owing. A collection of related records, such as all the Customer Balance records, comprises a file, or, in OS terminology, a "data set."

Many records contain a unique code in a specified position to identify the file to which they belong. Thus, the Customer Balance records could all contain '01' in the first two positions, and programs that read this file can check each record to ensure that the correct records are being entered. Also, the records are normally in ascending sequence by control field, in this case, customer number. If the program prints reports in sequence, the user can quickly locate any required customer number. Because the file may be submitted in an incorrect sequence, it is common practice for the program to *"sequence-check"* input records by their control fields.

We may define a field that contains character data: the numbers 0 through 9, the letters A through Z, and other characters as $, *, and @. Character data, like all other data, use binary representation through the bit on/off condition. One byte (8 bits) represents one character. The combinations of eight bits in a byte provide 256 (2^8) possible characters. The typical printer, however, can print about 60 different characters. Figure 2-2 depicts the standard printable characters. As can be seen, in storage the bits

$$\underbrace{1100}_{zone}\quad\underbrace{0010}_{numeric}$$

represent the letter B. On a card, the letter B is punched as a 12-zone and a 2. The zone portion of the byte, 1100, represents the card 12-zone punch. The numeric portion of the byte, 0010, represents the card numeric 2-punch. Also, the figure shows that the letter K, punched with an 11-zone and a 2, has a binary representation 1101 0010. The letter S, punched with a zero-zone and a 2, has a binary representation 1110 0010. The characters 0 through 9 are represented as 1111 0000 through 1111 1001, and in hexadecimal as F0 through F9.

CODE TRANSLATION TABLE

Dec.	Hex	Instruction (RR)	BCDIC	EBCDIC(1)	ASCII	EBCDIC Card Code	Binary
0	00			NUL	NUL	12-0-1-8-9	0000 0000
1	01			SOH	SOH	12-1-9	0000 0001
2	02			STX	STX	12-2-9	0000 0010
3	03			ETX	ETX	12-3-9	0000 0011
4	04	SPM		PF	EOT	12-4-9	0000 0100
5	05	BALR		HT	ENQ	12-5-9	0000 0101
6	06	BCTR		LC	ACK	12-6-9	0000 0110
7	07	BCR		DEL	BEL	12-7-9	0000 0111
8	08	SSK			BS	12-8-9	0000 1000
9	09	ISK			HT	12-1-8-9	0000 1001
10	0A	SVC		SMM	LF	12-2-8-9	0000 1010
11	0B			VT	VT	12-3-8-9	0000 1011
12	0C			FF	FF	12-4-8-9	0000 1100
13	0D			CR	CR	12-5-8-9	0000 1101
14	0E	MVCL		SO	SO	12-6-8-9	0000 1110
15	0F	CLCL		SI	SI	12-7-8-9	0000 1111
16	10	LPR		DLE	DLE	12-11-1-8-9	0001 0000
17	11	LNR		DC1	DC1	11-1-9	0001 0001
18	12	LTR		DC2	DC2	11-2-9	0001 0010
19	13	LCR		TM	DC3	11-3-9	0001 0011
20	14	NR		RES	DC4	11-4-9	0001 0100
21	15	CLR		NL	NAK	11-5-9	0001 0101
22	16	OR		BS	SYN	11-6-9	0001 0110
23	17	XR		IL	ETB	11-7-9	0001 0111
24	18	LR		CAN	CAN	11-8-9	0001 1000
25	19	CR		EM	EM	11-1-8-9	0001 1001
26	1A	AR		CC	SUB	11-2-8-9	0001 1010
27	1B	SR		CU1	ESC	11-3-8-9	0001 1011
28	1C	MR		IFS	FS	11-4-8-9	0001 1100
29	1D	DR		IGS	GS	11-5-8-9	0001 1101
30	1E	ALR		IRS	RS	11-6-8-9	0001 1110
31	1F	SLR		IUS	US	11-7-8-9	0001 1111
32	20	LPDR		DS	SP	11-0-1-8-9	0010 0000
33	21	LNDR		SOS	!	0-1-9	0010 0001
34	22	LTDR		FS	"	0-2-9	0010 0010
35	23	LCDR			#	0-3-9	0010 0011
36	24	HDR		BYP	$	0-4-9	0010 0100
37	25	LRDR		LF	%	0-5-9	0010 0101
38	26	MXR		ETB	&	0-6-9	0010 0110
39	27	MXDR		ESC	'	0-7-9	0010 0111
40	28	LDR			(	0-8-9	0010 1000
41	29	CDR			)	0-1-8-9	0010 1001
42	2A	ADR		SM	*	0-2-8-9	0010 1010
43	2B	SDR		CU2	+	0-3-8-9	0010 1011
44	2C	MDR			,	0-4-8-9	0010 1100
45	2D	DDR		ENQ	-	0-5-8-9	0010 1101
46	2E	AWR		ACK	.	0-6-8-9	0010 1110
47	2F	SWR		BEL	/	0-7-8-9	0010 1111
48	30	LPER			0	12-11-0-1-8-9	0011 0000
49	31	LNER			1	1-9	0011 0001
50	32	LTER		SYN	2	2-9	0011 0010
51	33	LCER			3	3-9	0011 0011
52	34	HER		PN	4	4-9	0011 0100
53	35	LRER		RS	5	5-9	0011 0101
54	36	AXR		UC	6	6-9	0011 0110
55	37	SXR		EOT	7	7-9	0011 0111
56	38	LER			8	8-9	0011 1000
57	39	CER			9	1-8-9	0011 1001
58	3A	AER			:	2-8-9	0011 1010
59	3B	SER		CU3	;	3-8-9	0011 1011
60	3C	MER		DC4	<	4-8-9	0011 1100
61	3D	DER		NAK	=	5-8-9	0011 1101
62	3E	AUR			>	6-8-9	0011 1110
63	3F	SUR		SUB	?	7-8-9	0011 1111

CODE TRANSLATION TABLE (Contd)

Dec.	Hex	Instruction (RX)	BCDIC	EBCDIC(1)	ASCII	EBCDIC Card Code	Binary
64	40	STH		Sp	Sp	@	no punches	0100 0000
65	41	LA				A	12-0-1-9	0100 0001
66	42	STC				B	12-0-2-9	0100 0010
67	43	IC				C	12-0-3-9	0100 0011
68	44	EX				D	12-0-4-9	0100 0100
69	45	BAL				E	12-0-5-9	0100 0101
70	46	BCT				F	12-0-6-9	0100 0110
71	47	BC				G	12-0-7-9	0100 0111
72	48	LH				H	12-0-8-9	0100 1000
73	49	CH				I	12-1-8	0100 1001
74	4A	AH		¢	¢	J	12-2-8	0100 1010
75	4B	SH	.	.	.	K	12-3-8	0100 1011
76	4C	MH	⊔)	<	<	L	12-4-8	0100 1100
77	4D		[	(	(	M	12-5-8	0100 1101
78	4E	CVD	<	+	+	N	12-6-8	0100 1110
79	4F	CVB	‡	|	|	O	12-7-8	0100 1111
80	50	ST	&+	&	&	P	12	0101 0000
81	51					Q	12-11-1-9	0101 0001
82	52					R	12-11-2-9	0101 0010
83	53					S	12-11-3-9	0101 0011
84	54	N				T	12-11-4-9	0101 0100
85	55	CL				U	12-11-5-9	0101 0101
86	56	O				V	12-11-6-9	0101 0110
87	57	X				W	12-11-7-9	0101 0111
88	58	L				X	12-11-8-9	0101 1000
89	59	C				Y	11-1-8	0101 1001
90	5A	A		!	!	Z	11-2-8	0101 1010
91	5B	S	$	$	$	[	11-3-8	0101 1011
92	5C	M	•	*	*	\	11-4-8	0101 1100
93	5D	D	]	)	)	]	11-5-8	0101 1101
94	5E	AL	;	;	;	¬ ^	11-6-8	0101 1110
95	5F	SL	Δ	⌐	⌐	_	11-7-8	0101 1111
96	60	STD	-	-	-	`	11	0110 0000
97	61		/	/	/	a	0-1	0110 0001
98	62					b	11-0-2-9	0110 0010
99	63					c	11-0-3-9	0110 0011
100	64					d	11-0-4-9	0110 0100
101	65					e	11-0-5-9	0110 0101
102	66					f	11-0-6-9	0110 0110
103	67	MXD				g	11-0-7-9	0110 0111
104	68	LD				h	11-0-8-9	0110 1000
105	69	CD				i	0-1-8-9	0110 1001
106	6A	AD		‖		j	12-11	0110 1010
107	6B	SD		,	,	k	0-3-8	0110 1011
108	6C	MD	%(	%	%	l	0-4-8	0110 1100
109	6D	DD	γ	_	_	m	0-5-8	0110 1101
110	6E	AW	\	>	>	n	0-6-8	0110 1110
111	6F	SW	⋈	?	?	o	0-7-8	0110 1111
112	70	STE				p	12-11-0	0111 0000
113	71					q	12-11-0-1-9	0111 0001
114	72					r	12-11-0-2-9	0111 0010
115	73					s	12-11-0-3-9	0111 0011
116	74					t	12-11-0-4-9	0111 0100
117	75					u	12-11-0-5-9	0111 0101
118	76					v	12-11-0-6-9	0111 0110
119	77					w	12-11-0-7-9	0111 0111
120	78	LE				x	12-11-0-8-9	0111 1000
121	79	CE				y	1-8	0111 1001
122	7A	AE	฿	:	:	z	2-8	0111 1010
123	7B	SE	‡•	#	#	{	3-8	0111 1011
124	7C	ME	@'	@	@	|	4-8	0111 1100
125	7D	DE	'	'	'	}	5-8	0111 1101
126	7E	AU	>	=	=	~	6-8	0111 1110
127	7F	SU	√	"	"	DEL	7-8	0111 1111

1. Two columns of EBCDIC graphics are shown. The first gives standard bit pattern assignments. The second shows the T-11 and TN text printing chains (120 graphics).

Note the following common Hex representations:

Hex			Hex			Hex		
40	ъ	Blank	50	&	Ampersand	61	/	Slash
4B	.	Period	5B	$	Dollar	6B	,	Comma
4E	+	Plus	5C	*	Asterisk	6C	%	Percent
4F	|	OR symbol	60	–	Minus	7D	'	Apostrophe

FIGURE 2-2 360/370 code representation.

41

CODE TRANSLATION TABLE (Contd)

Dec.	Hex	Instruction and Format	Graphics and Controls BCDIC	Graphics and Controls EBCDIC(1)	Graphics and Controls ASCII	EBCDIC Card Code	Binary
128	80	SSM -S				12-0-1-8	1000 0000
129	81			a	a	12-0-1	1000 0001
130	82	LPSW -S		b	b	12-0-2	1000 0010
131	83	Diagnose		c	c	12-0-3	1000 0011
132	84	WRD } SI		d	d	12-0-4	1000 0100
133	85	RDD } SI		e	e	12-0-5	1000 0101
134	86	BXH		f	f	12-0-6	1000 0110
135	87	BXLE		g	g	12-0-7	1000 0111
136	88	SRL		h	h	12-0-8	1000 1000
137	89	SLL		i	i	12-0-9	1000 1001
138	8A	SRA				12-0-2-8	1000 1010
139	8B	SLA -RS		{		12-0-3-8	1000 1011
140	8C	SRDL		≤		12-0-4-8	1000 1100
141	8D	SLDL		(		12-0-5-8	1000 1101
142	8E	SRDA		+		12-0-6-8	1000 1110
143	8F	SLDA		+		12-0-7-8	1000 1111
144	90	STM				12-11-1-8	1001 0000
145	91	TM		j	j	12-11-1	1001 0001
146	92	MVI } SI		k	k	12-11-2	1001 0010
147	93	TS -S		l	l	12-11-3	1001 0011
148	94	NI		m	m	12-11-4	1001 0100
149	95	CLI		n	n	12-11-5	1001 0101
150	96	OI } SI		o	o	12-11-6	1001 0110
151	97	XI		p	p	12-11-7	1001 0111
152	98	LM -RS		q	q	12-11-8	1001 1000
153	99			r	r	12-11-9	1001 1001
154	9A					12-11-2-8	1001 1010
155	9B			}		12-11-3-8	1001 1011
156	9C	SIO, SIOF		⌷		12-11-4-8	1001 1100
157	9D	TIO, CLRIO } S		)		12-11-5-8	1001 1101
158	9E	HIO, HDV		±		12-11-6-8	1001 1110
159	9F	TCH		■		12-11-7-8	1001 1111
160	A0			-		11-0-1-8	1010 0000
161	A1			~	°	11-0-1	1010 0001
162	A2			s	s	11-0-2	1010 0010
163	A3			t	t	11-0-3	1010 0011
164	A4			u	u	11-0-4	1010 0100
165	A5			v	v	11-0-5	1010 0101
166	A6			w	w	11-0-6	1010 0110
167	A7			x	x	11-0-7	1010 0111
168	A8			y	y	11-0-8	1010 1000
169	A9			z	z	11-0-9	1010 1001
170	AA					11-0-2-8	1010 1010
171	AB			L		11-0-3-8	1010 1011
172	AC	STNSM } SI		r		11-0-4-8	1010 1100
173	AD	STOSM } SI		[		11-0-5-8	1010 1101
174	AE	SIGP -RS		≥		11-0-6-8	1010 1110
175	AF	MC -SI		•		11-0-7-8	1010 1111
176	B0			•		12-11-0-1-8	1011 0000
177	B1	LRA -RX		1		12-11-0-1	1011 0001
178	B2	See below		2		12-11-0-2	1011 0010
179	B3			3		12-11-0-3	1011 0011
180	B4			4		12-11-0-4	1011 0100
181	B5			5		12-11-0-5	1011 0101
182	B6	STCTL } RS		6		12-11-0-6	1011 0110
183	B7	LCTL } RS		7		12-11-0-7	1011 0111
184	B8			8		12-11-0-8	1011 1000
185	B9			9		12-11-0-9	1011 1001
186	BA	CS } RS		J		12-11-0-2-8	1011 1010
187	BB	CDS } RS		⌐		12-11-0-3-8	1011 1011
188	BC			⌐		12-11-0-4-8	1011 1100
189	BD	CLM		]		12-11-0-5-8	1011 1101
190	BE	STCM } RS		+		12-11-0-6-8	1011 1110
191	BF	ICM } RS		—		12-11-0-7-8	1011 1111

CODE TRANSLATION TABLE (Contd)

Dec.	Hex	Instruction (SS)	Graphics and Controls BCDIC	Graphics and Controls EBCDIC(1)	Graphics and Controls ASCII	EBCDIC Card Code	Binary
192	C0		?	{		12-0	1100 0000
193	C1		A	A	A	12-1	1100 0001
194	C2		B	B	B	12-2	1100 0010
195	C3		C	C	C	12-3	1100 0011
196	C4		D	D	D	12-4	1100 0100
197	C5		E	E	E	12-5	1100 0101
198	C6		F	F	F	12-6	1100 0110
199	C7		G	G	G	12-7	1100 0111
200	C8		H	H	H	12-8	1100 1000
201	C9		I	I	I	12-9	1100 1001
202	CA					12-0-2-8-9	1100 1010
203	CB					12-0-3-8-9	1100 1011
204	CC			ſ		12-0-4-8-9	1100 1100
205	CD					12-0-5-8-9	1100 1101
206	CE			¥		12-0-6-8-9	1100 1110
207	CF					12-0-7-8-9	1100 1111
208	D0		!	}		11-0	1101 0000
209	D1	MVN	J	J	J	11-1	1101 0001
210	D2	MVC	K	K	K	11-2	1101 0010
211	D3	MVZ	L	L	L	11-3	1101 0011
212	D4	NC	M	M	M	11-4	1101 0100
213	D5	CLC	N	N	N	11-5	1101 0101
214	D6	OC	O	O	O	11-6	1101 0110
215	D7	XC	P	P	P	11-7	1101 0111
216	D8		Q	Q	Q	11-8	1101 1000
217	D9		R	R	R	11-9	1101 1001
218	DA					12-11-2-8-9	1101 1010
219	DB					12-11-3-8-9	1101 1011
220	DC	TR				12-11-4-8-9	1101 1100
221	DD	TRT				12-11-5-8-9	1101 1101
222	DE	ED				12-11-6-8-9	1101 1110
223	DF	EDMK				12-11-7-8-9	1101 1111
224	E0		‡	\		0-2-8	1110 0000
225	E1					11-0-1-9	1110 0001
226	E2		S	S	S	0-2	1110 0010
227	E3		T	T	T	0-3	1110 0011
228	E4		U	U	U	0-4	1110 0100
229	E5		V	V	V	0-5	1110 0101
230	E6		W	W	W	0-6	1110 0110
231	E7		X	X	X	0-7	1110 0111
232	E8		Y	Y	Y	0-8	1110 1000
233	E9		Z	Z	Z	0-9	1110 1001
234	EA					11-0-2-8-9	1110 1010
235	EB					11-0-3-8-9	1110 1011
236	EC			d		11-0-4-8-9	1110 1100
237	ED					11-0-5-8-9	1110 1101
238	EE					11-0-6-8-9	1110 1110
239	EF					11-0-7-8-9	1110 1111
240	F0	SRP	0	0	0	0	1111 0000
241	F1	MVO	1	1	1	1	1111 0001
242	F2	PACK	2	2	2	2	1111 0010
243	F3	UNPK	3	3	3	3	1111 0011
244	F4		4	4	4	4	1111 0100
245	F5		5	5	5	5	1111 0101
246	F6		6	6	6	6	1111 0110
247	F7		7	7	7	7	1111 0111
248	F8	ZAP	8	8	8	8	1111 1000
249	F9	CP	9	9	9	9	1111 1001
250	FA	AP		I		12-11-0-2-8-9	1111 1010
251	FB	SP				12-11-0-3-8-9	1111 1011
252	FC	MP				12-11-0-4-8-9	1111 1100
253	FD	DP				12-11-0-5-8-9	1111 1101
254	FE					12-11-0-6-8-9	1111 1110
255	FF			EO		12-11-0-7-8-9	1111 1111

FIGURE 2-2 (*Continued*)

42

Digits are normally read from cards into storage in character format, and are printed in this format. (However, to perform arithmetic, we must translate character data into packed or binary format.) Data is read into storage from such devices as card readers, disk, and tape. This chapter considers only card input. The card, punched with alphabetic and numeric data, reads into an 80-byte area, defined anywhere in available storage. *The card is read entirely in character format.* The following lists the contents of a punched card:

COLUMN	FIELD	PUNCHED WITH
1–2	Card code	01
3–5	Account number	123
6–18	Name	JP MCKINNON (Alphabetic data is punched beginning on the left in column 6, with blanks filled to the right up to column 18.)
19–25	Balance	0125000 (The balance is $1,250.00—we do not punch dollar sign or comma, nor usually the decimal point.)
26–80	Unused	Blank

Assume that the name of the 80-byte input area is CARDIN, and the name of the input file is CARD. The relevant instructions to read the record are:

```
            GET       CARD,CARDIN
              .
              .
              .
    CARD      DEFCD  ...
    CARDIN    DS        CL80
```

The GET instruction reads the 80-character input record into the 80-byte CARDIN area in main storage, byte-for-byte, as shown in Figure 2-3.

CARDIN   *card input area*   CARDIN+79

Char	0	1	1	2	3	J	P		M	C	K	I	N	N	O	N			0	1	2	5	0	0	0			...	
Hex	F0	F1	F1	F2	F3	D1	D7	40	D4	C3	D2	C9	D5	D5	D6	D5	40	40	F0	F1	F2	F5	F0	F0	F0	40	40	...	40

FIGURE 2-3 Character and hex representation of an input area.

Compare the character and the hexadecimal representation, two hex digits for each character read. Note especially that any *blank* card position appears in storage as X'40' (binary 0100 0000). Also, the numbers 0 through 9 become X'F0' through X'F9'. We may assign symbolic names to each field within the CARDIN area. We then process the data by referring to each field's symbolic name. For example, we may check that the card code (01) is correct. We may move the account number (123) and the name to another storage area in order to print them. Also, we may convert the balance field (1,250.00) into packed decimal format in order to add it to an accumulator. In order to perform these tasks, we must be able to do the following:

— Reference areas and fields in storage. For this purpose we use *declaratives* to tell the Assembler each field's name, length, and format (e.g. character, binary, packed).
— Instruct the computer step-by-step what is to be done. We use Assembler symbolic *instructions* in order, for example, to move, add, and compare data.

FLOWCHART LOGIC

Programming is more than simply coding instructions for the computer to execute. Usually there are several steps: analysis, design, flowcharting, and coding.

ANALYSIS.   The first step is to analyze the problem. This step may consist of interviewing people concerned with the problem, studying input data to be processed, and designing the output required. If other programs use the same input or require the output, then the new program must integrate with the present system.

DESIGN.   The data to be used may be at present on *source documents*. We may have to design a punched card so that the data can be keypunched. Next, we may have to design the printed report, depicting each print position to be used.

FLOWCHARTING.   The next step depicts the solution to the problem. Commonly, we draw a *flowchart,* a pictorial representation of the program's flow of logic, showing each step that the program coding is to take. If we can flowchart the program, we should be able to code it. A flowchart serves the following purposes:

— It ensures that the problem has been thoroughly analyzed.
— It aids in solving the problem and often reveals programming errors.
— It acts as documentation for future corrections and modifications.

Flowcharts are an important element of program design and documentation. There are special symbols for operations such as processing, input/output, decisions, and terminals. After analyzing the problem, we depict the flow of logic that the coded computer program is to follow, showing each step and action, in the sequence it will be executed. In this way we fully solve the problem at the detail level, and make adjustments as we proceed. When we code the instructions we follow the flowchart logic. The flowchart therefore simplifies coding and minimizes errors.

Flowcharts should be neat and legible, drawn on one side of the page only, in *pencil* to facilitate revisions. They provide the identical logic as the coded program. In the case of small programs, such as the ones that accompany many of the chapters, a single flowchart is adequate. Large programs may require an additional summary flowchart depicting the program's general overall logic. Computer manufacturers provide a standard flowchart template. The common symbols are described next.

SYMBOL	IDENTIFICATION
TERMINAL	Start or termination of the program.
DECISION	Indicates that a compare or test is made with more than one possible result. This is the only symbol that permits more than one exit.
PROCESS BLOCK	Describes normal computer instructions such as MOVE or ADD. Notation within the block describes the operation(s). Several similar operations in a row, such as adding various fields, may all be included in one block.
INPUT/ OUTPUT BLOCK	Depicts all input/output operations, such as read a card, or write a line.
ON-PAGE CONNECTOR	Used if a continuous line cannot easily be drawn from one block to another. One on-page connector is an exit from the block, and one is an entry to the other block. Unique letters, such as 'A', in each connector relate them.
OFF-PAGE CONNECTOR	Signifies that the next block is on a different page. One off-page connector is an exit from the block, and one is an entry to the other block. Two items are entered in the connector: the page number on which the block is to be found, and an unique letter, such as 'A', to relate the connectors.

EXAMPLE FLOWCHART.   Figure 2-4 illustrates most of the flowchart symbols. The flowchart depicts a program that reads Customer Balance records. Each record is identified by a customer number, and contains also customer name and balance owing. There may be only one record for a customer. The objective is to print the balance owing for each valid customer. Note the following points:

1. The program compares the customer number on each input record against the customer number from the previously processed record. If the new one is higher (Y), the program prints customer number, name and balance, and stores the new customer number in "previous" number for the next sequence-check. The program then branches back to read the next record and repeats the instructions.

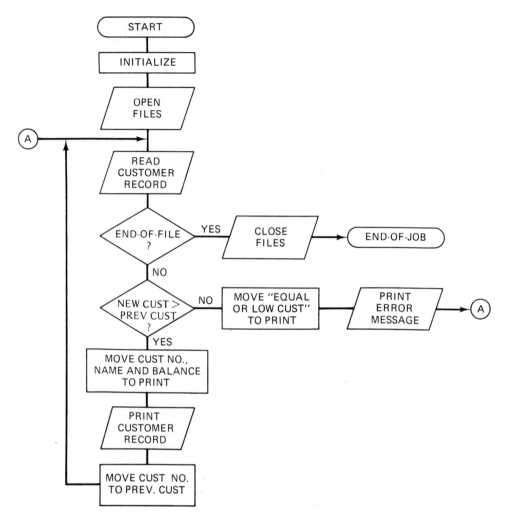

FIGURE 2-4 Flowchart for printing customer balances.

If the customer number is not higher, the program prints an error message and branches back to read the next record, indicated by a connector (A).

2. Immediately following the read operation is the end-of-file condition. If there are no more records to be processed, the program closes the files and terminates processing (END-OF-JOB).

Note a general flowcharting practice: the flow of logic is normally downward and to the right. The return of the flow is usually (but not always) upward and to the right.

JOB CONTROL

Medium and large sized 360/370 computers run under an operating system. In order to assemble or execute a program, we must submit "job control" entries that tell the operating system what action to perform. A "job" may consist of one or more programs that are to execute with required data. The system recognizes the start of a job, such as "Payroll", by means of the first job control card which contains an entry such as // JOB or //jobname JOB. Such entries that specify the job, and the action to perform comprise the "job control language" (JCL).

The two main IBM operating systems are Disk Operating System (DOS) for medium size computers, and Operating System (OS) for large ones. Job control language for these two systems is quite different, and even within a system may vary considerably between installations. Appendix D gives example job control for some typical situations. Check the particular JCL requirements for your own installation.

PROBLEMS

2-1. An input file is called "FILEIN" and an output file is called "FILEPR". Provide for your system: (a) The OPEN statement; (b) a properly defined area for input records; (c) the GET instruction; (d) a properly defined area for print records; (e) the write statement necessary to write and space two lines; (f) the CLOSE statement.

2-2. How does your system recognize the end of data for a file of cards?

2-3. A field tested in a program is found to be negative. What will be the condition code setting?

2-4. Given the Character, Hexadecimal or Binary, complete the representation.

	CHARACTER			HEX			BINARY		
Example	A	B	C	C1	C2	C3	1100 0001	1100 0010	1100 0011
(a)	3	7	0						
(b)	I	B	M						
(c)	S	a	m						
(d)	–	7	%						
(e)							1101 0111	1100 0001	1110 0011
(f)							0100 0000	1111 1001	1111 0000
(g)							0100 1101	0100 0000	0101 1101
(h)				C2	E4	C7			
(i)				E2	C1	D4			
(j)				5B	40	6B			

2-5. What is the purpose of the "flowchart"?

2-6. Draw a flowchart for the following problem. A card file contains sales data:

salesman number and amount of sales for the week. For each card, calculate sales commission as follows:

AMOUNT OF SALES	COMMISSION RATE
up to $1,000.00	5.0%
$1,000.01 to $3,500.00	7.5%
over $3,500.00	8.5%

Multiply sales amount by the required commission rate and print sales, rate, and commission. At the end of the file terminate processing.

2-7. Code the job control for your installation for assembly, link-edit, and execution of a card input program.

2-8. Code, assemble, and test a program that reads cards and prints their contents. If you call the input area CARDIN and the print area PRINT, then you can move the contents of each input record to the print area with:

```
MVC PRINT+20(80),CARDIN
```

PART II

BASIC ASSEMBLER CODING

CHAPTER 3

PROGRAMMING FOR CHARACTER DATA

The chapter introduces character format in which data is normally read and printed. The first part describes the Assembler declaratives that define character fields: *areas* in storage to handle input and output records, and *constants* such as report headings. Because programs must manipulate data that is read or defined, the next sections cover the basic instructions to move and compare data. A sample program illustrates the use of these instructions and how they may be organized into a working program.

DECLARATIVES

Declaratives are instructions that the Assembler recognizes and assigns storage locations. They do not generate an executable instruction. Declaratives provide for the entry of data to the program in two ways:

1. The declarative *Define Storage (DS) defines areas* for the program to receive data that varies in content, such as an input area.
2. The declarative *Define Constant (DC) defines constants,* such as a title for a report heading, or the numeric value '1' to count the pages being printed, or an accumulator initially set to zero.

51

DEFINE STORAGE (DS). The DS statement reserves an area of storage, for example, to define areas for reading cards and for printing. The general format of the DS statement on the coding sheet is:

NAME	OPERATION	OPERAND
[symbol]	DS	dTLn 'comments'

Optional: Symbol = the name assigned to the field. If the program needs to refer to the field by name, then we assign a name in columns 1–8. The name refers to the first (leftmost) byte of the field. Chapter 1 gives the requirements of symbolic names.

Optional: d = duplication factor which tells the Assembler *how many* repetitions of the same area are required. If we omit the factor, the Assembler assumes one area. If 2 is specified, the Assembler creates two adjacent areas; the name (if any) refers to the first area.

Required: T = type of format, such as C for Character, or P for Packed.

Optional: Ln = length of the field in bytes (n), positive values only. For example, L3 designates a 3-byte field. If length and comments are omitted (such as DS C), the Assembler assumes a length of one byte. The maximum length of a character DS field is 65,535 bytes.

Optional: 'comments' = a description within apostrophes of the purpose of the field. If we omit the length (Ln), the Assembler assumes that the length is the number of bytes within the apostrophes. For example, DS C'LIZ' defines a 3-byte area, but containing no such value—the contents are still "garbage".

Figure 3-1 depicts various DS statements in character format. Note the headings on the Assembler listing:

```
LOC   OBJECT CODE        STMT    SOURCE STATEMENT

                          7 *     ----------------------
                          8 *        DS    CHARACTER FORMAT
      Hex address of leftmost  9 *     ----------------------
003600 byte of defined field  10 FIELDA  DS    1CL5            RESERVES 5 BYTES CALLED FIELDA

003605                        12 FIELDB  DS    CL5             RESERVES 5 BYTES CALLED FIELDB

00360A                        14         DS    CL10            RESERVES 10 BYTES

003614                        16 CARDAREA DS   CL80            RESERVES 80 BYTES FOR CARD AREA

003664                        18         DS    80C             RESERVES 80 1-BYTE FIELDS

0036B4                        20 FIELDS  DS    3CL5            RESERVES 3 5-BYTE FIELDS

                              22 DATE    DS    CL8'DD/MM/YY'   RESERVES 8 BYTES. CONTENTS ARE ✦
0036C3                                                         DOCUMENTATION ONLY
```

FIGURE 3-1 Sample DS statements in character format.

SOURCE STATEMENT in the center lists our original source symbolic language code.

STMT, immediately to the left, gives the statement number of each source statement, as generated by the Assembler. FIELDA, for example, is statement-10. (Statement-11 is suppressed; it is a card with the instruction SPACE that causes the Assembler to space one line.)

LOC at the far left is the contents of the location counter that lists the hexadecimal address location of each statement. FIELDA is a 5-byte field beginning in location X'003600'. FIELDB begins immediately following in X'003605'. The Assembler defines declaratives in the same sequence that they are coded, in locations directly one after the other.

OBJECT CODE lists the assembled machine code: object code instructions and the contents of DC's. A DS lists no object code because it merely reserves space.

ADDR1 and ADDR2 refer to instructions, not declaratives. Each declarative is explained next. Comments on the right of each statement describe the defined area.

Statement-10: FIELDA is a 5-byte DS beginning in location X'003600'. The duplication factor 1 may be omitted, as shown in FIELDB.

Statement-12: FIELDB at X'003605' immediately follows FIELDA.

Statement-14: This DS is unnamed. Its address is X'360A' because FIELDB at X'3605' is five bytes: X'3605' + 5 = X'360A' (5 + 5 = 10 or A in hex).

Statement-16: CARDAREA defines an 80-byte area to be used for card input.

Statement-18: Because there is no length (Ln), the Assembler assumes that each of the 80 fields is one byte.

Statement-20: FIELDS defines three 5-byte fields. A reference to the name FIELDS is to the leftmost byte of the first 5-byte field.

Statement-22: DATE illustrates the use of comments. The programmer expects to store the date in the field in the specified format.

There are three problems to resolve:

1. *Where in storage will the field reside?* The Assembler assigns the field's location and accounts for the length of every instruction, storage area, and constant. For this task it uses a *location counter* (see Chapter 1).

2. *How does the computer know where the field resides and how long its length is?* The Assembler translates the symbolic addresses into machine object addresses. If it has assigned, for example, FIELDA with the address X'3600' then any instruction's reference to FIELDA is to address X'3600'. For certain instructions, the Assembler stores the length of the field as part of the instruction.

3. *What are the contents of the field?* The contents of a DS field are unknown, because the Assembler merely reserves the defined area. At the start of the program a DS area may contain data from a previous program. Therefore, we may have to initialize DS fields with valid data. For example, if the print area is defined as a DS, we should clear it to blanks at the start of the program so that "garbage" is not printed along with valid data. The only purpose of DS is to define an area of storage with a specified length. The fact that the field's format is *defined* as character, packed, etc., is irrelevant, *because at execution-time the field may*

contain data in any format. The defined format is merely a convenient reminder of what format we expect the field to contain. A major use of DS is to define input and output areas, covered next.

INPUT AREAS.   In order to define fields within a record, we use a DS with a zero duplication factor, as DS 0CL80, and define the fields immediately following.

The set of DS's in Figure 3-2 fully defines the input area for the card format given in Figure 2-3. The DS defines CARDIN as an 80-byte record. However, because of the "0" (zero) duplication factor, *the Assembler location counter is not incremented.* The Assembler assigns the next field, CODEIN, *the same address* as CARDIN (X'4201'). CODEIN, however, is a 2-byte field. Although both fields begin at X'4201', a reference to CARDIN is to an 80-byte field, whereas a reference to CODEIN is to a 2-byte field. Each DS following CARDIN defines a field *within* the CARDIN area. The sum of their lengths must equal 80, the length of CARDIN, in order to account for all card columns that read into the program's main storage area. We may now refer to the entire 80-byte CARDIN record, and to any field defined within the record.

The GET macro reads an 80-column card into an 80-byte area that we define, as in GET CARD,CARDIN. On input, card column 1 reads into the leftmost byte of CARDIN (location X'4201' on the assembled DS statement). Card column 2 reads into the next byte (X'4202'), and column 80 into the 80th byte (X'4250').

Note: The read operation erases the previous contents of the CARDIN area.

```
                  30 CARDIN   DS    0CL80    80-BYTE CARDIN AREA. DUPLICATION   +
004201                                       FACTOR IS ZERO
004201            31 CODEIN   DS    CL2      *    CARD CODE
004203            32 ACCTIN   DS    CL3      *    ACCOUNT NUMBER
004206            33 NAMEIN   DS    CL13     *    NAME
004213            34 BALANIN  DS    CL7      *    BALANCE OWING
00421A            35         DS    CL55     *    REST OF CARD
```

FIGURE 3-2   Area defined for card input.

OUTPUT AREAS.   Whereas a read operation erases the previous contents of the input area, a write operation leaves the contents of the output area unchanged. Therefore, if a DS defines the output area, we must ensure that the storage positions do not contain "garbage" from the previous program. At the beginning of our program, we should clear the output area to blanks (X'40'). An alternative soution is to use Define Constant (DC) to define the output area with an initial constant containing blanks. It is also often necessary to clear the print area after writing a line, so that it is blank for the next line to be printed.

Although the number of print positions varies with the printer used, a common requirement is to define a 133-byte print area as PRINT DS CL133 or DC CL133' '.

The 360/370 use the leftmost byte of PRINT for a printer *forms control character.* This character controls forms movement, such as print and space one line, or skip to a new page. We may use the other 132 positions to store data to be printed. Chapter 2 gives the requirements for the print macro, PUTPR.

We may also define the print area with a zero duplication factor, as PRINT DS 0CL133; with a DS to define each field within the record. Alternatively, we may reference PRINT by *relative addressing.* (It is possible to reference any field in main storage by relative addressing, or to define it with a zero duplication factor and redefine the fields within it.) Since the leftmost byte (the position labeled PRINT) is reserved for the control character, we may refer to the first printable position as PRINT+1, to the second as PRINT+2, etc.:

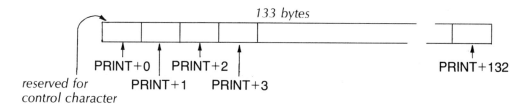

DEFINE CONSTANT (DC). The DC statement, like DS, reserves storage of a defined length. In addition, DC defines a constant (or value) such as a heading to be printed on a report. A DC may define a constant in any format, such as Character, Binary, Packed and Hexadecimal, and in various lengths. The general format for a DC statement is as follows:

NAME	OPERATION	OPERAND
[symbol]	DC	dTLn 'constant'

Optional: Symbol = the name that we may assign to the field.

Optional: d = duplication factor which tells the Assembler *how many* repetitions of the constant are required. The symbolic name (if any) refers to the first constant. If we omit the factor the Assembler assumes one constant.

Required: T = type of format, such as C for Character, P for Packed, X for Hexadecimal, Z for Zoned, etc.

Optional: Ln = length of the field in number (n) of bytes. If Ln is omitted the Assembler assumes the field length to be the number of bytes defined by the constant. For example, DC C'SAM' defines a 3-byte constant.

Required: 'constant' = the constant that is to be defined, contained within apostrophes. A DS "constant" is for documentation; a DC constant is stored.

The following are rules regarding *Character* constants:

1. Their length may be defined from one to 256 characters.
2. They may contain any character that may be keypunched or printed, including blanks.
3. If the length (Ln) is not coded, the Assembler assumes that the field length is that of the defined constant. Thus, DC C'SAM' defines a 3-character constant.
4. If the length (Ln) is specified, then the following may occur:
   a. The defined length *equals* the length of the constant:

FIELDA DC CL5'APRIL'

   The length of FIELDA is 5 bytes. The Assembler generates APRIL.
   b. The defined length is *less than* the length of the constant:

FIELDB DC CL4'APRIL'

   The defined length, 4, overrides the length of the constant. The length of FIELDB will be *four* bytes. The Assembler *left-adjusts the constant and truncates rightmost characters* that exceed the defined length. APRI is generated.
   c. The defined length is *greater* than the length of the constant.

FIELDC DC CL6'APRIL'

   The length of FIELDC will be *six* bytes. The Assembler left-adjusts the constant and *pads rightmost bytes with blanks*. APRILƀ is generated.
5. The apostrophe (') and the ampersand (&) have special meaning to the Assembler. If we define them within a constant, we must code them as two adjacent characters, although the Assembler counts and prints only one.

Figure 3-3 provides various character DC's with explanations. On the Assembler listing note the OBJECT CODE generated by each statement. LOC gives the hex address of the first byte of each constant. Under OBJECT CODE is the hex contents up to the first eight bytes (16 hex digits) of the constant. (The entire hex contents for constants exceeding eight bytes can be printed by means of the Assembler instruction PRINT DATA.)

The first pair of DC's defines fields containing blanks, or X'40' in object code. BLANK1 generates a 5-byte field containing five blanks. Its location is X'004301'. Under OBJECT CODE are the five bytes of blanks (X'40's). BLANK2 defines five 1-byte blank fields; its implicit length is therefore one.

The next section defines fields with zero values. ZERO1 generates a 5-byte field containing five zeros. Note that a character zero is X'F0'. ZERO2 is a 5-byte field as well. But because only one zero is specified, the Assembler left-adjusts the zero and fills the remaining bytes with blanks, a common coding error. ZERO3 generates five 1-byte fields, each containing a zero.

The third section defines numeric values. FIVEA and FIVEB show two ways to define a 1-byte field containing the value 5 (X'F5'). FIVEC generates 05, or X'F0F5'.

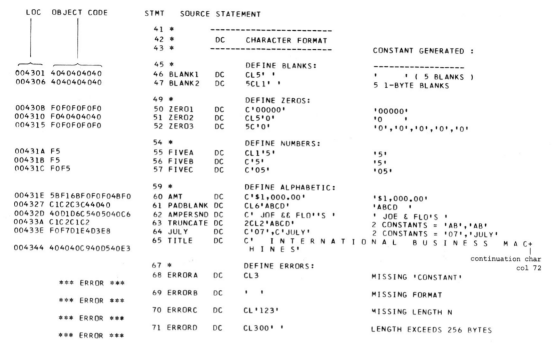

```
LOC    OBJECT CODE        STMT    SOURCE STATEMENT

                          41 *        ---------------------
                          42 *        DC    CHARACTER FORMAT
                          43 *        ---------------------               CONSTANT GENERATED :

                          45 *              DEFINE BLANKS:               --------------------
004301 4040404040         46 BLANK1   DC    CL5' '                      '     '  ( 5 BLANKS )
004306 4040404040         47 BLANK2   DC    5CL1' '                     5 1-BYTE BLANKS

                          49 *              DEFINE ZEROS:
00430B F0F0F0F0F0         50 ZERO1    DC    C'00000'                    '00000'
004310 F040404040         51 ZERO2    DC    CL5'0'                      '0     '
004315 F0F0F0F0F0         52 ZERO3    DC    5C'0'                       '0','0','0','0','0'

                          54 *              DEFINE NUMBERS:
00431A F5                 55 FIVEA    DC    CL1'5'                      '5'
00431B F5                 56 FIVEB    DC    C'5'                        '5'
00431C F0F5               57 FIVEC    DC    C'05'                       '05'

                          59 *              DEFINE ALPHABETIC:
00431E 5BF16BF0F0F04BF0   60 AMT      DC    C'$1,000.00'                '$1,000.00'
004327 C1C2C3C44040       61 PADBLANK DC    CL6'ABCD'                   'ABCD  '
00432D 40D1D6C5405040C6   62 AMPERSND DC    C' JOE && FLO''S '          ' JOE & FLO'S '
00433A C1C2C1C2           63 TRUNCATE DC    2CL2'ABCD'                  2 CONSTANTS = 'AB','AB'
00433E F0F7D1E4D3E8       64 JULY     DC    C'07','C'JULY'              2 CONSTANTS = '07','JULY'
                          65 TITLE    DC    C'  I N T E R N A T I O N A L   B U S I N E S S   M A C+
004344 404040C940D540E3                     H I N E S'
                                                                                  |
                                                                            continuation char
                                                                                  col 72
                          67 *              DEFINE ERRORS:
                          68 ERRORA   DC    CL3                         MISSING 'CONSTANT'
       *** ERROR ***
                          69 ERRORB   DC    ' '                         MISSING FORMAT
       *** ERROR ***
                          70 ERRORC   DC    CL'123'                     MISSING LENGTH N
       *** ERROR ***
                          71 ERRORD   DC    CL300' '                    LENGTH EXCEEDS 256 BYTES
       *** ERROR ***
```

FIGURE 3-3   Sample DC statements in character format.

The fourth section defines alphabetic fields. AMT generates a field with a dollar sign (X'5B'), a comma (X'6B'), and a decimal point (X'4B'). PADBLANK left-adjusts the constant and pads two blanks to the right. AMPERSND illustrates the use of the ampersand (&) and apostrophe ('), both of which must be defined twice. The generated constant in this case is 13 bytes long, although the Assembler prints only the first eight bytes under OBJECT CODE. TRUNCATE defines two constants, each two bytes long. The Assembler truncates the constant ABCD on the right to two bytes (because we coded L2) and generates AB twice (see the hex object code). JULY shows one statement that defines two character constants, separated by a comma. A reference to the name JULY is to the first 2-byte field. (This feature, providing for definition of more than one constant with one DC, is not available in every level of Assembler.)

TITLE illustrates the continuation character, in this case a plus sign (+) in column 72. The constant continues on the next line in column 16. (Even though there is an Assembler instruction TITLE, we can use TITLE for the name of a field.)

The last section defines some common coding errors. The comments on the right explain the cause of the error. The Assembler prints ERROR instead of the object code, and explains the cause at the end of the program listing (not shown). Any instruction in the program that references one of these invalid constants also causes an error message for that instruction.

Problems 3-1 and 3-2 should now be attempted.

CHARACTER INSTRUCTIONS

This section covers the movement and comparison of fields in character format. The content of these fields is made available to the program from an input record or declared as a constant value. There are two instruction formats that process data in main storage: Storage-to-Storage (SS) and Storage Immediate (SI). SS format processes data between two fields in main storage, whereas SI format processes between a one-byte constant built into the instruction and one main storage location.

STORAGE-TO-STORAGE FORMAT

Some instructions reference data in main storage only, others process data between main storage and the registers, and others process in registers only. Storage-to-storage (SS) format references only storage locations. In an instruction like MVC (Move Character), the operands are represented as S1,S2 meaning that both operand-1 (S1) and operand-2 (S2) reference main storage. Another representation in symbolic form is:

MVC D1(L,B1),D2(B2)

D1(L,B1) means that the operand-1 address consists of a base register (B1) and a displacement (D1).
L means that the length of operand-1 controls the number of bytes processed.
D2(B2) means that the operand-2 address consists of a base register (B2) and a displacement (D2). This feature may be ignored for now; Chapter 6 describes it in detail.

MOVE CHARACTERS—MVC

Frequently the program must move the contents of one field to another. Fields in the input area must be moved to other areas in order to save them from erasure by the next record that the program reads. Also, constants, headings, and calculated values must be moved to the print area for printing. The following instructions move character fields, bytes, and half-bytes from one storage location to another: Move Character (MVC), Move Numerics (MVN), Move Zones (MVZ), Move Immediate (MVI), and Move With Offset (MVO). This chapter describes MVC and MVI. Although MVC may move data in any format, we normally confine its use to character fields.

NAME	OPERATION	OPERAND
[symbol]	MVC	S1,S2 or D1(L,B1),D2(B2)

MVC is a Storage-to-Storage (SS) instruction. Its rules are:

1. MVC may move from one to 256 bytes, usually character data, but technically any format.
2. Data beginning in the byte specified by operand-2 is moved one byte at a time to the field beginning with the byte specified by operand-1. The move does not affect the contents of the operand-2 field; the bytes are *copied* into the operand-1 field. Thus, the instruction MVC FLDA,FLDB copies the contents of FLDB into FLDA.
3. Each operand specifies the *leftmost* byte of the field, and *movement is from left to right.*
4. *The length of the operand-1 field determines the number of bytes moved.* In the MVC instruction format there is a length code (L) for operand-1 only. The length of operand-2 is irrelevant to the operation. If the operand-1 field is five bytes long and operand-2 is six bytes, MVC moves only the first five bytes of operand-2 (from left to right one byte at a time) to the operand-1 field. If the operand-1 field is six bytes and operand-2 is five, MVC moves all five bytes of operand-2, plus one byte immediately to its right.

FIELD LENGTH. We may specify the number of bytes to be moved in one of two ways: *implicit* or *explicit length.* Assume the following DC's:

NAME	OPERATION	OPERAND
FIELD1	DC	C'JUNE'
FIELD2	DC	C'APRIL'

IMPLICIT LENGTH: MVC FIELD1,FIELD2. Operand-1, FIELD1, is implicitly defined as a 4-byte constant. Since the Assembler recognizes that a reference to FIELD1 is to a 4-byte field, the MVC moves only the first four bytes of FIELD2, APRI. The contents of FIELD2 are unaffected.

‚ĶFIELD1 ‚ĶFIELD2

before the MVC: J U N E A P R I L

after the MVC: A P R I A P R I L

EXPLICIT LENGTH: MVC FIELD1(3),FIELD2. Assume the same DC's as before. Operand-1 has an explicit length (3) that overrides the defined length of FIELD1. Therefore, MVC moves only the first three bytes of FIELD2 (APR) into the first three bytes of FIELD1. The fourth byte of FIELD1 is unaltered:

‚ĶFIELD1 ‚ĶFIELD2

before the MVC: J U N E A P R I L

after the MVC: A P R E A P R I L

EXPLICIT LENGTH: MVC FIELD1(5),FIELD2 moves 5 bytes. APRI is moved into FIELD1. The "L" is moved into the next byte to the right, the first byte of FIELD2, which immediately follows FIELD1:

FIELD1 FIELD2

before the MVC: J U N E A P R I L

after the MVC: A P R I L P R I L

RELATIVE ADDRESSING. Any operand that references main storage may use relative addressing. If we have to refer to a byte that has no name, we may refer to its position relative to a byte that has a name. For example, suppose we want to move the third and fourth bytes of FIELD2 to the second and third bytes of FIELD1: MVC FIELD1+1(2),FIELD2+2:

FIELD1 FIELD2

before the MVC: J U N E A P R I L

after the MVC: J R I E A P R I L

Note: In order to move two bytes, we code an explicit length (2) in operand-1. A relative address of +1 refers to the second byte, and +2 refers to the third byte.

SYMBOL LENGTH ATTRIBUTE. The Assembler permits explicit lengths coded *absolutely,* as was described, and *symbolically:*

> *absolute explicit length:* MVC FIELD1(5),FIELD2
> *symbolic explicit length:* MVC FIELD1(L'FIELD2),FIELD2

The symbol length attribute uses L' followed by a symbolic name. In this example, we want to move five bytes. Since the length of FIELD2 is five, the Assembler understands the explicit length to be 5.

Figure 3-4 depicts unrelated MVC operations. Note the OBJECT CODE generated for each statement. The Assembler lists under ADDR1 and ADDR2 the addresses of operand-1 and operand-2 respectively. For example, statement-17 is MVC X,Y. The address of X, a 3-byte field, is 03002 and the address of Y, a 5-byte field, is 03005. The instruction may be read as: Move the first three bytes of Y, starting in location 03005, to the field called X, starting in location 03002. The object code instruction is six bytes long, beginning in location 003012. Chapter 6 gives the interpretation of this machine language.

```
LOC    OBJECT CODE       ADDR1 ADDR2   STMT      SOURCE STATEMENT
                                        6  *      ----------------------
                                        7  ***    MVC   MOVE CHARACTERS
                                        8  *      ----------------------
003002 C1C2C3                          10  X       DC    C'ABC'           THESE FIELDS
003005 C4C5C6C7C8                      11  Y       DC    C'DEFGH'         ARE ADJACENT
00300A C9D1D2D3D4D5D6D7                12  Z       DC    C'IJKLMNOP'      IN STORAGE

                                       14  *                             ACTION OF MOVE:            RESULT OF MOVE:
                                       15  *                             --------------            --------------

                                       17  MOVE1   MVC   X,Y             1ST 3 BYTES OF Y INTO                 +
003012 D202 4000 4003 03002 03005                                          1ST 3 BYTES OF X        X= 'DEF'
                                       18  MOVE2   MVC   Z,X             ALL BYTES OF X &                      +
003018 D207 4008 4000 0300A 03002                                          Y INTO Z                Z= 'ABCDEFGH'
                                       19  MOVE3   MVC   Z(3),X          1ST 3 BYTES OF X INTO                 +
00301E D202 4008 4000 0300A 03002                                          1ST 3 BYTES OF Z        Z= 'ABCLMNOP'
                                       20  MOVE4   MVC   Z+2(3),X        1ST 3 BYTES OF X INTO                 +
003024 D202 400A 4000 0300C 03002                                          BYTES 3-5 OF Z          Z= 'IJABCNOP'
                                       21  MOVE5   MVC   Z+3(2),X+2      3RD BYTE OF X & 1ST                   +
00302A D201 400B 4002 0300D 03004                                          BYTE OF Y INTO Z        Z= 'IJKCDNOP'
                                       22  MOVE6   MVC   X+1(4),X        X TO X+1, X+1 TO X+2, X+2             +
003030 D203 4001 4000 03003 03002                                          TO Y, & Y TO Y+1        X= 'AAA'
                                                                                                   Y= 'AAFGH'
                                       23  MOVE7   MVC   X,X+1           LEFT SHIFT. MOVES X+1 TO X,           +
003036 D202 4000 4001 03002 03003                                          X+2 TO X+1, Y TO X+2    X= 'BCD'
                                       24  MOVE8   MVC   Z,X(3)          MVC DOES NOT PERMIT EXPLICIT LENGTH IN +
00303C 0000 0000 0000 00000 00000                                          OPERAND-2
          *** ERROR ***
```

FIGURE 3-4   Sample unrelated MVC operations.

Note *instruction alignment*—all the MVCs begin on an even storage location, as shown under LOC (location): X'003012', X'003018', etc. These examples illustrate some extreme cases, and although important to understand, most data movement is directly from one field to another defined with the same length.

MOVE1: Operand-1, X, is shorter than operand-2, Y. The implicit length (3) of X governs the number of bytes moved.

MOVE2: Operand-1, Z, is longer than operand-2, X. The implicit length (8) of Z governs the number of bytes moved.

MOVE3: The explicit length (3) overrides Z's implicit length of 8; only 3 bytes are moved. With symbol length attribute, the statement could be: MVC Z(L'X),X.

MOVE4 and MOVE5 illustrate explicit length and relative addressing. In each case the explicit length overrides the defined implicit length.

MOVE6 shows how to copy a character a specified number of positions to the right. The leftmost byte of X contains 'A', which MVC copies four bytes to the right. It is possible to propagate any character in this fashion because MVC moves one character at a time, from left to right. This technique is useful to clear areas to blanks.

MOVE7 shifts data one byte to the left. It may be useful to check the operation by following the data movement one byte at a time.

MOVE8: We want to move three bytes, but have erroneously coded an explicit length of 3 in operand-2 instead of operand-1. The Assembler generates six bytes of hex zeros as the object code "instruction". These will cause a "program interrupt" if the program is executed. MOVE3 shows the instruction correctly written.

For illustrative purposes, this text uses examples with declaratives named as X, Y, and Z, but does not advocate such cryptic names in programs.

Problem 3-3 should now be attempted.

COMPARE LOGICAL CHARACTER—CLC

It is often necessary to determine if the contents of one field are equal to, greater than, or less than, the contents of another field. Examples of the need to compare character fields include:

1. Testing for valid card codes;
2. Checking for valid dates on cards;
3. Testing for ascending sequence of account numbers in an input file. In this test, sequence-checking, the new account number just read is compared to the previously processed account number.

The instructions to compare character fields are Compare Logical Characters (CLC), and Compare Logical Immediate (CLI). All compare instructions and certain others set the *condition code* described in Chapter 2. As a result of the operation, the condition code is set as high, low, or equal, and may be interrogated with a *conditional branch* instruction. CLC may compare data in any format, but we normally confine its use to comparing character fields.

NAME	OPERATION	OPERAND
[symbol]	CLC	S1,S2 or D1(L,B1),D2(B2)

The rules for CLC are:

1. CLC may compare fields from one to 256 bytes long.
2. CLC compares data beginning in the byte specified by operand-1 to the data beginning with the byte specified by operand-2. Comparison is left to right, one byte at a time. The condition code is set as follows:

COMPARISON	CONDITION CODE SETTING
Operand-1 equals operand-2	0 (equal)
Operand-1 is lower	1 (low)
Operand-1 is higher	2 (high)

3. CLC terminates comparison as soon as an unequal condition is encountered, or if none, by the length of operand-1 (explicit or implicit).

Comparison is based on the binary contents of the bytes, and all possible bytes are valid. The lowest value is binary zeros (X'00'), and the highest is binary ones

(X'FF'). A "character" field contains what is called "logical" data—unsigned, nonarithmetic data. CLC is not suitable to compare arithmetic data in packed or binary format. For compares that consider a plus or minus sign, use CP for packed data, and C, CH, or CR for binary. Another logical compare operation on the 370, CLCL (Compare Logical Long), has rather restricted use.

Figure 3-5 provides examples of CLC operations which should be examined carefully.

```
LOC   OBJECT CODE      ADDR1 ADDR2  STMT    SOURCE STATEMENT
                                    28 *      ------------------------------
                                    29 ***    CLC   COMPARE LOGICAL CHARACTER
                                    30 *      ------------------------------
003042 C1C2C3C4C5                   31 FIELD1  DC    C'ABCDE'         THESE FIELDS
003047 C6C7C8                       32 FIELD2  DC    C'FGH'           ARE ADJACENT
00304A 5C5C                         33 FIELD3  DC    C'**'            IN STORAGE

                                    35 *                              DATA COMPARED:    COND'N CODE:
                                    36 *                              --------------    -----------
00304C D502 4045 4040  03047 03042  37 COMP1   CLC   FIELD2,FIELD1    'FGH'    > 'ABC'        HIGH
003052 D504 4040 4045  03042 03047  38 COMP2   CLC   FIELD1,FIELD2    'ABCDE' < 'FGH**'       LOW
003058 D502 4042 4045  03044 03047  39 COMP3   CLC   FIELD1+2(3),FIELD2  'CDE'  <'FGH'        LOW
00305F D504 4042 4045  03044 03047  40 COMP4   CLC   FIELD1+2,FIELD2  'CDEFG' < 'FGH**'       LOW
003064 D501 4048 4040  0304A 03042  41 COMP5   CLC   FIELD3,FIELD1    '**'    < 'AB'          LOW
                                    42 COMP6   CLC   FIELD2,FIELD1+2(3)  CLC DOES NOT PERMIT EXPLICIT
00306A 0000 0000 0000  00000 00000                                   LENGTH IN OPERAND-2
       *** ERROR ***
```

FIGURE 3-5   Sample unrelated CLC operations.

COMP1: The operand-1 field, FIELD2, is shorter. CLC compares the three bytes of FIELD2 against the first three bytes only of FIELD1. Because the data in FIELD2 is logically greater than that of FIELD1, the condition code is set to high.

COMP2: The operand-1 field is longer. CLC compares the five bytes of FIELD1 against the three bytes of FIELD2 plus the next rightmost two bytes of FIELD3 (two asterisks). Operand-1 is lower.

COMP3: Operand-1 uses relative addressing and explicit length. CLC compares bytes 3, 4 and 5 of FIELD1 against FIELD2.

COMP4: The instruction is similar to **COMP3**, with the explicit length omitted. The implicit length of operand-1 is therefore 5.

COMP5: An asterisk (X'5C') is lower than character 'A' (X'C1'), so the operation terminates as "low" after comparing only the first byte.

COMP6 illustrates erroneous use of explicit length in operand-2; omitting the length corrects the error.

BRANCHING.   CLC makes the comparison and sets the condition code. To test the condition code to determine what action to take (for example, was the result of the test high, low, or equal?), we use the following conditional branch instructions:

CONDITION CODE	CONDITIONAL BRANCHES	
0 = Equal/zero	**BE** (Branch equal)	**BNE** (Branch not equal)
1 = Low/minus	**BL** (Branch low)	**BNL** (Branch not low)
2 = High/plus	**BH** (Branch high)	**BNH** (Branch not high)

Each of the preceding conditional branch instructions is called an "extended mnemonic," and is a unique use of the Branch on Condition (BC) instruction, explained in detail in Chapter 6.

With normal processing, the computer executes instructions in storage, one after another. Conditional branch instructions permit the program to 'branch' to different addresses in the program. We may therefore code our program to test, for example, for valid card codes. If a card does not contain the correct code in a specified column, we may branch to an error routine that prints a warning message.

Example: Compare and conditional branch

NEW	DS	CL4	Contains the value of the account just read (assume '1347').
PREV	DS	CL4	Contains the value of the previous account read (assume '1208').
	CLC	NEW,PREV	Compare the contents of NEW to PREV.
	BH	R20HIGH	If NEW is higher, branch to R20HIGH (some address of a routine in the program).

The preceding instructions are read as follows: Compare the new account (containing 1347) to the previously read account (1208). NEW's contents being higher than PREV, the condition code is set to high (2). Next, BH tests if the high condition is set. Because the code is 'high', the program branches to R20HIGH. If the code was not "high", the computer would execute the next sequential instruction (NSI) following the BH.

Two other branch instructions are Unconditional branch (B), and No-operation (NOP). The unconditional branch tests if any condition (high, low, equal) exists. Since there is always at least one condition, we use B if a branch is always required. For example, after processing an input record, we may return to read the next record by means of an unconditional branch:

A10READ	GET	CARD	Read a card record
	.		Process the record
	B	A10READ	Branch to read the next record

NOP, which tests no condition, is only occasionally used.

COMPARE AND BRANCH.   The following examples illustrate the preceding discussion. Assume the declaratives X, Y, and Z contain data and are each defined as DS CL4:

Example: If X is greater than or equal to Y, branch to J10HIEQ (an address elsewhere in the program).

```
CLC   X,Y        Compare X to Y
BH    J10HIEQ    Branch if high
BE    J10HIEQ    Branch if equal
```

This example could also be coded more efficiently as:

```
CLC   X,Y        Compare X to Y
BNL   J10HIEQ    Branch if X is not lower (high or equal)
```

Example: If X is greater than Z, branch to J20HI. Else, if Z does not equal Y, branch to J30NEQ.

```
CLC   X,Z        Compare X to Z
BH    J20HI      Branch if high
CLC   Z,Y        Compare Z to Y
BNE   J30NEQ     Branch if unequal
```

Problem 3-4 should be be attempted.

STORAGE IMMEDIATE FORMAT

Storage-to-Storage (SS) format references two fields in main storage, whereas the Storage-Immediate (SI) format references only one field. The other data used is a 1-byte constant, built into the instruction itself. The Assembler stores the immediate constant in the second byte of the object code instruction. The constant is therefore part of the object instruction.

MOVE IMMEDIATE (MVI) AND COMPARE LOGICAL IMMEDIATE (CLI). The immediate instructions Move Immediate (MVI) and Compare Logical Immediate (CLI) are efficient instructions to move or compare 1-byte fields.

NAME	OPERATION	OPERAND	
[symbol]	MVI	S1,I2 or	D1(B1),I2
[symbol]	CLI	S1,I2 or	D1(B1),I2

The rules for MVI and CLI are similar to those for MVC and CLC, with the following exceptions:

1. Operand-1 references a single main storage location. The operand does not permit an explicit length code because the number of bytes is always one.
2. Operand-2 contains a 1-byte immediate constant. The immediate constant value may be character (C), hexadecimal (X), binary (B), or a decimal digit, but *not* zoned (Z) or packed (P).

Figure 3-6 depicts some typical use of immediate operations.

```
LOC   OBJECT CODE    ADDR1 ADDR2  STMT    SOURCE STATEMENT

003070 F0F0F0                     47 SAVE     DC    C'000'         SAVE=  |F0|F0|F0|
003073 F5                         48 CODEIN   DC    C'5'

                                  50 *        -----------------------
        MVI $                     51 ***      MVI   MOVE IMMEDIATE
        ↓↓                        52 *        -----------------------
003074 925B 406E      03070       53 MOVIMM1  MVI   SAVE,C'$'      SAVE=  |5B|F0|F0|
003078 925B 406E      03070       54 MOVIMM2  MVI   SAVE,X'5B'     X'5B'IS IDENTICAL TO C'$'
00307C 0000 0000      00000       55 MOVIMM3  MVI   SAVE(1),C'?'   ERROR IF LENGTH IN OP-1.
       *** ERROR ***
003080 0000 0000      00000       56 MOVIMM4  MVI   SAVE+1,=C'$'   ERROR: CANNOT USE LITERAL
       *** ERROR ***

                                  58 *        ----------------------------
        CLI 5                     59 ***      CLI   COMPARE LOGICAL IMMEDIATE
        ↓↓                        60 *        ----------------------------
003084 95F5 4071      03073       61 COMIMM1  CLI   CODEIN,C'5'    SETS CONDITION CODE EQUAL
003088 0000 0000      00000       62 COMIMM2  CLI   CODEIN(1),C'5' ERROR IF LENGTH IN OP-1.
       *** ERROR ***
00308C 0000 0000      00000       63 COMIMM3  CLI   CODEIN,P'5'    ERROR IF PACK OR ZONED
       *** ERROR ***
```

FIGURE 3-6   Sample unrelated MVI and CLI operations.

MOVIMMI moves a 1-byte dollar sign defined in character format. MOVIMM2 shows a hexadecimal dollar defined. Both statements generate identical object code, although C'$' provides better clarity to users. Note the object code for MOVIMM1 begins at 003074 and contains 925B406E: The machine code for MVI is hex 92, and the dollar sign, X'5B', is in the next (second) byte.

COMIMM1 compares the contents of a 1-byte field, CODEIN, to an immediate operand. Because both contain the character value '5', the condition code is set to equal.

MOVIMM3, MOVIMM4, COMIMM2, and COMIMM3 illustrates common coding errors that the Assembler recognizes. MOVIMM4 incorrectly uses a "literal." Literals are covered in the next section.

LITERALS

The use of literals is a short cut way of writing a DC. The literal begins with an equal (=) sign followed by a character for the type of constant, and the constant contained with apostrophes ('). The same basic rules that apply to DCs apply as well to literals.

Example: Use of a literal in place of a DC

```
   use of a DC:        HEADING  DC    C'INVENTORY'
                                MVC   PRINT+20(9),HEADING

   use of a literal:            MVC   PRINT+20(9),=C'INVENTORY'
```

Both operations accomplish the same results. However, the use of the literal, ='IN-VENTORY', saves us from writing the line of coding for the DC.

The Assembler recognizes that an operand beginning with an equal sign is a literal. The Assembler creates the object code constant, assigns an address, and stores the constant as part of the program in a "literal pool", without a name. Two or more literals defined identically within a program are usually set up as only one constant in the literal pool. Literals generated by IOCS (input/output system) macros are also included in the pool.

> *Note:* A literal is different from an immediate operand. Immediate instructions, such as MVI and CLI, must have a 1-byte constant in operand-2. A literal, however, must be preceded by the equal sign, and generates a constant in storage. For 1-byte nonarithmetic constants, immediate instructions should be used.

Example: Contrast of a literal and an immediate operand

use of a literal:	MVC	PRINT+20(1),=C'$'
use of immediate:	MVI	PRINT+20,C'$'

Although both operations accomplish identical results, note: (a) MVC requires a length (l) in operand-1 if PRINT is not defined with a length of one; (b) MVC uses a literal—the assembled address of operand-2 will contain the location of the constant ($); (c) MVI contains the $ as part of the assembled instruction; (d) MVI is more efficient coding here because it is only four bytes long. MVC requires six bytes for the instruction plus one for the constant defined by the literal =C'$'.

THE LITERAL POOL.   The Assembler organizes the literal pool into four sections, and within these sections, stores the literals in order of their appearance in the program.

SECTION	CONTENTS
1	All literals whose length is a multiple of eight.
2	All remaining literals whose length is a multiple of four.
3	All remaining literals whose length is a multiple of two.
4	All odd-length literals.

The Assembler stores the literal pool at the end of the program and prints it immediately following the END statement. However, the Assembler command LTORG can cause the Assembler to store literals anywhere in the program.

NAME	OPERATION	OPERAND
[symbol]	LTORG	Not used—omit

Wherever we use LTORG, the Assembler stores and prints the literals up to that point, from either the start of the program or from the previous LTORG. Figure 3-7 depicts various uses of literals. Note that the sequence of the literals in the literal pool after LTORG is different from the sequence in which they were originally coded. (The next chapter covers the ZAP and AP instructions.)

```
LOC    OBJECT CODE       ADDR1 ADDR2  STMT    SOURCE STATEMENT

                                      71  *                    ----------
                                      72  ***                  LITERALS
                                      73  *                    ----------
003091  4040404040404040              74  SAVLIT    DC    CL8' '
003099  00000C                        75  PAGECT    DC    PL3'0'
00309C  000C                          76  LINECT    DC    PL2'0'
00309E                                77  PRINT     DS    CL121

003117  00
003118  D207 408F 4136  03091 03138   79            MVC   SAVLIT,=C'COMPUTER'        MOVE CONSTANT
00311E  F820 4097 4146  03099 03148   80            ZAP   PAGECT,=P'0'               CLEAR PAGECT
003124  FA10 409A 4147  0309C 03149   81            AP    LINECT,=P'1'               ADD ONE TO LINECT
00312A  D205 40B0 413E  030B2 03140   82            MVC   PRINT+20(6),=X'40204B202060'  MOVE HEX CONSTANT
003130  D201 40B6 4144  030B8 03146   83            MVC   PRINT+26(2),=C'**'         MOVE ** TO PRINT

003138                                85            LTORG
003138  C3D6D4D7F4E3C5D9              86                  =C'COMPUTER'
003140  40204B202060                  87                  =X'40204B202060'  ⎫ Literal Pool
003146  5C5C                          88                  =C'**'            ⎬ generated by
003148  0C                            89                  =P'0'             ⎭ the Assembler
003149  1C                            90                  =P'1'
```

FIGURE 3-7   Sample use of literals.

EQUATE SYMBOL—EQU

EQU is used to equate one symbolic address to another. The Assembler only acts on EQU, and does not generate executable code.

NAME	OPERATION	OPERAND
[symbol]	EQU	an expression

1. We may assign more than one symbolic name to a field, just as a person may have a full name and a nickname:

```
PRINT  DC    CL133' '    Define PRINT
P      EQU   PRINT       Equate P to PRINT
```

In this example, the Assembler assigns the identical attributes to P as it has to PRINT. We may now use either symbol to reference the same location, with a length of 133 bytes. Note, however, the Assembler rule: the symbol in the EQU operand field, PRINT, *must be defined before the EQU statement.*

2. We may give symbolic names to an immediate operand:

```
CODE   EQU   C'5'              Assign '5' to the name CODE.
       CLI   CARDNO,CODE       Compare CARDNO to C'5'.
```

We may use CODE in place of C'5' in an immediate operand. The Assembler recognizes that CODE is a reference to a value C'5', and substitutes C'5' wherever it encounters the operand CODE. This technique facilitates program modifications. We may have to change the value of the immediate operand. Rather than change many instructions in the program, we merely change the operand in the EQU statement, and reassemble the program.

3. We can equate an address using the Assembler's location counter reference. An asterisk as an operand is a reference to the current value in the location counter:

```
LOC:  X'3012'    SAVE   DS    CL3
                 KEEP   EQU   *+5
```

After the Assembler processes SAVE, its location counter contains X'3015'. The address of KEEP is equated to the "address" in the operand, *+5, meaning the contents of the location counter plus 5. KEEP is therefore assigned the address X'3015' plus 5, or X'301A'. KEEP will have a length attribute of one.

Problem 3-5 should now be attempted.

SAMPLE PROGRAM—READ AND PRINT CUSTOMER RECORDS

Figure 3-8 depicts a flowchart for a simple program that reads customer records and prints selected fields, and Figure 3-9 provides the coding.

CARD COLUMN	DESCRIPTION	PRINT POSITIONS
1	Record code	
6–10	Customer number	11–15
11–30	Customer name	18–37
41–46	Balance owing	40–46 (prints as xxxx.xx)

PROCEDURE

1. A heading prints at the top of the first page (the program does not provide for printing headings at the top of every page printed).
2. The program checks column 1 of each input record for valid code (3). An invalid code causes an error message.
3. To ensure that each customer record is in ascending sequence (one record per customer), the program compares the current customer (CUSTIN) to the previously processed customer number (PREVCUST). If the new customer number is higher, the program stores CUSTIN in PREVCUST for the next input test. An equal or low customer number causes an error message.

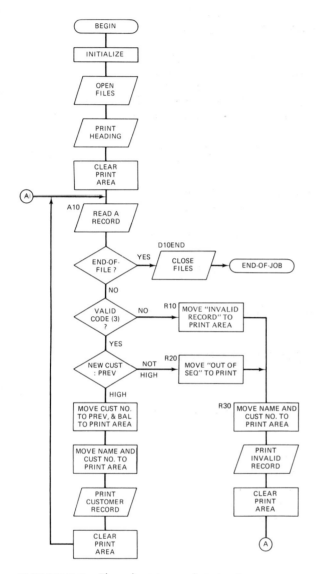

FIGURE 3-8 Flowchart to read and print customer records.

4. For valid records, the program moves customer name, number and balance owing to the print area, and inserts a decimal point in the balance field.
5. Immediately before PRINT is a 1-byte constant called BLANK. After printing, the program copies the contents of BLANK through the 133 bytes of PRINT. The blank character propagates through PRINT, clearing the entire field. (See MOVE6 in Figure 3-4 for an explanation.)

READING AND PRINTING CUSTOMER RECORDS

```
STMT    SOURCE STATEMENT

   4 *                    I N I T I A L I Z A T I O N
   5 *                    -------------------------
   6 PROG03     INIT                        INITIALIZE
  27          OPEN  CARD,PRINTER
  36          MVC   PRINT,BLANK             CLEAR PRINT AREA

  38          PUTPR PRINTER,PRINT,SK1   SKIP TO PAGE
  45          MVC   P+40(7),=C'BALANCE'
  46          MVC   P+14(8),=C'CUSTOMER'
  47          PUTPR PRINTER,PRINT,WSP2  PRINT HEADING
  54          MVC   PRINT,BLANK

  56 ***                  M A I N   P R O C E S S I N G
  57 *                    -------------------------
  58 A10READ    GET   CARD,CARDIN           READ RECORD
  64          CLI   CODEIN,C'3'           VALID RECORD CODE?
  65          BNE   R10INVCD             *   NO  - ERROR
  66          CLC   CUSTIN,PREVCUST       CUST NO. IN SEQ?
  67          BNH   R20SEQER             *   NO  - ERROR
  68          MVC   PREVCUST,CUSTIN       MOVE NEW CUST TO PREV
  69 *                                    MOVE TO PRINT:
  70          MVC   CENTSPR,BALIN+4      *     CENTS POSITIONS
  71          MVI   DECPR,C'.'          *     DECIMAL POINT
  72          MVC   DOLLPR,BALIN        *     DOLLAR POSITIONS
  73          MVC   NAMEPR,NAMEIN       *     NAME
  74          MVC   CUSTPR,CUSTIN       *     CUSTOMER NO.
  75          PUTPR PRINTER,PRINT,WSP1  PRINT CUST RECORD
  82          MVC   PRINT,BLANK
  83          B     A10READ

  85 ***                  E N D - O F - F I L E   R O U T I N E
  86 *                    -----------------------------------
  87 D10END     CLOSE CARD,PRINTER
  96          EOJ

 100 ***                  E R R O R   R O U T I N E S
 101 *                    -------------------------
 102 R10INVCD MVC   MESSAGPR,INVCARD      INVALID RECORD CODE
 103          B     R30

 105 R20SEQER MVC   MESSAGPR,OUTSEQ       OUT-OF-SEQUENCE

 107 R30        MVC   NAMEPR,NAMEIN        MOVE NAME &
 108          MVC   CUSTPR,CUSTIN        CUST NO. TO PRINT
 109          PUTPR PRINTER,PRINT,WSP1  PRINT ERROR MESSAGE
 116          MVC   PRINT,BLANK
 117          B     A10READ
```

FIGURE 3-9   Read and print customer records.

6. When the end-of-file is reached, the program branches to D10END, closes the files, and ends execution.

Although a relatively simple program, it is still organized into logical sections: Initialization, Main Processing, End-of-File, and Error routines. Also, program labels and data names are clear and meaningful, and along with the comments, the program is close to self-documenting.

```
120 ***              D E C L A R A T I V E S
121 *                ----------------------

123 CARD      DEFCD D10END            DEFINE INPUT FILE
147 PRINTER   DEFPR                   DEFINE PRINT FILE
```

```
172 CARDIN    DS    0CL80             INPUT RECORD:
173 CODEIN    DS    CL1               01-01 RECORD CODE
174           DS    CL4               02-05
175 CUSTIN    DS    CL5               06-10 CUST. NO.
176 NAMEIN    DS    CL20              11-30 CUST NAME
177           DS    CL10              31-40
178 BALIN     DS    CL6               41-46 BALANCE
179           DS    CL34              47-80
```

```
181 BLANK     DC    C' '              BLANK TO CLEAR PRINT
182 PRINT     DS    0CL133            PRINT AREA:
183           DC    CL11' '           *
184 CUSTPR    DS    CL05              *    CUST. NO.
185           DC    CL02' '           *
186 NAMEPR    DS    CL20              *    NAME
187           DC    CL02' '           *
188 DOLLPR    DS    CL04              *    $ POSITIONS
189 DECPR     DS    CL01              *    DECIMAL POINT
190 CENTSPR   DS    CL02              *    CENTS POS'NS
191           DC    CL03' '           *
192 MESSAGPR  DC    CL22' '           *    ERROR MESSAGE
193           DC    CL61' '           *
```

```
195 P         EQU   PRINT             EQUATE P TO PRINT

197 INVCARD   DC    CL22'INVALID RECORD CODE'
198 OUTSEQ    DC    CL22'RECORD OUT OF SEQUENCE'

200 PREVCUST  DC    CL5' '            PREV. CUST. NO.

202           LTORG
203                 =C'$$BOPEN '
204                 =C'CUSTOMER'
205                 =C'$$BCLOSE'
206                 =V(PCOCIT)
207                 =A(PRINTER)
208                 =A(PRINT)
209                 =A(CARD)
210                 =A(CARDIN)
211                 =C'BALANCE'

213           END   PROG03
```

```
    CUSTOMER              BALANCE

    12345   KE ANDERSON   1234.56
    24680   D  BAKER      5432.10
    33333   JW COUSTON    3333.33
    34567   AB DONOVAN              INVALID RECORD CODE
    12312   KM EDWARDS             RECORD OUT OF SEQUENCE
    99999   WM FISHER     3456.32
```

FIGURE 3-9 (Continued)

72

DEBUGGING TIPS

Even a program that performs no arithmetic stands a good chance of containing errors. Check first the diagnostics immediately following the assembled program for any errors that the Assembler has located (these may cause execution errors as well). The most common error that the Assembler identifies is spelling mistakes: an operation is misspelled, such as MCV for MVC, or an operand is not spelled the way it is defined. Such errors may cause the Assembler to generate a "dummy" instruction of hex zeros that will cause an "Operation Exception" if executed. Failure to initialize with INIT (or the instruction USING introduced in a later chapter) will cause a large number of "Addressability" errors.

Violating the rules of declaratives is also common, such as defining a DS with a constant, which is treated as a comment, and defining a DC without a constant. Watch for defining a constant length (Ln) that does not agree with the defined constant, as CL3'DATE'. It is easy to code the wrong constant; the constant DC CL5'0' generates '0bbbb' rather than '00000'.

Coding an explicit length in an MVI or CLI or in operand-2 of an MVC or CLC will cause Assembler errors. The program, when corrected and reassembled, may cause errors during execution. Be sure that the input definition agrees exactly with the actual input record format—any difference will cause incorrect results. Failure to clear the print area to blanks will cause "garbage" on the printed lines. A common error is caused by omitting the explicit length from an MVC used with relative addressing, as:

```
PRINT   DC    CL133' '
        MVC   PRINT+95,=C'DATE'
```

The computer will move 133 bytes, starting from the first byte of the literal 'DATE'— perhaps a good reason to minimize (or avoid?) use of relative addressing. The areas following PRINT will be clobbered, with often spectacular results that may not occur until later in the execution.

An error difficult to detect is caused by incorrect branching—reversing operands 1 and 2, or using, for example, BNH instead of BNL.

A disastrous error is caused by coding GET or PUT incorrectly, as, for example, GET CARDIN,CARD; the computer may end up executing outside of the program area, perhaps even executing garbage in the Supervisor.

Appendix B contains a list of program checks (interrupts) that can occur during program execution, along with possible causes of the errors.

PROBLEMS

3-1. DEFINE STORAGE. Define the following as DS's:
  (a) An 80-byte area called OUT to be used for card output.
  (b) A 100-byte area that does not increment the Location Counter.

(c) Five 10-byte areas defined with one statement.

(d) An area called DATE, subdivided with three 2-byte fields called respectively DAY, MONTH, and YEAR.

3-2. DEFINE CONSTANT. Define the following as DC's:

(a) A field called ASTER, one byte long, containing an asterisk.

(b) A field of ten blanks, called BLANKS.

(c) A constant containing "SAM'S".

(d) A constant of ten character zeros.

(e) Three 5-byte constants all containing blanks, defined with one statement.

3-3. MOVE CHARACTER. Given the declaratives shown, code the following *unrelated* questions. Show the contents of both fields after completion of the operation.

```
A    DC    C'123'         These fields are defined in storage
B    DC    C'4567'        adjacent to each other.
C    DC    C'XY'
```

Example: Move the contents of C to the leftmost two bytes of A: MVC A(2),C.

(a) Move the contents of C to the second and third bytes of B.

(b) Move the rightmost byte of A to the third byte of B.

(c) Move A to the bytes starting at the third byte of B.

(d) Use one MVC to change all the contents of A, B and C to character 1's.

(e) Use one MVC to shift both A and B one byte to the left, as follows:

```
before:   1 2 3 4 5 6 7
after:    2 3 4 5 6 7 7
          A      B
```

3-4. COMPARE AND BRANCH. Given the declaratives, code the following:

```
D    DC    C'ANN'
E    DC    C'MOE'
F    DC    C'SAL'
```

(a) If E is less than or equal to F, branch to G40.

(b) If D is greater than E but not less than F, branch to G50.

3-5. Show by an 'X' the Condition Code set by the following. D, E, and F refer to the DC's in Problem 3-4. Explain if invalid assemble or execute.

		High	Low	Equal
(a)	CLC D,F			
(b)	CLC F,E			
(c)	CLC D,=C'BOB'			

		High	Low	Equal
(d)	CLI E,C'P'			
(e)	CLI F,C'F'			
(f)	CLI D(1),=C'A'			

3-6. PROGRAM ASSIGNMENT.

Required: A program that reads Inventory records and prints selected data.

Input:

COLUMN	CONTENTS	COLUMN	CONTENTS
1	Record code ('4')	9–28	Description
2–3	Branch number	29–30	Month
4–8	Stock number	31–35	Quantity on hand
		36–42	Value (xxxxx.xx)

Output (including heading):

BRANCH	STOCK NO	DESCRIPTION	MONTH	QUANTITY	VALUE
xx	xxxxx	x--------x	xx	xxxxx	xxxxx.xx

Procedure:

— Check the record code ('4') to ensure that the program processes only valid records. By-pass invalid records and print a message 'INVALID RECORD'.

— To ensure that the records are in proper order, sequence-check them on Stock number. If out of sequence, print an error message 'OUT OF SEQUENCE'.

— Provide input data that tests for invalid record code and out-of-sequence condition.

— Print the fields as shown, in any suitable print positions. As an optional extra, code the program to convert the numeric input month into alphabetic for printing (i.e., '01' should be 'JANUARY').

— Flowchart, code, and test the program. Be sure to use the programming standards for your installation.

CHAPTER 4

DECIMAL DATA AND ARITHMETIC I

Chapter 3 covered the use of data in character format. Few programs are written using just this format, because generally we need to perform arithmetic—addition, multiplication, etc. The most common format for arithmetic is packed decimal. This chapter introduces three data formats: hexadecimal, zoned, and packed. The instructions, MVN and MVZ, although technically character operations, are covered here because they are mostly used with packed data. This chapter then covers the basic packed operations for packing, unpacking, addition, subtraction, and comparing.

HEXADECIMAL CONSTANTS

Two hexadecimal digits can represent any of the 256 different characters. They normally define constants that cannot easily be defined as character packed, zoned, or binary. A major use is in defining edit word constants (Chapter 5). The following rules apply to hexadecimal constants:

1. The constant may be defined in length from one byte (two hex digits) to 256 bytes (512 hex digits).

2. They may contain only the hex digits 0 through 9 and A through F.
3. A length (Ln) if defined specifies the number of bytes, *one byte for each pair of hex digits*. The Assembler right-adjusts hex constants. Therefore, if the defined length is less than the constant, the Assembler truncates the constant on the left. If the defined length is longer, the Assembler pads hex zeros to the left.

See Figure 4-1 for example hex DC's. Compare the defined constant to the object code:

```
LOC     OBJECT   STMT    SOURCE STATEMENT

                 6 *       --------------------------
                 7 *       DC    HEXADECIMAL FORMAT
                 8 *       --------------------------
003002 1A76      9 HEX1    DC    X'1A76'        |1A|76|
003004 76       10 HEX2    DC    XL1'1A76'      |76|              TRUNCATES
003005 001A76   11 HEX3    DC    XL3'1A76'      |00|1A|76|        PADS ZEROS
003008 012C     12 HEX4    DC    X'12C'         |01|2C|           PADS ZERO
00300A FFFFFF   13 HEX5    DC    3X'FF'         |FF|FF|FF|        3 CONSTANTS
```

FIGURE 4-1   Sample DC statements in hexadecimal format.

HEX1 defines a DC that requires two bytes of storage.

HEX2 has a length specified as one byte and a constant as two bytes. This is a possible coding error, because the Assembler truncated the constant on the left.

HEX3 has a length specified as three and a constant of two bytes. The Assembler pads zeros on the left.

HEX4 defines a constant with three hex digits—1½ bytes. The Assembler pads a hex zero to the left, resulting in a 2-byte constant.

HEX5 illustrates the duplication factor. Three constants each containing X'FF' are defined. The name HEX5 refers to the first constant with a length of one byte.

Hex constants should not be confused with constants of other formats. Note the difference between the following:

FORMAT	CONSTANT	BYTES	HEX REPRESENTATION
character	DC C'ABCD'	4	/C1/C2/C3/C4/
hexadecimal	DC X'ABCD'	2	/AB/CD/

MOVE NUMERIC (MVN) AND MOVE ZONES (MVZ)

NAME	OPERATION	OPERAND		
[symbol]	MVN	S1,S2	or	D1(L,B1),D2(B2)
[symbol]	MVZ	S1,S2	or	D1(L,B1),D2(B2)

These move operations are mainly used to manipulate half-bytes for decimal arithmetic. The rules for both instructions are similar to those for MVC, with the following exceptions:

MVN moves only the numeric portion of the half-byte, the rightmost four bits, numbered 4 to 7. From one to 256 numeric portions may be moved from the operand-2 field to the operand-1 field. The zone portion is undisturbed.

MVZ moves only the zone half of the byte, the leftmost four bits, numbered 0 to 3. From one to 256 zones may be moved. The numeric portion is undisturbed.

Figure 4-2 provides examples of MVN and MVZ operations:

The first MVN moves the numeric portion of each byte of A (1, 2, and 3) to the numeric portion of each byte of B. The second MVN, illustrating relative addressing and explicit length, moves two numerics, starting from A to B+1.

The first MVZ moves zone portions (X'F's). The second MVZ moves one zone from B+1 to B+2.

```
LOC    OBJECT CODE      ADDR1 ADDR2  STMT     SOURCE STATEMENT

00300D F1F2F3                         18 A       DC    C'123'         A= |F1|F2|F3|
003010 45678C                         19 B       DC    X'45678C'      B= |45|67|8C|

                                      21 *       -------------------
                                      22 ***     MVN   MOVE NUMERICS
                                      23 *       -------------------
003013 00
003014 D102 400E 400B 03010 0300D     24         MVN   B,A            B= |41|62|83|
00301A D101 400F 400B 03011 0300D     25         MVN   B+1(2),A       B= |45|61|82|

                                      27 *       -----------------
                                      28 ***     MVZ   MOVE ZONES
                                      29 *       -----------------
003020 D302 400E 400B 03010 0300D     30         MVZ   B,A            B= |F5|F7|FC|
003026 D300 4010 400F 03012 03011     31         MVZ   B+2(1),B+1     B= |45|67|6C|
```

FIGURE 4-2 Sample unrelated MVN and MVZ operations.

Problem 4-1 should now be attempted.

ZONED DECIMAL DATA

Zoned decimal data is similar to character data, but is of limited use. Zoned is sometimes used, for example, to define a field containing data that will be later packed, such as an amount read from an input file. The following rules govern zoned declaratives:

1. The length may be defined from one to 16 bytes.
2. The constant may contain only the digits 0 through 9, a sign (+ or −), and a decimal point. The Assembler does not translate or store the decimal point—we code it only for documentation, where we intend the decimal to be.
3. We may define more than one zoned constant with one DC, separated by commas.
4. Except for the rightmost digit of the constant, the Assembler converts each zoned digit 0 through 9 to X'FO' through X'F9'. If the constant is positive, the Assembler generates a plus sign X'C', and if negative a minus sign, X'D'. For example, DC Z'123.45' becomes /F1/F2/F3/F4/C5/. The rightmost byte X'C5' contains the plus sign in the zone portion. The zone 'C' is equivalent to the plus sign (12-zone) on the punched card. The minus zone 'D' is equivalent to the punched card minus sign (11-zone).
5. We code the sign (+ or −) to the left of the constant, such as DC Z'−1.25'. To represent a positive value, we code a + sign, or omit the sign altogether.
6. We may specify length (Ln) as for hexadecimal format. If the constant is shorter than the specified length, the Assembler right-adjusts the constant and pads leftmost zeros:

DC   ZL3'25'   /F0/F2/C5/

If the constant is longer than the specified length, the Assembler truncates the constant on the left:

DC   ZL2'1234'   /F3/C4/

Figure 4-3 illustrates zoned declaratives explained as follows:

ZONE0 defines a DS as five bytes long, to be used for zoned data.

ZONE1 is a DC with a decimal point in the constant. Note the generated object code on the left.

ZONE2 shows a DC with a minus sign coded to the left. The Assembler stores the sign in object code on the right as X'D'.

```
LOC     OBJECT CODE   STMT    SOURCE STATEMENT

                      35 *    --------------------
                      36 *    DC     ZONED FORMAT
                      37 *    --------------------
00302C                38 ZONE0   DS     ZL5              5-BYTE ZONED AREA
003031  F1F2F3C5      39 ZONE1   DC     Z'123.5'         |F1|F2|F3|C5|        IGNORES DEC
003035  F5F0F0F0D0    40 ZONE2   DC     Z'-500.00'       |F5|F0|F0|F0|D0|     MINUS
00303A  F0F1F2C3      41 ZONE3   DC     ZL4'123'         |F0|F1|F2|C3|        PADS ZEROS

00303E  F2C3          43 ZONE4   DC     ZL2'123'         |F2|C3|              TRUNCATES
003040  F0C0F0C0F0C0  44 ZONE5   DC     3ZL2'0'          |F0|C0|F0|C0|F0|C0|  3 CONSTANTS
003046  F1F2C3C4F6C7  45 ZONE6   DC     Z'123,4,67'      |F1|F2|C3|C4|F6|C7|  3 CONSTANTS
```

FIGURE 4-3   Sample zoned declaratives.

ZONE3 and ZONE4 use the length indication (Ln). In ZONE3, X'F0' is padded on the left, and in ZONE4 the constant is truncated.

ZONE5 defines three identical constants. A reference to ZONE5 is to the first 2-byte constant.

ZONE6 defines three constants, each separated by a comma. The comma is not stored. A reference to ZONE6 is to the first 3-byte constant.

Note the difference between the generated code for the following character and zoned DC's:

character:	DC C'1,234.56'	/F1/6B/F2/F3/F4/4B/F5/F6/
zoned:	DC Z'1,234.56'	/C1/F2/F3/F4/F5/C6/

2 constants generated by the comma

PACKED DECIMAL DATA

Ordinary decimal data is performed on fields in packed format. We define these fields either initially as packed, or we use the PACK instruction to translate character or zoned data into packed. Each packed byte contains two digits, one in each half-byte. The plus or minus sign is the rightmost half-byte of the field. For example, the packed value +125 requires two bytes, as $\boxed{12 \mid 5C}$. The binary representation of this field is $\boxed{0001 \mid 0010 \mid 0101 \mid 1100}$. The standard plus sign (X'C' or binary 1100) is equivalent to the plus (12-zone) on a punched card. The standard minus sign (X'D' or binary 1101) is equivalent to the punched card minus (11-zone). All packed fields must conform to the following rules:

1. All digit positions (all half-bytes other than the rightmost sign) may contain only digits 0 through 9 (binary 0000 through 1001).

2. The rightmost half-byte must contain a sign. There are four valid plus signs and two valid minus signs:

BINARY	HEX	SIGN		BINARY	HEX	SIGN
1010	A	+		1101	D	− *standard minus sign*
1011	B	−		1110	E	+
1100	C	+ *standard plus sign*		1111	F	+

3. Packed fields may be a minimum of one byte long (one digit plus a sign) and a maximum of 16 bytes (31 digits plus a sign).

PACKED DECIMAL CONSTANTS.   Constants are defined as packed for use in decimal arithmetic. The rules for packed, which are similar to zoned, are as follows:

1. The length may be defined from one to 16 bytes.
2. A packed constant, like zoned, may contain only the digits 0 through 9, and optionally a decimal point (.) and a sign (+ or −). The Assembler does not store the decimal point, which is chiefly for program documentation.
3. One DC may define more than one packed constant, each separated by a comma.
4. We may also use length indication (Ln). The Assembler right-adjusts the constant to permit padding leftmost zeros or truncating on the left.

The Assembler converts the packed constant to object code as follows:

1. The rightmost half-byte (numeric portion) of the assembled constant contains the sign, X'C' for plus and X'D' for minus. For example, DC PL3'1234' is converted to packed as /01/23/4C/.
2. All other half-bytes contain a digit. Other than the rightmost byte which has a digit and a sign, all bytes contain two digits. A packed constant, therefore, always has an odd number of digits, one to 31.

Figure 4-4 depicts packed DC's, explained as follows:

PACK1 packs three digits into two bytes. The plus (+) sign is optional.

PACK2 defines a negative constant.

PACK3 packs four digits into three bytes. The Assembler inserts a zero digit in the leftmost half-byte. Note that a packed constant defined as an even number of digits results in an odd number of packed digits. Also, the decimal point acts as a comment, and is not stored.

PACK4 defines the length longer than the constant. The Assembler pads zeros on the left.

PACK5 defines the length shorter than the constant. The Assembler truncates the leftmost digit.

PACK6 defines three identical constants containing zeros.

PACK7 defines three constants, each separated by a comma, which is not stored. A reference to PACK7 is to the first 2-byte field.

```
  LOC   OBJECT CODE   STMT    SOURCE STATEMENT

                      49 *        --------------------
                      50 *        DC    PACKED FORMAT
                      51 *        --------------------
00304C 370C           52 PACK1   DC    P'+370'           |37|0C|              PLUS SIGN
00304E 500D           53 PACK2   DC    P'-500'           |50|0D|              MINUS SIGN
003050 01234C         54 PACK3   DC    P'12.34'          |01|23|4C|           IGNORES DEC
003053 0012345C       55 PACK4   DC    PL4'12345'        |00|12|34|5C|        PADS ZERO

003057 345C           57 PACK5   DC    PL2'12345'        |34|5C|              TRUNCATES
003059 000C000C000C   58 PACK6   DC    3PL2'0'           |00|0C|00|0C|00|0C|  3 CONSTANTS
00305F 125C215C387C   59 PACK7   DC    PL2'125,215,387'  |12|5C|21|5C|38|7C|  3 CONSTANTS
003065 007CD1E4D3E8   60 PACK8   DC    P'07',C'JULY'     |00|7C|D1|E4|D3|E8|  2 CONSTANTS
```

FIGURE 4-4   Sample DC statements in packed format.

PACK8 defines two constants, the first packed and the second character. A reference to PACK8 is to the first field, the 2-byte packed constant.

PACKED OPERATIONS

The computer can perform arithmetic only on valid numeric fields (packed decimal and binary). Since input data from cards is in character format, it is necessary to convert into packed, using the PACK operation. In packed format, operations such as AP, SP and ZAP can perform arithmetic, and CP can perform comparisons. The UNPK operation (and ED in the next chapter) converts the packed data into printable characters.

PACKING FIELDS—PACK.   Data normally appears in packed format by (1) a constant defined as packed, or (2) an instruction, PACK, that converts character or zoned fields into packed. The standard steps to process decimal arithmetic are:

1. Read an input record. We may define card amount fields as character or zoned, but regardless of our definition, the card content is read in character format.
2. Convert (PACK) character amount fields into packed.
3. Perform decimal arithmetic on packed fields.
4. Prepare the output area. Output on tape and disk may be any format. Output on a printer or card punch is usually in character format; the packed fields must be either unpacked or "edited" into the print area (the next chapter covers editing).
5. Write the output record.

Although PACK is normally used to convert character and zoned to packed, PACK executes regardless of the format. There is no checking for valid data, and PACK can easily generate "garbage" if applied to the wrong data field.

NAME	OPERATION	OPERAND
[symbol]	PACK	S1,S2 or D1(L1,B1),D2(L2,B2)

The rules for PACK are as follows:

1. The maximum length of each operand is 16 bytes. Either operand may specify an explicit length (L1 and L2).
2. Bytes referenced by operand-2 are packed one byte at a time from right to left into the operand-1 field. In the rightmost byte the half-bytes are reversed:

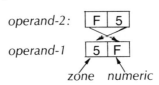

In the example, the zone portion of the rightmost byte of operand-2 (X'F') is placed in the numeric portion of the rightmost byte of operand-1. The numeric portion of operand-2 (X'5') is placed in the zone portion of operand-1. It becomes the rightmost, or units, digit.

3. Other than the rightmost byte, all other zones of operand-2 are ignored. PACK extracts numeric portions from operand-2 one at a time from right to left, and places them adjacent to one another in the operand-1 field. The following instruction packs the contents of ZONED into PACKED:

ZONED   DC   Z'12345'   /F1/F2/F3/F4/C5/

PACKED   DS   PL3
         PACK PACKED,ZONED   /12/34/5C/

Note that the zoned sign C becomes the packed sign. The zoned 5 becomes the rightmost digit, and each other numeric ZONED digit is extracted and placed in PACKED. PACKED now contains data on which we may perform arithmetic.

4. PACK terminates when all digits are transmitted. If operand-1 is too short to receive all the digits, the remaining leftmost digits of operand-2 are ignored. If operand-1 is longer than necessary to receive all the digits, its leftmost bytes are filled with zeros (X'0'). In any event, PACK fully erases the previous contents of the receiving field.

Figure 4-5 gives various unrelated PACK examples which should now be studied:

PACKA illustrates a conventional PACK operation. H, a 5-byte zoned field, requires 3 bytes when converted to packed format.

In PACKB, operand-1, G, is one byte longer than necessary for the PACK operation. PACK pads leftmost zeros in the leftmost byte.

PACKC depicts a common programming error. A 6-byte field, K, is packed into a

```
LOC    OBJECT CODE      ADDR1 ADDR2  STMT    SOURCE STATEMENT

                                     64 *         ------
                                     65 ***       PACK
                                     66 *         ------
00306B                               67 G         DS    PL3
00306E  F1F2F3F4C5                   68 H         DC    Z'12345'       H=  |F1|F2|F3|F4|C5|
003073  F1F2F3                       69 J         DC    C'123'         J=  |F1|F2|F3|
003076  F1F2F3F4F5C6                 70 K         DC    Z'123456'      K=  |F1|F2|F3|F4|F5|C6|

00307C  F224 4069 406C  0306B 0306E  72 PACKA     PACK  G,H            G=  |12|34|5C|
003082  F222 4069 4071  0306B 03073  73 PACKB     PACK  G,J            G=  |00|12|3F|
003088  F225 4069 4074  0306B 03076  74 PACKC     PACK  G,K            G=  |23|45|6C|

00308E  F244 406C 406C  0306E 0306E  76 PACKD     PACK  H,H            H=  |00|00|12|34|5C|
003094  F221 4069 406D  0306B 0306F  77 PACKE     PACK  G,H+1(2)       G=  |00|02|3F|
00309A  F212 4077 406D  03079 0306F  78 PACKF     PACK  K+3(2),H+1(3)  K=  |F1|F2|F3|23|4F|C6|
```

FIGURE 4-5   Sample unrelated pack operations.

3-byte field, G. PACK proceeds from right to left, terminating before packing all the digits in G.

PACKD shows the effect of packing a field into itself. Although the operation works correctly, *this practice is not always desirable.* First, the field is defined as zoned, but now contains packed data. Second, the defined length is five bytes, but the field now contains only three bytes of significant data. It is generally preferable to pack into a field defined with the correct format and length.

PACKE and PACKF illustrate valid use of relative addressing and explicit lengths. In the case of PACKF, the second, third, and fourth bytes of H are packed into the fourth and fifth bytes of K—the other bytes are not affected by the operation. The example is illustrative, because there are few practical reasons to code in this way.

UNPACKING FIELDS—UNPK.   UNPK performs the reverse of PACK. Its main purpose is to convert packed data into zoned, in order, for example, to print the zoned field. However, UNPK may be used to manipulate data in any format; there is no checking for validity of data. Unpacking data that is not packed may result in "garbage".

NAME	OPERATION	OPERAND
[symbol]	UNPK	S1,S2 or D1(L1,B1),D2(L2,B2)

The rules for UNPK are as follows:

1. The maximum length for each field is 16 bytes. Either operand may specify an explicit length (L1 and L2).
2. Bytes referenced by operand-2 are unpacked one byte at a time from right to left into the operand-1 field.
3. As done also by PACK, the half-bytes of the rightmost byte of the operand-2 field are reversed in the operand-1 field.
4. UNPK successively places all other digits in operand-2 from right to left in the numeric portion of each byte in operand-1. The zone portions are filled with hex 'F'. The following unpacks PACKED into ZONED:

```
PACKED   DC    P'12345'            /12/34/5C/

ZONED    DS    PL5         /F1/F2/F3/F4/C5/
         UNPK  ZONED,PACKED
```

Note that UNPK reverses the PACKED sign C and the digit '5' in the receiving field, ZONED. All other digits are placed in ZONED with a zone 'F'. The data in ZONED is now in a format that we can print, whereas PACKED contains bytes that are invalid for printing. (In practice, rather than use UNPK to translate packed data for printing, we normally use the ED operation covered in the next chapter.)

5. UNPK normally terminates when all digits are transmitted. If the operand-1 field is too short to receive all the digits, the remaining leftmost bytes of operand-2 are ignored. If the operand-1 field is longer than necessary to receive all the digits, its leftmost bytes are filled with character zeros (X'F0').

In Figure 4-6, UNPACK1 illustrates a 3-byte field unpacked into a 5-byte field, the correct size.

In UNPACK2, operand-1 is one byte longer than necessary. The unpack fills a character zero (X'F0') to the left.

In UNPACK3, operand-1 is two bytes too short to receive all the unpacked data. Therefore, the two leftmost digits of the operand-2 field are not unpacked.

UNPACK4 and UNPACK5 depict the use of relative addressing and explicit length, fancy coding, but dangerous.

UNPACK6 and UNPACK7 unpack fields into themselves. The result is correct only if the field is one or two bytes long. The danger of this practice is seen by the results.

UNPACK6 attempts to unpack a 3-byte field called L into itself. Because L contains five digits which cannot fully unpack into a 3-byte field, the two leftmost digits (1 and 2) are erased.

UNPACK7 unpacks a 5-byte field called Q into itself, propagating an error. The error can be best understood if we consider the rule of UNPK: *one byte at a time is extracted and unpacked from right to left:*

— The zone and numeric portions of Q+4 are reversed.

— Q+3 containing 78 is extracted. F8 is stored in Q+3 and F7 is stored in Q+2.

— Q+2, *now containing F7,* is extracted. F7 is stored in Q+1 and FF is stored in Q. The operation having filled all five bytes is now complete, but incorrect.

```
LOC     OBJECT CODE      ADDR1 ADDR2   STMT    SOURCE STATEMENT

                                       82 *        ---------------
                                       83 ***      UNPK  UNPACK
                                       84 *        ---------------
0030A0  12345C                         85 L        DC    P'12345'        L= |12|34|5C|
0030A3                                 86 M        DS    ZL5
0030A8  F9F9F9F9F9C9                   87 N        DC    Z'999999'       N= |F9|F9|F9|F9|F9|C9|
0030AE                                 88 P        DS    CL3
0030B1  123456789C                     89 Q        DC    P'123456789'    Q= |12|34|56|78|9C|

0030B6  F342 40A1 409E   030A3 030A0   91 UNPACK1  UNPK  M,L             M= |F1|F2|F3|F4|C5|
0030BC  F352 40A6 409E   030A8 030A0   92 UNPACK2  UNPK  N,L             N= |F0|F1|F2|F3|F4|C5|
0030C2  F322 40AC 409E   030AE 030A0   93 UNPACK3  UNPK  P,L             P= |F3|F4|C5|
0030C8  F321 40AC 409F   030AE 030A1   94 UNPACK4  UNPK  P,L+1(2)        P= |F3|F4|C5|

0030CE  F342 40A7 409E   030A9 030A0   96 UNPACK5  UNPK  N+1(5),L        N= |F9|F1|F2|F3|F4|C5|
0030D4  F322 409E 409E   030A0 030A0   97 UNPACK6  UNPK  L,L             L= |F3|F4|C5|
0030DA  F344 40AF 40AF   030B1 030B1   98 UNPACK7  UNPK  Q,Q             Q= |FF|F7|F7|F8|C9|
```

FIGURE 4-6 Sample unrelated unpack operations.

— The computer continues processing with no indication that an "error" occurred.

PACKED DECIMAL ARITHMETIC—ZAP, AP, AND SP.   All decimal arithmetic is performed in main storage using valid packed data and the appropriate packed decimal instructions. This chapter introduces operations for simple arithmetic, and the next chapter covers multiply and divide.

NAME	OPERATION	OPERAND		
[symbol]	ZAP	S1,S2	or	D1(L1,B1),D2(L2,B2)
[symbol]	AP	S1,S2	or	D1(L1,B1),D2(L2,B2)
[symbol]	SP	S1,S2	or	D1(L1,B1),D2(L2,B2)

We use ZAP, Zero and Add Packed, to transfer packed data, just as MVC is used to transfer character data. However, if the receiving field is longer than the sending field, ZAP fills the leftmost bytes with zeros. We use AP, Add Packed, and SP, Subtract Packed, for addition and subtraction of packed fields. The rules for ZAP, AP, and SP are as follows:

1. The maximum length of each field is 16 bytes. Either operand may contain an explicit length (L1 and L2), up to 16.
2. The operand-2 sending field must be a packed field with a valid sign (hex 'A' to hex 'F'). If the field is not valid, a program interrupt "data exception" will occur. On the 370, if the sign is invalid the operation may be suppressed rather than terminated.
3. For AP and SP the operand-1 receiving field must be a packed field with a valid sign. In the case of ZAP, the operand-1 field may be any format.
4. If the operand-1 field is shorter than the operand-2 field, a program interrupt overflow may occur. Normally an arithmetic field should be defined so that it can contain the largest answer that could ever occur, plus a byte for insurance.
5. The rules of algebra determine the resulting sign. A positive sum yields a plus (hex 'C') sign, and a negative sum yields a minus (hex 'D') sign. A zero result yields a positive (hex 'C') sign. X'C' and X'D' are the standard plus and minus signs, although X'A', X'B', X'E', and X'F' are valid.

> *Note:* An arithmetic operation changes an X'F' sign to X'C'. If an input field contains the value '12345', its hex representation in main storage is X'F1F2F3F4F5'. If we pack the field, it becomes X'12345F', still with the F-sign. If we perform any arithmetic upon this packed field, its sign changes: X'C' if positive and X'D' if negative. This feature is algebraically correct, but confusing to the learner.

6. ZAP, AP, and SP set the condition code, so that we may test the results if necessary:

CODE	CONTENTS OF THE RESULT FIELD
0	Zero
1	Minus (less than zero)
2	Plus (greater than zero)
3	Overflow

The following conditional branches may then test for these conditions:

CONDITION CODE	CONDITIONAL BRANCHES	
0 = Zero	BZ (Branch Zero)	BNZ (Branch not Zero)
1 = Minus	BM (Branch Minus)	BNM (Branch not Minus)
2 = Plus	BP (Branch Plus)	BNP (Branch not Plus)
3 = Overflow	BO (Branch Overflow)	

Example testing of the condition code:

```
ACCUM   DC   PL2'0'
TOTAL   DC   PL3'0'
        AP   TOTAL,ACCUM      Add and set the condition code.
        BM   P10NEG           (Assume P10NEG is any valid address.)
```

Assume the contents of ACCUM and TOTAL are unknown. If the result of adding the contents of ACCUM to TOTAL is negative, the program branches to P10NEG. If the result is positive or zero, the program continues with the next instruction. Figure 4-7 provides various unrelated ZAP, AP, and SP examples:

ZAP1, ADD1, and SUBTR1 illustrate conventional ZAP, AP, and SP operations. ZAP2 and ADD2 depict a coding error in which operand-1 is shorter than operand-2. The result at execute-time is an overflow condition.

ZAP3 and ADD3 also are coding errors not recognized by the Assembler. The explicit length P3(3) causes only the first three bytes to be processed. Since there is no sign in the explicitly defined field, the instruction will "bomb" with a "Data Exception."

ZAP4 shows how we may correctly use explicit length and relative addressing.

ZAP5 tests the contents of a packed field. If we ZAP a field into itself the value is unchanged, but the condition code is set. Since P1 contains a positive value, the condition code is set to high/plus.

ZAP6 and SUBTR2 both clear a field to packed zeros. Subtracting a field from itself, as in SUBTR2, is more efficient, but requires valid packed data in operand-1. ZAP requires a constant defined for operand-2, in this case a literal =P'0'.

ADD4 depicts a common coding error caused by an operand-1 field that is too short:

Contents of P1	/12/3C/	Because P1 is only two bytes and the total
Add '999'	/99/9C/	requires three, there is an overflow
		interrupt, and an answer of 122 instead
Total	/12/2C/	of 1,122.

```
LOC   OBJECT CODE        STMT    SOURCE STATEMENT


003002 123C                 7 P1      DC    P'123'          P1= |12|3C|
003004 04567C               8 P2      DC    P'4567'         P2= |04|56|7C|
003007 0890123C             9 P3      DC    P'890123'       P3= |08|90|12|3C|
                           10 *       --------------------------
                           11 ***     ZAP   ZERO AND ADD PACKED
                           12 *       --------------------------
00300B 00
00300C F821 4002 4000      13 ZAP1    ZAP   P2,P1           P2= |00|12|3C|
003012 F823 4002 4005      14 ZAP2    ZAP   P2,P3           ERROR - P2 IS TOO SHORT
003018 F822 4002 4005      15 ZAP3    ZAP   P2,P3(3)        ERROR - NO SIGN IN OPERAND-2
00301E F822 4002 4006      16 ZAP4    ZAP   P2,P3+1(3)      P2= |90|12|3C|
003024 F811 4000 4000      17 ZAP5    ZAP   P1,P1           SETS CONDITION CODE HIGH/PLUS
00302A F810 4000 40C4      18 ZAP6    ZAP   P1,=P'0'        P1= |00|0C|

                           20 *       --------------------
                           21 ***     AP    ADD PACKED
                           22 *       --------------------
003030 FA21 4002 4000      23 ADD1    AP    P2,P1           P2= |04|69|0C|
003036 FA12 4000 4002      24 ADD2    AP    P1,P2           ERROR - P1 IS TOO SHORT
00303C FA21 4005 4000      25 ADD3    AP    P3(3),P1        ERROR - NO SIGN IN OPERAND-1
003042 FA11 4000 40BE      26 ADD4    AP    P1,=P'999'      P1= |12|2C| ERROR - OVERFLOW

                           28 *       ----------------------
                           29 ***     SP    SUBTRACT PACKED
                           30 *       ----------------------
003048 FB21 4002 4000      31 SUBTR1  SP    P2,P1           P2= |04|44|4C|
00304E FB11 4000 4000      32 SUBTR2  SP    P1,P1           P1= |00|0C|
```

FIGURE 4-7   Sample unrelated ZAP, AP, and SP operations.

Problem 4-2 should now be attempted.

COMPARISON OF PACKED DECIMAL FIELDS—CP.   It is often necessary to test if a packed field is plus, minus, or zero, and to compare the result of one calculation to another. We compare packed decimal fields with CP, Compare Packed.

NAME	OPERATION	OPERAND
[symbol]	CP	S1,S2 or D1(L1,B1),D2(L2,B2)

The rules for CP are as follows:

1. Maximum field lengths are 16 bytes. Either operand may contain an explicit length (L1 and L2).
2. Both operands must contain valid packed data. Invalid data results in a program interrupt ("data exception"); the 370 suppresses the operation.
3. If the fields are not the same length, CP extends the shorter field (not in storage) with leftmost zeros (the value is not changed algebraically, and the test is still valid). There can be no overflow.
4. CP compares the contents of operand-1 *algebraically* to that of operand-2. That is, the positive value P'+001' is algebraically greater than P'−001'. (However,

+0 is equal to −0.) CP sets the condition code, which we may then test with conditional branches, as for CLC.

COMPARISON	CONDITION CODE
Operand-1 equals operand-2	0 (equal)
Operand-1 is lower	1 (low)
Operand-1 is higher	2 (high)

Example: Contrast between CP and CLC. The following illustrates why we should use the correct operation for the data format, CLC for Character data and CP for Packed.

```
AMTCHAR   DC      C'123'              /F1/F2/F3/
AMTPACK   DS      PL2
          PACK    AMTPACK,AMTCHAR     /12/3F/
          CP      AMTPACK,=P'123'     EQUAL
          CLC     AMTPACK,=P'123'     HIGH
```

AMTCHAR packed into AMTPACK gives the hex value /12/3F/. Using both CP and CLC, we compare AMTPACK to a literal =P'123'. The literal generates a constant /12/3C/. For CP, /12/3F/ and /12/3C/ are algebraically equal (+123); the condition code is set to *equal*. For CLC, the two fields do not contain identical bits. Because F is greater than C, the condition code is set to *high*. Figure 4-8 depicts various CP operations:

COMP1 compares A to B. Because A's algebraic value is less, the condition code is set to low/minus.

```
LOC    OBJECT CODE      STMT    SOURCE STATEMENT

                        36  *        --------------------
                        37  ***      CP      COMPARE PACKED
                        38  *        --------------------
003054 012C             39  A        DC      P'12'            |01|2C|
003056 345C             40  B        DC      P'345'           |34|5C|
003058 05000C           41  C        DC      P'5000'          |05|00|0C|
00305B 025D             42  D        DC      P'-25'           |02|5D|
00305D 012A             43  E        DC      X'012A'          |01|2A|

                        45  *                                 DATA COMPARED:      COND'N CODE:
                                                              -------------       -----------
00305F 00
003060 F911 4052 4054   46  COMP1    CP      A,B             '12+'  < '345+'      LOW
003066 F921 4056 4052   47  COMP2    CP      C,A             '5000+' > '12+'      HIGH
00306C F911 4052 4059   48  COMP3    CP      A,D             '12+'  > '25-'       HIGH
003072 F911 4054 4057   49  COMP4    CP      B,C+1(2)        '345+' > '000+'      HIGH

003078 F910 4052 40C4   51  COMP5    CP      A,=P'0'         '12+'  > '0+'        HIGH
00307E F911 4052 405B   52  COMP6    CP      A,E             '012+' = '012+'      EQUAL
003084 F911 4056 4054   53  COMP7    CP      C(2),B          ERROR - NO SIGN IN OP-1
00308A F911 4052 40C0   54  COMP8    CP      A,=C'12'        ERROR - NO SIGN IN OP-2
```

FIGURE 4-8   Sample compare packed operations.

COMP2 shows that CP correctly compares packed fields of unequal length.

COMP3 compares a positive amount in A against D's negative value. A's value is algebraically higher.

COMP4 uses relative addressing and explicit length to compare the two bytes of B against the second and third bytes of C.

COMP5 compares A to a literal containing packed zero.

COMP6 compares A against a hex constant, E, containing valid packed data. The sign in E is X'A', which, although a valid plus sign, is rarely used.

COMP7 and COMP8 depict common programming errors made with packed data: the fields *as used* do not contain valid packed data. COMP7 should be coded with no explicit length, because C(2) means the first two bytes of C, containing no sign. In COMP8, the character literal does not define valid packed data. The literal should be defined as packed. Although these instructions assemble with no error message, at execute-time they will cause a program interrupt.

Problem 4-3 should now be attempted.

FORMATTING THE PRINT AREA

No problem was encountered in the previous chapter printing character data. Packed fields, however, contain nonprintable characters and must be unpacked for printing. A small problem arises when we print unpacked data. Assume we read a card field QTYIN containing the value 12345 (F1F2F3F4F5). We pack QTYIN into QTYPACK, add '50', and unpack QTYPACK into QTYOUT for printing:

```
QTYPACK   DC     PL3'0'
QTYOUT    DS     CL5
          PACK   QTYPACK,QTYIN      QTYPACK:   /12/34/5F/   sign
          AP     QTYPACK,=P'50'     QTYPACK:   /12/39/5C/
          UNPK   QTYOUT,QTYPACK     QTYOUT:    /F1/F2/F3/F9/C5
```

Note that AP changed the sign in QTYPACK from X'F' to X'C'. Now QTYOUT will print as 1239E. (The printer graphic for X'C5' is an alphabetic E.) But we want to print 12395. Because a character 5 is X'F5', then we need to change X'C5' to X'F5'. We can, therefore, move one of the other zone positions of QTYOUT into the units zone position. QTYOUT will now print correctly as 12345:

MVZ   QTYOUT+4(1),QTYOUT+3   /F1/F2/F3/F9/C5/

Another problem arises if the field is negative. Assume that QTYOUT contains /F1/F2/F3/F9/D5/. Inserting an F-zone to replace the D-zone changes the field's value from negative to positive. If we want the field to print, if positive as 12395, and if negative as 12395−, we may use the routine shown in Figure 4-9.

```
STMT    SOURCE STATEMENT

59              PACK    QTYPK,QTYIN         PACK QTYIN
60              AP      QTYPK,=P'50'        ADD 50 TO QTYPK
61              BNM     D10                 IF NOT MINUS, GO TO D10

63              MVI     QTYOUT+5,C'-'       MOVE MINUS SIGN TO PRINT
64 D10          UNPK    QTYOUT,QTYPK        UNPACK QTYPK INTO QTYOUT
65              MVZ     QTYOUT+4(1),QTYOUT+3 CORRECT ZONE IN SIGN
66 *              .
67 *              .
68 *              .
69 QTYIN        DS      ZL5                 ZONED INPUT FIELD
70 QTYPK        DS      PL3                 PACKED FIELD
71 QTYOUT       DS      ZL5                 ZONED OUTPUT FIELD
```

FIGURE 4-9   Formatting plus and minus unpacked amounts.

This procedure is quite cumbersome and inefficient. We would like an instruction or routine that better facilitates printing the unit position digit and the minus sign. Indeed, there is an instruction, ED, described in the next chapter, which does just that, and much more.

PAGE OVERFLOW.   The standard 11″ form provides for up to 60 lines of printing. Up to now we have not considered the possibility that the printer would reach the bottom of the form. Unless action is taken, the program will continue printing lines to the bottom of the page, over the horizontal perforation, and onto the top of the next page. Desirably, the program should know when printing has reached near to the bottom of the page, and the forms should eject to the top of the next page. Then the routine that printed the heading at the beginning of the program should be repeated, and normal printing of detail resumed.

The procedure to accommodate page overflow is for the program to count the lines that have been printed or spaced. The count is compared to some number, such as 40 or 50, that has been deemed the maximum number of print lines on a page. If the count exceeds this maximum, the program is directed to repeat the heading routine. The program at the end of this chapter provides for simple page overflow and should be carefully studied.

SAMPLE PROGRAM—BUDGET STATEMENT

The flowchart in Figure 4-10 depicts a program that reads company cost records containing Budget expense and Actual expense for the current period. The cards are sequence-checked by general account number. The program calculates the variance: Budget less Actual expense. A negative variance means that the Actual expense exceeds the Budget. If this variance exceeds -500.00, the program prints a message "OVER LIMIT". At the end of the run, the total variance is printed.

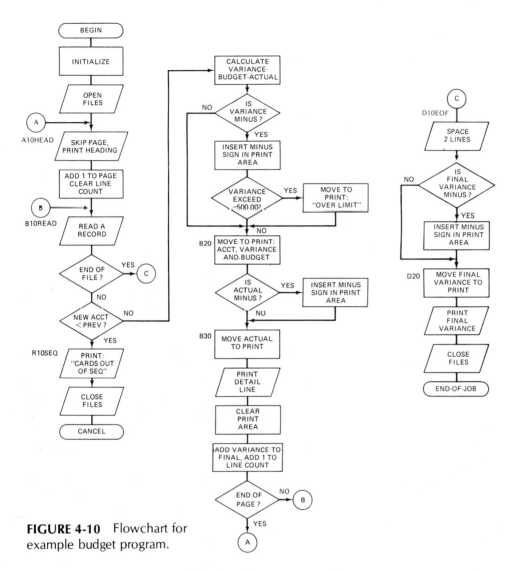

FIGURE 4-10 Flowchart for example budget program.

For reasons of brevity, the program omits many common procedures such as: checking for valid record code, printing total budget amount and actual expense, and providing for the current date on the report. Figure 4-11 gives the assembled and executed program. The input format is as follows:

COLUMN	CONTENTS	COLUMN	CONTENTS
1	Record code	16–21	Budget expense
2–5	General account number	22–27	Actual expense (plus or minus)
6–15	Expense description	28–80	Unused

```
              LIST OF BUDGET, ACTUAL EXPENSE AND VARIANCE           PAGE   1

STMT    SOURCE STATEMENT

  2             PRINT ON,NOGEN,NODATA

  4 *                  I N I T I A L I Z A T I O N
  5 *                  --------------------------
  6 PROG04    INIT                             INITIALIZE
 27           OPEN   CARD,PRTR
 36           MVC    PRINT,BLANK               CLEAR PRINT AREA

 38 *                  P A G E  H E A D I N G  R O U T I N E
 39 *                  --------------------------------
 40 A10HEAD   PUTPR  PRTR,PRINT,SK1            SKIP TO NEW PAGE
 47           UNPK   PAGEPR,PAGEPK             SET UP
 48           MVZ    PAGEPR+2(1),PAGEPR           PAGE NO.
 49           PUTPR  PRTR,PRHEAD,WSP2          PRINT HEADING
 56           AP     PAGEPK,=P'1'             ADD TO PAGE NUMBER
 57           ZAP    LINEPK,=P'0'             CLEAR LINE COUNTER

 59 *                  M A I N  P R O C E S S I N G  R O U T I N E
 60 *                  -----------------------------------------
 61 B10READ   GET    CARD,CARDIN              READ RECORD
 67           CLC    ACCIN,PREV               NEW ACCOUNT < PREV ACCT?
 68           BL     R10SEQER                    YES - CANCEL JOB
 69           MVC    PREV,ACCIN               MOVE NEW ACCOUNT NO. TO PREV
 70           PACK   VARPK,BUDGETIN           PACK BUDGET &
 71           PACK   ACTPK,ACTUALIN              ACTUAL AMOUNTS
 72           SP     VARPK,ACTPK              CALCULATE VARIANCE
 73           BNM    B20                      IS VARIANCE NEGATIVE?
 74           MVI    VAROUT+7,C'-'              YES - INSERT '-' SIGN

 76           CP     VARPK,=P'-500.00'        VARIANCE > 500.00 NEGATIVE?
 77           BNL    B20                        NO  - BYPASS
 78           MVC    MESSAGOT,=C'OVER LIMIT'     YES - PRINT WARNING

 80 B20       MVC    ACCOT,ACCIN              MOVE ACCOUNT NO. TO PRINT AREA
 81           MVC    DESCROT,DESCRIN          MOVE DESCRIPTION
 82           UNPK   VAROUT,VARPK             UNPACK VARIANCE INTO PRINT AREA
 83           MVZ    VAROUT+6(1),VAROUT+5     CORRECT ZONE IN UNITS POSITION
 84           MVC    BUDGOUT,BUDGETIN         MOVE BUDGET TO PRINT AREA
 85           ZAP    ACTPK,ACTPK             IS ACTUAL NEGATIVE?
 86           BNM    B30                        NO  - BYPASS
 87           MVI    ACTOUT+6,C'-'              YES - INSERT MINUS SIGN

 89 B30       MVC    ACTOUT,ACTUALIN          MOVE ACTUAL EXPENSE
 90           MVZ    ACTOUT+5(1),ACTOUT+4     CORRECT ZONE IN UNITS POSITION
 91           PUTPR  PRTR,PRINT,WSP1          PRINT ACCOUNT
 98           MVC    PRINT,BLANK              CLEAR PRINT AREA
 99           AP     VFINPK,VARPK             ADD TO FINAL TOTAL VARIANCE
100           AP     LINEPK,=P'1'             ADD 1 TO LINE COUNTER
101           CP     LINEPK,=P'10'            END OF PAGE?
102           BL     B10READ                    NO  - READ NEXT RECORD
103           B      A10HEAD                    YES - GO TO PRINT HEADING *
                                                      FOR NEXT PAGE
```

FIGURE 4-11 List of budget, actual expense, and variance. Output record.

LIST OF BUDGET, ACTUAL EXPENSE AND VARIANCE   PAGE 2

```
STMT    SOURCE STATEMENT

105 *               E N D - O F - F I L E   R O U T I N E
106 *               -------------------------------------
107 D10EOF   PUTPR  PRTR,PRINT,SP2            SPACE 2 LINES
114          ZAP    VFINPK,VFINPK            FINAL AMOUNT NEGATIVE?
115          BNM    D20                       *    NO
116          MVI    P+69,C'-'                 *    YES - INSERT MINUS SIGN

118 D20      UNPK   P+60(9),VFINPK            MOVE TOTAL TO PRINT
119          MVZ    P+68(1),P+67             CORRECT ZONE IN UNITS POSITION
120          MVC    DESCROT(11),=C'FINAL TOTAL'
121          PUTPR  PRTR,PRINT,WSP1          PRINT FINAL TOTAL
128          CLOSE  CARD,PRTR
137          EOJ                              NORMAL END-OF-JOB

141 *               E R R O R   R O U T I N E
142 *               -------------------------
143 R10SEQER MVC   MESSAGOT(17),MESSEQ       PRINT ERROR MESSAGE
144          PUTPR  PRTR,PRINT,WSP3
151          CLOSE  CARD,PRTR
160          CANCEL ,                         ABNORMAL JOB TERMINATION

165 *               D E C L A R A T I V E S
166 *               -----------------------

168 CARD     DEFCD  D10EOF                    DEFINE CARD FILE
192 PRTR     DEFPR                            DEFINE PRINTER FILE

217 CARDIN   DS     0CL80                     INPUT AREA:
218 CODEIN   DS     CL1                       01-01 RECORD CODE
219 ACCIN    DS     CL4                       02-05 ACCOUNT NO.
220 DESCRIN  DS     CL15                      06-20 DESCRIPTION
221 BUDGETIN DS     ZL6                       21-26 BUDGETTED EXPENSE
222 ACTUALIN DS     ZL6                       27-32 ACTUAL EXPENSE
223          DS     CL48                      33-80 UNUSED

225 PRHEAD   DS     0CL133                    HEADING AREA:
226          DC     CL20' '                   *
227          DC     CL24'ACCT   DESCRIPTION'  *
228          DC     CL34'BUDGET    ACTUAL  VARIANCE    PAGE'
229 PAGEPR   DS     CL03                      *
230          DC     CL52' '                   *

232 BLANK    DC     C' '                      BLANK FOR CLEARING PRINT AREA
233 PRINT    DS     0CL133                    PRINTER AREA:
234 P        DS     CL1                       *
235          DS     CL19                      *
236 ACCOT    DS     CL4                       *   ACCOUNT NO.
237          DS     CL2                       *
238 DESCROT  DS     CL15                      *   DESCRIPTION
239          DS     CL3                       *
240 BUDGOUT  DS     ZL6                       *   BUDGETTED EXPENSE
241          DS     CL3                       *
242 ACTOUT   DS     ZL6                       *   ACTUAL EXPENSE
243          DS     CL3                       *
244 VAROUT   DS     ZL7                       *   VARIANCE
245          DS     CL4                       *
246 MESSAGOT DS     CL10                      *   OVER BUDGET MESSAGE
247          DS     CL50                      *
```

FIGURE 4-11 (*Continued*)

```
                    LIST OF BUDGET, ACTUAL EXPENSE AND VARIANCE          PAGE  3

STMT    SOURCE STATEMENT

 249 ACTPK      DC     PL4'0'              PACKED CONSTANTS
 250 LINEPK     DC     PL2'0'             *
 251 PAGEPK     DC     PL2'1'             *
 252 VARPK      DC     PL4'0'             *
 253 VFINPK     DC     PL5'0'             *

 255 MESSEQ     DC     C'RECORD OUT OF SEQ'

 257 PREV       DC     XL4'00'            PREVIOUS ACCOUNT NUMBER

 259            LTORG
 260                   =C'$$BOPEN '
 261                   =C'$$BCLOSE'
 262                   =V(PCOCIT)
 263                   =A(PRTR)
 264                   =A(PRINT)
 265                   =A(PRHEAD)
 266                   =A(CARD)
 267                   =A(CARDIN)
 268                   =C'OVER LIMIT'
 269                   =P'10'
 270                   =P'1'
 271                   =P'0'
 272                   =P'-500.00'
 273                   =C'FINAL TOTAL'

 275            END    PROGC4
```

ACCT	DESCRIPTICN	BUDGET	ACTUAL	VARIANCE	PAGE 001
5301	LABOR	250000	268315	0018315-	
5302	SUPERVISION	100000	100000	0000000	
5315	HEAT, LIGHT	022000	029526	0007526-	
5328	REPAIRS	000000	065315	0065315-	OVER LIMIT
6001	SALES SALARIES	123450	123450	0000000	
6051	DELIVERY EXPEN	003333	005010	0001677-	
6059	DEPRECIATION	015000	013356	0001644	
6061	FREIGHT	008500	011520	0003020-	
6075	ADVERTISING	005000	000000	0005000	
6081	TRAVEL EXPENSE	010000	112016	0102016-	OVER LIMIT

ACCT	DESCRIPTICN	BUDGET	ACTUAL	VARIANCE	PAGE 002
6084	INSURANCE	002500	002500	0000000	
7011	OFFICE SUPPLIES	003500	001516	0001984	
7029	BAD DEBTS	002500	068500	0066000-	OVER LIMIT
7082	POSTAGE	001000	001215	0000215-	
	FINAL TOTAL			000255456-	

FIGURE 4-11 (Continued)

Note on sequence-checking: PREV, the previously stored account number, is initially defined with hexadecimal zeros (XL4'00'). This represents binary zeros, or all bits OFF, the lowest possible value. The punched card code for X'00' is 12-0-1-8-9. It is virtually impossible for a data record to contain the value of hex zeros in the account number field. The *first* input record will therefore always be higher than contents of PREV. (PREV could be defined in character format as CL4' ' or C'0000', but the first record could conceivably contain blanks or zeros in the account number. Such a record would therefore be treated as *equal* to PREV, resulting in an invalid error message.)

The program is organized by sections. The Initialization opens the files and clears the print area (this clearing could be omitted if the contents of the PRINT area were fully defined with DC blanks). Under OS, the OPEN and CLOSE are coded differently.

The Page Heading routine prints headings and page number at the top of each page printed.

The Main Processing routine reads records, calculates, and prints the variance.

The End-of-File routine prints the total variance and closes the files.

The Error routine prints a message and terminates on an out-of-sequence record. Under OS, the ABEND macro would replace the CANCEL.

DEBUGGING TIPS

Expect considerably more bugs in both the assembly and execution phases as your programs become larger and involve arithmetic data. Finding a bug for the first time is quite often time-consuming, but in time you can become proficient in tracing errors (especially if you have enough of them!).

New assembly errors that can occur involve, for example, coding packed DC's with characters other than 0-9, decimal point, and sign. Watch for coding hex constants: DC XL3'FF' generates '0000FF', not 'FFFFFF'.

More likely, however, are errors during program execution. Packing a field that contains a blank (X'40') in its rightmost position generates a packed field with an invalid sign (X'04'); an attempt to perform arithmetic using this field will cause a "Data Exception". A likely cause of the blank position is a blank input field, or an improperly defined input record. Another popular cause of Data Exceptions is adding to a field that has not been initialized as a DC, or is defined as Character or Hex, so that it contains invalid packed data.

Watch out also for using MVC and CLC on packed data (incorrect execution), or ZAP and CP on character data (Data Exceptions). Improper relative addressing and missing explicit lengths are always good for a few bugs.

ERROR DETECTION. The system is designed to terminate a run on a "program check" interrupt, such as a "Data Exception" or an "Operation Exception" (Appendix B contains a complete list). The Supervisor's error diagnostics vary considerably by operating system.

ERRORS UNDER DOS.   On a processing error, the DOS Supervisor interrupts the program and prints the location of the invalid instruction and the type of error, as:

PROGRAM CHECK INTERRUPTION—HEX LOCATION 051340—CONDITION CODE 3—DATA EXCEPTION

The "hex location" is the address of the instruction in error. If the program's START instruction specifies the program "load point" (starting storage location for execution), then we simply have to check the program listing:

```
LOC
51340  ...  AP  TOTAL,AMOUNT      (Instruction causing the error)
51346  ...  ZAP  ...
```

A "Data Exception" means that the instruction has attempted to perform arithmetic on invalid packed data. An examination of the two defined operands reveals:

```
51780  AMOUNT  DC  PL3'0'
51783  TOTAL   DS  PL4'0'
```

TOTAL is incorrectly defined as a DS. The Supervisor can also print a hexadecimal dump of the contents of storage, which we can examine. The dump could indicate for locations 51783–51786 the hex value 00000000. The cause of the error is explained—TOTAL does not contain a valid sign because it was defined as a DS instead of a DC.

ERRORS UNDER OS.   OS provides a mass of processing messages, telling us more than we want to know, but supplies useful error diagnostics only if requested. Insert the following with the //GO statements:

//GO.SYSUDUMP DD SYSOUT=A

The system will now supply the load or entry point of the program, the address of the instruction following the error, and a hex dump of the registers and program storage area. If the program encounters an error (program check interrupt), check the printout following the program listing and any output. The first diagnostics could appear as:

```
JOB xxxxxx STEP GO

COMPLETION CODE SYSTEM 0C⑦     indicates "data exception"

PSW AT ENTRY TO ABEND FFB5000D C0051346     "instruction address"
```

"Completion Code" indicates the type of program check. In this case, the code '7' is for "Data Exception"—see Appendix B for all codes. (Incredibly, the system prints several hundred lines of diagnostics, but identifies errors only with this crumby code!)

The PSW (Program Status Word) indicates the "instruction address" in the rightmost six hex digits, in this case 051346. This is the address of the instruction following the one in error. When the program was assembled, we did not know where it would load for execution, and indicated the START location as zero. We can determine the load point in the diagnostics under the CDE section. The first statement there could appear as:

.... **NM MAIN (or NM GO) USE 01 EPA 051210**

The entry point address (EPA) is therefore 05120, the "relocation factor". Now we can calculate the address in the program listing:

Address in the PSW	51346
Relocation factor	51210
Location of instruction following the error	136

```
LOC
130   ...   AP    TOTAL,AMOUNT
136   ...   ZAP   ...
```

The instruction preceding 136 is the AP at 130. The Data Exception indicates invalid packed data in one or both operands. The next steps are to check the definitions of TOTAL and AMOUNT, and to examine the hex dump of storage, as was done for the DOS example.

ERROR RECOVERY. Program checks cause the program to terminate, but when testing, we usually want to push the program through to detect as many errors as possible. There are special macros that provide for error recovery, STXIT under DOS and SPIE under OS. The IBM Supervisor and Macros manuals provide details.

PROBLEMS

4-1. MVN and MVZ. Given the following declaratives, code the following unrelated questions. Give results in hex and character.

```
HAM     DC   C'HAL'
EGGS    DC   C'2472'
TOAST   DC   X'C9E2C4E0'
```

(a) Move the first 3 numeric ½-bytes of TOAST to the numerics of HAM.
(b) Move the zone ½-bytes of TOAST to those of EGGS.

4-2. Complete the hex representation for the following. Except for a and for b, questions are unrelated.

			L	F3	F4	F5	F6	F7	F8
Example:	L	DC	C'345678'	M						
	M	DC	C'1234'	N						
	N	DC	Z'123'	P						
	P	DC	P'−123'	Q						
	Q	DC	P'12.34'	P						
(a)	{PACK	P,N	L						
	{UNPK	L,P	Q						
(b)	{PACK	Q,L	N						
	{UNPK	N,Q	Q						
(c)	PACK	Q+1(2),N+1(2)	P						
(d)	PACK	P,=CL2' '	M						
(e)	PACK	M,M	P						
(f)	UNPK	P,P	Q						
(g)	ZAP	Q,P	P						
(h)	ZAP	P,Q	Q						
(i)	AP	Q,=P'5'	Q						
(j)	AP	Q,=X'5C'	Q						

4-3. Check the *condition code* set by the following. Symbolic names refer to Problem 4-2. Explain if invalid.

			HI	LO	EQ
(a)	CP	P,Q			
(b)	CP	Q,P			
(c)	CP	M,Q			
(d)	CLC	M,N			

4-4. PROGRAM ASSIGNMENT.

Required: A program that reads Accounts Receivable records, prints the detail, and accumulates totals.

Input: Data records similar to the format of the example program at the end of Chapter 3, with some additions:

COLUMN		COLUMN	
1	Record code (3)	31–32	Current month
4–5	Store number	41–46	Balance owing
6–10	Customer number	47–52	Customer limit
11–30	Customer name		

Procedure:

— Check for valid record code (3).

— Sequence-check the file according to Store-Customer number. Within a Store, the Customer numbers are in ascending sequence.

— Check that the current month is the same for all cards. If not, print a suitable message.

— Compare Customer balances to their credit limits. If the balance exceeds the limit, print 'OVER LIMIT'.

— Print all the data except record code from each record. At the end of each Store, print the total balance owing for all Customers for that Store (minor total). At the end of the run, print the total balance owing for all Stores (final total).

— Provide test input data that will test all possible conditions in the program.

— Flowchart, code, and test the program. Be sure to use the programming standards for your installation.

CHAPTER 5

DECIMAL ARITHMETIC II

This chapter continues with the additional decimal instructions commonly used in programming: edit, multiply, and divide. Editing involves sign and punctuation control to format packed fields for printing. The sections on multiply and divide provide practical techniques for handling various field lengths and decimal-point precision and more realistic programming examples and problems.

EDITING—ED

The purpose of ED is to make packed data suitable for printing. ED converts packed data into zoned format and provides for punctuation and sign. Once understood, ED greatly facilitates print formatting.

NAME	OPERATION	OPERAND
[symbol]	ED	S1,S2 or D1(L,B1),D2(B2)

Editing normally consists of two operations:

1. We define an edit word, or pattern, specifying where we want commas, decimal point, and sign to print. We use MVC to move this edit word to the print positions where the amount is to be printed.

2. We then use ED to modify the packed field according to the edit word definition. ED unpacks the amount field and provides the required editing for commas, decimal point, and minus sign.

The following simple example edits a 2-byte (3-digit) packed field called COUNT into a print field called COUNPR. (There is no provision for commas or decimal point.)

```
COUNT    DS    PL2                        3-digit packed field
COUNPR   DS    CL4                        Print field for edited result
         MVC   COUNPR,=X'40202020'        Move editword to print field
         ED    COUNPR,COUNT               Edit the packed field into
                                          print field
```

THE EDIT WORD.   The edit word consists of pairs of hex digits. Each pair represents one print position. The commonly used edit characters are:

HEX	NAME	PURPOSE
40	Fill character	Used for "zero suppression"—to fill or pad leftmost unwanted zeros with blanks. For example, ED can suppress 00025 so that it prints as 25. We may use any other character such as asterisk (5C) as a fill character, although X'40' is the commonly used EBCDIC blank.
20	Digit selector	One X'20' in the edit word represents each packed digit to be printed. Since a packed field always contains an odd number of digits, there must be an odd number of X'20's (including X'21's, if any). In the example earlier, COUNT contains three digits. Our edit word, therefore, contains three X'20's. ED selects one packed digit for each X'20'. It unpacks the digit in the X'20' position. However, if the digit is a leading (leftmost) zero, ED replaced the X'20' with the X'40' fill character.
6B	Comma (,)	X'6B' is coded in the edit word wherever a comma is to be printed.
4B	Decimal point (.)	X'4B' is coded in the edit word wherever a decimal point is to be printed.
60	Minus sign (−)	If the amount could be negative, we code X'60' to print a minus sign to the right of the edited amount.
C3D9	Credit (CR)	To print CR instead of minus, we use X'C3D9'.
21	Significance starter	A "significant" digit is 1 through 9 (nonzero). In the value 000.25, the '2' is the first significant digit in the field. The fill character X'40' "zero suppresses" the leftmost zeros by filling them with blanks: bbbb25. We may want to *force significance* so that a leftmost zero prints as bb0.25. For this purpose we code X'21', the

significance starter. Normally, we code only one X'21'. It acts the same as the digit selector, but in addition X'21' forces significance—all characters to its right are forced to print, whether they contain a significant digit or not.

BASIC RULES OF EDITING.

1. We move the required edit word into the print area.
2. The operands of the ED operation work as follows: Operand-1 references the leftmost byte of the edit word. This is normally the print area, the same position and length as specified by the MVC. Operand-2 references the packed field to be edited.
3. Editing proceeds from left to right. ED examines each character in the edit word to determine what action to take:
   — The leftmost hex byte is always assumed to be the fill character, which is normally X'40', but may be any other required character.
   — For each X'20', ED selects a packed digit. If the digit is nonzero, it is unpacked, replacing the X'20'. If zero, and significance has not been encountered, then ED replaces the X'20' with the fill character (usually X'40'). Significance is forced either by a significant digit or by the significance starter (X'21').
   — If the hex byte X'6B' (comma) or X'4B' (decimal), and significance has been encountered, they are preserved. If significance has not been encountered, ED replaces them with the fill character.
   — If the packed field is negative, then the CR or minus (X'60') is preserved. If positive, ED replaces them with the fill character. The condition code for minus, zero, and plus is set.
4. The length of operand-1 terminates the operation. The maximum length is 256 bytes. Only operand-1 may have an explicit length.

EXAMPLE EDIT OPERATION.   A 3-byte packed field, PACKAMT, is to be edited. The edit word must provide for decimal point, minus sign, and zero suppression of the three leftmost digits.

```
PACKAMT   DC   PL3'5'                    (contains /00/00/5C/)
EDWORD    DC   X'402020214B202060'
```

The defined edit word, EDWORD, provides the necessary sign and punctuation control. Note that there is an X'20' or X'21' for each packed digit. The instructions to edit are:

```
MVC   P+90(8),EDWORD      / 40/20/20/21/4B/20/20/60/
ED    P+90(8),PACKAMT     /40/40/40/40/4B/F0/F5/40/
                            |    |    |    |    |
                          P+90 |+92 |+94 |+96 |
                            +91   +93   +95   +97
```

MVC moved EDWORD into the required print positions. ED then edits PACKAMT into the same print positions. *The explicit length (8) in the ED operand refers to the length of the edit word* in the print area, not to the length of PACKAMT. Editing proceeds from left to right, starting at P+90:

P+90: X'40', assumed to be the fill character, is not changed.

P+91: Because the position contains X'20', ED examines the first digit of PACKAMT. It contains zero, and therefore the fill character X'40' replaces the X'20'.

P+92: Because of the X'20' here, ED examines the second digit of PACKAMT. It also contains a zero, so the X'20' is changed to X'40'.

P+93: Because of the X'21' significance starter here, all characters to the right are to be printed. Also, ED examines the third digit of PACKAMT, a zero, and replaces the X'21' with X'40'.

·P+94: X'4B' is a decimal point. Because X'21' has signalled to force printing, the X'4B' is not changed. (Had the X'21' not been encountered yet, the fill character would replace the X'4B'.)

P+95: Because of the X'20', ED examines the fourth digit of PACKAMT, a zero. Because of the preceding X'21', ED unpacks the zero and replaces the X'20' with X'F0'.

P+96: Because of the X'20', ED unpacks the fifth digit of PACKAMT, 5. X'F5' replaces the X'20'.

P+97: X'60' means that if the next half-byte of PACKAMT contains X'D' (a minus sign), the field is considered negative and the X'60' is not changed. Because PACKAMT is positive (X'C'), ED replaces the X'60' with the fill character, X'40'.

At this point the length (8) of operand-1 is exhausted, and the operation terminates. The edited amount will print as .05 (if EDWORD contained X'402021204B202060', the result would be 0.05). Figure 5-1 illustrates four example edit operations:

EDWD1 shows simple zero suppression. The packed amount in COUNTER is to print with leftmost zeros suppressed. The edit word, EDWD1, therefore consists of an X'40' fill character and an X'20' for each packed digit.

EDWD2 edits and prints a 4-byte packed field. The edit word provides for zero suppression, comma, decimal point, and minus sign.

EDWD3 depicts use of the CR symbol commonly used in financial statements.

EDWD4 is explained in the next section.

DOLLAR SIGN AND ASTERISK. The dollar sign (X'5B') and the asterisk (X'5C') when used in the edit word create certain problems. Normally we use the dollar sign ($) to print Supplier and Employee checks and Customer bills, with the $ to the left of the amount. If X'5B' is coded on the left, ED improperly uses it as the fill character.

```
STMT    SOURCE STATEMENT

   6 *         ------------
   7 ***    ED    EDIT
   8 *         ------------
   9 *               ZERO SUPPRESSION:    HEX CONTENTS:
  10 *               ----------------     ------------
  11 P       DS    CL121
  12 COUNTER DC    P'0015'              |00|01|5C|
  13 EDWD1   DC    X'402020202020'      |40|20|20|20|20|20|

  15         MVC   P+20(6),EDWD1        |40|20|20|20|20|20|
  16         ED    P+20(6),COUNTER      |40|40|40|40|F1|F5|

  18 *               COMMA, DECIMAL, MINUS SIGN:
  19 *               --------------------------
  20 AMOUNT  DC    P'-2345.00'          |02|34|50|0D|
  21 EDWD2   DC    X'4020206B2020214B202060'


  23         MVC   P+30(11),EDWD2       |40|20|20|6B|20|20|21|4B|20|20|60|
  24         ED    P+30(11),AMOUNT      |40|40|F2|6B|F3|F4|F5|4B|F0|F0|60|   +
                                              2  ,  3  4  5  .  0  0  -
  25 *               CREDIT (CR) SIGN:
  26 *               ----------------
  27 TOTAL   DC    P'-0000.05'          |00|00|00|5D|
  28 EDWD3   DC    X'4020206B2021204B2020C3D9'

  30         MVC   P+50(12),EDWD3       |40|20|20|6B|20|21|20|4B|20|20|C3|D9|
  31         ED    P+50(12),TOTAL       |40|40|40|40|40|40|F0|4B|F0|F5|C3|D9|  +
                                              0  .  0  5  C  R
  32 *               ASTERISK AND DOLLAR SIGN:
  33 *               ------------------------
  34 ACCUM   DC    P'12.34'             |01|23|4C|
  35 EDWD4   DC    X'5B402020214B2020605C'


  37         MVC   P+70(10),EDWD4       |5B|40|20|20|21|4B|20|20|60|5C|
  38         ED    P+71(08),ACCUM       |5B|40|40|F1|F2|4B|F3|F4|40|5C|   +
                                         $      1  2  .  3  4     *
```

FIGURE 5-1   Sample edit operations.

Also, many installations print asterisks (*) to the right of the amount field to denote the level of total:

     *   Minor total
     **   Intermediate total
     ***   Major total

       If one or more X'5C's are coded to the right of the edit word, ED leaves the asterisks undisturbed only if the amount is negative. If positive, ED replaces asterisks with the fill character, thus erasing them. One solution is to omit both X'5B' and X'5C' from the edit word and use separate operations to move $ and * to the print area. Another solution is to use the technique in Figure 5-1, in which $ and * are defined as part of the edit word but do not participate in the ED operation. MVC moves the full edit word, starting in P+70. The ED operation begins in P+71, leaving the $ intact. Further, ED specifies editing only 8 bytes, although the MVC moved 10. The operation terminates just prior to the * at P+79, leaving it also intact.

Another instruction, EDMK, providing for floating dollar sign and asterisk is covered in a later chapter.

Problems 5-1, 5-2, and 5-3 should now be attempted.

MULTIPLY PACKED—MP

We use MP to multiply one packed field (the multiplicand) by another (the multiplier). Common examples are multiplying hours by rate-of-pay in payroll, and quantity by unit cost in inventory programs.

NAME	OPERATION	OPERAND
[symbol]	MP	S1,S2 or D1(L1,B1),D2(L2,B2)

The rules for MP are:

1. Either operand may contain an explicit length (L1 and L2).
2. The operand-1 field is the *multiplicand* and must contain valid packed data. The *product* is developed in this field, and replaces the multiplicand. The maximum length of operand-1 is 16 bytes, providing 31 digits. We should define the operand-1 field large enough to accommodate the largest possible product that the two operands can develop. Generally, the product length should equal at least the length in bytes of the multiplicand plus the multiplier.
3. Operand-2 references the *multiplier* in valid packed format. The maximum length is 8 bytes.
4. MP is governed by the normal rules of algebra: like signs yield a positive product, and unlike signs yield a negative product. A zero amount in either operand causes a zero product. MP does not set the condition code.

PRODUCT LENGTH.   Good programming practice defines the product length equal at least to the length *in bytes* of the multiplicand plus multiplier. From another point of view, prior to execution of the MP, for each byte in the multiplier, the product field must contain one byte of zeros to the left of the significant digits in the multiplicand. Consider the following:

```
MULTPLD   DC    PL4'1234560'        4-byte multiplicand
MULTPLR   DC    PL2'950'            2-byte multiplier
PRODUCT   DS    PL6                 6-byte product
          ZAP   PRODUCT,MULTPLD     /00/00/12/34/56/0C/
          MP    PRODUCT,MULTPLR     /01/17/28/32/00/0C/
```

Since MULTPLD is four bytes and MULTPLR is two, we define PRODUCT as six bytes (PRODUCT may be defined longer). We ZAP MULTPLD into PRODUCT. After the MP, PRODUCT contains a 6-byte product. If PRODUCT were shorter, the MP would cause a program interrupt.

DECIMAL PRECISION.   Neither the Assembler nor the computer handles the decimal position. With all decimal arithmetic we must provide for the implied decimal point. The following is a useful rule: *the number of decimal positions in the product equals the number of decimals in the multiplicand plus multiplier.* For example, if the multiplicand has three decimals and the multiplier has two, then the product will have five decimal positions.

ROUNDING, OR HALF-ADJUSTING.   In many program languages after multiplying we round by adding 5 to the unwanted decimal position. Then we drop the unwanted decimal position(s). If the product is negative, we subtract 5. The following examples round a 3-decimal and a 5-decimal value:

3-DECIMAL VALUE		5-DECIMAL VALUE	
123.456	Require a 2-decimal answer	123.45678	Require a 2-decimal answer
5	Round by adding 5	500	Add 500
123.461	Answer is 123.46	123.46178	Answer is 123.46
	(Drop the unwanted 1)		

Before rounding, however, we should check if the product is negative to determine whether to add or subtract five. A convenient technique in Assembler programming is to add all the unwanted decimal positions to the product, regardless of the sign:

3-DECIMAL VALUE		5-DECIMAL VALUE	
123.456	Require a 2-decimal answer	123.45678−	Require a 2-decimal answer
6	Add 6	678−	Add minus 678
123.462	Answer is 123.46	123.46356−	Answer is 123.46−

The restriction is that we may adjust only an *odd-number* of unwanted decimal positions, because of the presence of the sign. For example, the value 123.4567 requires a 2-decimal answer. In storage, the value is /12/34/56/7C/. We would like to add the rightmost two digits, 67. This is impossible—we can add either one byte, /7C/, or two bytes, /56/7C/. We solve this problem by shifting the value one digit to the right as /01/23/45/6C/, and then add the 6C: /01/23/46/2C/, or 123.462. The next sections should further clarify this.

Figure 5-2 illustrates multiply operations. The first example multiplies a 2-byte field, QTY, by a 2-byte field, PRICE. The product, AMT, is therefore defined as four bytes in length. Since PRICE contains two decimals and QTY none, there are two decimal positions generated in the product. This example requires a 2-decimal answer, and therefore no rounding is done.

```
42 *        ---------------------
43 ***    MP     MULTIPLY PACKED
44 *        ---------------------

46 *               MULTIPLY, GENERATE 2 DECIMALS, NO ROUNDING:
47 *               ---------------------------
48 QTY      DC     P'475'          |47|5C|
49 PRICE    DC     P'3.50'         |35|0C|
50 AMT      DS     PL4

52          ZAP    AMT,QTY         |00|00|47|5C|
53          MP     AMT,PRICE       |01|66|25|0C|  AMT = 1662.50

55 *               MULTIPLY, GENERATE 3 DECIMALS, ROUND TO 2 DECIMALS:
56 *               ---------------------------
57 HRS      DC     P'120.5'        |01|20|5C|
58 RATE     DC     P'3.55'         |35|5C|
59 WAGE     DS     PL5

61          ZAP    WAGE,HRS        |00|00|01|20|5C|
62          MP     WAGE,RATE       |00|04|27|77|5C|  MULTIPLY 427.775
63          AP     WAGE,WAGE+4(1)  |00|04|27|78|0C|  ROUND    427.780
64          MVO    WAGE,WAGE(4)    |00|00|42|77|8C|  SHIFT    427.78
```

FIGURE 5-2   Sample multiply packed operations.

The second example multiplies a 3-byte field, HRS, by a 2-byte field, RATE. The product, WAGE, is therefore five bytes long. Since HRS contains one decimal and RATE two, the product has three decimal positions. Because only two decimals are required, this example rounds the unwanted rightmost decimal digit. That is, the rightmost byte of WAGE is added to WAGE. Next, an MVO operation shifts the product one digit to the right, leaving two decimal positions, as explained in the next section.

A later chapter covers a 370 instruction, SRP, which greatly facilitates rounding and shifting.

MOVE WITH OFFSET—MVO

The MVO operation moves data an odd number of half-bytes to the right. Although MVO may be used on any format, its most common use is on packed data—to shift off unwanted decimal positions generated by MP and DP operations. For example, an MVO could shift a field containing 12/34/56/7C three digits to the right, yielding 00/01/23/4C.

NAME	OPERATION	OPERAND
[symbol]	MVO	S1,S2 or D1(L1,B1),D2(L2,B2)

The rules for MVO are:

1. The maximum length of each operand is 16 bytes. Either operand may specify an explicit length (L1 and L2).
2. MVO moves the operand-2 data to the operand-1 field and shifts to the right an odd number of half-bytes. (To shift an even number of half-bytes requires two MVOs.) The rightmost half-byte of operand-1 (if packed, the sign position) is not altered.
3. MVO fills leftmost shifted half-bytes with X'0'.
4. The length of operand-2 determines how many bytes MVO moves into the operand-1 field, and shifts to the rightmost half-byte of operand-1.

Refer now to the examples in Figure 5-3:

```
STMT     SOURCE STATEMENT

  68 *           -----------------------
  69 ***      MVO    MOVE WITH OFFSET
  70 *           -----------------------
  71 X        DC     P'123456789'    |12|34|56|78|9C|
  72 Y        DC     PL5'0'          |00|00|00|00|0C|

  74 MVO1     MVO    Y,X(4)          |01|23|45|67|8C| SHIFT 1 DIGIT
  75 MVO2     MVO    Y,X(3)          |00|01|23|45|6C| SHIFT 3 DIGITS
  76 MVO3     MVO    Y,X(2)          |00|00|01|23|4C| SHIFT 5 DIGITS


  78 *              MULTIPLY, GENERATE 4 DECIMALS, ROUND TO 2 DECIMALS:
  79 *              ----------------------------
  80 HOUR     DC     P'20.5'         |20|5C|
  81 RATEPY   DC     P'03.250'       |03|25|0C|
  82 PAY      DS     PL5

  84          ZAP    PAY,HOUR        |00|00|00|20|5C|
  85          MP     PAY,RATEPY      |00|06|66|25|0C| MULTIPLY  66.6250
  86          MVO    PAY,PAY(4)      |00|00|66|62|5C| SHIFT     66.625
  87          AP     PAY,PAY+4(1)    |00|00|66|63|0C| ROUND     66.630
  88          MVO    PAY,PAY(4)      |00|00|06|66|3C| SHIFT     66.63
```

FIGURE 5-3 Sample MVO operations.

MVO1 moves the first four (leftmost) bytes of X into Y. The packed digits from X are right-shifted, one half-byte, to the rightmost half-byte of Y. MVO2 moves the first three bytes of X into Y and right-shifts 3 half-bytes, to the rightmost half-byte of Y. MVO3 moves the first two bytes of X into Y and right-shifts 5 half-bytes, to the rightmost half-byte of Y..

Figure 5-3 also illustrates a multiply operation that generates four decimal positions. Because only two are required, two MVO's are used to shift the unwanted two decimals to the right. The rounding operation, AP, is immediately after the first MVO. This is because we must round beginning with the first unwanted decimal position, in this case '5'. In the product, /00/06/66/25/0C/, the '5' is shifted one position so that it becomes the leftmost digit of the next byte, /00/00/66/62/5C/. We now round and shift off the unwanted '5'.

Problems 5-4 and 5-5 should now be attempted.

DIVIDE PACKED—DP

We use DP to divide one packed field (the dividend) by another (the divisor). Common examples include dividing inventory value by number of units to calculate unit cost, and computing ratios and percentages.

NAME	OPERATION	OPERAND
[symbol]	DP	S1,S2 or D1(L1,B1),D2(L2,B2)

The rules for DP are:

1. Either operand may contain an explicit length (L1 and L2).
2. Operand-1 is the *dividend,* and must contain valid packed data. The *quotient* and *remainder* are developed in this field. The maximum length is 16 bytes. Operand-1 should be defined large enough to accommodate the largest possible quotient, plus remainder.
3. Operand-2 is the *divisor* containing valid packed data. The maximum length is 8 bytes.
4. The length of the generated remainder is the length of the divisor.
5. DP is governed by the normal rules of algebra: like signs yield a positive quotient, and unlike signs yield a negative quotient. A zero divisor is invalid—it causes a program interrupt. DP does not set the condition code.

QUOTIENT LENGTH. Since we do not normally know the contents of arithmetic fields, we should provide for the worst possible case, in which the divisor contains the value 1 (zero divisors are not permitted). With a divisor of 1, the quotient will equal (and cannot exceed) the value of the dividend.

$$dividend \overbrace{\frac{1234567}{1}} = \underbrace{1234567}_{quotient} \quad (quotient = dividend)$$

As good programming practice, therefore, we should define the length of the quotient equal at least to the length of the dividend. Also, the length of the remainder always equals the length of the divisor. The remainder is generated in the operand-1 field to the right of the quotient. Both quotient and remainder contain a sign. Technically, the quotient length needs to be only long enough to contain the significant digits developed. If the quotient field is longer than necessary, DP inserts leftmost zeros. If the quotient field is too short to contain all the significant digits generated in the quotient, an overflow interrupt occurs. The following rule always provides adequate field lengths: *define the operand-1 field equal at least to the length of the dividend plus divisor:*

DIVIDEND	DC	PL4'1234567'	/12/34/56/7C/	4-byte dividend
DIVISOR	DC	PL1'3'	/3C/	1-byte divisor
ANSWER	DS	PL5		5-byte answer
	ZAP	ANSWER,DIVIDEND		
	DP	ANSWER,DIVISOR	/00/12/34/56/7C/	
			/04/11/52/2C/1C/	

$$\underbrace{\qquad\qquad}\quad\underbrace{\qquad}$$
quotient   remainder

Since DIVIDEND contains four bytes and DIVISOR one, ANSWER (to be used for the resulting quotient and remainder) should contain five bytes. (ANSWER may be defined longer.) We ZAP DIVIDEND into ANSWER. After the DP, the first four bytes of ANSWER contain the quotient, with a sign. The fifth byte contains the signed remainder, one byte long, the same length as the divisor.

DECIMAL PRECISION. We must provide for the implied decimal point. The following rule is always valid: *the number of decimal positions in the quotient equals the number of decimals in the dividend minus divisor.* For example, if the dividend contains four decimals and the divisor one, then the quotient has three decimal positions. If the dividend does not contain sufficient decimal positions for our division, we may generate the required extra decimal positions by shifting the dividend to the left, using an MP that multiplies by 100 (1.00). Thus, 12.34 × 1.00 = 12.3400, a product that is the same algebraic value, provided that we in the program always account for the new implied decimal point.

It may facilitate programming to mentally "clear" the divisor of decimal positions first. For example, the following divisor can be "cleared" of its decimal places with no added programming steps, by definition:

$$\frac{12.3400}{1.23} = \frac{1234.00}{123}$$

ROUNDING, OR HALF-ADJUSTING. In the earlier example, the remainder in ANSWER was 1/3, not .1. The remainder is not usually rounded or required. The quotient, however, is rounded, similar to rounding the product. If we want added precision for rounding we may shift the dividend to the left. Note that after the left shift, the length of the dividend is longer, so that the quotient will have to be correspondingly longer. For example, assume a 3-byte dividend and a 2-byte divisor. If we shift the dividend left 2 digits (one byte), the dividend is now effectively 4 bytes, so that the quotient/remainder should be 6 bytes. We may generate one more decimal position than we need, and round it off. The following examples each divide 246.79 by 31:

Require a 1-decimal quotient:

$$\frac{246.79}{31} = 7.96 \qquad \text{(may be rounded to 8.0)}$$

Require a 2-decimal quotient—multiply the dividend by 1.0:

$$\frac{246.79 \times 1.0}{31} = \frac{246.790}{31} = 7.960 \qquad \text{(may be rounded to 7.96)}$$

```
92 *              --------------------
93 ***      DP    DIVIDE PACKED
94 *              --------------------
95 DIST     DC    P'2356.5'           |23|56|5C|
96 GALS     DC    P'150.0'            |01|50|0C|

98 *              DIVIDE, NO DECIMAL, NO ROUNDING:
99 *              -------------------------------
100 ANS1    DS    PL6

102         ZAP   ANS1,DIST           |00|00|00|23|56|5C|            +
                                      QUOTIENT|REMAINDER
103         DP    ANS1,GALS           |00|01|5C|01|06|5C|

105 *             DIVIDE, ROUND TO NO DECIMALS:
106 *             ---------------------------
107 ANS2    DS    PL7

108         ZAP   ANS2,DIST           |00|00|00|00|23|56|5C|
109         MP    ANS2,=P'10'         |00|00|00|02|35|65|0C|         +
                                      QUOTIENT    |REMAINDER
110         DP    ANS2,GALS           |00|00|15|7C|00|15|0C|  DIVIDE 15.7
111         AP    ANS2(4),ANS2+3(1)   |00|00|16|4C|00|15|0C|  ROUND  16.4
112         MVO   ANS2(4),ANS2(3)     |00|00|01|6C|00|15|0C|  SHIFT  16

114 *             DIVIDE, ROUND TO ONE DECIMAL:
115 *             ---------------------------
116 ANS3    DS    PL7

117         ZAP   ANS3,DIST           |00|00|00|00|23|56|5C|
118         MP    ANS3,=P'100'        |00|00|00|23|56|50|0C|         +
                                      QUOTIENT    |REMAINDER
119         DP    ANS3,GALS           |00|01|57|1C|00|00|0C|  DIVIDE 15.71
120         AP    ANS3(4),ANS3+3(1)   |00|01|57|2C|00|00|0C|  ROUND  15.72
121         MVO   ANS3(4),ANS3(3)     |00|00|15|7C|00|00|0C|  SHIFT  15.7

123 *             DIVIDE, ROUND TO TWO DECIMALS:
124 *             ---------------------------
125 ANS4    DS    0PL8                ZERO DUPLICATION FACTOR
126 QUOT    DS    PL5                 QUOTIENT AREA
127 RMDR    DS    PL3                 REMAINDER AREA

129         ZAP   ANS4,DIST           |00|00|00|00|00|23|56|5C|
130         MP    ANS4,=P'1000'       |00|00|00|02|35|65|00|0C|      +
                                      QUOTIENT    |REMAINDER
131         DP    ANS4,GALS           |00|00|15|71|1C|00|00|0C|  15.710
132         AP    QUOT,QUOT+4(1)      |00|00|15|71|1C|00|00|0C|  15.710
133         MVO   QUOT,QUOT(4)        |00|00|01|57|1C|00|00|0C|  15.71
```

FIGURE 5-4 Sample divide packed operations.

Require a 3-decimal quotient—multiply the dividend by 1.00:

$$\frac{246.79 \times 1.00}{31} = \frac{246.7900}{31} = 7.9609 \quad \text{(may be rounded to 7.961)}$$

Each increase in precision provides a more accurate result. Required accuracy depends on the application and the user's needs, and should be determined before starting the program. The examples in Figure 5-4 divide distance (DIST) by gallons (GALS) to calculate miles-per-gallon. Both DIST and GALS contain one decimal position. Division results in no decimal positions, as in ANS1. To produce a quotient with no decimal places, but rounded, as in ANS2, the dividend must be shifted to the left one digit (2356.5 becomes 2356.50). This is now the dividend that we must consider when defining the quotient-remainder area. Since the divisor (GALS) is three bytes, and the dividend is now four bytes, the answer area (ANS2) is defined as seven bytes.

ANS3 requires a one-decimal quotient. Therefore, to generate two decimal places we multiply the dividend by 100. Since the divisor is three bytes and the dividend is now four, ANS3 is defined as seven bytes. After the DP we round and shift the second decimal place.

ANS4 requires a two-decimal quotient. Multiplying the dividend by 1000 generates three extra decimal positions. Since the divisor is three bytes and the dividend is now five, ANS4 is defined as eight bytes. This example also illustrates redefining the answer area. ANS4 is defined with a zero duplication factor (0PL8). It contains two subfields: QUOT defines the five-byte quotient area, and RMDR defines the three-byte remainder. We may reference by name the entire area ANS4, or the subfield QUOT.

Problem 5-6 should now be attempted.

SAMPLE PROGRAM—INVENTORY UPDATE

In a typical business system, there are two common types of records. *Master records* contain data of a relatively permanent nature, such as Customer name and address, or Stock description and price. Other data can be temporary and subject to periodic change, such as current Customer balance or current Stock quantity on hand.

Transaction records contain data for the current period that affects the Master records. For example, a payment or sale must be applied to the balance owing in the Customer Master record, and a Stock receipt or issue must be applied to the quantity on hand in the Inventory Master record.

A "control break" occurs when the input records make a significant change in the control fields. In the example program next, it is necessary to break control and print totals by changes in Stock number (minor totals), and by Branch number (major totals). There can be any number of Receipt records for a Stock item, and any number

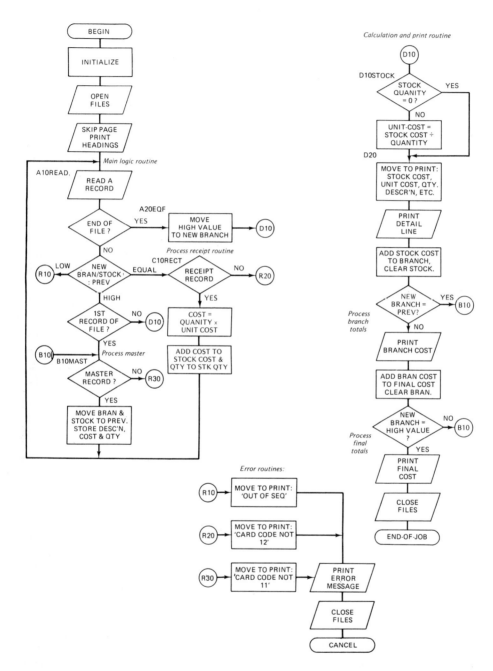

FIGURE 5-5   Flowchart for sample inventory program.

of Stock items in a Branch. The program is organized into logical, separated sections that perform specific functions.

The flowchart in Figure 5-5 depicts an inventory update program. There are two types of records, Inventory masters (code 11) and Inventory receipts (12).

COLUMN	INVENTORY MASTER	RECEIPTS
1–2	Record code (11)	Record code (12)
3–4	Branch number	Branch number
5–8	Stock number	Stock number
9–24	Description	
25–28	Quantity on hand	
29–35	Cost on hand	
11–13		Quantity received
14–17		Unit cost of receipt

— For each Stock number there may be only one master record (code 11) but any number of receipts (code 12). The master record precedes its receipt records.
— Missing masters, invalid record codes, and out-of-sequence conditions on Branch-Stock number cause errors.
— For each receipt record that contains the same Stock number as the master record, the program calculates quantity times unit cost. The calculated cost is added to total cost on hand for the Stock, and the quantity received is added to total quantity on hand for the Stock.
— The program checks sequence on Stock number (minor) and on Branch (major). The program uses a control word composed of Branch-Stock number. If the new control word is greater than the previous, then the program prints the stored Stock number data and calculates and prints new unit cost. (This is a "control break" on the Stock number.) New unit cost is calculated by dividing Stock cost-on-hand by quantity-on-hand.
— If the input Branch number is also higher than the one in the previous record, total Branch cost is printed. At the end of the run, the program prints total cost for all Branches.
— The first record condition is handled by hex zeros in "PREVCTL". On a high Branch/Stock, if PREVCTL contains hex zeros, the program recognizes a "false control break" on the first record. End-of-file is handled by storing hex F's in the input Branch/Stock number to force printing the last stored Stock and Branch.

Figure 5-6 provides the program listing. The program has two new features, ORG and PDUMP, which the next sections explain. Carefully study the flowchart and listing and work through all conditions. For purposes of brevity, the program omits some features that we would normally include, such as printing the current date and page overflow.

INVENTORY UPDATE AND CALCULATE UNIT COST

```
  4 *                  I N I T I A L I Z A T I O N
  5 *                  ---------------------------
  6 PROG05    INIT                              INITIALIZE
 27           OPEN    CARD,PRTR

 37           PUTPR   PRTR,PRINT,SK1            SKIP TO NEW PAGE
 44           PUTPR   PRTR,PRHEAD1,WSP2         PRINT HEADING-1
 51           PUTPR   PRTR,PRHEAD2,WSP2         *       HEADING-2

 59 *                  M A I N   L O G I C
 60 *                  -------------------
 61 A10READ   GET     CARD,CARDIN
 67           CLC     CTLIN,PREVCTL             BRANCH/STOCK NO. SEQUENCE?
 68           BE      C10RECT                   *     EQUAL - PROCESS RECEIPT
 69           BL      R10SEQ                    *     LOW   - OUT-OF-SEQUENCE
 70 *                                           *     HIGH  - NEW STOCK NO.
 71           CLC     PREVCTL,LOWVALUE          FIRST RECORD OF FILE?
 72           BNE     D10STOCK                  *     NO - CONTROL BREAK
 73           B       B10MAST                   *     YES- PROCESS MASTER

 75 A20EOF    MVC     CTLIN,HIVALUE            EOF - STORE HI VALUE, FORCE
 76           B       D10STOCK                 *     CONTROL BREAK & EOJ

 78 *                  P R O C E S S   I N V E N T O R Y   M A S T E R
 79 *                  -----------------------------------------------
 80 B10MAST   CLC     CODEIN,=C'11'            MASTER RECORD?
 81           BNE     R30NOMAS                 *     NO - ERROR
 82           MVC     PREVCTL,CTLIN            STORE BRANCH-STOCK IN PREV
 83           MVC     DESCRN,DESCRPIN          STORE STOCK FIELDS
 84           PACK    STCOSTPK,COSTIN          *
 85           PACK    STOQTYPK,QTYIN           *
 86           B       A10READ

 88 *                  P R O C E S S   R E C E I P T S   R E C O R D
 89 *                  ---------------------------------------------
 90 C10RECT   CLC     CODEIN,=C'12'            RECEIPT RECORD?
 91           BNE     R20NOREC                 *     NO - ERROR
 92           PACK    QTYPK,QTYRECIN
 93           AP      STOQTYPK,QTYPK           ADD QUANTITY RECEIVED TO STOCK
 94           PACK    COSTPK,UNCOSTIN          QUANTITY X UNIT-COST = COST
 95           MP      COSTPK,QTYPK             |XX|XX|XX|XC| 2 DEC
 96           AP      STCOSTPK,COSTPK          ADD COST OF RECEIPT TO STOCK
 97           B       A10READ

 99 *                  C A L C U L A T E   N E W   U N I T   C O S T
100 *                  ---------------------------------------------
101 D10STOCK  ZAP     UNCOSTPK,=P'0'          CLEAR UNIT-COST FIELD
102           ZAP     STOQTYPK,STOQTYPK       STOCK QUANTITY = 0?
103           BZ      D20                      *     YES - BYPASS DIVIDE
104           ZAP     UNCOSTPK,STCOSTPK       |00|00|00|00|XX|XX|XX|XC| 2 DEC
105           MP      UNCOSTPK,=P'10'         |00|00|00|0X|XX|XX|XX|0C| 3 DEC
106           DP      UNCOSTPK,STOQTYPK       |00|00|XX|XX|XC|XX|XX|XC| 3 DEC
107           AP      UNCOSTPK(5),UNCOSTPK+4(1) ROUND, THEN SHIFT 1 DIGIT
108           MVO     UNCOSTPK(5),UNCOSTPK(4) |00|00|0X|XX|XC|XX|XX|XC| 2 DEC

110 D20       MVC     COSTPR,EDCOST            EDIT STOCK FIELDS
111           ED      COSTPR,STCOSTPK          *     COST

113           MVC     UNCOSPR,EDUNIT           *
114           ED      UNCOSPR,UNCOSTPK+2       *     UNIT COST
```

FIGURE 5-6 Inventory update.

```
116          MVC    QTYPR,EDQTY              *
117          ED     QTYPR,STOQTYPK           *        QUANTITY

119          MVC    DESCRIPR,DESCRN
120          MVC    STOCKPR,PREVSTK
121          MVC    BRANPR,PREVBR

123          PUTPR  PRTR,PRINT,WSP1          PRINT STOCK RECORD
130          MVC    PRINT,BLANK
131          AP     BRCOSTPK,STCOSTPK        ADD COST TO BRANCH TOTAL
132          ZAP    STCOSTPK,=P'0'           CLEAR STOCK COST

134          CLC    BRANCHIN,PREVBR          NEW BRANCH = PREVIOUS?
135          BNE    E10BRAN                      NO  - PROCESS BRANCH TOTAL
136          B      B10MAST                      YES - PROCESS MASTER

139 *               P R O C E S S   B R A N C H   T O T A L
140 *               -------------------------------------
141 E10BRAN PUTPR  PRTR,PRINT,SP1           SPACE 1 LINE
148          MVC    COSTPR(L'EDCOST+1),EDCOST
149          ED     COSTPR,BRCOSTPK          EDIT TOTAL BRANCH COST
150          MVC    DESCRIPR(12),=C'BRANCH TOTAL'
151          PUTPR  PRTR,PRINT,WSP2          PRINT BRANCH TOTAL
158          MVC    PRINT,BLANK

160          AP     FINCOSPK,BRCOSTPK        ADD BRANCH COST TO FINAL
161          ZAP    BRCOSTPK,=P'0'           CLEAR BRANCH COST

163          CLC    CTLIN,HIVALUE            END-OF-FILE CONDITION REACHED?
164          BE     F10FINAL                     YES- PROCESS FINAL TOTAL
165          B      B10MAST                      NO - PROCESS MASTER

167 *               P R O C E S S   F I N A L   T O T A L
168 *               -------------------------------------
169 F10FINAL MVC   COSTPR(L'EDCOST+2),EDCOST
170          ED     COSTPR,FINCOSPK          EDIT FINAL TOTAL COST
171          MVC    DESCRIPR(12),=C'FINAL  TOTAL'
172          PUTPR  PRTR,PRINT,WSP1          PRINT FINAL TOTAL LINE

180          PDUMP  BRCOSTPK,P+132           DEMONSTRATION OF PDUMP MACRO

186          CLOSE  CARD,PRTR
195          EOJ

199 *               E R R O R   R O U T I N E S
200 *               ---------------------------------
201 R10SEQ   MVC    P+41(L'SEQERR),SEQERR    OUT-OF-SEQUENCE BRANCH/STOCK
202          B      R80

204 R20NOREC MVC    P+41(L'RECTERR),RECTERR  SAME STOCK, RECORD NOT RECEIPT
205          B      R80

207 R30NOMAS MVC    P+41(L'MASTERR),MASTERR  NEW STOCK RECORD, NOT MASTER

209 R80      MVC    STOCKPR,PREVSTK
210          MVC    BRANPR,PREVBR
211          PUTPR  PRTR,PRINT,WSP3          PRINT ERROR MESSAGE
218          CLOSE  CARD,PRTR
227          CANCEL .                        ABNORMAL TERMINATION

233 *               D E C L A R A T I V E S
234 *               ------------------------

236 CARD     DEFCD  A20EOF                   DEFINE CARD FILE
260 PRTR     DEFPR                           DEFINE PRINTER FILE
```

FIGURE 5-6 (*Continued*)

117

```
285 BRCOSTPK  DC    PL4'0'                    PACKED DECLARATIVES:
286 COSTPK    DC    PL4'0'                    *
287 FINCOSPK  DC    PL4'0'                    *
288 QTYPK     DC    PL2'0'                    *
289 STCOSTPK  DC    PL4'0'                    *
290 STCQTYPK  DC    PL3'0'                    *
291 UNCOSTPK  DC    PL8'0'                    *

293 DESCRN    DC    CL16' '
294 SEQERR    DC    C'RECORD OUT-OF-SEQUENCE ON BRANCH/STOCK'
295 RECTERR   DC    C'SAME BR/STOCK, NOT RECEIPT RECORD'
296 MASTERR   DC    C'DIFF BR/STOCK, NOT MASTER RECORD'

298 LOWVALUE  DC    XL6'00'                   LOW VALUE FOR 1ST RECORD TEST
299 HIVALUE   DC    6X'FF'                    HIGH VALUE FOR EOF PROCESSING
300 PREVCTL   DS    0CL6                      PREVIOUS BRANCH/STOCK
301 PREVBR    DC    XL2'00'                   *    BRANCH NO.
302 PREVSTK   DC    XL4'00'                   *    STOCK NO.
303 *                                         EDIT WORDS :
304 EDCOST    DC    X'402020 6B20 2021 4B20 20C3D9',C'**'
305 EDUNIT    DC    X'402020 2021 4B20 20'
306 EDQTY     DC    X'402020 2020 20C3D9'

308 CARDIN    DS    0CL80                     INPUT RECORD COLUMNS:
309 CODEIN    DS    CL2                       01-02   RECORD CODE
310 CTLIN     DS    0CL6                              BRANCH/STOCK CTL FIELD:
311 BRANCHIN  DS    CL2                       03-04   BRANCH
312 STOCKIN   DS    CL4                       05-08   STOCK NO.
313           DS    CL72

315           ORG   CARDIN
316           DS    CL8                                         INVENTORY MASTER:
317 DESCRPIN  DS    CL16                      09-24   * DESCRIPTION
318 QTYIN     DS    ZL4                       25-28   * QUANTITY
319 COSTIN    DS    ZL7'00000.00'             29-35   * COST

321           ORG   CARDIN
322           DS    CL10                                        RECEIPTS :
323 QTYRECIN  DS    ZL3                       11-13   * QUANTITY
324 UNCOSTIN  DS    ZL4'00.00'                14-17   * UNIT COST
325           ORG   *                         RESET LOCATION COUNTER

327 BLANK     DC    C' '                      BLANK FOR CLEARING PRINT AREA
328 PRINT     DS    0CL133                    PRINT AREA:
329 P         DC    CL1' '                    *
330           DC    CL17' '                   *
331 BRANPR    DS    CL2                       *       BRANCH NO.
332           DC    CL4' '                    *
333 STOCKPR   DS    CL4                       *       STOCK NO.
334           DC    CL2' '                    *
335 DESCRIPR  DS    CL16                      *       DESCRIPTION
336 QTYPR     DS    ZL8                       *       QUANTITY
337           DC    CL4' '                    *
338 UNCOSPR   DS    ZL7                       *       UNIT COST
339 COSTPR    DS    ZL12                      *       COST
340           DC    CL56' '                   *

342 PRHEAD1   DC    CL18' '                   PRINT AREA FOR HEADING-1
343           DC    CL115'I N V E N T O R Y   U N I T - C O S T   R E P O R T'

345 PRHEAD2   DC    CL16' '                   PRINT AREA FOR HEADING-2
346           DC    CL29'BRANCH  STOCK'       *
347           DC    CL88'QUANTITY    UNITCOST      COST'
348           END   PROG05
```

FIGURE 5-6 (*Continued*)

```
  I  N  V  E  N  T  O  R  Y     U  N  I  T  -  C  O  S  T     R  E  P  O  R  T

 BRANCH   STOCK                        QUANTITY      UNITCOST         COST

   01     1234   PLYWCOD  1/4            107           2.58         319.00
   01     2468   PLYWOOD  3/8            150           5.50         825.00

                 ERANCH TOTAL                                     1,144.00   *

   33     1234   PLYWCOD  1/4              5CR         3.05           15.25CR
   33     2468   PLYWOOD  3/8            305           4.63        1,412.50
   33     2470   PLYWOOD  1/2            160           5.48          676.25

                 ERANCH TOTAL                                     2,273.50   *

   40     1234   PLYWCOD  1/4             25           3.06           76.50
   40     2470   PLYWCOD  1/2                           .00            .00
   40     2844   PLYWOOD  3/4              2           6.75           13.50

                 ERANCH TOTAL                                        90.00   *

                 FINAL    TOTAL                                   3,507.50   **
```

FIGURE 5-6 (*Continued*)

ORG—SET LOCATION COUNTER

ORG is a command to the Assembler to alter or *reoriginate* the value of the location counter during assembly. We generally use ORG to redefine data areas in the program, that is, one on top of the other.

NAME	OPERATION	OPERAND
[omit]	ORG	A symbol or not used

The *name* is normally used only in macro writing, and is otherwise omitted. The *operand*, if any, is a symbolic address with or without relative addressing (i.e., A30, or A30+1000), or a reference to the location counter itself (as *+20). The Assembler sets the location counter to the value of the expression. The operand may not be an absolute address, such as 8192 or X'2000'. Note: if the operand is omitted, the Assembler sets the location counter to the maximum value that it has been set up to this point.

Beware of ORG with no operand, because the Assembler may mistakenly use a comment for its operand. In the following, the Assembler will use the asterisk in column 41 as the ORG operand. Instead of setting the location counter to the previous high setting, it is set incorrectly to the current setting of the location counter:

column 10   16   41
       ORG   * RESET LOCATION COUNTER

The solution as shown in the program is to insert a comma in column 16, which tells the Assembler explicitly that there is no operand.

Figure 5-7 provides the object code for declaratives defined in the previous program. ORG is used to redefine the input area, which starts with column 1 at X'DA61D' in statement 308. First, the fields common to both types of records, Master and Receipts, are defined. Then the other fields for both record formats are uniquely defined.

```
                        233 *                    D E C L A R A T I V E S
                        234 *                    ---------------------------

                        236 CARD     DEFCD A20ECF
                        260 PRTR     DEFPR

0DA55A 0C00000C         285 BRCOSTPK DC    PL4'0'
0DA55E 0000000C         286 COSTPK   DC    PL4'0'
0DA562 0C00000C         287 FINCOSFK DC    PL4'0'
0DA566 000C             288 QTYPK    DC    PL2'0'
0DA568 0C00000C         289 STCOSTPK DC    PL4'0'
0DA56C 00000C           290 STCQTYPK DC    PL3'0'
0DA56F 000000000000000C 291 UNCOSTPK DC    PL8'0'
                          .                .
                          .                .
                          .                .
0DA61D                  308 CARDIN   DS    0CL80    INPUT RECORD COLUMNS:
0DA61D                  309 CODEIN   DS    CL2      01-02   RECORD CODE
0DA61F                  310 CTLIN    DS    0CL6             CTL FIELD:
0DA61F                  311 BRANCHIN DS    CL2      03-04   BRANCH
0DA621                  312 STOCKIN  DS    CL4      05-08   STOCK NO.
0DA625                  313          DS    CL72

0DA66D                  315          ORG   CARDIN
0DA61D                  316          DS    CL8              MASTER:
0DA625                  317 DESCRPIN DS    CL16     09-24  * DESCRIPTION
0DA635                  318 QTYIN    DS    ZL4      25-28  * QUANTITY
0DA639                  319 COSTIN   DS    ZL7'00000.00' 29-35 * COST

0DA640                  321          ORG   CARDIN
0DA61D                  322          DS    CL10             RECEIPTS :
0DA627                  323 QTYRECIN DS    ZL3      11-13  * QUANTITY
0DA62A                  324 UNCOSTIN DS    ZL4'00.00' 14-17 * UNIT COST
0DA62E                  325          ORG   .        RESET LOCATION COUNTER

0DA66D 40               327 BLANK    DC    C' '
0DA66E                  328 PRINT    DS    0CL133   PRINT AREA:
0DA66E 40               329 P        DC    CL1' '   *
0DA66F 4040404C40404040 330          DC    CL17' '  *
0DA680                  331 BRANPR   DS    CL2      *       BRANCH NO.
0DA682 4C404040         332          DC    CL4' '   *
0DA686                  333 STOCKPR  DS    CL4      *       STOCK NO.
0DA68A 4040             334          DC    CL2' '   *
0DA68C                  335 DESCRIPR DS    CL16     *       DESCRIPTION
0DA69C                  336 QTYPR    DS    ZL8      *       QUANTITY
0DA6A4 40404040         337          DC    CL4' '   *
0DA6A8                  338 UNCOSPR  DS    ZL7      *       UNIT COST
0DA6AF                  339 COSTPR   DS    ZL12     *       COST
0DA6BB 404C404040404040 340          DC    CL56' '  *

0DA6F3 404C404040404040 342 PRHEAD1  DC    CL18' '
```

FIGURE 5-7   Use of the ORG instruction.

STATEMENT   EXPLANATION

313   The statement DS CL72 at X'DA625' increments the location counter by 72 (X'48'): X'DA625' + X'48' = X'DA66D' (as shown at statement 315).

315   ORG CARDIN resets the location counter from X'DA66D' to the address of CARDIN X'DA61D'. It now references column 1, the start of the input area. The Master record fields are defined next.

321   ORG CARDIN again resets the location counter to CARDIN, X'DA61D'. The Receipts record fields are defined next.

325   Since the ORG here has no operand, the Assembler sets the location counter to its highest previous setting, X'DA66D', achieved after statement 313. Note: the address of the next field, BLANK, is defined at X'DA66D'. Check the accuracy: CARDIN is defined at X'DA61D', and is 80 bytes long (X'50'). X'DA61D' + X'50' = X'DA66D', the correct location for the first field following CARDIN.

All fields for both types of records may now be referenced by name, without an explicit length. In a similar manner, we may use ORG to redefine the print area.

PDUMP—PARTIAL DUMP OF MAIN STORAGE

The DOS PDUMP macro is a convenient device for program debugging. (The macro differs under operating systems.) PDUMP enables us to see the contents of any storage area during program execution. When the program encounters PDUMP, it transfers control to the Supervisor, which produces a hexadecimal printout of the contents of the registers and of the specified storage area. At termination of the dump, control returns to the statement immediately following the PDUMP.

NAME	OPERATION	OPERAND
[symbol]	PDUMP	address1,address2

Address1 and address2 reference the start and end positions of the area to be dumped. The addresses may be symbolic (as A10,CARDIN+80), or hexadecimal (as X'3015',X'3420'). We normally use PDUMP in a program that contains a bug, and we want to know the contents of certain accumulators and work areas at some specific point. We can insert PDUMPs in the program wherever storage contents are required. When the program is corrected and working, we take the PDUMP out.

Refer again to the sample program. Statement (STMT) 180 specifies PDUMP BRCOSTPK,P+132 to print hex contents from BRCOSTPK (location X'DA55A') through to P+132 (location X'DA6F2', hex address not printed). Although the program works correctly, PDUMP is inserted so that it executes after the printing of the

```
GR 0-7   000DA810 000DA808 000E9FFF 400DA07A    000CB07A 000DC07A 8000CC25 000E9FFF
GR 8-F   800CB4B0 0A16180C 00000000 182F07F1    000CA078 000DA09C AF0CA2C6 000DA900
FP REG   418C0000 00000000 43CFB00C 0000000C    0C000000 00CCC000 0C0CCCC0 00000000
CR 0-7   8C400CE0 04014E00 FFFFFFFF FFFFFFFF    00C00000 00000000 00000C00 00000000
CR 8-F   C0000000 00000000 CC000000 0000000C    00C0000C 00000000 EF000000 00000200

                                                          DA558          BRCOSTPK   COSTPK
0DA540              FINCOSPK   QTYPK                              40400000 000C0000
0CA560   700C0350 750C001F 0000000C 00002C00    0000675C 00000CD7 D3E8E6D6 D6C440F3
0DA580   61F44040 404040D9 C5C3D6D5 C440D6E4    E360D6C6 60E2C5D8 E4C5D5C3 C540D6D5
0DA5A0   40C2D5C1 D5C3C861 E2E3D6C3 D2E2C1D4    C540C2D9 61E2E3D6 C3D26840 D5C6E340
0DA5C0   D9C5C3C5 C9D7E340 D5C5C3D6 D9C4C4C9    C6C640C2 D961E2E3 D6C3D26B 40D5D6E3
0DA5E0   40D4C1E2 E3C5D940 D5C5C3D6 D9C40000    00000000 FFFFFFFF FFFFF4F0 F2F8F4F4
0DA600   4020206B 2020214B 2020C3D5 5C5C4020    20214B20 20402020 202020C3 D9F1F2FF
0CA620   FFFFFFFF FF4040F0 F0F1F0F7 F0F04040    40404040 40404040 40404040 40404040
0CA640   40404040 --SAME--
0CA66C   40404040 40404040 40404040 40400940    40404040 40404040 40404040 40404040
0CA680   40404040 40404040 40404040 C6C9D5C1    C34040E3 D6E3C1D3 40404040 4C404040
0CA6A0   40404040 40404040 40404040 40404040    40F368F5 F0F74BF5 F040405C 5C404040
0CA6C0   40404040 --SAME--
0DA6E0   40404040 40404040 40404040 40404040    40404011
```

FIGURE 5-8   Hexadecimal storage dump.

final total. Refer now to the dump itself in Figure 5-8. (Some dump versions may differ from this one.)

— Lines 1 and 2 print the hex contents of the 16 general registers, GR 0-7 and GR 8-F, or registers 0-7 and 8-15.
— The next line lists the hex contents of the floating-point registers, FP REG.
— The lines following with CR 0-7 and CR 0-F show the contents of the 16 ''Control Registers'' of the 370 that the operating system uses.

   The contents of storage print next. Each line lists 32 bytes, with the hex contents to the left, and the character contents—if the character is printable—to the right (not shown in the figure). The vertical spacing between each 4 bytes (8 hex digits) is for readability, and may be ignored. At the extreme left is the address X'DA540', of the first location to be printed on the line. The address of the first byte in each group of 4 bytes after DA540 is DA544, DA548, and DA54C. The address of the first byte at the center is DA550. Now PDUMP begins printing with the group that contains the first byte specified, BRCOSTPK at DA55A. Thus, DA558 and DA559 are printed (and contain '4040'). Next print the contents of BRCOSTPK, a 4-byte field, containing '0000000C'. The next field defined in the program, COSTPK, is 4 bytes beginning at DA55E, and contains '0000700C' (spilling onto the next line).

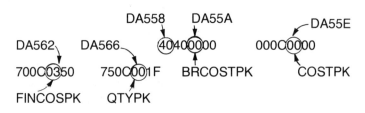

Check the names and locations to Figure 5-7 to ensure that the dump represents the storage contents correctly.

Thus, PDUMP provides the starting address on a line, and to locate the contents of any field, we must count across the line, using each pair of digits as one byte. Note the line beginning at DA640: All the locations on that line contain the same character X'40'. PDUMP minimizes printing and simply prints —SAME—.

Under Operating System (OS), a partial dump requires the SNAP macro and other complex coding—see the IBM Supervisor manual.

DEBUGGING TIPS

The ED instruction offers almost unlimited scope for new bugs. Before assembly, double-check the MVC/ED operations. Allow in the edit word X'20's and X'21's for each packed digit to be edited (there should be an odd number). Be sure that the print area field is the same size as the edit word.

The most common error with MP seems to be ignoring the rule that the product field must be at least the length of the multiplicand plus multiplier in bytes, regardless of the contents. If too short, then count on a much-deserved Data Exception.

DP suffers from the similar problem of field length: the quotient/remainder area must be at least as long as the dividend (after the MP left-shift, if any) plus divisor. Another popular error is attempting to divide by a zero value—check for a zero divisor first! Both errors cause "Decimal Divide Exceptions".

If the bug cannot be located, rerun the program with a request for a dump of storage, and trace the hex contents of the concerned storage areas. Almost always the error is in your program or data, rarely in the operating system, and never is it the computer.

As well as the technical misuse of instructions, there are the problems with programming logic—wrong compares, wrong branches, wrong calculations. Perhaps the worst error is misunderstanding the problem, and coding the incorrect solution. Analyze the program specifications carefully before flowcharting and coding the program.

PROBLEMS

5-1. *Editing.*
   (a) What characters other than X'40' may be used as the fill character?
   (b) An amount field containing zero is defined as TOTAL DC PL3'0'. Define an edit word to cause TOTAL to print as all blanks.
   (c) Why must the edit word contain an odd number of X'20's and X'21's?
   (d) Refer to the IBM Principles of Operation manual and define the purpose of the "field separator."

5-2. Complete the following Edit words and Edit operations as indicated.

If zero amount, the edited field should print as:

(a) AMT2 DS PL4
    ED2 DC X'
        MVC PRINT+20,
        ED

.00 (Use comma, decimal point, minus sign)

(b) AMT3 DS PL5
    ED3 DC X'
        MVC PRINT+40,
        ED

0.00 (Use commas, decimal point, minus sign)

(c) AMT4 DS PL4
    ED4 DC X'
        MVC PRINT+60,
        ED

.00 (Use $, comma, decimal point, CR, and two asterisks)

5-3. Use MVO to shift the contents of the following DC. Indicate the results in hex. Questions are unrelated.

PKFIELD DC P'123456789'

(a) Shift right one digit.
(b) Shift right two digits.
(c) Shift right four digits.

5-4. *Rounding.* Why are two MVO's used to shift an even number of digits right? If the field is to be rounded as well, why is the AP between the two MVO's and not before or after them?

5-5. *Multiply Packed.* Use a coding sheet to write the instructions as indicated. Show results in hex representation. Define the product area called PROD in each example.

A DC P'82.5'
B DC P'940.5'
C DC P'78.55'
D DC P'92.345'

(a) Multiply A × B. Round and shift to 1 decimal position.
(b) Multiply B × C. Round and shift to 2 decimal positions.
(c) Multiply B × D. Round and shift to 2 decimal positions.
(d) Multiply C × D. Round and shift to 2 decimal positions.
(e) Explain the error (if any): MP C,=P'2'.

5-6. *Divide Packed.* Use a coding sheet to write the required instructions. Show the hex results, and define the quotient-remainder area as RESULT.

A DC P'017'
B DC P'127.5'
C DC P'613.57'
D DC P'925.365'

(a) Divide B/A, round and shift to 1 decimal position.

(b) Divide C/B, round and shift to 2 decimal positions.

(c) Divide D/A, round and shift to 1 decimal position.

(d) Divide D/B, round and shift to 0 decimal positions.

(e) Explain the error (if any): DP D,=P'2'.

5-7. PROGRAM ASSIGNMENT.

Required: A program that reads Sales records containing selling price and cost, and calculates gross profit, percent gross profit, and sales commission.

Input: Sales records, containing in each column:

1–2	Record code (25)	11–13 Commission rate (e.g. .155 = 15.5%)
3–4	Store number	14–27 Category description
5–7	Salesman number	28–33 Selling price (xxxx.xx)
8–10	Category (type of sale,	36–41 Cost price (xxxx.xx)
	such as TV, furniture, appliance)	

Procedure:

— Check for valid record code (25) and that records are in sequence by Salesman (minor) within Store (major).

— For each record, calculate and print:
    Gross profit = Selling Price − Cost (Cost can exceed Selling Price).
    Percent Gross Profit = Gross Profit ÷ Cost.
    Commission = Gross Profit × Commission rate.

— For each Salesman, print totals of Sales, Cost, Gross Profit, and Commission. Calculate Percent Gross Profit. For each Store and for final total, print and calculate as for Salesman.

— Provide test data that checks all conditions. Flowchart, code, and test. Take a hex dump of storage and analyze the contents.

CHAPTER 6

BASE REGISTERS AND INSTRUCTION FORMAT

Up to now we have used only instructions that access data in main storage—the storage-to-storage (SS) and storage immediate (SI) formats. The next step is to use the registers to perform binary arithmetic and to manipulate addresses. These operations enable the explicit use of registers in addressing for powerful programming capability, such as table look-up. For these purposes we must learn how to use registers for arithmetic and for addressing, and what is the *machine language object code format* for each instruction.

THE GENERAL PURPOSE REGISTERS

The 16 general purpose registers are separate from main storage. They are numbered from 0 through 15, and are referenced by number.* Each register contains 32 bits of data, numbered from left to right 0 through 31. The registers have two main purposes, binary arithmetic and addressing.

> *We can use EQU to assign a name to a register: e.g., LINKREG EQU 7 tells the Assembler to substitute the number 7 for each reference to the name LINKREG in the program. Thus, the instruction BAL LINKREG,H10HEAD becomes BAL 7,H10HEAD.

1. *Binary Arithmetic.* The general registers perform all binary arithmetic. For binary values, bit 0 is the sign bit, and bits 1–31 are data. Chapter 7 covers binary arithmetic in detail.

bit: 0 1   31

2. *Addressing.* The general registers perform all the addressing involved in referencing main storage. A register used for addressing purposes is called a *base register*. Addressing uses only the rightmost 24 bits of the register (bits 8–31), giving a maximum address of $2^{24}-1$, or 16,777,215. Certain instructions of "RX" format have the facility to modify or "index" an address; a register used for this purpose is called an "*index register*".

	Unused	Address

bit: 0   7 8   31

Some of the registers have special functions, and the following restrictions apply:

REGISTER	RESTRICTIONS
0–1	We may use 0 and 1 freely for temporary calculations, but Supervisor operations such as CALL and PUT destroy their contents. Also, because the Supervisor uses register-0 as its own base register, the system does not permit us to use register-0 as a base register.
2	2 is available as a base register or for binary arithmetic, with one exception: the TRT instruction uses register-2 to store a generated value, thus limiting its use as a base register.
3–12	Registers 3–12 are always available for binary arithmetic or as base registers.
13	Control program routines including the input/output system use register-13. We use it when performing special linkage to a "subprogram," and otherwise should not use it.
14–15	Control program and subprogram routines also use these. Their use is restricted as for 0 and 1, for temporary calculations.

BASE REGISTER ADDRESSING

On earlier computers, instructions directly referenced main storage locations by their assigned number. The computer may have had an Add instruction (coded as 21) to add the contents of location 01056 to 01232, coded as 21 01232 01056. Such a direct addressing system is simple, but limits the highest address, in this case to 99999. Modern large computers require considerably more storage because of (a) more complex input/output facilities, (b) complex operating systems, and (c) the capability of multiprogramming—the executing of two or more programs in storage concurrently.

For addressing main storage locations, the 360/370 use the rightmost 24 bits of a register, providing a maximum address of 16,777,215. Every instruction operand that references a main storage location consists of more than just a direct reference to that location; the computer architecture compresses the addresses by splitting them into two parts, a base address and a displacement:

1. *Base Address.* This is an address of the beginning of an area of storage. We code BALR to load this address into a register, and code USING to tell the Assembler that this register is to be the program's base register containing the address of the start of the program. The INIT macro has performed these functions up to now. We can allocate any registers (preferably 2 through 12) for the base address, and may not use it for any other purpose in the program.
2. *Displacement.* The Assembler calculates the displacement for each instruction and declarative in the program, the number of bytes that the actual location is from the base address.

Each address referenced therefore consists of two parts: the contents of the base register combined with the displacement provides the effective address. Refer to Figure 6-1a. Assume that register-3 is the base register for a small program in main storage. Register-3 contains the value X'4200', which is the location of the first byte of the program in main storage. (Do not be concerned for now how X'4200' loads into register-3 or how the Assembler knows this value.)

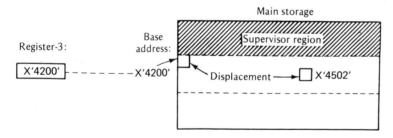

FIGURE 6-1a   Base register addressing—one base register.

Every location within the program is relative to the first byte, X'4200'. For example, location X'4502' is X'302' bytes from the start, and therefore location X'4502' has a *displacement* of X'302' bytes. The computer then references location X'4502' by adding: base address X'4200' plus displacement X'302' equals the effective address X'4502'. Any instruction referencing this location does so by means of the contents of the base register (X'4200') plus the displacement (X'302').

The Assembler calculates the displacement for every instruction and declarative in the program. For every instruction that references a main storage location, the Assembler forms an operand in object code comprised of the base register number and the displacement, and stores this as two bytes within the instruction:

$$\boxed{\text{B} \mid \text{D} \quad \text{D} \quad \text{D}}$$
bits: 0–3   4–15

Bits 0–3 provide four bits to reference a base register, as X'1' through X'F'. Bits 4–15 provide for a displacement from X'000' through X'FFF' (up to 4095 bytes). Thus, in Figure 6-1a an instruction referencing X'4502' would contain as its operand the hex value $\boxed{3 \mid 302}$. To reference X'4502' the computer adds the contents of the base register-3, X'4200', with the displacement, X'302'. An MVC instruction would move data to the address X'4200' plus X'302'.

Example: Assume that a program defines PRINT+30 at location X'4502'. The Assembler would translate the instruction MVI PRINT+30,C'*' into hex object code as:

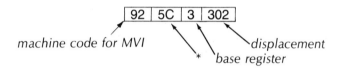

$$\boxed{92 \mid 5C \mid 3 \mid 302}$$
machine code for MVI   `displacement`
            * `base register`

At execution-time, the computer processes the MVI instruction by combining the contents of base register-3 with the displacement, and moves the asterisk into the calculated effective address, X'4502'.

MORE THAN ONE BASE REGISTER. Since the maximum displacement is X'FFF', or 4095, the area covered by a base register and its displacement is X'000' through X'FFF', giving X'1000' or 4096 bytes. Each 4096 (4K) bytes of program being executed requires a base register. A program up to 12K bytes in size requires three base registers, as shown in Figure 6-1b.

The first 4K area begins with base address X'4200', and any position defined within this area is subject to base register-3 and a displacement relative to the base address. The second 4K area begins at a location X'1000' higher, at X'5200'. In the example, the base register is register-4 (although it could have been some other available register), and any position defined within this area is subject to base register-4 and a displacement. Also, in the example, any position defined within the third 4K area beginning at X'6200' is subject to base register-5 and a displacement.

There are two advantages to base/displacement addressing:

1. Instruction length is reduced because each address requires only two rather than three bytes.

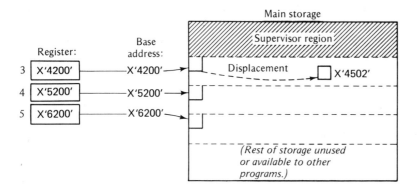

FIGURE 6-1b   Base register addressing—three base registers.

2. Such a system facilitates *program relocatability*. The Assembler does not assign specific locations for each address. Instead, it determines where each address is relative to a base address. At execute-time the base address may be almost any location, loaded in a base register. Accordingly, the system may locate a program almost anywhere in main storage for execution. For example, the program may be executed beginning in X'4200' today, and next week in X'6840'. The purpose of relocatability is to facilitate *multiprogramming*—the executing of two or more programs in storage concurrently. (Although there are several programs in main storage, the computer can execute only one instruction at a time, and it "flip-flops" between programs, as available time permits.)

INSTRUCTION FORMAT

This section examines the instruction format in detail to make clear how the Assembler converts symbolic to machine language code and how it converts base registers and displacements. Each format has a specific purpose. RR format processes data between registers; RS and RX process data between registers and storage; SI and SS process data between storage positions, as follows:

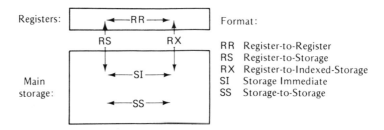

Figure 6-2 depicts the five formats. The column under Format contains the general symbolic coding format. For example, RR means that both operand-1 and operand-2 reference a register. SS means that both operands reference storage addresses. The other symbols, explained in the next section, are:

D = displacement
B = base register
X = index register
I = immediate operand

Format	Length in bytes	Explicit symbolic operands	Object code format					
RR	2	R1, R2	OP	R1R2				
RS	4	R1, R3, D2 (B2)	OP	R1R3	B2D2	D2D2		
RX	4	R1, D2 (X2, B2)	OP	R1X2	B2D2	D2D2		
SI	4	D1 (B1), I2	OP	I I	B1D1	D1D1		
SS (1)	6	D1 (L, B1), D2 (B2)	OP	L L	B1D1	D1D1	B2D2	D2D2
SS (2)	6	D1 (L1, B1), D2 (L2, B2)	OP	L1L2	B1D1	D1D1	B2D2	D2D2
		Bits	0–7	8–15	16–23	24–31	32–39	40–47
		Byte	1	2	3	4	5	6

FIGURE 6-2   Instruction formats.

Under Object Code Format is the hex representation of machine language—the format in which the Assembler converts from symbolic code and which the system loads into main storage for execution. The first byte, bits 0–7, is the operation code. For example, the CLC code is X'D5'. (The exception is the 370 S-format—not covered—that uses the first two bytes for the operation code.) IBM supplies a convenient and indispensable reference card, Form GX20-1850, containing all instruction codes, formats, and bit configurations.

The next sections explain the remaining bytes in the instruction format. The SI and SS formats, the most familiar at this point, are covered first.

SI, STORAGE IMMEDIATE FORMAT. SI instructions include MVI and CLI. Operand-1 in symbolic code references a storage location and operand-2 represents a 1-byte immediate constant. In object code, the second byte (two hex digits) stores the immediate constant, X'00' through X'FF' (this is the reason why immediate operands may be coded as only one byte). Byte-3 and byte-4 store the address as BD | DD .

```
       OP  IM  B1D1  D1D1
      /      |   \      _____
operation immediate base/displacement
         constant      address
```

No length indication is permitted because immediate operations are defined as one byte. For example, MVI, machine code 92, moves an asterisk to PRINT: MVI PRINT+48,C'*'. The Assembler generates four bytes of object code and converts the asterisk X'5C' into the second byte as | 92 | 5C | BD | DD | (assume some base/displacement reference for PRINT+48).

SS, STORAGE-TO-STORAGE FORMAT.   SS format instructions include MVC, ZAP, and CP. Both operands reference a storage address. There are two types, Character instructions of the form D1(L,B1),D2(B2) that provide a length only for operand-1, and Packed operations of the form D1(L1,B1),D2(L2,B2) that provide lengths for both operands.

1. *Character instructions* such as MVC and CLC permit a length up to 256 bytes of data. These use the length of operand-1 to govern the number of bytes that are processed. Assume that MVC is used to move a field to the print area: MVC PRINT+20(6),=C'RECORD'. Given register-3 as the base register and displacements of 426 for PRINT+20 and 62A for the literal, the generated object code is

D2	05	34	26	36	2A
(a)	(b)	(c)		(d)	

(a) D2 is the machine code for MVC.

(b) The length of operand-1 is explicitly coded as 6. However, *the Assembler deducts 1 from the length when converting to object code. At execute-time the computer increments the length by 1.* This process permits lengths of 256 rather than 255. If we code a length of 256 in an instruction, the Assembler deducts 1, giving 255 or X'FF'.

(c) The third and fourth bytes contain base/displacement for operand-1, | BD | DD |. The Assembler inserts base register-3 and the displacement 426 in these positions.

(d) The fifth and sixth bytes contain base register-3 and displacement 62A for operand-2.

At execute-time, the computer increments the length code 05 by 1, to 06. Also, it combines the contents of base register-3 with the displacement. If register-3 contained X'4200', then the effective addresses are:

	OPERAND-1	OPERAND-2
Contents of base register	X'4200'	X'4200'
Displacement	X'0426'	X'062A'
Effective address	X'4626'	X'482A'

The instruction says, in effect, Move (D2) for six bytes (05 + 1) the contents beginning at location X'482A' to the field beginning at X'4626'.

2. *Packed operations* permit a length code for both operands, but limited to 16 bytes. Assume we use AP to add packed fields as: AP PAGEPK,=P'1'. Given base register-3 and displacements of 624 for PAGEPK and 94E for the literal, the generated object code is

```
FA | 10 | 36  24 | 39  4E
ⓐ   ⓑ     ⓒ        ⓓ
```

ⓐ FA is the machine code for AP.

ⓑ The lengths of operand-1 and 2 are stored in the second byte. Assume PAGEPK DC PL2'0'. The Assembler decrements the defined length 2 by 1, and stores 1 as the length. The literal =P'1' creates a 1-byte constant; the Assembler decrements and stores the length as 0. For the maximum length, 16, the Assembler decrements the length to 15 and stores X'F'.

ⓒ The third and fourth bytes contain base/displacement for operand-1. The Assembler inserts base register-3 and displacement 624 in these positions.

ⓓ The fifth and sixth bytes contain base register-3 and displacement 94E for operand-2, the literal.

At execute-time the computer increments the two length codes and combines the contents of the base register with the displacement. The effective addresses are:

	OPERAND-1	OPERAND-2
Contents of base register	X'4200'	X'4200'
Displacement	X'0624'	X'094E'
Effective address	X'4824'	X'4B4E'

RR, REGISTER-TO-REGISTER FORMAT.   RR format is used to process data between registers. The second byte in object code contains the reference to both registers. The four bits in a half byte provide for decimal values 0 to 15, or X'0' to X'F'. (A reference to register-15 is converted to F.) Because registers are fixed length 32 bits, no length indication is required or permitted—the length is implicitly known. For example, to add the contents of register-8 to register-6, we code AR 6,8. The machine language code for AR (Add Register) is 1A. The Assembler converts the instruction to two bytes as `1A | 68`. Another instruction, AR 10,11 converts to `1A | AB`.

> *Exception:* Branch on Condition, BCR, is specified as M1,R2. Operand-1 is a mask or a reference to the condition code in the PSW, not to a register. See the Technical Note at the end of this chapter.

RS, REGISTER-TO-STORAGE FORMAT.   Both RS and RX formats provide the facility to process data between registers and storage. RS also permits three operands. For example, we may code the Load Multiple operation (covered in Chapter 9) as LM

5,7,FIELDS (load registers 5, 6, and 7 with the three 4-byte fields in storage beginning at the address of FIELDS). The machine language code for LM is 98. The Assembler translates symbolic to four bytes of object code as 98 | 57 | BD | DD . The two bytes referencing FIELDS in storage, BD | DD , are filled by the Assembler. Given a base register to use, it inserts the register number (0 through F) in the specified half byte. The Assembler calculates and stores the displacement in 1½ bytes.

Some RS instructions, such as shift, use only two operands. For these, we omit R3 as shown in Figure 6-2, and the Assembler inserts a zero in the machine language position. (Register-0 is not used as the third operand.)

RX, REGISTER-TO-INDEXED-STORAGE.   RX format also processes data between registers and storage, and is quite similar to RS format.

Operand-2 references a storage location with base and displacement. The operation determines the length of operand-2. For example, there are two operations that add binary data in storage to a register. A (Add Fullword) adds four bytes of storage to a register, and AH (Add Halfword) adds two bytes of storage.

As an example, assume the AH (Add Halfword) instruction, coded as AH 5,=H'7'. The literal, =H'7' defines a binary halfword (2-byte) constant. The operation adds the halfword value defined in storage to register-5. There is no length specification, because the operation AH indicates a 2-byte length for operand-2, and register length is always four bytes. The machine code for AH is X'4A', and assume that the base register is 3, containing X'4200'. If the literal =H'7' is stored at X'4704', then its displacement from the base address is X'504'. The Assembler completes the machine code as:

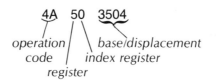

In this case, the Assembler sets the "index register" position to zero. In many cases, including this one, a reference to register-0 means no register reference. If the instruction is one that can specify an index register or an index register is explicitly coded, the Assembler inserts the register number into the machine code position. An index register is simply a specific use of one of the general registers, just as is a base register. Indexing is a feature that does not have too many uses, but an example is given in a later chapter under the LA (Load Address) instruction.

Exception: Branch on Condition, BC, is specified as M1,D2(X2,B2). Operand-1 is a mask, a reference to the condition code in the PSW. See the Technical Note at the end of this chapter.

Problems 6-1 through 6-5 should now be attempted.

CONTROL SECTIONS

For practical purposes, only eleven registers (2 through 12) are available as base registers. It would appear that the largest program we can assemble and execute is 11 × 4K, or 44K. But many programs require considerably more storage. We may write such large programs and, indeed, any program requiring more than 2 or 3 base registers in separate sections. These *control sections* (CSECTS) are assembled separately, each with its own set of base registers. They may then be combined (link-edited) into one object program. We have written programs comprised of one control section. By definition a control section is "a block of coding that can be relocated (independent of other coding) without altering the operating logic of the program". Neither the Assembler nor the Linkage-Editor recognizes a "program"—they process one or more control sections.

Under Operating System, OS, where multiprogramming is common, there is often more than one program being executed in storage. On any given day these programs are located in storage depending on the sequence in which they are first required. Therefore, under such a system when we code a program we do not know where it will be located for execution. Under smaller systems where generally single programs are run, programs are normally loaded following the Supervisor area, beginning in an available location that is evenly divisible by eight, a "doubleword" address.

The first or only control section of a program is identified by either the START or CSECT instruction. Subsequent control sections, if any, are identified by CSECT. Because we are still concerned with small programs we may code them in one section using START. Chapter 15 covers program sectioning and CSECT.

NAME	OPERATION	OPERAND
[symbol]	START	a decimal or hex value, or blank

The START instruction specifies the beginning of the first or only control section (CSECT may also be used for this purpose). The Assembler treats the name, if any, as the name of the control section. If we know where the program will be loaded, we may code an initial value (evenly divisible by eight) for the Assembler location counter. If the value is omitted the location counter is set to zero. The following three examples illustrate various uses of START:

1. PROGA   START   X'4800'   The name of the control section is PROGA. The location counter is set to X'4800' or 18,432, where we expect the program to be loaded.

2.   START   18432   The control section is unnamed. The location counter is set to 18,432 or X'4800'.

3. PROGB   START   The name is PROGB. Because the operand is blank the location counter is set to zero. This coding practice is common under OS, where it is generally not known in advance where the program will reside during execution.

Up to this point, the INIT macro has performed the START statement functions, as well as the BALR/USING, covered in the next section.

The Assembler location counter assigns storage addresses to program statements. These are relative addresses that are printed under the LOC column. The content of the location counter has no effect on program execution. Displacements are all relative to the contents of a base register. We may, for example, omit the operand in the START statement so that the location counter is set to zero. But at execute-time the program may be loaded at X'4200'. The first statement shown on the listing at X'0000' is actually at X'4200'. When debugging the program we have to reconcile the listing with the storage dump—a statement listed under LOC at X'0048' is in storage at X'4200' + X'0048', or X'4248'.

ASSIGNING BASE REGISTERS

It is our responsibility to notify the Assembler which registers are available as a base register. For this purpose we code the USING instruction. Subject to the restrictions discussed earlier, we may assign any registers (generally 2 through 12)—*but the program should not use them for any other purpose.* The USING instruction simply tells the Assembler which register(s) to use for base addressing. No executable code is generated.

NAME	OPERATION	OPERAND
blank	USING	S1,R1, . . .,Rn

S1 in the operand field designates the address from which the Assembler calculates displacements. R2, . . . , Rn specifes the base registers (1 through 15) and their sequence. When coding the program we can only guess how much storage is required. Assume about 25 coding sheets for each 4K of storage, excluding any large declaratives. Consider the following three examples:

1. USING *,3   The asterisk in the operand references the current value in the Assembler location counter. The statement tells the Assembler

that from this point on (for the next 4096 bytes) to use register-3 as the base register. In effect, the Assembler inserts a '3' as the base register into any address that references this region. The Assembler also calculates the displacement from this beginning address and inserts the displacement into the object code instruction.

2.   **USING A10,5**
         A 10   MVC   P+30(10),NAME   At assembly-time the current value of the location counter is the address of A10. Here, register-5 becomes the assigned base register. The exact same effect is achieved by USING *,5.

3. USING *,3,9,4   Each 4096 bytes of storage referenced by the program requires one base register. In this case we expect to require between 8K and 12K of storage. We designate three base registers, and the Assembler uses them as required in the sequence coded. Suppose that the current value in the location counter is X'3802'. Then base register-3 is to apply to all locations from X'3802' through the next 4095 bytes. Since 4096 equals X'1000', when the location counter reaches X'4802', the Assembler assigns base register-9 for the next 4K region. At X'5802' and for the next region, register-4 becomes the base register.

LOADING THE BASE REGISTER

USING merely notifies the Assembler which base registers to use. *It is our responsibility to code the program to load the register with a base address.* For this purpose we use the BALR instruction, Branch and Link Register.

NAME	OPERATION	OPERAND
[symbol]	BALR	R1,R2

BALR is an RR (register-to-register) format instruction. The rules are:

1. Both operands specify any general purpose register.
2. The instruction loads bits 32–63 of the Program Status Word into the operand-1 register. The rightmost 24 bits contain the address of the next sequential instruction in the program. (The other 8 bits include the condition code and are not used for addressing.)
3. If operand-2 specifies registers 1 through 15, the program branches to the address in that register (assuming one is already there):

X'4000'   BALR   6,9   Load the address of the next instruction, X'4002', into
X'4002'   MVC   . . .   register-6, and branch to the address in register-9.

4. For certain instructions like BALR and BCTR, register-0 has special properties. When operand-2 specifies register-0, the computer assumes that there is no register reference. For BALR, if operand-2 is register-0, no branch is taken. The program continues with the next sequential instruction:

X'5800'	BALR	3,0	Load the address of the next instruction, X'5802', into
X'5802'	MVC	...	register-3, and execute the next instruction, the MVC in X'5802'. This is the most common use of BALR. (0 in operand-2 means no register.)

Figure 6-3 shows how BALR and USING are combined at the beginning of a program to initialize and assign a base register. This is a skeleton program for illustrative purposes—we would not normally move such a constant into the first position of PRINT, which is reserved for the printer forms control character. Carefully distinguish in the example between assembly and execute operations.

```
LOC    OBJECT CODE      ADDR1 ADDR2  STMT   SOURCE STATEMENT

003800                               4             START X'3800' INIT LOC'N COUNTER
003800 0530                          5 BEGIN       BALR  3,0      LOAD BASE REGISTER
003802                               6             USING *,3      ASSIGN BASE REG

003802 D20E 3006 307F 03808 03881    8             MVC   PRINT(15),HEADING


003808                              10 PRINT  DS    CL121
003881 C9D5E5D6C9C3C540             11 HEADING DC   CL15'INVOICE LISTING'


003800
```

FIGURE 6-3 Base register initialization.

AT ASSEMBLY-TIME. The START statement initializes the Assembler location counter to X'3800' where we expect the program to load at execute-time. Therefore, under LOC the program listing shows the initial value 003800, and the location counter is incremented to show where each assembled statement is located. This is the only effect of START—it has nothing to do with initializing base registers or telling the system where to load the program. Under OS, START or CSECT usually contain a blank or zero operand.

BALR is the first executable instruction. BALR is RR format with machine code 05. The Assembler generates the two bytes of object code 0530, and increments the location counter to 3802. USING next tells the Assembler from this point (X'3802') to use register-3 as the base register. USING generates no object code. The next instruction, MVC, is assigned to X'3802'. The generated MVC instruction is

D2	0E	30	06	30	7F
(a)	(b)	(c)		(d)	

(a) D2 is the machine language code for MVC.

(b) The length of operand-1 is explicitly coded as 15. The Assembler deducts 1 from this length and inserts 14 (X'0E') in the second byte of the object code. *The machine length code is therefore always one less than the actual length.* At execute-time, the computer in effect "adds" one to this length. For any operand that references main storage, the object code length is one less than its length in the source program.

(c) Operand-1, X'3006', references PRINT. The Assembler inserts 3 for base register-3 in the first half byte. Note that PRINT is defined at location X'3808'. Its displacement from USING at X'3802' is 6 bytes. Therefore, the Assembler inserts the displacement 006 into the three half bytes.

(d) Operand-2, X'307F', references HEADING. The Assembler inserts 3 for base register into the object code. The displacement of HEADING is 127 bytes from USING, or X'07F'.

AT EXECUTE-TIME.   After assembly and link-edit, the program is ready to execute. It is loaded beginning at X'3800'. The first instruction, BALR, loads into register-3 the instruction address of the PSW containing the address of the next instruction, X'003802'. When MVC is executed, the computer calculates the effective addresses as:

	OPERAND-1	OPERAND-2
Contents of base register-3	X'3802'	X'3802'
Displacement	X'0006'	X'007F'
Effective address	X'3808'	X'3881'

These effective addresses agree with those shown under ADDR1 and ADDR2, and for the location of PRINT and HEADING. The computer adds 1 to the length (14 + 1 = 15), and moves 15 bytes beginning at X'3881' to X'3808'.

> *Note: We must reserve a base register and ensure that it is loaded with the correct value. The Assembler cannot check that the base register is correctly initialized. It is possible to get an error-free assembly, but one that at execute-time references the wrong locations!* One way to cause such an execute error is to code the USING before the BALR. The Assembler sets the location counter to X'3800' instead of X'3802', and calculates displacements from X'3800'. But at execute-time BALR loads the base register with X'3802', causing all displacements to be incorrect by two bytes.

OS INITIALIZATION

Both DOS and OS require the BALR/USING initialization instructions, used identically. But OS is a more complex system, and its Supervisor treats all users' programs like "subprograms". There is added code to supply a linkage between the Supervisor and our program, as Figure 6-4 illustrates.

```
 1                      START
 2                      SAVE    (14,12)         STORE SUPERVISOR'S REGISTERS
 3                      BALR    ...
 4                      USING   ...
 5                      ST      13,SAVEAREA+4    STORE REGISTER 13
 6                      LA      13,SAVEAREA      LOAD ADDRESS OF SAVEAREA
 7                      OPEN    ...
                          •
                          •
                          •
 8                      CLOSE ...
 9                      L       13,SAVEAREA+4    RE-LOAD REGISTER 13
10                      RETURN (14,12)          RE-LOAD REGS. RETURN TO SPVR

11 SAVEAREA             DS      18F             SAVE AREA, 18 FULLWORDS
```

FIGURE 6-4 OS initialization and return linkage.

Statement 1 is the usual START, under OS omitting the operand or coding it as 0. At execute-time the system tells us where the program has loaded by means of a "Location Factor". If the Load or Entry Point is X'50000' (the starting address) and the program listing indicates that a field called AMOUNT is at location (LOC) X'68A', then its actual location during the particular execution is X'50000' plus X'68A', or X'5068A'.

Statement 2 is a special macro that immediately saves the contents of the registers for the Supervisor. The program will change the register contents for its own purposes, but will restore the original values before returning to the Supervisor.

Statements 3 and 4 are conventional BALR and USING instructions, coded after the SAVE.

Statement 5 stores the contents of register-13 in a special register save area, called SAVEAREA in statement 11. Statement 6 loads into register-13 the address of the SAVEAREA. Register-13 is important to such linkage between two programs, and should not be used for any other purpose. There is continual traffic between the user program and the Supervisor, for all I/O operations and program checks.

Statements 9 and 10 are coded following the CLOSE at the end of all processing, and are equivalent to the DOS EOJ macro. They reload the registers that were saved at the start, and return control to the Supervisor.

Statement 11 defines SAVEAREA as 18 "fullwords" (each four bytes long), for storing the contents of the 16 registers and two other values.

Later chapters cover in detail these register operations, and the linkage is explained in the chapter "Subprograms and Overlays". When using this linkage, be sure to code it exactly as illustrated, using the same instructions and registers, in the same sequence. The Assembler does not check for accuracy, and any variation could be disastrous at execution-time.

Problems 6-6 through 6-10 should now be attempted.

TECHNICAL NOTE RE BCR AND BC

BCR, although RR format, is designated as M1,R2, and BC, although RX format, is M1,D2(X2,B2). M1 is a *mask*, a reference to the condition code in the PSW, not to a register. The common "extended mnemonic" for BCR is BR (Branch Register), an unconditional branch to an address in a register. The instruction BR addr may also be written as BC 15,addr. The extended mnemonics such as BE, BH, and BNL are unique cases of the BC operation. We may test the condition code with BC or the extended mnemonics. (The following discusses BC but applies also to BCR.) The two bits in the condition code are:

CONDITION CODE BITS	VALUE	INDICATION
00	0	Equal/Zero
01	1	Low/Minus
10	2	High/Plus
11	3	Overflow

Figure 6-5 provides the four-bit mask for the nine common branch conditions. We can test for *Equal/Zero* with either BE addr or BC 8,addr. The Assembler translates the 8 to binary 1000 in the object code mask position. Note that bits are numbered from left to right, beginning with zero for the leftmost bit, as 0, 1, 2, 3. On execution, the computer checks the mask—binary 1000 asks if bit 0 is on, meaning: does the condition code value equal zero?

The 4-bit Mask

Condition	Eq/zero 0	Low/min 1	High/plus 2	Over-flow 3	Branch on condition	Extended mnemonic		
0 = Equal/zero	1	0	0	0	BC 8,addr	BE	addr BZ	addr
1 = Low/minus	0	1	0	0	BC 4,addr	BL	addr BM	addr
2 = High/plus	0	0	1	0	BC 2,addr	BH	addr BP	addr
3 = Overflow	0	0	0	1	BC 1,addr	BO	addr	
No branch	0	0	0	0	BC 0,addr	NOP	addr	
1,2,3 = Not equal	0	1	1	1	BC 7,addr	BNE	addr BNZ	addr
0,2,3 = Not low	1	0	1	1	BC 11,addr	BNL	addr BNM	addr
0,1,3 = Not high	1	1	0	1	BC 13,addr	BNH	addr BNP	addr
0,1,2,3 = Any	1	1	1	1	BC 15,addr	B	addr	

FIGURE 6-5   Branch on condition mask.

For *Not Equal,* we could code either BNE addr or BC 7,addr. The Assembler translates the 7 to binary 0111 in the mask. On execution, the computer checks the mask:

If bit number 1 is on, does the condition code value equal 1?
If bit number 2 is on, does the condition code value equal 2?
If bit number 3 is on, does the condition code value equal 3?

If any one of these conditions exists, then the condition is not equal. The Assembler provides the extended mnemonics to save us coding and memorizing the mask. But whichever way we code, for example BNE addr or BC 7,addr, the Assembler generates the identical object code.

In the interests of clarity and reducing program bugs, this text recommends using the extended mnemonics. An understanding of the mask and the condition is useful, however, to aid in deciphering machine language code.

DEBUGGING TIPS

Except for the special OS initialization, the only new instructions introduced in this chapter are BALR and USING. Typical errors are:

— Omission of either BALR or USING. Omitting BALR causes an unpredictable error at execute-time, and omitting USING prevents the Assembler from generating machine code for instructions that require an implicit base register (addressability errors).
— Failure to assign and load enough base registers for a large program (Assembler addressability errors). A fairly common error is to load the second and third base registers with incorrect values.
— Using the base register for some other purpose in the program, thereby destroying the base address reference.
— Reversing BALR/USING, as USING/BALR. BALR will load the base register with a value of two bytes more than the Assembler expects when calculating displacements. The following code is sometimes used to initialize and adjust the base register to the correct value:

```
USING *,3
BALR 3,0
BCTR 3,0    Decrement register-3 by 1
BCTR 3,0    Decrement register-3 by 1
```

PROBLEMS

6-1. What are the two main purposes of the general registers?

6-2. What are the two main advantages of base/displacement addressing?

6-3. Why is explicit length indication permitted only for SS format?

6-4. Give the machine language code generated for the following. Assume base register-2 contains X'4800'.

    (a) BALR 9,10

    (b) LM   3,15,SAVE   Assume SAVE is at location 4920.

    (c) CLI   CODE,C'X'   Assume CODE is at location 4A26.

    (d) CLC   NEW,OLD   NEW is 3 bytes at 521A and OLD is 3 bytes at 5308.

    (e) ZAP   LINECT,=P'0'   LINECT is 2 bytes at 522B and =P'0' is at 5444.

6-5. Explain how the instruction format limits: (a) the number of registers to 16; (b) character lengths to 256; (c) packed lengths to 16; (d) maximum displacement to 4095 bytes.

6-6. ·Does the operand in START X'5000' affect where the program loads for execution? Explain.

6-7. Code a USING instruction for a program requiring 19,000 bytes.

6-8. Distinguish between BALR and USING. What is the purpose of each? Explain what happens at assembly and at execute-time by:

        X'5800'   **BALR   3,0**   Load base register-3

                USING *,4   Assign base register-4

6-9. Revise any previous program for base register initialization. Replace the INIT macro (or whatever macro you used for initialization). If under OS, code the linkage carefully.

6-10. The first base register is loaded using BALR, and additional ones with L, LA, or LM. Assign and load registers 6, 7, and 8 as base registers, and define any required declaratives. (*Hint:* Look ahead in the book.)

    (a) Use one LM instruction to load registers 7 and 8.

    (b) Use LA instructions to load registers 7 and 8.

6-11. Give the extended mnemonics for the following: (a) BC 8,C90; (b) BC 2,D90; (c) BC 11,E90; (d) BC 15,F90.

6-12. Code the following in machine language (assuming base register-3 contains X'5200' and B30 is at X'5C38'): (a) B B30; (b) BNL B30; (c) BAL 5,B30; (d) BR 5.

6-13. What would BC 9,addr mean?

CHAPTER 7

INPUT AND OUTPUT

Input/output on the 360 and 370 is significantly complex and for this reason its discussion has been delayed until now. This chapter covers only a fraction of the technical material available. (See especially the IBM Supervisor manuals.)

Earlier computers transmitted data directly between storage and I/O devices. Such computers used to read records directly into storage in a specified area and wrote out of an area. Indeed many small computers still function this way. During the I/O operation, all other processing was suspended until transmission was completed. Such a system considerably delays processing, especially when many devices are attached. I/O processing has been improved by:

— At the software (programming) level, *buffers* are used (covered in a later section).
— The I/O devices now generally are faster.
— CPU processing and data transmission are designed to *overlap*. For example, while a print operation transmits data to the printer, the CPU continues executing instructions. This advantage is achieved by the use of a hardware feature, *channels,* covered in the chapter on Operating Systems.
— Many more I/O devices are available, requiring more powerful I/O capability.

144

INPUT/OUTPUT CONTROL SYSTEM

A 360/370 program always executes in one of two states—the *Problem* and the *Supervisor state*. At any given time, the computer is either in the problem state executing a user's ("problem") program, or in the Supervisor state, executing the Supervisor program. The Supervisor program handles the transition between jobs and all interrupts, which include program and machine checks and all input/output operations. The problem program cannot actually issue I/O operations—these are *privileged instructions* that only the Supervisor can execute. The PSW indication is in bit 15 : 0 means supervisor and 1 means the problem program is being executed. Privileged instructions execute only when the program is in the supervisor state (PSW bit 15 = 0). For all I/O, the problem program interrupts and transfers control to the Supervisor.

For its I/O operations, the Supervisor uses the privileged instructions: Start I/O, Test I/O, Halt I/O, and Test Channel. We can (but usually do not) code I/O operations for the channel program by linking to the Supervisor with SVC (Supervisor Call) and CCW (Channel Command Word). This detailed level requires that we synchronize I/O operations with the program and provide for channel scheduling and interrupts. Few programmers code at this level. Instead, there is available a generalized Input/Output Control System, IOCS (called Data Management Services under OS). We can simplify I/O programming considerably by coding IOCS macro instructions. There are two main forms of IOCS: *physical IOCS (PIOCS) and logical IOCS (LIOCS)*.

PHYSICAL IOCS.   This level is still close to the actual machine operation, and coding is similar to that already discussed. We code the channel program using the macros EXCP (Execute Channel Program), WAIT, and CCB (Command Control Block). This level initiates execution of channel commands, and handles I/O interrupts and channel scheduling, but we must still synchronize I/O operations with our program. Chapter 16 provides more information on Physical IOCS.

LOGICAL IOCS.   This level uses the capabilities of physical IOCS, but provides many more features. On input, LIOCS locates the required record and delivers it to the program as a *logical record*. On output, LIOCS delivers the logical record to the channel program. LIOCS handles end-of-file conditions and many more functions not yet discussed, including:

— Switching ("flip-flopping") between I/O areas (*"buffers"*) if more than one buffer is designated.
— *"Blocking"* and *"unblocking"* tape and disk records.
— Checking and writing tape and disk *"labels."*

To obtain a record using logical IOCS we simply code the GET macro, and to write a record we code the PUT macro (sometimes READ and WRITE in special cases). IOCS saves us from coding the complex but repetitious input/output routines. The rest of this chapter covers programming using logical IOCS. We have already used Logical IOCS for OPEN, CLOSE, and GET. This chapter explains these and other macros in detail.

BUFFERS.   Under a conventional unbuffered input/output system, we read a record, then process it, then read another record:

Read-1	Process-1	Read-2	Process-2	etc. . . .

time ⟶

Better efficiency can be achieved by overlapping reading with processing. We read a record, *then while processing this record, read the next record:*

Read-1	Process-1	Process-2	Process-3	
	Read-2	Read-3	Read-4	etc. . . .

time ⟶

As can be seen, reading and processing are overlapped. The input records are read into areas in our program called *buffers* or *I/O areas.* We can extend this facility by increasing the number of buffers (up to 2 for DOS and 256 for OS). Similarly, writing can be overlapped with processing. Under DOS the programmer must designate the buffer areas, but OS automatically supplies them.

There are two types of IOCS macros: *file definition macros* and *imperative macros.*

FILE DEFINITION MACROS.   These describe the file that is to be processed. We define, for example, the symbolic name of the file, the length of the records, the buffers, and the actual device to be used. The Assembler is then able to construct a table of applicable channel commands. Under DOS, the DTFnn macro (Define The File) defines a file. For example, DTFCD means define a card file, and DTFPR means define a printer file. OS uses a Data Control Block, DCB, to define a "data set". Both are more fully described later in this chapter and in chapters on magnetic tape and disk.

IMPERATIVE MACROS

These initiate the input/output operation and include OPEN, CLOSE, GET, and PUT. These macros relate to the generalized DTF's channel commands and link to the Supervisor to issue the data transmission.

THE OPEN MACRO.   OPEN makes a file available to the program. Control is passed to the Supervisor which checks that the file exists and that the device is ready. (IOCS does considerably more when opening disk and tape.) One OPEN may open from one to 16 files. For example, assume the following statements:

```
CARD      DTFCD or DCB...        Define the card file
PRINTER   DTFPR or DCB...        Define the print file
          OPEN       CARD,PRINTER   Activate the files
```

THE CLOSE MACRO.   CLOSE deactivates all files previously opened and no longer required. We may close a file any time, and should close all files before terminating the program. A file closed in a program may be reopened and further processed. (IOCS does considerably more when closing disk and tape.)

> *Note:* In a *multiprogramming system,* a file that has been fully processed should be closed promptly. The device is then available to other programs.

Many systems now provide for automatic *self-relocating programs.* If the system does not have this capability, then to facilitate program self-relocatability under DOS, the macros should be coded OPENR and CLOSER. The IBM Supervisor manual provides the details.

THE GET MACRO.   GET makes available the next record from a sequential input file. The input record erases the previous contents of the input area.

OPERATION	OPERAND
GET	filename,workarea
or GET	(1),(0)

The file name is that of the DTF for the file. IOCS delivers the record to the workarea specified in operand-2. For instance:

```
CARD     DTFCD or DCB...     Define the card file
CARDIN   DS     CL80         Card workarea
         GET    CARD,CARDIN  Read a record into CARDIN
```

In this example, the filename is CARD and the workarea is CARDIN. The 80-character card record is transmitted to CARDIN. We may also load the DTF or DCB address and the workarea address into registers 1 and 0, as follows:

```
LA    1,CARD      Load the address of CARD
LA    0,CARDIN    Load the address of CARDIN
GET   (1),(0)     Read a record into CARDIN
```

Figure 7-1a depicts the relationship of the GET statement with two buffers. The first GET issued in the program reads record-1 into the first buffer, I/O area1. Record-1 is transferred to CARDIN, available for processing. Then while the program processes the record in CARDIN, IOCS reads record-2 into the second buffer, I/O area2:

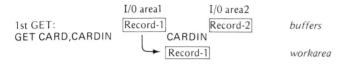

FIGURE 7-1a

In Figure 7-1b the second GET issued in the program transfers record-2 to CARDIN, and while the program processes CARDIN, IOCS reads record-3 into the first buffer:

FIGURE 7-1b

We must inform IOCS where to branch when it encounters the end-of-file (the /* trailer card). We designate the address where the system is to branch in the DCB or DTF statement. IOCS reads the /* record directly into a buffer. When a GET attempts to transfer the /* record to our workarea, the system instead will automatically direct the program to our end-of-file address.

THE PUT MACRO.   PUT writes or punches our record from our output (work) area. The rules for coding PUT are similar to those for GET.

OPERATION	OPERAND
PUT	filename,workarea
or PUT	(1),(0)

For example:

```
PRINTER   DTFPR or DCB...          Define the print file
PRINT     DS          CL121        The print workarea
          PUT         PRINTER,PRINT  Write a record
```

The PUT macro causes the contents of the workarea PRINT to write onto the device called PRINTER. *Note: The contents of the workarea and the buffers are not erased.* If we move data into the print area, we should clear the area after writing.

Before printing, we must insert a special forms control character into the first byte of the print workarea. (An alternative method is to use the CNTRL macro—see the IBM Supervisor Macro manuals.) The character informs the channel what action to take, such as print, space, eject. Punching cards may also require a special control character before the punch area. The common forms control characters in hex are:

	NO WRITE	WRITE
Space 1 line	0B	09
Space 2 lines	13	11
Space 3 lines	1B	19
Skip to new page	8B	89

Note also: X'01' is Write, space 0 lines.

For example, write and space two lines:

```
PRINT   DS    CL121          The print workarea
        MVI   PRINT,X'11'    Insert control character
        PUT   PRINTER,PRINT  Print & space 2 lines
```

If we use X'13' as the control character, the printer spaces two lines, *without printing, regardless of the contents of PRINT.* "Skip to a new page" is actually "skip to channel 1". The printer is equipped with a carriage control tape punched with a hole in "channel 1". The hole usually aligns with the printer forms at the top of the page as shown in Figure 7-2. Punches and control channels are available for channels 1 through 12 to permit skipping to various lines on the page. Most tapes are punched with channel 1, but not necessarily with the other channels.

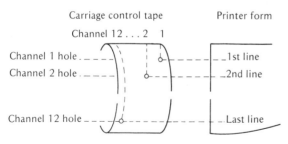

FIGURE 7-2   Carriage control tape.

ASA CONTROL CHARACTER.   An alternative forms control character that is more universal for different computers is the American Standards Association set, which is less efficient on the 360/370. Following are the more common characters:

blank	Space 1 line, then print
0	Space 2 lines, then print
−	Space 3 lines, then print
+	Print without spacing
1	Skip to the next page, then print

The next two example programs both illustrate the same program, using DOS and OS imperative and file definition macros. The programs simply read and write card records. They load register-3 as the base register and open the files; this initialization need be performed only once, at the start of the program execution.

At A10HEAD the program skips to a new page to print the heading. Note that CTLCHAR is defined as the first byte of the print area. At A20READ a card is read into CARDIN. This field is moved to the print area and printed. The line counter is incremented and checked for page overflow as in previous programs.

When all the input records have been read, IOCS recognizes the end-of-file (/* trailer record under DOS), and directs the program to the end-file address, Z10END, where the files are closed and execution terminates. Both file definition macros, DTF and DCB, are *keyword macros*. That is, the entries are recognized by specific names, and may be coded in any sequence. The keyword is followed by an equal sign (=) and a 'parameter', such as EOFADDR=Z10END. One entry is coded per line, followed immediately by a comma to separate the entries. We punch a continuation character in column 72 to indicate that the macro continues on the next line, in column 16. (It is possible to code several entries per line, but this practice makes the listing difficult to read and to change.) The last entry has no comma or continuation character. Some entries may be omitted; in these cases the Assembler assumes an entry—such assumptions are called *"default values"*. Precise entries and defaults vary by version of operating system, so that it is necessary to refer to the appropriate IBM Supervisor manual.

THE DOS DTF FILE DEFINITION MACRO

Figure 7-3 provides the requirements for a program written under DOS. The specifications for DTFCD and DTFPR follow:

DTFCD—DEFINE THE CARD FILE.   The name in Figure 7-3 given to the card file is CARD (any unique name may be given). The entries are:

BLKSIZE=80 tells IOCS that the size of each block of data to be read is 80 bytes, or 80 card columns. If this entry is omitted, the Assembler assumes a default of 80 (depending on the device).

DEVADDR=SYSIPT gives the entry SYSIPT, the primary system input device. Depending on the system, we may designate SYSRDR (the system reader device), or a "programmer logical unit", SYSnnn appropriate to the computer installation.

```
  5 ***              I N I T I A L I Z A T I O N
  6 PROG7A   START X'9AC78'
  7          BALR  3,0                        INITIALIZE BASE REGISTER
  8          USING *,3
  9          OPEN  CARD,PRINTER               ACTIVATE FILES

 19 ***              P A G E   O V E R F L O W
 20 A10HEAD  MVI   CTLCHAR,X'88'             MOVE FORMS CONTROL CHARACTER
 21          PUT   PRINTER,PRINT             SKIP TO NEW PAGE
 27          ZAP   LINECT,=P'0'             CLEAR LINE COUNT

 29 ***              M A I N   P R O C E S S I N G
 30 B10READ  GET   CARD,CARDIN
 36          MVC   RECPR,CARDIN              MOVE RECORD TO PRINT AREA
 37          MVI   CTLCHAR,X'09'            MOVE CONTROL CHARACTER
 38          PUT   PRINTER,PRINT            PRINT, SPACE 1 LINE
 44          AP    LINECT,=P'1'            ADD TO LINE COUNT
 45          CP    LINECT,=P'50'           END OF PAGE ?
 46          BH    A10HEAD                   YES - SKIP PAGE
 47          B     B10READ                   NO  - READ NEXT RECORD

 49 ***              E N D - O F - F I L E
 50 Z10END   CLOSE CARD,PRINTER              DE-ACTIVATE FILES
 59          EOJ                             NORMAL END-OF-JOB

 63 ***              D E C L A R A T I V E S

 65 LINECT   DC    PL2'0'                   LINE COUNTER

 67 CARDIN   DS    CL80                     INPUT WORKAREA

 69 PRINT    DS    0CL121                   PRINT AREA :
 70 CTLCHAR  DS    0CL1                     *    CONTROL CHAR POSITION
 71          DC    CL20' '                  *
 72 RECPR    DS    CL80                     *      RECORD PRINT AREA
 73          DC    CL21' '                  *
```

```
 75 CARD     DTFCD BLKSIZE=80,         DEFINE THE CARD FILE          +
                   DEVADDR=SYSIPT,                                   +
                   DEVICE=2501,                                      +
                   EOFADDR=Z10END,     END-OF-FILE ADDRESS           +
                   IOAREA1=IOARCD1,                                  +
                   IOAREA2=IOARCD2,                                  +
                   RECFORM=FIXUNB,                                   +
                   TYPEFLE=INPUT,                                    +
                   WORKA=YES

117 IOARCD1  DC    CL80' '             CARD BUFFER 1
118 IOARCD2  DC    CL80' '             CARD BUFFER 2
```

```
120 PRINTER  DTFPR BLKSIZE=121,        DEFINE THE PRINTER FILE       +
                   CTLCHR=YES,                                       +
                   DEVADDR=SYSLST,                                   +
                   DEVICE=1403,                                      +
                   IOAREA1=IOARPR1,                                  +
                   IOAREA2=IOARPR2,                                  +
                   RECFORM=FIXUNB,                                   +
                   WORKA=YES

142 IOARPR1  DC    CL121' '            PRINT BUFFER 1
143 IOARPR2  DC    CL121' '            PRINT BUFFER 2
```

```
145          END   PROG7A
```

FIGURE 7-3 DOS input/output macros.

DEVICE=2501 designates the card reader device to be used by the file. If the oper-
and is omitted, the Assembler assumes a 2540 reader.

EOFADDR=Z10END indicates the address of our end-of-file routine, and may be
any unique program name. IOCS recognizes the /* trailer card and links to our
end-of-file address. Never branch to this address from any other point.

IOAREA1=IOARCD1 is a required entry that specifies the name of the first buffer (or
I/O area). We have defined this buffer elsewhere in the program as IOARCD1
DS CL80. Any unique name could be used. IOCS reads input records into this
area.

IOAREA2=IOARCD2 gives the name of the second buffer (or I/O area). It is defined
elsewhere in the program as IOARCD2 DS CL80. A second buffer is optional,
but provides more efficient processing.

RECFORM=FIXUNB means that the format of records to be read is "fixed length,
unblocked." All card records are in this format normally, but tape and disk
records may be variable in length, and "blocked"—several records per block. If
this entry is omitted, the Assember assumes FIXUNB.

TYPEFLE=INPUT means that the type of file is input. The operand for punched
output is OUTPUT, and for a combined punch-feed-read device is CMBND. If
the entry is omitted, the Assembler assumes INPUT.

WORKA=YES tells IOCS that we want to process records in a "workarea" rather than
directly in a buffer. IOCS is to transfer records from the buffers to our workarea,
as specified in the macro GET CARD,CARDIN. CARDIN is defined elsewhere as
DS CL80. This entry may be omitted, but if so, we must specify another entry as
IOREG=(r), and process the input records directly in the buffers. This practice
may be done with DTFCD, but is illustrated later under DTFDI.

Other entries may also be coded; however, IOCS varies by operating system,
and many programs have unique needs. The Supervisor manual for each system
gives more specific details.

DTFPR—DEFINE THE PRINTER FILE.   The name in Figure 7-3 given to the printer is
PRINTER. Note that there is no entry for TYPEFLE because DTFPR is understood to be
an output file. The entry EOFADDR is omitted because it is only for input files.
DTFPR also permits entries other than the ones shown in the example.

BLKSIZE=121 tells IOCS that the size of the block of output data is 121 bytes. The
first (leftmost) byte is reserved for the forms control character, so that only 120
bytes are printed. The maximum block length depends on the particular printer
device.

CTLCHR=YES means that the program is using the 360/370 forms control character
set. Alternatively, coding CTLCHR=ASA stipulates the American Standards Association set.

DEVADDR=SYSLST defines SYSLST, the primary system printing device to be used
by this file. Depending on the system, we may also designate a programmer
logical unit, as SYSnnn appropriate to the computer installation.

DEVICE=1403 designates the printer device for the file, such as 1443, 3203, etc.

IOAREA1=IOARPR1 specifies the name of the first buffer (I/O area). We have defined this buffer elsewhere in the program as IOARPR1 DS CL121. Any unique name could be used. The entry is required.

IOAREA2=IOARPR2 gives the name of the second (optional) buffer. It is defined elsewhere as IOARPR2 DS CL121. The use of more than one buffer provides more efficient processing.

RECFORM=FIXUNB means that the output format is "fixed length, unblocked."

WORKA=YES tells IOCS that we want to process records in a "workarea" rather than in buffers. IOCS is to transfer records from our workarea to the buffers, in the example by means of the macro PUT PRINTER,PRINT. PRINT is defined elsewhere as DS CL121, and is our workarea for defining output records.

IOCS MODULES.   For each file, the *Linkage Editor* includes an IOCS logic module immediately following the program. A macro such as PUT PRINTER,PRINT links to the DTFPR, which in turn links to the printer logic module following the program.

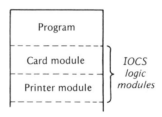

The size and location of these modules are available on the Linkage Editor Map (use the control statement ACTION MAP). An example of the Linkage Editor Map and names of the IOCS logic modules are given in Chapter 15.

The IOCS modules are preassembled and catalogued, and the Linkage Editor includes the appropriate modules with all programs that require input/output.

THE OS DCB FILE DEFINITION MACRO

DCB, Data Control Block, is equivalent to the DOS DTF macro, and is used to define a "data set." Because OS has considerable device independence capability, a recommended approach is to define all data sets as disk in order to facilitate this feature. Many of the entries required for DTF's are omitted for DCB's. Under OS, we may specify additional I/O attributes at execute-time by means of the DD, Data Definition, job control cards. This feature permits some programming changes concerned with I/O without reassembling the program.

The Assembler completes as much of the "data control block" as possible from the DCB entries. Prior to execution, the system checks for missing entries, and

```
***               I N I T I A L I Z A T I C N
PROG7B    START  0

          SAVE   (14,12)                    SAVE REGISTERS FOR SUPERVISOR

          BALR   3,0                        INITIALIZE BASE REGISTER
          USING  *,3

          ST     13,SAVEAREA+4              SAVE ADDRESSES FOR RETURN
          LA     13,SAVEAREA               *    TO SUPERVISOR

          OPEN   (FILEIN,(INPUT),FILEOT,(CUTPUT))

***               P A G E   O V E R F L O W

A10HEAD   MVI    CTLCHAR,X'8B'              MOVE FCRMS CONTROL CHARACTER
          PUT    FILEOT,PRINT               SKIP TO NEW PAGE
          ZAP    LINECT,=P'0'               CLEAR LINE COUNT

***               M A I N   P R O C E S S I N G

B10READ   GET    FILEIN,INAREA
          MVC    RECPR,INAREA               MOVE RECORD TO PRINT AREA
          MVI    CTLCHAR,X'09'              MOVE CONTRCL CHARACTER
          PUT    FILEOT,PRINT               PRINT, SPACE 1 LINE

          AP     LINECT,=P'1'              ADD TO LINE COUNT
          CP     LINECT,=P'50'             END OF PAGE ?
          BH     A10HEAD                          YES - SKIP PAGE
          B      B10READ                          NO  - READ NEXT RECORD

***               E N D - O F - F I L E

Z10END    CLOSE  (FILEIN,,FILECT)

          L      13,SAVEAREA+4             END-OF-JOB,  RETURN
          RETURN (14,12)                   *    TO SUPERVISOR

***               D E C L A R A T I V E S

LINECT    DC     PL2'0'                    LINE COUNTER

INAREA    DS     CL80                      INPUT WORKAREA

PRINT     DS     0CL133                    PRINT AREA :
CTLCHAR   DS     0CL1                      *    CONTROL CHAR POSITION
          DC     CL20' '                   *
RECPR     DS     CL80                      *      RECCRD PRINT AREA
          DC     CL33' '                   *
```
```
FILEIN    DCB    BLKSIZE=80,               DEFINE THE INPUT FILE        +
                 DDNAME=SYSIN,                                          +
                 DEVD=DA,                                               +
                 DSORG=PS,                                              +
                 EODAD=Z10END,                                          +
                 MACRF=(GM)
```
```
FILEOT    DCB    BLKSIZE=133,              DEFINE THE PRINTER FILE      +
                 DDNAME=SYSPRINT,                                       +
                 DEVD=DA,                                               +
                 DSORG=PS,                                              +
                 MACRF=(PM),                                            +
                 RECFM=FM
```
```
SAVEAREA  DS     18F                       REGISTER SAVE AREA
          END    PROG7B
```

FIGURE 7-4 OS input/output macros.

accesses them from the DD statement. In this way, entries in the DCB have priority over those in the DD statement. If there is information not provided, the system may make a default assumption, or if not possible, the program will possibly "bomb" when attempting an I/O operation.

Figure 7-4 illustrates the OS DCB macro and initialization, using the same example as the previous one for OS, reading and writing card records.

DCB FOR INPUT.   In the example, the name of the data set is FILEIN. Some of the DCB entries may be made on the DD job control cards.

BLKSIZE=80 means that the size of each data block is 80 bytes.

DDNAME=SYSIN tells Data Management that the "data definition name" is the logical address SYSIN (or whichever unit applies).

DEVD=DA means that the device for the data set is "direct access", or disk. The use of this entry instead of RD for card reader facilitates device independence, so that, for example, card records may be "spooled" onto disk for later processing.

DSORG=PS means that the data set organization is "physical sequential" (that is, the data is organized as sequential, rather than as direct access or indexed sequential—two disk processing methods). This entry may appear only in the DCB macro, and not in the DD job statement.

EODAD=Z10END tells Data Management that the end-of-data address is Z10END (or any other program label designated as the end routine). Data Management (like IOCS) directs the program to this address on encountering the end-of-file indication on the input data set (/* on cards).

MACRF=(GM) means that the "macro format" to be used in the program is "Get and Move" to a workarea (the coding is to be GET FILEIN,workarea).

We may provide other definitions at execute-time with the DD (Data Definition) job control card, such as assigning the actual I/O device to be used (printer, tape, disk, etc.). Also, we do not define the buffers with the DCB. The DD card specifies the number of buffers; if omitted, OS assumes two buffers by default.

DCB FOR OUTPUT.   In Figure 7-4, the name of the DCB printer data set is FILEOT, and provides one possible coding:

BLKSIZE, DEVD, and DSORG are similar to the definitions for the input data set.

DDNAME=SYSPRINT means that the system printer is the device for this data set.

MACRF=(PM) means that the macro format is "Put and Move" from a workarea (the coding is to be PUT FILEOT,workarea).

RECFM=FM. F means "fixed, unblocked". M is for "machine code", the format for the regular 360/370 print control characters. For ASA characters, use A. The requirements for other installations may be quite different. Some systems block print records onto disk prior to printing, and the entry may be FBM or FBSM.

LOCATE MODE

It is possible to process input/output records directly in the buffers. The advantage (not very great) is that the workarea need not be defined. GET and PUT are coded without specifying a workarea in operand-2, as

GET FILEIN   and   PUT FILEOUT

The DTF and DCB requirements differ. For the DTF, the entry IOREG replaces WORKA, as IOREG=(reg) specifying an available general register. IOCS is to load the register with the address of the buffer that contains the next record to be processed. The DCB entry to denote processing in a buffer ("Locate Mode") is MACRF=(GL) for input and MACRF=(PL) for output. The system uses register-1 for the address of the buffer that contains the record to be processed.

The example in Figure 7-5a shows the first GET executed. IOCS reads record-1 into buffer-1 and loads the address of buffer-1 into "register-r". Then, while the program processes the record in buffer-1, IOCS reads record-2 into buffer-2:

	I/O area1	I/O area2	Register-r
1st GET:	Record-1	Record-2	A (I/O area1)
GET FILEIN	Buffer-1	Buffer-2	

FIGURE 7-5a

The example cites "register-r" to mean the specified register in the DTF or register-1 for the DCB.

Figure 7-5b shows the second GET executed. IOCS loads the address of buffer-2 (which contains record-2) into register-r. Then, while we process record-2, IOCS reads record-3 into buffer-1:

	I/O area1	I/O area2	Register-r
2nd GET:	Record-3	Record-2	A (I/O area2)
GET FILEIN			

FIGURE 7-5b

Processing continues "flip-flopping" between the two buffers (or more under OS). GET reads a record into one of the buffers, but which one? After the GET, the register will contain the address of the first byte of the buffer in which the next input record is located. For the programmer, the simplest action is to move the contents of the buffer to a workarea for processing. We can use the address in the register explicitly in an MVC operation immediately following the GET. The symbolic format for MVC is

MVC D1(L,B1),D2(B2)

We can use explicit base/displacement addressing in either operand. In this case, since register-r contains the address of the buffer, we can code the following:

```
GET    FILEIN          Read File—Load Register with Buffer Address
MVC    INAREA,0(r)     Move Buffer to INAREA
```

The MVC instruction works as follows: Using the address in register-r (base register-r, no displacement), move from the specified storage location to INAREA (an 80-byte move, based on the length of INAREA). The GET operation is basically the same for DOS and OS, although OS requires the use of register-1 only. The PUT statements and file definitions differ.

DOS CODING FOR LOCATE MODE. The changes required to process in the buffer are compared in Figure 7-6 with the conventional use of a workarea. The example arbitrarily selects register-4 for the input register and register-5 for the output one, with the IOREG entry replacing the WORKA entry. Any available register (2 through 12) will work, but not the base register(s). For printing, the OPEN statement establishes in register-5 (in this case) the address of the first available print buffer. Before the PUT, we move the contents of the PRINT area to the buffer: operand-1 of the MVC, coded as 0(121,5) uses base register-5, displacement zero and length 121 explicitly to move the contents of PRINT to the designated storage locations. The following PUT statement initializes register-5 with the address of the next available buffer.

Macro	Using workarea	Using locate mode
Read	GET CARD,CARDIN	GET CARD MVC CARDIN,0(4)
Write	PUT PRTR,PRINT	MVC 0(121,5),PRINT PUT PRTR
Input file definition	DTFCD . . WORKA=YES	DTFCD . . IOREG=(4)
Output file definition	DTFPR . . WORKA=YES	DTFPR . . IOREG=(5)

FIGURE 7-6 DOS locate mode.

OS CODING FOR LOCATE MODE. Under OS, the DCB entry for processing in the buffer for the input data set is MACRF=(GL) for Get Locate, and the entry for the output data set is MACRF=(PL) for Put Locate. Figure 7-7 compares the conventional use of a workarea with Locate Mode. Since the DCB contains the entry for (PL), we

Macro	Using workarea	Using locate mode
Read	GET FILEIN,INAREA	GET FILEIN MVC INAREA,0(1)
Write	PUT FILEOT,OUTAREA	PUT FILEOT MVC 0(133,1),OUTAREA

Input file definition	DCB .
	     .
	    MACRF=(GM)
		DCB .
		     .
		    MACRF=(GL)

Output file definition	DCB .
	     .
	    MACRF=(PM)
		DCB .
		     .
		    MACRF=(PL)

FIGURE 7-7   OS locate mode.

must code the PUT with no operand-2. PUT inserts into register-1 the address of the first byte of the buffer that is to receive the next output record. We code PUT to locate the output buffer, and then can use register-1 explicitly to move data into the buffer. But watch out—the coding for PUT and MVC under OS is reverse to that for DOS.

We are not yet fully ready for explicit use of base/displacement, covered in a later chapter. What have we accomplished? Using standard workareas, IOCS would perform these functions automatically. Processing fully in a buffer without moving to a workarea requires extensive use of explicit base/displacement processing. Chapter 15, under DSECT, does provide a sophisticated method of processing within a buffer, and giving names to the various fields in that area. Meanwhile, feel free to continue using workareas, the approach most commonly used in handling input/output.

DEVICE INDEPENDENCE UNDER DOS

With DTFCD and DTFPR we can normally read and write data only on the card reader, punch, and printer. Some situations, however, require more I/O flexibility. For example, assume a multiprogramming system that is executing two programs. The first program fully uses the only printer, but the second program also needs the printer. We may ask the system to direct the second program's output onto magnetic tape, which can later be used to print the output when the printer is available. We can enhance the flexibility of *device independence* (assigning tape output for a printer, for example) with the use of the macro DTFDI (Define the File Device Independent) in place of DTFCD and DTFPR. OS and larger DOS/VS versions, designed for device independence, do not require such a special macro.

The module that DTFDI generates is larger than those for DTFCD and DTFPR, but is more versatile. Among restrictions, records must be fixed length, unblocked, and with no workarea specified. Figure 7-8 illustrates DTFDI macros for input and for output.

```
FILEIN     DTFDI DEVADDR=SYSIPT,        DEFINE INPUT FILE            +
                 EOFADDR=Z10END,                                     +
                 RECSIZE=80,                                         +
                 IOAREA1=BUFFIN1,                                    +
                 IOAREA2=BUFFIN2,                                    +
                 IOREG=(4)

BUFFIN1  DC    CL80' '                   INPUT BUFFER 1
BUFFIN2  DC    CL80' '                   INPUT BUFFER 2
```

```
PRTR       DTFDI DEVADDR=SYSLST,         DEFINE PRINT FILE           +
                 RECSIZE=121,                                        +
                 IOAREA1=BUFFOUT1,                                   +
                 IOAREA2=BUFFOUT2,                                   +
                 IOREG=(5)

BUFFOUT1 DC    CL121' '                  OUTPUT BUFFER 1
BUFFOUT2 DC    CL121' '                  OUTPUT BUFFER 2
```

FIGURE 7-8   DOS DTFDI macros.

DTFDI FOR INPUT.   The name in the figure given to the file is FILEIN. Entries EOFADDR, IOAREA1, and IOAREA2 are coded the same as for DTFCD.

DEVADDR uses only the primary system input device names SYSIPT and SYSRDR.
IOREG=(4) tells IOCS to load register-4 with the address of the buffer that contains the current input record. Any available register, 2 through 12, may be assigned. With IOREG, we code GET filename (with no workarea indicated).
RECSIZE=80 designates the length of the input area as 80 bytes, the maximum length allowed.

Note the use of RECSIZE instead of BLKSIZE. We do not code DEVICE (because it is device independent), RECFORM (always fixed, blocked), TYPEFLE (files can be input or output), or WORKA (processing is in a buffer, not a workarea).

DTFDI FOR OUTPUT.   The name given to the output file in the figure is PRTR. Note that we do not code CTLCHR, DEVICE, RECFORM, or TYPEFLE. Entries DEVADDR, IOAREA1, and IOAREA2 are the same as for DTFPR.

IOREG=(5) tells IOCS to load register-5 with the address of the buffer that is next to be used for output. Initially, the OPEN macro loads register-5, and subsequently the PUT macro as executed. Any available register, 2 through 12, may be assigned. With IOREG, we code PUT filename (with no workarea indicated).
RECSIZE=(121) defines the length of the output record. The first byte is reserved for the control character. The maximum length is normally 121 for SYSLST (printer) and 81 for SYSPCH (card punch).

ABNORMAL TERMINATION

Both DOS and OS have macros that are used to terminate the program abnormally when a serious error condition is encountered. Both provide a hexadecimal dump of the registers and the program storage area. The DOS macro is DUMP and the OS one is ABEND.

NAME	OPERATION	OPERAND
	DUMP ABEND	Ignored, use for comments completion-code,DUMP

THE DOS DUMP MACRO.   DUMP terminates program execution and provides a storage dump. Generally, PDUMP is more convenient to use when testing a program because it continues processing the program. The CANCEL macro also terminates processing, and flushes all input records through to the /& Job End card. If we precede program execution with a // OPTION DUMP job card, the Supervisor automatically produces a storage dump after the CANCEL. (// OPTION PARTDUMP on some larger systems.)

THE OS ABEND MACRO.   To provide for a serious error condition where we want an "abnormal end" of the program, we code the ABEND macro. The operand includes a "completion-code", any decimal value up to 4095, as ABEND 25,DUMP. There could be several ABENDs in the program, but the completion code 25 identifies which ABEND when it prints at termination. The DUMP operand invokes the ABDUMP macro (abnormal DUMP) which prints a hexadecimal dump of the registers and relevant parts of main storage.

DEBUGGING TIPS

Coding errors based on input/output are many and serious. The Assembler can identify the most obvious spelling errors, but others include:

— Under DOS, failure to open a file.
— Use of an invalid forms control character. An invalid IBM machine code causes a terminating "I/O error", and an invalid ASA causes a default to space and print.
— Conflicting record lengths defined in the file definition macro, in workareas, in DOS buffers, and in OS DD entries. This type of error is easy to make but difficult to trace. If the input workarea or buffer is too small, a GET operation will destroy the data immediately following. When at some later point the program tries to execute the "garbage", the results will be unpredictable.

— Incomplete file definition macro entries, allowing the Assembler to default to unexpected values (such as ASA forms control character).
— Confusion in use of Locate Mode with file definition, imperative macro, or register.

PROBLEMS

7-1. What is the difference between "Supervisor" and "Problem" state?

7-2. What is a "privileged" instruction?

7-3. What is the advantage (if any) of buffers?

7-4. What is a "file definition" macro and an "imperative" macro?

7-5. Give the MVI and the PUT to print and space 3 lines, using file PRTR and workarea PRINT.

7-6. Provide the file definition macro for a card reader called READER, end-of-file address P35END, device 2540, and a workarea. If using DOS, define two buffers.

7-7. Provide the file definition macro for a printer called PRTR, device 1403, and a workarea of 133 bytes. If using DOS, define two buffers.

7-8. Redefine the file in Problem 7-6 for Locate Mode. Provide the GET statement.

7-9. Redefine the file in Problem 7-7 for Locate Mode. Provide a PUT and MVI for print space 2.

7-10. Recode any previous program. Assign base registers and use full IOCS. Replace any special macros such as INIT, DEFCD, DEFPR, and PUTPR.

CHAPTER 8

STRATEGY, STYLE, AND STANDARDS

Up to now, most of the emphasis in this book has been with the technical aspects of Assembler programming. In this chapter we take a break, and examine program organization, style, and standards. Much of this material is relevant to any programming language.

PROGRAMMING OBJECTIVES

The goal of a computer system is to produce information. We reach this goal by means of three objectives: accuracy, efficiency, and clarity.

1. *Accuracy*. A program must produce 100 percent accurate results, since the recipient of the report may base decisions on the information. For example, if a report detailing delinquent customer payments is incorrect, the company may start badgering customers who are fully paid up.
2. *Efficiency*. In these days of large main storage, "virtual" storage, and fast execute-time, efficiency is no longer such a consideration as once it was. There may even be justification for some inefficiency, where the added cost of pro-

gramming time exceeds the expected cost of CPU time, or when there is an urgent need for information. However, in the interests of less execute-time and storage space, an efficient program is always a reasonable objective.

3. *Clarity.* Since many installations devote considerable time to program corrections and revisions, it is vital to design programs that are clear and maintainable. In the past, there have been many programmers with great technical skill who coded incredibly complex routines, and used the most sophisticated instructions where simple ones would work equally well. Today's emphasis is on code that is simple, clear, and well-organized.

This chapter first examines an approach to program organization, subroutines, then Programming Style, and finally Standardization and Documentation.

SUBROUTINES AND LINKAGE

A subroutine is a section of program coding that acts almost as an independent part of the program. Sometimes more than one part of the main program uses the subroutine. For example, we can treat the section of coding for page overflow as a separate part of the main program. It can be written as a subroutine used by different parts of the main program. Each time a line is printed, the program can check if the maximum number of lines per page has been reached. If so, the program branches, or links, to the subroutine. The subroutine executes the following:

— Skips to a new page.
— Prints the heading.
— Initializes the line counter.
— Adds one to the page count.
— Returns, or links, to the point of invocation in the main program.

The use of subroutines has several advantages: (a) It simplifies program writing. Commonly used routines, or complex routines, may be separated from the main program. The main program logic then is simplified. (b) A subroutine may be written once, then catalogued as a permanent part of the system, available for use by other programs. (c) It facilitates teams of programmers working on one program.

SUBROUTINE LINKAGE—BAL AND BR. We perform subroutine linkage by means of two instructions that use a register: BAL and BR.

NAME	OPERATION	OPERAND
[symbol]	BAL	R1,X2 or R1,D2(X2,B2)
[symbol]	BR	R1

BRANCH AND LINK—BAL.   BAL is similar to BALR, covered earlier. The rules are:

1. Operand-1 specifies a register to be used for subroutine linkage.
2. Operand-2 references an address, generally the subroutine.
3. On execution, BAL loads the address of the next instruction into the operand-1 register (the instruction address, bits 32–63 of the PSW). Then BAL branches unconditionally to the operand-2 storage address.

For example, BAL 8,P10PAGE means: load the address of the next instruction in register-8, and branch to the address of P10PAGE.

BRANCH ON CONDITION REGISTER—BR.   BR is an unconditional branch to an address in a register. We commonly use BR to return from a subroutine. For example, BR 8 branches unconditionally to an address stored in register-8. BR is an "extended mnemonic," and is actually a BCR (Branch Condition Register) operation.

USE OF LINKAGE.   We allocate any available register for subroutine linkage. We should be careful, however, not to change the contents of the register between the time BAL loads the address and the time BR returns from the subroutine. In Figure 8-1, the main program has two linkages to the subroutine, statements 1 and 5. The program executes as follows:

STATEMENT	DESCRIPTION
1	BAL loads the address of the next instruction, statement 2, into register-8, and branches to P10PAGE, statement 9.
9–12	The subroutine, P10PAGE, is executed. At statement 12 the program branches to the address stored in register-8, statement 2.
2–4	Statements 2, 3, and 4 are executed.
5	BAL loads the address of the next instruction, statement 6, in register-8, and branches to P10PAGE, statement 9.
9–12	Statements 9, 10, and 11 are executed. At statement 12 the program branches to the address stored in register-8, statement 6.

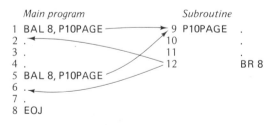

```
    Main program                Subroutine
1 BAL 8, P10PAGE ───────────▶ 9 P10PAGE   .
2 .  ◀─                       10             .
3 .                           11             .
4 .                           12          BR 8
5 BAL 8, P10PAGE
6 .  ◀─
7 .
8 EOJ
```

FIGURE 8-1   Subroutine linkage.

6–8   Statements 6, 7, and 8 are executed. Statement 8 terminates program execution.

We must ensure that the subroutine is a separate part of the program. The only way this subroutine should be normally entered is with BAL 8,P10PAGE. The normal exit in this example is back through register-8. The program, however, may branch out of the subroutine to any address, such as to an error routine.

SUBROUTINE FLOWCHARTING.   Both the subroutine coding and the subroutine flowchart are separated from the main program. The only new requirements are the flowchart symbols for linkage to and from the subroutine. The main program uses one symbol that represents the entire processing in the subroutine, as shown in Figure 8-2, one of several ways to represent subroutines.

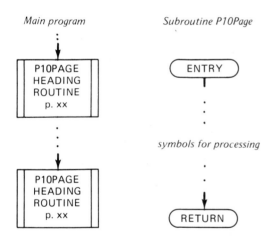

FIGURE 8-2   Subroutine symbols.

The symbol in the main program that represents the subroutine processing shows:

1. The name of the subroutine (P10PAGE),
2. A description of the subroutine (HEADING ROUTINE), and
3. The flowchart page number on which the subroutine detail is given.

For a complete example of main logic and subroutines, refer to the flowchart and program at the end of this chapter.

PROGRAMMING STYLE

A subroutine need not be limited in use to a common section of code, such as the example page heading. Good programming practice today is in the style of "structured programming". Now, Assembler language does not lend itself well to structured programming requirements, which are better facilitated by high-level languages like PL/I and COBOL. But we can adhere to some of its main features:

— Organization of the program into a "main logic" section with various subsidiary routines (subroutines). The main logic handles input and testing for record code or sequence to determine the action to take. It then uses BAL to perform the required subroutine.
— Each subroutine has a specific identifiable purpose and contains only logic related to its purpose. In a Payroll program, for example, one subroutine calculates income tax, another calculates pension deduction, etc.
— The main logic and the subroutines are each contained within one page of printed code (or the number of lines on a visual display terminal). By this limitation, the mind can grasp (hopefully!) the entire processing logic of the routine. Routines that continue for pages become incomprehensible. (One exception could be for a routine that performs many repetitive Move/Edit operations.)
— Each subroutine has one entry-point, at its start, and one exit-point, at its end. The program accordingly organizes itself into clear, logical sections, with no confusing branches back and forth between routines.
— Within a subroutine, branch statements should go forward as much as possible. The only statements that branch backwards are those that loop (e.g., branch back to read the next input record). The following example illustrates an unnecessary branch backwards caused by an illogical approach:

```
         UNNECESSARY BRANCH                          PROPER CODING
     CP    CUSTBAL,CREDLIM                      CP    CUSTBAL,CREDLIM
     BH    D30                                  BNH   D20
D20  •                                          MVC   MESSOUT,=C'OVER LIMIT'
     •                                  D20  •
     •                                          •
D30  MVC   MESSOUT,=C'OVER LIMIT'               •
     B     D20
```

Fully structured programming as used in PL/I and COBOL entirely eliminates the GO TO statement (in Assembler, B, BH, BNE, etc.) because of their powerful "macro statements", DO WHILE and PERFORM.

The example program at the end of this chapter illustrates a Payroll program that is organized according to the foregoing conventions. The objective of such programming style is to gain better clarity and to facilitate program maintenance.

Because a large part of programming effort is in correcting and revising programs, there is an urgent need for clear, concise, and well-organized programs.

Good programming style is only one way to provide better clarity. Others are:

— The use of meaningful names that describe the fields being defined, such as TOTALTAX instead of AMOUNTA, or worst of all, cryptic one-letter names such as A and X.
— A systematic labelling convention that provides easy locating of branch points and clearly identifies the section in which it belongs. In the example program at the end of this chapter, the Main Logic routine has labels that all begin with 'A': A10READ, A20, A30; the Wage Calculation subroutine labels are 'B'; and Employee Total subroutine labels begin with 'D'; etc.
— Assigning certain registers always with specific purposes, such as 3, 4, and 5 for base registers; 6 and 7 for subroutine linkage; etc. Such conventions help minimize errors in register usage.

PROGRAM DOCUMENTATION

An important element of program maintenance is adequate documentation. There is certainly no universal standard of documentation. Some installations keep a program listing only, well-documented with comments, sometimes stored on disk and available to users through visual display terminals. Others keep a record of each program in files or binders for quick reference, along with other related material, such as flowcharts and test runs. This text does not advocate any particular method of documentation. Programmers quickly develop bad habits in areas that are non-productive and uninteresting (such as documentation). Learners should at least begin developing good habits and apply them to their installation's standards.

THE PROGRAM DOCUMENTATION FILE. The following is an example of one possible documentation file, by section.

1. *Title Page.* The first page could contain program number, program name, the names of the programmers who wrote it, and the date completed. It might also specify who authorized the program originally, and the date. This section could also contain the dates of any revisions, who requested them, and who made them.
2. *Contents Page.* If the size of the program warrants it, a contents page may be useful.
3. *Program Objective.* This section consists of one or two paragraphs providing the objective(s) of the program, in effect what the program is to accomplish.
4. *Operator's Guide.* Many installations have a preprinted operator's guide that the programmer completes to facilitate running of the program. The guide contains inputs and their sequence, output devices, printer forms, control totals, and error

messages, listing of job control cards (if any), and approximate run time. A copy of this guide is often usefully included in the program documentation file.

5. *Layouts for Input and Output Records and the Printed Report.* The report layout shows the print position of every field in the headings, detail line, total lines, and error messages.

6. *Flowcharts.* The current program flowchart (or decision tables in some installations) should be filed. A large program could also have an overall summary flowchart.

7. *The Program Listing.* The current program listing is included, with the date clearly identified.

8. *Example Test Data.* A program using tape or disk input generally is tested using "live" data. If input is from punched cards, it is not difficult to arrange and list sample data for testing the program. The test cards should be kept for use in testing the program whenever it is revised. On the listing of the data, each input field should be clearly indicated, along with any intentional errors. The list of input data should show *expected results* (the totals that we expect the run to produce), and a random sample of calculations (such as hour × rate in the documented program following).

9. *Program Report Output.* This section gives a sample of the program's printed output, either from "live" data or from test data, with adding machine tapes to prove the accuracy of the test.

10. *Previous Listing.* The previous program listing should be preserved in case revisions turn out to be wrong, or the revision is cancelled and we have to reverse the changes.

The next section illustrates an Assembler program fully documented according to the preceding discussion. The example is somewhat overdocumented to make it clearer to readers not familiar with Assembler language. The only topic in the program not yet covered is table look-up.

DOCUMENTED PROGRAM

TITLE PAGE

Program Number: PROG08
Program Name: Weekly Wage Calculation
Programmer: Oliver Twit
Completion Date: January 28, 19xx
Authorization: J. P. Megabuck
                    Payroll Department
                    January 27, 19xx
Language: Assembler
Status: Tested and fully working.
Revisions:

WEEKLY WAGE CALCULATION PROGRAM PROG08

CONTENTS

PROGRAM OBJECTIVE   1

To calculate employees' wages for the current pay period, and to produce the weekly wage report.

169

PROGRAM:	PROG08, Weekly Wage Calculation
INPUT FILE:	Employee weekly time records (code 04) for the current pay period.
SEQUENCE:	Employee number
RUN TIME:	10 minutes
FREQUENCY OF RUN:	Weekly
OUTPUT:	Printer:

Employee Weekly Wage Report
Forms: 8½ × 14 management report form
2-part
standard carriage control tape

RECIPIENT OF REPORT:	Payroll Department, both parts
CONTROL TOTALS:	The program produces total hours and wages by employee number (indicated by *) and for final total (indicated by **). Final total hours on the report must agree with the precalculated hours in the Payroll Control Register before continuing with the next payroll job. Total wages from the report is to be entered in the Control Register.

ERROR MESSAGES: CAUSE:

'INVALID RECORD CODE'	A record does not contain '04' in columns 1–2.
'RECORD OUT OF SEQUENCE'	An employee number read is lower than the preceding record.
'JOB NO. NOT IN TABLE'	A job number on an input record is not in the table of jobs in the program.

Action: The program prints the error message and continues processing with the next input record. Invalid records should be corrected and the job rerun.

The program is organized into the following sections:
SECTION A: MAIN LOGIC (READ & CHECK VALIDITY & SEQUENCE)
Checks each record for valid code. Sequence-checks on Employee number:
   Equal — Process the record (Section B).
   Low   — Sequence error (Section R).
   High — Control break; tests for first record of file:
          First record — **Bypasses control break (goes to Section B).**
          Not first   — Performs Employee totals (Section D).
On end-of-file, links to address A50END (see DTFCD in program). This routine performs Employee Totals, Section D, then Final Totals, Section E, and terminates processing.
SECTION B: PROCESS EMPLOYEE RECORD
Uses Job number from the input record to locate related rate-of-pay in a stored table. (A Job not found in the table is an error.) For example, Job number is '02' and located rate-of-pay is $6.15. The program multiplies Hours worked (21.5) by rate to calculate Wage:

$$21.5 \times \$6.15 = \$132.225 \text{ (rounded to } \$132.23)$$

Accumulates total Employee hours and wages, and prints Employee detail line (see print layout). Returns to read the next record (Section B).
SECTION D: EMPLOYEE TOTALS
Prints total Employee hours and wages (one *), accumulates final total hours and wages, and clears Employee totals.
SECTION E: FINAL TOTALS
Prints total hours and wages (two **'s).
SECTION H: PAGE OVERFLOW & HEADINGS
Prints page heading at the start of the run and on reaching the end of each page.
SECTION P: PRINT SUBROUTINE
Performs all printing and adding to line counter.
SECTION R: ERROR ROUTINES
The Operator's Guide describes the three error routines.

REGISTERS USED:	Register:	Purpose:
	3	Base register for addressing
	7	Subroutine linkage
	9	Table look-up for Job number

SWITCHES USED: None.

MULTIPLE-CARD LAYOUT FORM

Company _____

Application __Weekly Wage Report__ by __P. R. Ogram__ Date __July 7, 19xx__ Job No. __PROG08__ Sheet No. _____

INPUT RECORD FORMAT

Code (04) | Emp. no. | Employee name | Job no. | Hours

9999999999999999999999999999999999999999999999999999999999999999999999999999999
1 2 3 4 5 6 7 8 9 10 11 12 13 14 15 16 17 18 19 20 21 22 23 24 25 26 27 28 29 30 31 32 33 34 35 36 37 38 39 40 41 42 43 44 45 46 47 48 49 50 51 52 53 54 55 56 57 58 59 60 61 62 63 64 65 66 67 68 69 70 71 72 73 74 75 76 77 78 79 80

9999999999999999999999999999999999999999999999999999999999999999999999999999999
1 2 3 4 5 6 7 8 9 10 11 12 13 14 15 16 17 18 19 20 21 22 23 24 25 26 27 28 29 30 31 32 33 34 35 36 37 38 39 40 41 42 43 44 45 46 47 48 49 50 51 52 53 54 55 56 57 58 59 60 61 62 63 64 65 66 67 68 69 70 71 72 73 74 75 76 77 78 79 80

9999999999999999999999999999999999999999999999999999999999999999999999999999999
1 2 3 4 5 6 7 8 9 10 11 12 13 14 15 16 17 18 19 20 21 22 23 24 25 26 27 28 29 30 31 32 33 34 35 36 37 38 39 40 41 42 43 44 45 46 47 48 49 50 51 52 53 54 55 56 57 58 59 60 61 62 63 64 65 66 67 68 69 70 71 72 73 74 75 76 77 78 79 80

9999999999999999999999999999999999999999999999999999999999999999999999999999999
1 2 3 4 5 6 7 8 9 10 11 12 13 14 15 16 17 18 19 20 21 22 23 24 25 26 27 28 29 30 31 32 33 34 35 36 37 38 39 40 41 42 43 44 45 46 47 48 49 50 51 52 53 54 55 56 57 58 59 60 61 62 63 64 65 66 67 68 69 70 71 72 73 74 75 76 77 78 79 80

9999999999999999999999999999999999999999999999999999999999999999999999999999999
1 2 3 4 5 6 7 8 9 10 11 12 13 14 15 16 17 18 19 20 21 22 23 24 25 26 27 28 29 30 31 32 33 34 35 36 37 38 39 40 41 42 43 44 45 46 47 48 49 50 51 52 53 54 55 56 57 58 59 60 61 62 63 64 65 66 67 68 69 70 71 72 73 74 75 76 77 78 79 80

9999999999999999999999999999999999999999999999999999999999999999999999999999999
1 2 3 4 5 6 7 8 9 10 11 12 13 14 15 16 17 18 19 20 21 22 23 24 25 26 27 28 29 30 31 32 33 34 35 36 37 38 39 40 41 42 43 44 45 46 47 48 49 50 51 52 53 54 55 56 57 58 59 60 61 62 63 64 65 66 67 68 69 70 71 72 73 74 75 76 77 78 79 80

5

PROGRAM TITLE __PROG08 Weekly Wage Calculation__

PROGRAMMER OR DOCUMENTALIST: __Oliver Twit__

CHART TITLE

PRINT CHART

DATE __Jan. 28, 19xx__

```
 1  HEADING 1:        WEEKLY  WAGE  REPORT                        PAGE XXX
 3  HEADING 2:  EMPLOYEE NAME        JOB   RATE  HOURS        WAGE
 5  DETAIL:     XXXXX X-------X       XX    X.XX  XX.X-     XXX.XX CR
 7  EMPLOYEE TOTAL:   X,XXX.X *           X,XXX,XXX.XXCR*
 9  FINAL TOTAL:      X,XXX.X **          X,XXX,XXX.XXCR**
13  ERRORS:     XXXXX X-------X                 INVALID RECORD CODE
15              XYYYYY X-------X                 JOB NO. NOT IN TABLE
17              XXXXX X-------X                 RECORD OUT OF SEQUENCE

                                    REPORT FORMAT
```

173

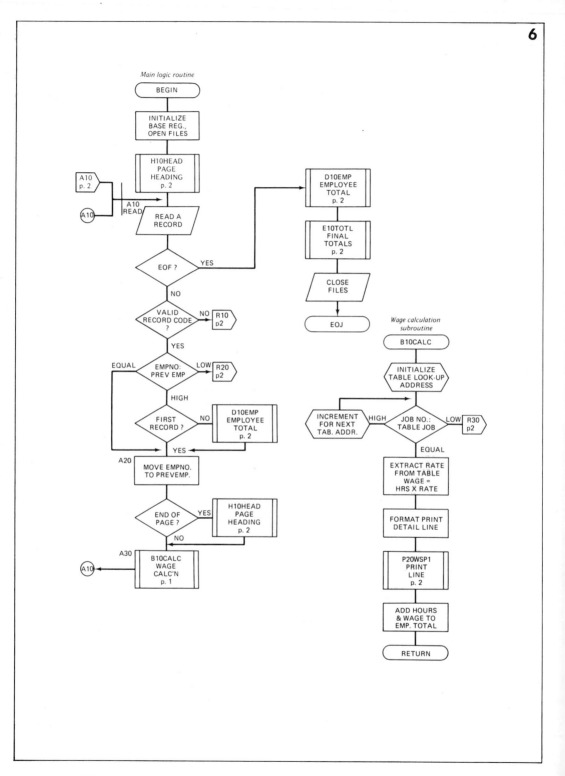

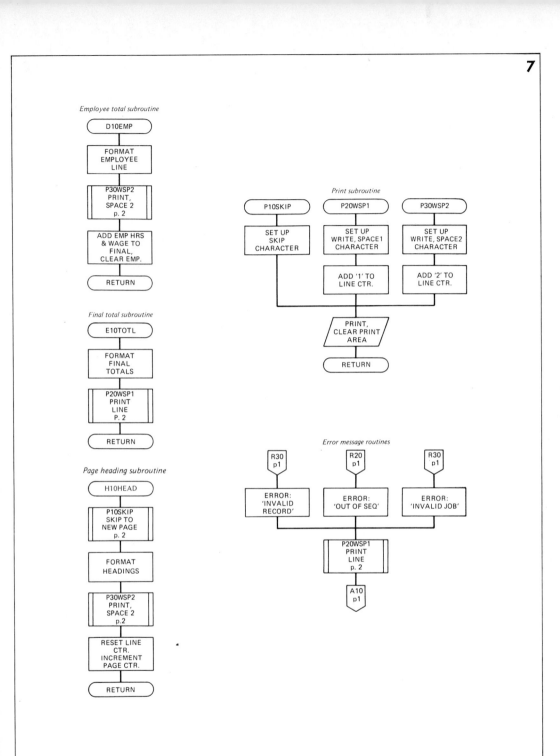

Employee total subroutine

(D10EMP)

FORMAT
EMPLOYEE
LINE

P30WSP2
PRINT,
SPACE 2
p. 2

ADD EMP HRS
& WAGE TO
FINAL,
CLEAR EMP.

(RETURN)

Final total subroutine

(E10TOTL)

FORMAT
FINAL
TOTALS

P20WSP1
PRINT
LINE
P. 2

(RETURN)

Page heading subroutine

(H10HEAD)

P10SKIP
SKIP TO
NEW PAGE
p. 2

FORMAT
HEADINGS

P30WSP2
PRINT,
SPACE 2
p.2

RESET LINE
CTR.
INCREMENT
PAGE CTR.

(RETURN)

Print subroutine

(P10SKIP)   (P20WSP1)   (P30WSP2)

SET UP
SKIP
CHARACTER

SET UP
WRITE, SPACE1
CHARACTER

SET UP
WRITE, SPACE2
CHARACTER

ADD '1' TO
LINE CTR.

ADD '2' TO
LINE CTR.

PRINT,
CLEAR PRINT
AREA

(RETURN)

Error message routines

R30 p1   R20 p1   R30 p1

ERROR:
'INVALID
RECORD'

ERROR:
'OUT OF SEQ'

ERROR:
'INVALID JOB'

P20WSP1
PRINT
LINE
p. 2

A10
p1

```
   4 ***      I N I T I A L I Z A T I O N

   6 PROG08   START 0
   7          BALR  3,0              INITIALIZE BASE REGISTER
   8          USING *,3
  10          OPEN  FILEIN,PRTR      ACTIVATE FILES
  19          BAL   7,H10HEAD        PRINT HEADING

  21 ***      M A I N   L O G I C

  23 A10READ  GET   FILEIN,INAREA    READ A RECORD
  29          CLC   CODEIN,=C'04'    VALID RECORD CODE?
  30          BNE   R10CODE                NO - ERROR

  32          CLC   EMPNOIN,PREVEMP  EMPLOYEE SEQUENCE?
  33          BE    A20                    EQU - PROCESS
  34          BL    R20SEQ                 LOW - ERROR
  35 *                                     HI  - NEW EMPLOYEE
  36          CLC   PREVEMP,LOVALUE  FIRST INPUT RECORD?
  37          BE    A20                    YES - BYPASS CTL BREAK
  38          BAL   7,D10EMP               NO  - PRINT EMPL TOTALS

  40 A20      CP    LINECTR,ENDPAGE  END OF PAGE?
  41          BL    A30                    NO
  42          BAL   7,H10HEAD              YES - PRINT HEADINGS

  44 A30      BAL   7,B10CALC        PERFORM CALCULATIONS
  45          B     A10READ

  47 ***      E N D - O F - F I L E

  49 A50END   BAL   7,D10EMP         EMPLOYEE TOTALS
  50 A60      BAL   7,E10TOTL        FINAL TOTALS
  52          CLOSE FILEIN,PRTR
  61          EOJ                    TERMINATE RUN


  65 **       CALCULATION OF WAGE - SUBROUTINE

  67 B10CALC  LA    9,JOBTAB         INIT. SEARCH FOR JOB RATE
  68 B20      CLC   JOBIN,0(9)       COMP JOB NO. TO TABLE ENTRY
  69          BL    R30JOB                 LOW - NOT IN TABLE
  70          BE    B30                    EQU - FOUND
  71          AH    9,=H'4'                HI  - INCREM. NEXT ADDRESS
  72          B     B20

  74 B30      ZAP   RATEPK,2(2,9)    EXTRACT RATE FROM TABLE
  75          PACK  HRSPK,HRSIN
  76          ZAP   WAGEPK,HRSPK     CALCULATE WAGE =
  77          MP    WAGEPK,RATEPK          HOURS X RATE
  78          SRP   WAGEPK,63,5            SHIFT & ROUND 1 DIGIT

  80          MVC   WAGEPR,EDAMT3    EDIT:
  81          ED    WAGEPR,WAGEPK+1        WAGE
  82          MVC   HOURSPR,EDHRS2
  83          ED    HOURSPR,HRSPK          HOURS
  84          MVC   RATEPR,EDRATE2
  85          ED    RATEPR,RATEPK          RATE
  86          MVC   JOBPR,JOBIN

  88          CLC   EMPNOIN,PREVEMP  IF NEW EMPLOYEE NO.
  89          BNE   B40                    OR
  90          CP    LINECTR,TOPAGE   IF TOP OF PAGE
  91          BNE   B50                    MOVE
  92 B40      MVC   NAMEPR,NAMEIN          NAME &
  93          MVC   EMPNOPR,EMPNOIN        EMPLOYEE NO. TO PRINT
```

```
 95 B50      MVC    PRINT,DETALINE
 96          BAL    8,P20WSP1              PRINT & SPACE 1
 97          MVC    DETALINE,BLANK        CLEAR PRINT AREA
 98          AP     EMPHRPK,HRSPK         ADD TOTAL HOURS & WAGES
 99          AP     EMPWGPK,WAGEPK            FOR EMPLOYEE
100          MVC    PREVEMP,EMPNOIN
101          BR     7


103 **          OUTPUT TOTAL HOURS & WAGES FOR EMPLOYEE - SUBROUTINE -

105 D10EMP    MVC    TOTWAGPR,EDAMT4       EDIT EMPLOYEE TOTALS:
106          ED     TOTWAGPR,EMPWGPK          WAGES
107          MVC    TOTHRSPR,EDHRS3
108          ED     TOTHRSPR,EMPHRPK         HOURS
109          MVC    PRINT,TOTALINE
110          BAL    8,P30WSP2             PRINT & SPACE 2

112          AP     TOTHRPK,EMPHRPK       ADD TO FINAL TOTAL HOURS
113          AP     TOTWGPK,EMPWGPK          & WAGES
114          ZAP    EMPHRPK,=P'0'         CLEAR EMPLOYEE HOURS
115          ZAP    EMPWGPK,=P'0'            & WAGES
116          BR     7                     BRANCH TO ADDR REG7-A20 OR A60


119 **          PRINT FINAL TOTALS - SUBROUTINE

121 E10TOTL   MVC    ASTERPR2(2),=C'**'
122          MVC    TOTWAGPR,EDAMT4       EDIT FINAL TOTAL:
123          ED     TOTWAGPR,TOTWGPK         WAGES
124          MVC    ASTERPR1(2),=C'**'
125          MVC    TOTHRSPR,EDHRS3
126          ED     TOTHRSPR,TOTHRPK         HOURS
127          MVC    PRINT,TOTALINE
128          BAL    8,P20WSP1             PRINT & SPACE 1
129          BR     7


131 **          PAGE HEADING SUB-ROUTINE

133 H10HEAD   BAL    8,P10SKIP            SKIP TO NEXT PAGE
134          MVC    PAGEPR,EDPAGE         SET UP HEADING LINE 1
135          ED     PAGEPR,PAGECTR
136          MVC    PRINT,HEADING1
137          BAL    8,P30WSP2             PRINT & SPACE 2

139          MVC    PRINT,HEADING2
140          BAL    8,P30WSP2             PRINT & SPACE 2
141          ZAP    LINECTR,TOPAGE        INITIALIZE LINE COUNT
142          AP     PAGECTR,=P'1'         INCREMENT PAGE NO.
143          BR     7                     RETURN


146 **          PRINT  SUBROUTINE

148 P10SKIP   MVI    CTLCHAR,SKIP         SKIP CHARACTER
149          B      P90

151 P20WSP1   MVI    CTLCHAR,WSP1         WRITE & SPACE CHARACTER
152          AP     LINECTR,=P'1'        ADD TO LINE COUNTER
153          B      P90

155 P30WSP2   MVI    CTLCHAR,WSP2         WRITE & DOUBLE-SPACE CHARACTER
156          AP     LINECTR,=P'2'        ADD TO LINE COUNTER

158 P90       PUT    PRTR,PRINT           PRINT
164          BR     8                     RETURN
```

```
166 SKIP      EQU    X'88'
167 WSP1      EQU    X'09'
168 WSP2      EQU    X'11'


171 **        ERROR  ROUTINES

173 R10CODE   MVC    DETALINE+60(L'ERRCODE),ERRCODE
174           B      R50

176 R20SEQ    MVC    DETALINE+60(L'ERRSEQ),ERRSEQ
177           B      R50

179 R30JCB    MVC    DETALINE+60(L'ERRJOB),ERRJOB

181 R50       MVC    EMPNOPR,EMPNOIN
182           MVC    NAMEPR,NAMEIN
183           MVC    PRINT,DETALINE
184           BAL    8,P20WSP1               PRINT ERROR MESSAGE
185           MVC    DETALINE,BLANK
186           B      A10READ


188 *         D E C L A R A T I V E S

190 FILEIN    DTFCD  BLKSIZE=80,             DEFINE INPUT FILE      +
                     DEVADDR=SYSIPT,                                +
                     DEVICE=1442,                                   +
                     EOFADDR=A50ENC,                                +
                     IOAREA1=INBUFF1,                               +
                     IOAREA2=INBUFF2,                               +
                     TYPEFLE=INPUT,                                 +
                     WORKA=YES

212 INBUFF1   DC     CL80' '                 INPUT BUFFER-1
213 INBUFF2   DC     CL80' '                 INPUT BUFFER-2

215 INAREA    DS     0CL80                   INPUT AREA
216 CODEIN    DS     CL2              *      RECORD CODE
217 EMPNOIN   DS     CL5              *      EMPLOYEE NO.
218 NAMEIN    DS     CL15             *      EMPLOYEE NAME
219 JOBIN     DS     CL2              *      JOB NO.
220 HRSIN     DS     CL3              *      HOURS WORKED (XX.X)
221           DS     CL53             *      UNUSED

223 PRTR      DTFPR  BLKSIZE=133,            DEFINE PRINTER FILE    +
                     CTLCHR=YES,                                    +
                     DEVADDR=SYSLST,                                +
                     DEVICE=1403,                                   +
                     IOAREA1=PRBUFF1,                               +
                     IOAREA2=PRBUFF2,                               +
                     WORKA=YES

245 PRBUFF1   DC     CL133' '                PRINTER BUFFER-1
246 PRBUFF2   DC     CL133' '                PRINTER BUFFER-2

248 PRINT     DS     0CL133                  PRINT OUTPUT AREA
249 CTLCHAR   DS     CL1                     PRINT CTL CHARACTER
250           DC     CL132' '         *

252 HEADING1  DS     0CL133                  1ST HEADING LINE
253           DC     CL23' '
254           DC     CL48'W E E K L Y   W A G E   R E P O R T'
255           DC     CL5'PAGE'
256 PAGEPR    DS     ZL4
257           DC     CL53' '
```

```
259 HEADING2 DS      OCL133                    2ND HEADING LINE
260          DC      CL13' '
261          DC      CL26'EMPLOYEE   NAME'
262          DC      CL94'JOB    RATE   HOURS         WAGE'

264 BLANK    DC      C' '                      BLANK TO CLEAR PRINT AREA
265 DETALINE DS      OCL133                    EMPLOYEE DETAIL PRINT LINE
266          DC      CL15' '
267 EMPNOPR  DS      CL5
268          DC      CL3' '
269 NAMEPR   DS      CL15
270          DC      CL2' '
271 JOBPR    DS      CL2
272          DC      CL2' '
273 RATEPR   DS      ZL5
274          DC      CL2' '
275 HOURSPR  DS      ZL6
276          DC      CL6' '
277 WAGEPR   DS      ZL9
278          DC      CL61' '

280 TOTALINE DS      OCL133                    TOTAL WAGE PRINT LINE
281          DC      CL48' '
282 TOTHRSPR DS      ZL9
283 ASTERPR1 DC      CL3'*'
284 TOTWAGPR DS      ZL12
285 ASTERPR2 DC      CL61'*'

287 ERRCODE  DC      C'INVALID RECORD CODE'
288 ERRJOB   DC      C'JOB NO. NOT IN TABLE'
289 ERRSEQ   DC      C'RECORD OUT OF SEQUENCE'
290 PREVEMP  DC      XL5'00'
291 LOVALUE  DC      XL5'00'
292 *                                          PACKED DECLARATIVES:
293 HRSPK    DC      PL2'0'                    |XX|.XC|
294 RATEPK   DC      PL2'0'                    |X.X|XC|
295 WAGEPK   DC      PL4'0'
296 EMPHRPK  DC      PL3'0'
297 EMPWGPK  DC      PL4'0'
298 TOTHRPK  DC      PL3'0'
299 TOTWGPK  DC      PL4'0'
300 LINECTR  DC      PL2'0'
301 PAGECTR  DC      PL2'1'
302 TOPAGE   DC      P'5'
303 ENDPAGE  DC      P'40'
304 *                                          EDIT WORDS:
305 EDPAGE   DC      X'40202020'
306 EDHRS2   DC      X'4020214B2060'
307 EDRATE2  DC      X'40204B2020'
308 EDAMT3   DC      X'40202021482020C3D9'
309 EDHRS3   DC      X'40206B2020214B20605C5C'
310 EDAMT4   DC      X'40202068202021482020C3D95C5C'

312 JOBTAB   DC      C'01',P'7.25'             TABLE OF JOB NOS. & RATES
313          DC      C'02',P'6.15'             *
314          DC      C'04',P'7.45'             *
315          DC      C'05',P'8.55'             *
316          DC      C'06',P'7.50'             *
317          DC      C'08',P'9.25'             *
318          DC      C'10',P'8.95'             *
319          DC      X'FFFF',P'0.00'           * END OF TABLE

             END     PROG08
```

RUN #1

VALID TEST INPUT DATA

04 1 1 1 1 1 ANDERSON	04 105	
04 1 1 1 1 1 ANDERSON	01 215	
04 1 1 1 1 1 ANDERSON	01 315	
04 1 1 1 1 1 ANDERSON	01 105	
04 1 1 1 1 1 ANDERSON	04 105	
04 2 2 2 2 2 BROWN	02 400	
04 2 2 2 2 2 BROWN	02 500	
04 2 2 2 3 3 CARPENTER	01 999	neg.
04 2 2 2 3 3 CARPENTER	04 010	hrs.
04 2 2 2 3 3 CARPENTER	02 250	
04 2 2 2 3 5 DIXON	02 400	
04 2 2 2 4 0 EMMETT	01 150	
04 2 2 2 4 0 EMMETT	01 150	
04 2 2 2 4 0 EMMETT	04 050	
04 2 2 3 0 1 FLANDERS	01 255	
04 2 2 3 0 1 FLANDERS	01 255	
04 2 2 3 0 1 FLANDERS	01 050	
04 2 2 3 5 5 GAROWSKI	04 015	
04 2 2 3 5 5 GAROWSKI	04 015	
04 2 2 3 5 5 GAROWSKI	04 015	
04 2 2 3 6 0 HENDERSON	02 080	
04 2 2 3 6 0 HENDERSON	02 080	
04 2 2 3 6 0 HENDERSON	02 080	
04 2 2 3 6 0 HENDERSON	02 080	
04 2 2 3 6 0 HENDERSON	02 080	

Total hours   473.9

Expected results:

Employee 22233:

Job 01   7.25 x
Hours   99.9
         724.28 *

Job 04   7.45-x
Hours   01.0
         7.45-*

Job 02   6.15 x
Hours   25.0
         153.75 *

Total   724.28
wages   7.45-
         153.75
         870.58 *

Employee 22360:
Job 02   6.15 x
Hours   8.0
         49.20 *

Total   49.20 x
wages   5
         246.00 *

RUN #2

INVALID TEST INPUT DATA

04 1 1 1 1 1 ANDERSON	04 105	
04 1 1 1 1 1 ANDERSON	01 215	
04 1 1 1 1 1 ANDERSON	01 315	
04 1 1 1 1 1 ANDERSON	01 105	
04 1 1 1 1 1 ANDERSON	04 105	
04 2 2 2 2 2 BROWN	02 400	
03 2 2 2 2 2 BROWN	02 500	INVALID CODE
04 2 2 2 2 2 BROWN	02 500	
04 2 2 2 2 2 BROWN	03 200	INVALID JOB
04 1 1 1 1 1 ANDERSON	04 105	OUT-OF-SEQUENCE
04 2 2 2 2 2 BROWN	02 400	

Code Emp.# Name   Job Hours

<u>OUTPUT RUN #1</u>   W E E K L Y   W A G E   R E P O R T   PAGE   1

EMPLOYEE	NAME	JOB	RATE	HOURS	WAGE	
11111	ANDERSON	04	7.45	10.5	78.23	
		01	7.25	21.5	155.88	
		01	7.25	31.5	228.38	
		01	7.25	10.5	76.13	
		04	7.45	10.5	78.23	
				84.5 *	616.85	*
22222	BROWN	02	6.15	40.0	246.00	
		02	6.15	50.0	307.50	
				90.0 *	553.50	*
22233	CARPENTER	01	7.25	99.9	724.28	
		04	7.45	1.0-	7.45CR	
		02	6.15	25.0	153.75	
				123.9 *	870.58	*
22235	DIXON	02	6.15	40.0	246.00	
				40.0 *	246.00	*
22240	EMMETT	01	7.25	15.0	108.75	
		01	7.25	15.0	108.75	
		04	7.45	5.0	37.25	
				35.0 *	254.75	*
22301	FLANDERS	01	7.25	25.5	184.88	
		01	7.25	25.5	184.88	
		01	7.25	5.0	36.25	
				56.0 *	406.01	*
22355	GAROWSKI	04	7.45	1.5	11.18	
		04	7.45	1.5	11.18	
		04	7.45	1.5	11.18	
				4.5 *	33.54	*
22360	HENDERSON	02	6.15	8.0	49.20	

Agrees with expected results for Emp. 22233 (annotation beside CARPENTER rows)

- -

          W E E K L Y   W A G E   R E P O R T   PAGE   2

EMPLOYEE	NAME	JOB	RATE	HOURS	WAGE	
22360	HENDERSON	02	6.15	8.0	49.20	
		02	6.15	8.0	49.20	
		02	6.15	8.0	49.20	
		02	6.15	8.0	49.20	
				40.0 *	246.00	*

Agrees with expected results for Emp. 22360 (annotation beside HENDERSON rows)

Agrees with "Total Hrs" in expected results → (473.9) ** (3,227.23) ** *Total checked*

_____

<u>OUTPUT RUN #2</u>   W E E K L Y   W A G E   R E P O R T   PAGE   1

EMPLOYEE	NAME	JOB	RATE	HOURS	WAGE	
11111	ANDERSON	04	7.45	10.5	78.23	
		01	7.25	21.5	155.88	
		01	7.25	31.5	228.38	
		01	7.25	10.5	76.13	
		04	7.45	10.5	78.23	
				84.5 *	616.85	*
22222	BROWN	02	6.15	40.0	246.00	
22222	BROWN				INVALID RECORD CODE	
		02	6.15	50.0	307.50	
22222	BROWN				JOB NO. NOT IN TABLE	
11111	ANDERSON				RECORD OUT OF SEQUENCE	
		02	6.15	40.0	246.00	
				130.0 *	799.50	*
				214.5 **	1,416.35	**

DEBUGGING TIPS

"Preventative programming" can minimize the bugs in the program. A recommended approach is to organize the program into logical segments—a main logic routine to handle input processing, and various subroutines, each containing related processing. With such an approach, we are more likely to keep a firm grip on the logic, and can more readily locate execution bugs.

When using subroutines, be especially careful in the use of registers. If all subroutines are at the same "level", then the main logic could link to every subroutine using the same register, as:

```
BAL   9,subroutine
```

Sometimes, however, it is necessary to link from one subroutine to another. In large programs, the linkage can become complex and confusing. Doublecheck the linkage, and ensure that the return register is the correct one.

PROBLEMS

8-1. Three programming objectives are accuracy, efficiency and clarity. Discuss the significance of each objective.

8-2. What are the advantages (if any) of organizing a program into subroutines?

8-3. Consider the following code. Is there a bug? If so, explain.

```
BALR  3,0
USING *,3
  .
  .

BAL   3,P10PAGE            P10PAGE ·
                                     .
                                     .
                            BR  3
```

8-4. Consider the following code. If there is a bug, explain.

```
BALR  3,0
USING *,3
  .
  .

BAL   5,P10PAGE            P10PAGE ·
                                     .
                            BR  3
```

8-5. What are the features of "structured programming" that can be applied to Assembler programs?

8-6. What are the purposes (if any) of program documentation?

8-7. Revise a previous program, organizing it into a main logic routine and various subroutines, each containing related processing, in a logical sequence.

PART III

BINARY OPERATIONS

CHAPTER 9

REGISTERS AND BINARY PROGRAMMING

Chapter 6 introduced registers and their use in base addressing. The registers may also perform binary arithmetic and manipulate data in binary format. Indeed, binary arithmetic is done only in the general registers, and conversely the registers perform arithmetic only in binary format. This chapter covers basic binary and register operations: first, defining of binary data and then the instructions for binary arithmetic. Binary data may enter the program from sources such as:

— Defined in storage as a constant, as binary (B-type), fullword (F-type), and halfword (H-type).
— Generated in a register by such operations as CVB, LA, BAL, EDMK.
— Received from external input such as disk or tape where the data was written in binary format.

Although processing binary data in registers is extremely fast, there may be additional steps converting data from character input to packed and to binary, and then into printable format: binary to packed to edited character. Binary format does have useful applications, however, especially in manipulating addresses for table searching, as covered in the next chapter.

BINARY DATA REPRESENTATION

Binary numbers, whether defined in storage by constants of types B, F, and H, or used in the general registers, have the following features:

1. For reference, bits are numbered from left to right, with the leftmost bit numbered zero:

> Binary value: 00000000
> Position: 01234567 etc.

2. The sign is the leftmost bit, position zero: a 0-bit indicates a positive value, and a 1-bit indicates negative. A zero value is always positive.

3. The rules of binary addition are:

$$0 + 0 = 0 \qquad 1 + 1 = 10$$
$$0 + 1 = 1 \quad 1 + 1 + 1 = 11$$

For simplicity, the following examples of decimal and binary addition assume 5-bit fields, with the leftmost bit the sign:

DEC	BINARY	DEC	BINARY	DEC	BINARY
4	0 0100	7	0 0111	7	0 0111
+2	0 0010	+2	0 0010	+7	0 0111
6	0 0110	9	0 1001	14	0 1110

4. Negative numbers are expressed in what is called *two's complement* form. To obtain a negative binary number, reverse all the bits of its positive value (a 0-bit becomes 1, and a 1-bit becomes 0), then add 1. The same procedure converts negative values to positive values. For example, what is the binary representation of −7, assuming a 5-bit field?:

> Decimal value 7 = 0 0111
> Reverse bits   = 1 1000
> Add 1   = 1 1001   (two's complement representation of −7)
>   ↑
>   *sign bit*

5. For subtraction, the field being subtracted is converted to its two's complement, and then added:

> Decimal value 7   0 0111   0 0111
> Subtract   −5 = −0 0101 = 1 1011   (add two's complement of 5)
> Result   2   0 0010   (binary value 2)

Note that there is a *carry into and out of* the sign position. Where there is both a carry into and out of the sign bit, the result is correct, not an overflow.

6. *Invalid overflows* occur on the following conditions:

    a. Overflow caused by carry into the sign position:

Decimal value	9	0 1001
Add	+9 =	0 1001
Result	18	1 0010

    (negative value, minus 14)

    There is a carry into the sign position, and none out of it. The sum is an incorrect negative value. (To determine the value of 1 0010, reverse the bits (0 1101), then add '1' (0 1110). Since this value is +14, then 1 0010 has a value of −14, but was supposed to be +18.)

    b. Overflow caused by carry out of the sign position:

Decimal value	−9	1 0111
Add	+(−9) =	1 0111
Result	−18	0 1110

    (positive value, plus 14)

    There is no carry into the sign position but one out of it. The sum is an incorrect positive value, +14 instead of −18.

Problem 9-1 should now be done.

BINARY CONSTANTS

Both DS and DC may define a binary field. There are three types: B (ordinary binary), F (fullword fixed-point), and H (halfword fixed-point). The following sections describe DC's; DS statements are written similarly except that the constant is optional and acts as a comment.

BINARY CONSTANT—B. Type B constants contain binary ones and zeros. A common use is for immediate operands for instructions such as NI, OI, XI, and TM, covered in a later chapter. Although the format has some specialized uses, its use is limited by the fact that the binary instruction set is designed to work better with F and H formats.

NAME	OPERATION	OPERAND
[symbol]	DC	dBLn'constant'

Optional: d = duplication factor.
Required: B specifying binary constant.

Optional: Ln = length of the field in bytes, maximum 256.

Required: 'constant,' containing ones and zeros. If the length of the defined constant is different from the specified length (Ln), the Assembler pads or truncates the constant on the left.

Example B-format declaratives:

			LENGTH IN BYTES	ASSEMBLED AS		DECIMAL VALUE
BIN1	DC	B'00010011'	1	00010011		19
BIN2	DC	BL1'110'	1	00000110		6
BIN3	DC	BL2'100010011'	2	00000001	00010011	275

BINARY (FIXED-POINT) CONSTANTS—F AND H.   Fixed-point constants are commonly used in register arithmetic.

NAME	OPERATION	OPERAND	
[symbol]	DC	dF'constant'	(Fullword)
		dH'constant'	(Halfword)

Optional: d = duplication factor.

Required: Type: F = Fullword (4 bytes) and H = Halfword (2 bytes). For F-type, the Assembler generates a binary constant in a 4-byte field, aligned on a *fullword boundary* (a storage address evenly divisible by four). For H-types, the Assembler generates a 2-byte constant aligned on a *halfword boundary* (a storage address evenly divisible by two). These are the normal required formats for binary arithmetic.

Required: 'constant', containing a *decimal number* which the Assembler converts to a binary number. If the length of the constant is greater than the explicit or implicit length, the Assembler truncates it on the left.

With bit 0 (the leftmost bit) as the sign, maximum and minimum values are:

	BITS	MAXIMUM	MINIMUM
Halfword	16	$2^{15}-1 = 32,767$	$-2^{15} = -32,768$
Fullword	32	$2^{31}-1 = 2,147,483,647$	$-2^{31} = -2,147,483,648$

Figure 9-1 depicts Fullword and Halfword declaratives.

BINVAL1 is a DS that simply causes the location counter to align on a fullword boundary. (Check the hex address for the statement.)

BINVAL2 defines a 2-byte field aligned on a halfword boundary.

```
                        24 *    -------------------------------------
                        25 *    DS & DC FULLWORD & HALFWORD DECLARES
                        26 *    -------------------------------------
003834                  27 BINVAL1  DS   0F        SETS LOC'N CONTER TO FULLWORD ADDR.
003834                  28 BINVAL2  DS   H         A HALFWORD AREA
003838                  29 BINVAL3  DS   3F        3 FULLWORD AREAS
003844 0019             30 BINVAL4  DC   H'25'     A HALFWORD WITH POSITIVE VALUE
003846 0000
003848 FFFFFFFB         31 BINVAL5  DC   F'-5'     A FULLWORD WITH NEGATIVE VALUE
00384C 8001             32 BINVAL6  DC   H'32769'  CONSTANT EXCEEDS MAXIMUM 32767
          *** ERROR ***
```

FIGURE 9-1   Defining Fullword and Halfword constants.

BINVAL3 defines three adjacent fullwords; a reference to the name BINVAL3 is to the first fullword.

BINVAL4 is a halfword that defines the decimal value 25. The Assembler converts 25 to a binary value 00011001, shown in object code on the left as X'19'.

BINVAL5 defines a fullword containing −5. Note the two's complement of 5 in object code. Try converting binary +5 (00000101): flip the bits (11111010), add '1' (11111011), which equals X'FB'.

BINVAL6 depicts an error in coding: the halfword defines a value exceeding 32,767. The Assembler generates an error message and truncates the leftmost bits changing the value of the field. In terms of dollars and cents, the maximum halfword value is $327.67, a trivial amount in many computer problems, and is easily exceeded.

There may be occasions when it is necessary to define a binary H or F field without the Assembler's alignment. One case occurs when an input or output record for tape or disk contains a binary field. Consider the following input record:

```
LOC
8420   RECORDIN   DS   0CL29
8420   ACCTIN     DS   CL5
8428   AMTIN      DS   F      (F-format causes alignment here)
842C   NAMEIN     DS   CL20
```

In the example, the Assembler location counter for ACCTIN is at X'8420'. Since it is a 5-byte field, the next field (AMTIN) would normally begin at 8425. But AMTIN is defined as DS F, so the Assembler aligns its address on a fullword boundary following: 8428. There are now three "slack" bytes between the two fields, causing the record to be defined with 32 bytes instead of the expected 29. Unfortunately, an input operation would read the 29-byte record byte-for-byte beginning at RECORD-IN. The first three bytes of the binary amount will be in the slack bytes, and the program will reference incorrect data in AMTIN and NAMEIN.

A simple remedy is to code the binary fullword as FL4 rather than F. If a fullword or halfword declarative contains a length (Ln), the Assembler does not align the field.

ADDRESS CONSTANTS—A.   It is often necessary to define the address of a declarative or of an instruction. For example, BALR initializes the first base register. Address constants may be used to initialize additional base registers. Of the four types of address constants, this chapter discusses only the common A-format.

NAME	OPERATION	OPERAND
[symbol]	DC	A(address-1,address-2, . . .,address-n)

The rules for A-type constants are:

1. The address constant is enclosed within brackets. We may define more than one address, each separated by a comma. The constant may be either an absolute value (rarely used) or a symbolic name.
2. The Assembler generates a fullword constant, aligned on a fullword boundary (provided no length indication is coded). The constant is right-adjusted in the field. The maximum value is $2^{31}-1$ (the highest fullword value).

Figure 9-2 gives a number of examples. (At A10, the LM instruction loads the three addresses into registers 4, 5, and 6. A later section describes this way to initialize base registers.)

ADDRESS1 depicts an address constant with an absolute value. Absolute addresses are rarely defined, since we do not normally know where the Assembler assigns addresses or where the program resides for execution.

ADDRESS2 defines the address of DECLAR. The object code hex value generated by the statement (X'3806'), is the same as the hex address of DECLAR.

ADDRESS3 defines the address of A10. Compare the object code address constant with that of the actual address of A10.

```
                          4  *         -----------------------
                          5  *         DC    ADDRESS CONSTANTS
                          6  *         -----------------------
003800 0530               7  BEGIN     BALR  3,0                         INITIALIZE BASE REGISTER 3
                          8            USING *,3,4,5,6                    ASSIGN BASE REGISTERS
003802 9846 3026          9  A10       LM    4,6,ADDRESS5                 LOAD REGISTERS 4, 5, 6
                         10  *           .
                         11  *           .
003806 C1C4C4D9C5E2F240  12  DECLAR    DC    C'ADDRESS CONSTANTS'
00380F C3D6D5E2F3C1D5E3
003816 E2
003817 00
003818 00004E20          13  ADDRESS1  DC    A(20000)                    ADDRESS OF 20000
00381C 00003806          14  ADDRESS2  DC    A(DECLAR)                   ADDRESS OF DECLAR
003820 00003802          15  ADDRESS3  DC    A(A10)                      ADDRESS OF A10
003824 00004802          16  ADDRESS4  DC    A(A10+4096)                 ADDRESS OF A10 + X'1000'
003828 0000480200005802  17  ADDRESS5  DC    A(A10+4096,A10+2*4096,A10+3*4096) A10+X'1000',
003830 00006802
                         18  *                                           A10+X'2000', A10+X'3000'
```

FIGURE 9-2   Defining address constants.

ADDRESS4 illustrates a relative address, A10+4096. The Assembler converts the decimal value 4096 to X'1000'. Therefore, the object code address is X'3802' + X'1000', or X'4802'.

ADDRESS5 illustrates three address constants, separated by commas. Note the use of Assembler arithmetic: 2*4096 = 8192.

> *Note on Alignment:*   On the 360, instructions such as CVB and CVD require doubleword alignment; L, A, C, M, and D require fullword alignment; and those like LH, AH, and CH require halfword alignment. The purpose, especially on larger models, was to ensure faster processing of binary operations. On the 370, such alignment is not necessary—operand-2 of these instructions need not reference an aligned storage location during execution. However, if the instructions are aligned, they will require fewer machine cycles and will execute faster. This text therefore recommends providing for alignment on the 370. (On the 370, only channel command words and operands of certain privileged instructions must align on integral boundaries.)

CONVERSION OF DECIMAL AND BINARY DATA—CVB AND CVD

Convert to Binary, CVB, converts packed decimal data in storage into binary in a register. The packed data must be contained in a *doubleword* field (8 bytes), aligned on a doubleword boundary (evenly divisible by eight). For this purpose, the definition DS D is often conveniently used. (A D-type DC normally defines floating-point values, but a DS may store data in any format.) Similarly, Convert to Decimal, CVD, converts binary data in a register into packed decimal in storage, also defined as a doubleword.

NAME	OPERATION	OPERAND
[symbol]	CVB	R1,X2 or R1,D2(X2,B2)
[symbol]	CVD	R1,X2 or R1,D2(X2,B2)

For both operations, operand-1 specifies a general register, and operand-2 references a storage location defined as a doubleword, aligned, containing packed data. Note a significant difference. CVB converts data from operand-2 (storage) to operand-1 (a register); CVD converts data from operand-1 (a register) to operand-2 (storage). We can use CVB to convert packed to binary in a register, perform binary arithmetic, use CVD to convert back to packed, and then edit for printing.

In Figure 9-3, the packed field, AMTPK, is moved to a doubleword field, DBLWD1. CVB converts the packed contents of DBLWD1 into binary format in register-6. CVD converts the binary contents of register-6 into packed format in a doubleword, DBLWD2.

```
              37 *        -------------------------
              38 *        CVB    CONVERT TO BINARY
              39 *        -------------------------
00384E F871 305E  40        ZAP    DBLWD1,AMTPK          MOVE TO DOUBLE WORD
003854 4F60 305E  41        CVB    6,DBLWD1             CONVERT DBLWD1 TO BINARY

              43 *        --------------------------------
              44 *        CVD    CONVERT TO PACKED DECIMAL
              45 *        --------------------------------
003858 4E60 3066  46        CVD    6,DBLWD2             CONVERT BINARY TO PACKED
              47 *        •
              48 *        •
              49 *        •
00385C 125C       50  AMTPK   DC    P'125'
003860            51  DBLWD1  DS    D                   ALIGNED DOUBLEWORD
003868            52  DBLWD2  DS    D                   ALIGNED DOUBLEWORD
```

FIGURE 9-3   Conversion of packed and binary data: CVB, CVD.

LOADING REGISTERS—L, LH, LR, LM, LA

To load binary fullwords and halfwords in registers, we use load operations. The most common load instructions are L (Load Fullword), LH (Load Halfword), LR (Load Register), LM (Load Multiple), and LA (Load Address). These do not set the condition code. The next section gives a number of less-used Load operations: LCR, LNR, LPR, and LTR.

NAME	OPERATION	OPERAND
[symbol]	L	R1,X2 or R1,D2(X2,B2)
	LH	R1,X2 or R1,D2(X2,B2)
	LR	R1,R2
	LM	R1,R3,S2 or R1,R3,D2(B2)
	LA	R1,X2 or R1,D2(X2,B2)

LOAD FULLWORD—L.   The L operation loads a binary fullword value into a register. The rules are:

1. Operand-1 specifies any general register.
2. Operand-2 references a fullword in storage, aligned on a fullword boundary. Typically we use a declarative or literal with F-format.
3. The contents of the fullword are loaded into the register, replacing the previous contents.

   Figure 9-4 illustrates four L operations, under LOADFULL. The first loads a fullword literal into register-2. (The Assembler aligns H and F literals the same as declaratives.) The second example loads the fullword FULWRD1 into register-8. The third depicts a coding error: operand-2 is a halfword literal rather than a fullword. (The Assembler does not generate an error message, even if the literal is not a fullword. The error occurs at execute-time, when the computer loads the halfword plus the following two bytes.) The fourth example loads a literal address constant into register-5.

LOAD HALFWORD—LH.   LH is similar to L, with the following differences:

1. Operand-2 specifies a halfword aligned on a halfword storage boundary. LH loads its contents into the operand-2 register.
2. LH expands the halfword to a fullword by propagating the sign-bit through the 16 leftmost positions, in the register. If the halfword is negative, LH fills 1-bits to the left, maintaining the correct two's complement value.

Figure 9-4 depicts LH under LOADHALF. The first example loads a halfword literal into register-9. The second loads a halfword constant into register-0. The third example illustrates a coding error: operand-2 is a fullword rather than a halfword. Again the Assembler does not generate an error message. At execute-time LH loads only the leftmost two bytes of the fullword into register-8, causing an error that may be difficult to locate.

LOAD REGISTER—LR.   Both operands reference a register. LR loads the contents of the register specified by operand-2 into the operand-1 register. Figure 9-4 illustrates the LR operation under LOADREG. First an L instruction loads a fullword into register-8. Then LR loads the contents of register-8 into register-7.

LOAD MULTIPLE—LM.   LM can load more than one register in one operation. LM is an RS-format instruction, with three operands. The rules are:

1. Operands 1 and 2 each specify a register. They represent a *span* of registers. That is, 8,10 means registers 8 through 10, or 8, 9, and 10.
2. Operand-3 references a fullword address in storage, the first of a number of adjacent fullword values—one for each register that LM is to load successively into the designated registers.

Figure 9-4 illustrates LM under LOADMULT. The first example loads registers 6, 7, and 8 with FULWRD1, FULWRD2, and FULWRD3 respectively. The second example shows how the registers may "wrap around". Because registers 15 through 1 are referenced, LM loads registers 15, 0, and 1 with the fullwords.

LM has two common uses. One is to restore registers that were saved when the program links to a subprogram (covered in Chapter 15). The other use is in base register initialization. We have used BALR to initialize the first base register. LM may load subsequent registers with base addresses, although LM is restricted to sequential register loading. Figure 9-2 gave an example of the use of LM to load base registers 4, 5, and 6. But watch out—after the BALR only base register-3 is initialized, and the LM will execute correctly only if the constant ADDRESS5 is defined within the first 4K of the program.

```
                         55  *        -----------------------
                         56  *        L      LOAD FULLWORD          DECIMAL
                         57  *        -----------------------  REG:   VALUE
003870  5820 31A6        58  LOADFULL L      2,=F'123456'      2:    123456
003874  5880 309A        59           L      8,FULWRD1         8:    6936
003878  5810 31AE        60           L      1,=H'287'         ERROR: OP-2 SHOULD BE FULLWORD
00387C  5850 31AA        61           L      5,=A(TABLE)       5: ADDRESS OF TABLE


                         63  *        ---------------------
                         64  *        LH     LOAD HALFWORD
                         65  *        ---------------------
003880  4890 31B0        66  LOADHALF LH     9,=H'500'         9:     0500
003884  4800 3098        67           LH     0,HALFWRD1        0:     0595
003888  4880 309A        68           LH     8,FULWRD1         ERROR: OP-2 SHOULD BE HALFWORD


                         70  *        ---------------------
                         71  *        LR     LOAD REGISTER
                         72  *        ---------------------
00388C  5880 309E        73  LOADREG  L      8,FULWRD2         8:     4174
003890  1878             74           LR     7,8               7:     4174


                         76  *        ---------------------
                         77  *        LM     LOAD MULTIPLE
                         78  *        ---------------------
                         79  LOADMULT LM     6,8,FULWRD1       6:     6936    7:     4174
003892  9868 309A                                             8:     5637
                         80           LM     15,1,FULWRD1     15:     6936    0:     4174
003896  98F1 309A                                             1:     5637

00389A  0253             82  HALFWRD1 DC     H'595'
00389C  00001B18         83  FULWRD1  DC     F'6936'
0038A0  0000104E         84  FULWRD2  DC     F'4174'
0038A4  00001605         85  FULWRD3  DC     F'5637'
0038A8                   86  TABLE    DS     50CL5
0039A8                   87           LTORG
0039A8  0001E240         88                  =F'123456'
0039AC  000038A8         89                  =A(TABLE)
0039B0  011F             90                  =H'287'
0039B2  01F4             91                  =H'500'
```

FIGURE 9-4   Load register operations: L, LH, LR, LM.

LOAD ADDRESS—LA.   Load Address is a convenient RX instruction to load base registers and to initialize an address in a register for table look-up. The rules are:

1. Operand-1 specifies any general register.
2. Operand-2 contains a storage address of the form D2(X2,B2).
3. LA loads the operand-2 address into bits 8–31 of the operand-1 register and clears bits 0-7 to zero. The 24 bits used give a maximum address of $2^{24}-1$.

The following illustrates several uses of LA:

1. **LA 9,A10**: Assume A10 is subject to base register-3 containing X'4200' with a displacement of X'0660'. The object code instruction is

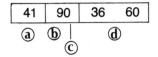

ⓐ The machine language code for LA is X'41'.
ⓑ The operand-1 register is 9.
ⓒ There is no index register signified.
ⓓ The base register is 3 and displacement is 660.
The instruction adds the contents of the base register (X'4200') plus the displacement (X'0660'). The sum X'004860', the address of A10, is loaded into register-9.

2. **LA 9,5(0,0)**: This example illustrates explicit use of base/displacement. (The next chapter covers this practice more fully.) The object code instruction is ⎡41│90│00│05⎤ —assume no base register, no index register, but load the displacement X'005' into register-9. In effect, the value 5 loads into register-9. *Note:* The 5 is a displacement, not a register.

3. **LA 9,5**: The Assembler treats operand-2 as if it were coded like example-2:5(0,0). This is a convenient way to load a value into a register, up to a maximum displacement of 4095.

4. **LA 9,1(0,9)**: The generated object code is ⎡41│90│90│01⎤ —load the contents of "base" register-9 plus a displacement of 001 into register-9. In effect, the contents of register-9 are incremented by 1. This method of adding to a register, although efficient, works only for increments up to 4095 (the maximum displacement), and only if the value in the register is positive and does not exceed 24 bits (because LA clears bits 0–7 to zero).

Figure 9-5 illustrates an efficient way to load additional base registers by means of the index register feature. The program is assumed to load at X'4800'. BALR loads register-3 with X'4802'. We now want to load registers 4, 5, and 6 with each base address successively containing X'5802', X'6802' and X'7802'. We first load 2048 or X'0800' into register-6. We then load register-4 with:

Contents of base register-3	X'4802'
Contents of index register-6	X'0800'
Displacement	X'0800'
Total generated address	X'5802'

					REG-3	REG-4	REG-5	REG-6
004800			2	START X'4800'				
			3 *		-----	-----	-----	-----
			4 *					
004800	0530		5	BALR 3,0	4802			
004802			6	USING *,3,4,5,6				
004802	4160	0800	7	LA 6,2048	4802			0800
004806	4146	3800	8	LA 4,2048(6,3)	4802	5802		0800
00480A	4156	4800	9	LA 5,2048(6,4)	4802	5802	6802	0800
00480E	4166	5800	10	LA 6,2048(6,5)	4802	5802	6802	7802

FIGURE 9-5   Initialization of four base registers with LA.

(In hex, 800 + 800 = 1000.) Check the generated object code for each LA operation. Registers 5 and 6 are loaded accordingly.

> *Note:*   LA is a "logical" instruction (like MVC and CLC) that treats data as unsigned.

OTHER LOAD OPERATIONS—LCR, LNR, LPR, LTR.   There may be occasional use for these load register (RR) instructions. Each sets the condition code.

LOAD COMPLEMENT—LCR.   LCR loads the contents of the operand-2 register (R2) into the operand-1 register (R1), and reverses the sign.

LCR 5,8   Load the contents of register-8 into register-5, reverse the sign, and set the condition code.

LOAD NEGATIVE—LNR.   LNR loads the contents of R2 into R1 and sets the value to negative. The condition code is set to 0 (zero) or 1 (nonzero minus).

LNR 5,5   Load the contents of register-5 into register-5, force a negative sign, and set the condition code.

LOAD POSITIVE—LPR.   LPR loads the contents of R2 into R1 and sets the value to positive. The condition code is set to 0 (zero) or 2 (nonzero plus).

LPR 9,7   Load the contents of register-7 into register-9, force a positive sign, and set the condition code.

LOAD AND TEST—LTR.   LTR loads the contents of R2 into R1, just as LR, but in addition sets the condition code for zero, minus, and plus.

LTR 4,4   Load the contents of register-4 into register-4 and set the condition code. This example sets the condition code only, a useful technique to test a register's contents for sign.

STORE REGISTER OPERATIONS—ST, STH, STM

We use store operations to store or "save" the contents of registers. A large program may require the use of many registers for base addressing, binary calculations, subroutines, and input/output operations. It is necessary then to save the contents of registers, use them for other purposes, and then use L or LM to reload them.

NAME	OPERATION	OPERAND		
[symbol]	ST	R1,X2	or	R1,D2(X2,B2)
	STH	R1,X2	or	R1,D2(X2,B2)
	STM	R1,S2	or	R1,R3,D2(B2)

The Store operations, ST, STH, and STM, are effectively the reverse of L, LH, and LM, respectively. They store the contents of registers in storage, on fullword or halfword boundaries. Note that like CVD, these store instructions move the contents of operand-1 (a register) to operand-2 (storage).

STORE—ST.   ST stores the contents of the operand-1 register (R1) into the fullword in storage referenced by operand-2. The fullword should be aligned on a fullword boundary.

STORE HALFWORD—STH.   STH stores the rightmost 16 bits of R1 into the operand-2 halfword, aligned in storage.

STORE MULTIPLE—STM.   R1 and R3 specify the span of registers to be stored. STM stores the fullword contents of R1 and the fullword contents of each register up to and including R3 consecutively starting with the operand-2 address. If R1 references a higher register than R3 (such as 14,3) then the registers stored are 14, 15, 0, 1, 2, and 3.

Figure 9-6 illustrates the Store operations. LM initializes registers 4, 5, and 6 with fullword values. In STORE1, the Store (ST) instruction stores the contents of register-5 in the fullword SAVEFULL. In STORE2, STH stores the rightmost 16-bit contents of register-6 in the halfword SAVEHALF.

In STORE3, the first STM stores the contents of registers 4, 5, and 6 in three

```
0039B4 00000675      96 FULLA     DC    F'1653'
0039B8 00000138      97           DC    F'312'
0039BC 00002103      98           DC    F'8451'
0039C0               99 SAVEFULL  DS    F
0039C4              100 SAVEHALF  DS    H
0039C8              101 THREEFW   DS    3F
                    102 FIVEFW    DS    5F
0039D4
0039E8 9846 31B2    103           LM    4,6,FULLA      REGS 4,5,6 : 1653, 312, 8451

                    105 *         --------------------
                    106 *         ST    STORE FULLWORD
                    107 *         --------------------
0039EC 5050 31BE    108 STORE1    ST    5,SAVEFULL     SAVEFULL : 312

                    110 *         --------------------
                    111 *         STH   STORE HALFWORD
                    112 *         --------------------
0039F0 4060 31C2    113 STORE2    STH   6,SAVEHALF     SAVEHALF : 8451

                    115 *         --------------------
                    116 *         STM   STORE MULTIPLE
                    117 *         --------------------
0039F4 9046 31C6    118 STORE3    STM   4,6,THREEFW    THREEFW  : 1653, 312, 8451
                    119           STM   15,3,FIVEFW    FIVEFW RECEIVES CONTENTS OF
0039F8 90F3 31D2                                       *    REGISTERS 15,0,1,2,3
```

FIGURE 9-6   Store register operations: ST, STH, STM.

fullwords labelled THREEFW. The second STM stores the contents of registers 15, 0, 1, 2, and 3 in five fullwords labelled FIVEFW.

Problems 9-2 and 9-3 should now be attempted.

BINARY ARITHMETIC—A, S, AH, SH, AR, SR

The following instructions perform binary addition and subtraction in registers. These operations all treat the leftmost sign bit as a plus or minus sign, not data.

NAME	OPERATION	OPERAND		
[symbol]	A	R1,X2	or	R1,D2(X2,B2)
	S	R1,X2	or	R1,D2(X2,B2)
	AH	R1,X2	or	R1,D2(X2,B2)
	SH	R1,X2	or	R1,D2(X2,B2)
	AR	R1,R2		
	SR	R1,R2		

For valid results, all data must be in binary format. These instructions all set the condition code (to zero, minus, or plus), which the usual BC operation may interrogate.

ADD AND SUBTRACT—A AND S. Operand-1 references a register. Operand-2 references a storage location aligned on a fullword boundary, containing data in binary format. All 31 data bits of the fullword are algebraically added to or subtracted from the contents of the register.

ADD AND SUBTRACT HALFWORD—AH AND SH. Operand-1 references a register, and operand-2 references a storage location aligned on a halfword boundary, containing binary data. Before the add or subtract, the halfword is expanded to a fullword by filling the sign-bit through the 16 leftmost bit positions. All 31 data bits are then algebraically added or subtracted, as A and S. Remember that a halfword has a maximum of 32,767.

ADD AND SUBTRACT REGISTER—AR AND SR. Both operands reference a register. All 32 bits of operand-2 are algebraically added or subtracted from operand-1.

Figure 9-7 illustrates the preceding. Each example is unrelated to the others. Note that because of the rules of halfword and fullword alignment for RX instructions, we define binary fields in H and F format, not B. In ADDFULL, a fullword

```
                      7  *        ---------------------------
                      8  *       A      ADD  FULLWORD                  DECIMAL
                      9  *       S      SUBTRACT  FULLWORD             VALUE:
                     10  *        ---------------------------         -----
003002  5850 402A    11  ADDFULL  L      5,FWD1                REG-5:   125
003006  5A50 402E    12          A      5,FWD2                REG-5:   195
00300A  5B50 4046    13          S      5,=F'50'              REG-5:   145

                     15  *        ---------------------------
                     16  *       AH     ADD  HALFWORD
                     17  *       SH     SUBTRACT  HALFWORD
                     18  *        ---------------------------
00300E  5880 402A    19  ADDHALF  L      8,FWD1                REG-8:   125
003012  4A80 404A    20          AH     8,=H'50'              REG-8:   175
003016  4B80 404C    21          SH     8,=H'25'              REG-8:   150

                     23  *        ---------------------------
                     24  *       AR     ADD  REGISTER
                     25  *       SR     SUBTRACT  REGISTER
                     26  *        ---------------------------
00301A  4F10 4036    27  ADDREG   CVB    1,DBPK1               REG-1:   250
00301E  4F00 403E    28          CVB    0,DBPK2               REG-0:   075
003022  1A01         29          AR     0,1                   REG-0:   325
003024  1B11         30          SR     1,1                   REG-1:   000
003026  4E00 4036    31          CVD    0,DBPK1               CONVERT  325 TO  PACKED

00302A  0000
00302C  0000007D     33  FWD1     DC     F'125'                BINARY  FULLWORD
003030  00000046     34  FWD2     DC     F'70'                 BINARY  FULLWORD
003038               35          DS     0D                    FORCE  DOUBLEWORD  ALIGN
003038  000000000000250C 36 DBPK1 DC    PL8'250'              PACKED  VALUE
003040  000000000000075C 37 DBPK2 DC    PL8'075'              PACKED  VALUE
003048               38          LTORG
003048  00000032     39                 =F'50'
00304C  0032         40                 =H'50'
00304E  0019         41                 =H'25'
```

FIGURE 9-7   Binary addition and subtraction.

containing 125 (in decimal notation) is loaded into register-5. A fullword containing 70 is added, and a fullword literal containing 50 is subtracted. Although notation is in decimal format for ease of reading, the fields and registers actually contain binary values.

In ADDHALF, a fullword is loaded into register-8, a halfword is added, and a halfword is subtracted. In ADDREG, two packed fields are defined as doublewords. DS 0D forces alignment on a doubleword boundary. The packed values are converted to binary in registers 0 and 1. (These registers should be used only for temporary calculations.) AR adds the contents of register-1 to register-0. Then SR clears register-1, and CVD converts the contents of register-0 to packed format.

BINARY COMPARISON—C, CH, CR

These operations compare binary data, just as CLC compares character data, and CP compares packed data. Each of these operations algebraically compares the contents of operand-1 to operand-2, and sets the condition code (to equal, low, or high).

NAME	OPERATION	OPERAND	
[symbol]	C CH CR	R1,X2 or R1,D2(X2,B2) R1,X2 or R1,D2(X2,B2) R1,R2	

COMPARE—C. Operand-1 references a register. Operand-2 references a fullword aligned on a fullword boundary, containing binary data.

COMPARE HALFWORD—CH. Operand-2 references a halfword, aligned on a halfword boundary containing binary data. Before the compare, CH expands the halfword to a full word by filling of the sign-bit value through the leftmost 16 bits.

COMPARE REGISTER—CR. Both operands specify a register. CR compares the contents of operand-1 to that of operand-2.

Figure 9-8 illustrates compare operations. Note how each sets the condition code. COMP1 loads a fullword FWD3 into register-6. C then compares register-6 to the contents of FWD4 in storage. COMP2 loads a halfword HWD1 into register-7 and compares its contents to HWD2, another halfword in storage. COMP3 loads FWD3 into register-8 and a fullword literal into register-9. Then CR compares registers 8 and 9.

```
                          46  *        ----------------------
                          47  *        C      COMPARE FULLWORD     DATA        COND'N
                          48  *        ---------------------- COMPARED:        CODE:
003050 5860 406A          49 COMP1     L      6,FWD3               --------    ----
003054 5960 406E          50           C      6,FWD4        1250 < 2575        LOW

                          52  *        ----------------------
                          53  *        CH     COMPARE HALFWORD
                          54  *        ----------------------
003058 4870 4072          55 COMP2     LH     7,HWD1
00305C 4970 4074          56           CH     7,HWD2         365  >  215       HIGH

                          58  *        ----------------------
                          59  *        CR     COMPARE REGISTERS
                          60  *        ----------------------
003060 5880 406A          61 COMP3     L      8,FWD3
003064 5890 4076          62           L      9,=F'975'
003068 1989               63           CR     8,9           1250 >  975        HIGH

00306A 0000
00306C 000004E2           65 FWD3      DC     F'1250'
003070 00000A0F           66 FWD4      DC     F'2575'
003074 016D               67 HWD1      DC     H'365'
003076 00D7               68 HWD2      DC     H'215'
003078                    69           LTORG
003078 000003CF           70                  =F'975'
```

FIGURE 9-8 Binary compare operations: C, CH, CR.

MULTIPLICATION—M, MH, MR

M, MH, and MR multiply fields in binary format. They do not set the condition code.

NAME	OPERATION	OPERAND
[symbol]	M	R1,X2 or R1,D2(X2,B2)
	MH	R1,X2 or R1,D2(X2,B2)
	MR	R1,R2

Certain binary operations require a pair of registers to express values greater than $2^{31}-1$. A double register permits values up to $2^{63}-1$. The registers are an *even-odd numbered pair*, such as 4 and 5, or 8 and 9, with the sign bit in the leftmost bit of the even register.

Both M and MR require an even-odd pair of registers. We load the multiplicand into the odd-numbered register. The product is developed in the pair of registers, with one sign bit and 63 data bits. For *most* multiplication operations, the product never exceeds $2^{31}-1$ or 2,147,483,647.* Therefore only one register (the odd one) is sufficient to contain the product. In this case, the leftmost bit of the odd register contains the correct sign, the same as that of the even register. Provided we are sure the product cannot exceed $2^{31}-1$, we may treat the value in the odd register as the correct signed product.

	EVEN REGISTER	ODD REGISTER
Before the M or MR:	(Garbage)	Multiplicand
After the multiply:	(Product)	Product

MULTIPLY FULLWORD—M.   Operand-1 specifies the even register of an even-odd pair. The odd register contains the multiplicand. Operand-2 references a fullword in storage, aligned, containing the multiplier in binary format. The product is developed in the even-odd pair, and erases the multiplicand. Note: The even register need not be initially cleared to zero (M ignores its contents).

MULTIPLY HALFWORD—MH.   MH is similar to M, with the following exceptions:

1. Operand-1, the mutiplicand, specifies any register, not necessarily an even one. The mutiplicand is assumed to be 31 data bits.

*When we compute averages and ratios, a value such as 21,474.83647 may be easily exceeded. Ensure that such a value is not exceeded regardless of the decimal position (see Double-precision in a later section).

2. Operand-2 references the multiplier—a halfword of binary data aligned on a halfword boundary in storage.

3. On execution, MH expands the halfword to a fullword by filling the sign-bit value through the 16 leftmost bits. The 32-bit product is developed in the Operand-1 register only, and erases the multiplicand.

MULTIPLY REGISTER—MR.   MR is similar to M except that operand-2 references a register containing the multiplier. We may load the multiplier in the even register, although the product erases it.

Figure 9-9 provides examples of multiply operations. In MULT1, the even-odd pair of registers is 4 and 5. The fullword MULTCAND is loaded into register-5. The Load instructions are for data in binary format, and CVB if in packed. To multiply, we specify the even register (4) in operand-1. Operand-2 specifies the fullword multiplier in storage. The product is generated in registers 4 and 5.

MULT2, because MH is used, needs only one register. A fullword is loaded into register-7, and then MH multiplies register-7 by a halfword in storage. The product is generated in register-7.

In MULT3, the even-odd pair of registers is 8 and 9. Registers 3 and 9 are loaded with fullwords which are to be multiplied. For MR we specify the multiplicand in the even register (8) as operand-1. The multiplier in register-3 is operand-2. The product is developed in registers 8 and 9.

In MULT4, the MR operation uses only two registers. Registers 8 and 9 are the even-odd pair. The multiplicand is loaded into register-9, and the multiplier in

```
                            74 *                               REG:      REG:
                            75 *      ------------------------
                            76 *      M      MULTIPLY FULLWORD
                            77 *      ------------------------
00307C 5850 409E            78 MULT1  L      5,MULTCAND                    5: 03333
003080 5C40 40A2            79        M      4,MULTPLER         4: 00000   5: 66660

                            81 *      ------------------------
                            82 *      MH     MULTIPLY HALFWORD
                            83 *      ------------------------
003084 5870 409E            84 MULT2  L      7,MULTCAND         7: 03333
003088 4C70 40A6            85        MH     7,MULTHALF         7: 09999

                            87 *      ------------------------
                            88 *      MR     MULTIPLY REGISTER
                            89 *      ------------------------
00308C 5830 40A2            90 MULT3  L      3,MULTPLER         3: 00020
003090 5890 409E            91        L      9,MULTCAND                    9: 03333
003094 1C83                 92        MR     8,3                8: 00000   9: 66660

003096 5880 40A2            94 MULT4  L      8,MULTPLER         8: 00020
00309A 5890 409E            95        L      9,MULTCAND                    9: 03333
00309E 1C88                 96        MR     8,8                8: 00000   9: 66660

0030A0 00000D05             98 MULTCAND DC   F'3333'
0030A4 00000014             99 MULTPLER DC   F'20'
0030A8 0003               100 MULTHALF DC    H'3'
```

FIGURE 9-9   Binary multiplication: M, MH, MR.

register-8. In spite of its appearance, MR 8,8 does not mean multiply the contents of register-8 and register-8. Operand-1 refers to the multiplicand in the odd register (9) of an even-odd pair (8 and 9). Operand-2 refers to the multiplier that happens to be in register-8. It is erased by the multiplication.

Warning: In these examples, the product does not exceed the capacity of a single register, which is $2^{31} - 1$ or 2,147,483,647. If there is a possibility of such a large product, then we must provide additional programming. The technique is given later in this chapter in Conversion of Double Precision Binary to Decimal Format.

REGISTER SHIFT INSTRUCTIONS

We can shift binary data in a register either left or right a specified number of bit positions. This feature, for example, can clear unwanted bit positions from a field, or multiply or divide a field by a power of two. The following operations shift the bit contents of registers, other than the leftmost sign bit which is unaffected. Bits shifted out of the register are lost. The condition code is set.

NAME	OPERATION	OPERAND		
[symbol]	SRA	R1,S2	or	R1,D2(B2)
	SLA	R1,S2	or	R1,D2(B2)
	SRDA	R1,S2	or	R1,D2(B2)
	SLDA	R1,S2	or	R1,D2(B2)

SHIFT RIGHT ALGEBRAIC—SRA.   The rules for SRA are:

1. Operand-1 specifies a register whose 31-bit contents other than the sign bit are to be shifted to the right. The leftmost sign bit is not moved.
2. Operand-2 denotes the number of bits to be shifted. Normally we code the shift factor as a decimal number less than 32.
3. Bits shifted off to the right are lost. The sign bit replaces leftmost shifted bits. There is no overflow or program interrupt.

We may use SRA to divide the contents of a register by a power of 2. For example, shifting right one bit is equivalent to dividing by 2^1, or 2; shifting right two bits is equivalent to dividing by 2^2, or 4, etc. Consider a 4-bit register containing initially (a) 1000, and (b) 1111:

	(a) CONTENTS		(b) CONTENTS	
Initial value:	1000	(8)	1111	(15)
Shift right 1:	0100	(4)	0111	(7)
Shift right 2:	0010	(2)	0011	(3)
Shift right 3:	0001	(1)	0001	(1)

SHIFT LEFT ALGEBRAIC—SLA. SLA is similar to SRA with the following differences:

1. SLA shifts up to 31 bit positions to the left. The leftmost sign bit is unaffected.
2. SLA replaces rightmost shifted bit positions with 0-bits. For example, shift left three bits: 00001011 becomes 01011000.
3. A leftmost bit shifted out that is *different* from the sign bit may cause an overflow and interrupt.

We may use SLA to multiply the contents of a register by a power of 2. For example, shifting left three bits is equivalent to multiplying by 2^3, or 8.

SHIFT RIGHT DOUBLE ALGEBRAIC—SRDA. SRDA is similar to SRA except that the contents of *two* registers shift as a single unit. SRDA is commonly used with binary divide operations.

1. Operand-1 specifies the even-numbered register of an even-odd pair of registers. The pair is treated as a single doubleword.
2. Up to 63 bits may be shifted. The sign bit in the even register, considered the sign for the pair, replaces leftmost shifted bits in both registers. The sign bit in the odd registers is treated as *data,* therefore yielding 63 bits of data.

SHIFT LEFT DOUBLE ALGEBRAIC—SLDA. SLDA is similar to SLA except that, like SRDA, operand-1 specifies the even-numbered register of an even-odd pair. The sign bit of the pair is that of the even register. The sign bit of the odd register is treated as a data-bit, giving a 63-bit doubleword.

For each shift operation, if operand-2 contains *zero,* the instruction executes without shifting. This use of shift is a convenient way to set the condition code. If we want to *vary* the number of bits shifted throughout the program, we may use the base-displacement facility of operand-2, D(B). For example, register-3 contains the value 12. Given SRA 9,0(3) the contents of register-9 shift right according to the contents of register-3, that is 12 bits.

Figure 9-10 illustrates shift operations. Check the hex representation for the fullword constants, and the effect of the shift. Note that it is the *bits* that shift. For example, if a binary value containing 0001 (X'1') is left-shifted two bits, the result is 0100 (X'4').

In SHIFT1, SRA shifts the contents of register-9 two bits to the right. This shift is equivalent to dividing by four. The second example specifies zero in operand-2. No shift occurs, but, since the value is positive, the condition code is set to high/plus.

In SHIFT2, SLA shifts the contents of register-7 two bits to the left. This shift is equivalent to multiplying by four. The second example explicitly uses a base register.

```
              123 *                           HEX CONTENTS:
              124 *      ------------------------------
              125 *      SRA    SHIFT RIGHT ALGEBRAIC
              126 *      ------------------------------
0039FC 5890 322A  127 SHIFT1  L      9,FULLWD2        00004327
003A00 8A90 0002  128         SRA    9,2              000010C9

003A04 8A90 0000  130         SRA    9,0         NO SHIFT. SET COND'N CODE
                                                          TO HIGH/PLUS
              132 *      ------------------------------
              133 *      SLA    SHIFT LEFT   ALGEBRAIC
              134 *      ------------------------------
003A08 5870 3256  135 SHIFT2  L      7,=F'17191'      00004327
003A0C 8B70 0002  136         SLA    7,2              00010C9C

003A10 4180 0003  138         LA     8,3         LOAD 3 IN REG 8
003A14 8B70 8000  139         SLA    7,0(8)      SHIFT REG-7 LEFT 3 BITS

              141 *      ------------------------------
              142 *      SRDA   SHIFT RIGHT DOUBLE ALGEBRAIC
              143 *      ------------------------------
003A18 9867 3226  144 SHIFT3  LM     6,7,FULLWD1      0000013F/00004327
003A1C 8E60 0004  145         SRDA   6,4              00000013/F0000432

              147 *      ------------------------------
              148 *      SLDA   SHIFT LEFT   DOUBLE ALGEBRAIC
              149 *      ------------------------------
003A20 9889 3226  150 SHIFT4  LM     8,9,FULLWD1      0000013F/00004327
003A24 8F80 0012  151         SLDA   8,18             04FC0001/0C9C0000


003A28 0000013F  153 FULLWD1  DC     F'319'           0000013F
003A2C 00004327  154 FULLWD2  DC     F'17191'         00004327
```

FIGURE 9-10 Binary algebraic shift operations.

The value 3 is loaded into register-8. Then register-8 is referenced explicitly in operand-2 of the SLA to cause a left shift of 3 bits.

In SHIFT3, SRDA shifts the contents of the even-odd registers 6 and 7 four bits to the right. In SHIFT4, SLDA shifts the contents of the even-odd registers 8 and 9 eighteen bits to the left.

Problems 9-4, 9-5, and 9-6 should now be attempted.

BINARY DIVISION—D, DR

The D and DR instructions divide fields in binary format. (Unexpectedly, there is no Divide Halfword operation.)

NAME	OPERATION	OPERAND
[symbol]	D	R1,X2 or R1,D2(X2,B2)
	DR	R1,R2

DIVIDE AND DIVIDE REGISTER.   Both D and DR, like M and MR, require the use of a doubleword of 63 bits plus a sign in an even-odd pair of registers. D and DR treat the pair of registers, all 63 bits, as a dividend field. Possibly, for example, an M or MR operation generated a two-register product, and it is now necessary to divide this product by some value. Often, however, the programmer loads the dividend into a register, and only one register is required to contain the fullword dividend. In this case, the dividend is in the odd register, but *the even register must be initialized so that it contains the same sign as the dividend.* We may force similar signs by the following practice:

— Load the dividend into the even register.
— Using SRDA, shift the dividend 32 bits out of the even into the odd register. The even register now is cleared of "garbage" from any previous operation, and initialized with the correct sign.

EVEN REGISTER, INITIALIZED	ODD REGISTER, DIVIDEND SIGN
Binary zeros	Positive
Binary ones	Negative

The rules for D and DR are:

1. Operand-1 specifies the even register of an even-odd pair of registers containing the dividend.
2. Operand-2 references the 32-bit divisor. For D, the divisor is a fullword aligned in storage. For DR the divisor is a register.
3. After execution, the remainder is in the even register and the quotient is in the odd register. Both contain 31 data bits and a leftmost sign bit. A quotient that exceeds 31 bits plus the sign causes an overflow and program interrupt. Dividing by zero will cause this condition.

	EVEN REGISTER	ODD REGISTER
Before the D or DR:	Dividend	Dividend
After the divide:	Remainder	Quotient

4. The sign of the quotient is determined by normal algebraic rules. The remainder's sign is the same as the dividend. The condition code is not set, but we can ZAP the quotient into itself to set it.

Figure 9-11 illustrates the D and DR operations. For D, the even-odd pair is registers 0 and 1. The binary fullword DIVD is loaded into register-0. Then the contents of register-0 are shifted into register-1, leaving register-0 correctly initialized. The fullword divisor DIVSR divides into the even-odd pair. Register-1 now contains the quotient, 326, and register-0 contains the remainder, 5.

```
             158 *          --------------
             159 *          D     DIVIDE            REG:        REG:   DECIMAL
             160 *          --------------          ---         ---    FORMAT:
003A30 5800 324A  161          L     0,DIVD           0: 4569
003A34 8E00 0020  162          SRDA  0,32             0: 0000    1: 4569
003A38 5D00 324E  163          D     0,DIVSR          0: 0005    1: 0326

             165 *          ------------------------
             166 *          DR    DIVIDE REGISTER
             167 *          ------------------------
003A3C 58C0 324E  168          L     12,DIVSR        12: 0014
003A40 58A0 324A  169          L     10,DIVD         10: 4569
003A44 8EA0 0020  170          SRDA  10,32           10: 0000   11: 4569
003A48 1DAC       171          DR    10,12           10: 0005   11: 0326


003A4A 0000
003A4C 000011D9  173 DIVD     DC    F'4569'          FULLWORD DIVIDEND
003A50 0000000E  174 DIVSR    DC    F'14'            FULLWORD DIVISOR
```

FIGURE 9-11   Binary division operations: D and DR.

For DR, the even-odd pair is registers 10 and 11. The divisor and dividend are loaded respectively into registers 12 and 10. The contents of register-10 are shifted into register-11, leaving register-10 correctly initialized. DR then divides register-12 into the even-odd pair. Register-11 now contains the quotient, 326, and register-10 contains the remainder.

SCALING AND ROUNDING.   Assembler performs arithmetic on integers only. The problem of scaling, that is, providing for the decimal point, is similar to that for DP. We must mentally account for the implicit decimal point. *It simplifies programming to think of binary as decimal values.*

```
0038C6 23565C          87 DISTPK   DC    P'2356.5'
0038C9 01500C          88 GALSPK   DC    P'150.0'
0038D0                 89 DISTDW   DS    D
0038D8                 90 GALSDW   DS    D
0038E0                 91 ANSWER   DS    D

0038E8 F872 30CE 30C4  93 DIVIDE   ZAP   DISTDW,DISTPK    REG CONTENTS AS DECIMAL FORMAT :
0038EE F872 30D6 30C7  94          ZAP   GALSDW,GALSPK

                      118 *   ROUND TO TWO DECIMALS :
003936 4F90 30D6      119 DIVID30  CVB   9,GALSDW         9: 0000001500
00393A 4F60 30CE      120          CVB   6,DISTDW         6: 0000023565
00393E 8E60 0020      121          SRDA  6,32             6: 0000000000   7: 0000023565
003942 4C70 3188      122          MH    7,=H'1000'       6: 0000000000   7: 0023565000
003946 1D69           123          DR    6,9              6: 0000000000   7: 0000015710
003948 1267           124          LTR   6,7              LOAD QUOTIENT INTO REG-6,
00394A 4740 3154      125          BM    DIVID32          *     TEST CONDITION CODE
00394E 4A60 3186      126          AH    6,=H'5'          6: 0000015715   7: 0000015710
003952 47F0 3158      127          B     DIVID34
003956 4B60 3186      128 DIVID32  SH    6,=H'5'
00395A 8E60 0020      129 DIVID34  SRDA  6,32             6: 0000000000   7: 0000015715
00395E 5D60 317E      130          D     6,=F'10'         6: 0000000005   7: 0000001571
003962 4E70 30DE      131          CVD   7,ANSWER         ANSWER CONTAINS PACKED 15.71
```

FIGURE 9-12   Binary division with decimal point scaling.

Refer to Figure 9-12, which is similar to a DP example in Figure 5-4 which divides distance (DISTPK) by gallons (GALSPK) to calculate miles-per-gallon (AN-SWER). Both DISTPK and GALSPK are transferred to aligned doublewords to permit CVB to convert them to binary. Distance, in register-6, is shifted all 32 bits into register-7 to initialize register-6 with the correct sign. We require a 2-decimal quotient after rounding. Since both distance and gallons contain one decimal position, we must generate three additional positions.

To generate three decimal places, we multiply by 1000. (Note that shift operations, such as SLA, multiply by powers of 2, not 10.) LTR is used to set the condition code: if positive we add 5; if negative we subtract 5. LTR as well loaded the quotient from register-7 into register-6, erasing the remainder. This move is done because the quotient is to be divided again, by 10. Before dividing, we shift the quotient out of register-6 back into register-7, thereby clearing and initializing register-6 to the correct sign. The division by 10 adjusts for the required number of decimal positions.

The following facts should be clearly understood: LTR cleared the remainder from register-6 because of the subsequent divide by 10. If the remainder were left in register-6 the second divide would have treated the contents of registers 6 and 7 as one extremely large 63-bit value. The contents of the registers and fullwords are in binary format. However, we code decimal format to conveniently *represent* the binary values.

CONVERSION OF DOUBLE-PRECISION BINARY TO DECIMAL FORMAT

A binary multiplication may develop a product that exceeds the capacity of one register (2,147,483,647). The result is a double-precision, or a two-register, product. This situation requires additional programming in order to convert the result to decimal format. Consider a situation in which registers 4 and 5 contain only four bits, 0011 and 0111. The sign is the leftmost bit of register-4. The decimal value of this quantity is $32 + 16 + 0 + 4 + 2 + 1 = 55$. Converting register-4 to decimal yields the decimal value 3, instead of $32 + 16 = 48$. To correct this value 3, we may multiply it by a constant value 16, or $3 \times 16 = 48$. The constant 16 is used because the "register" contains four bits, and the maximum value is $2^4 = 16$. (Determine the constant required if the registers contain 5, 6, or 32 bits.) With register-4 correctly converted to decimal value 48, we may now process register-5. Conversion of register-5 to decimal results in the value 7, which when added to 48 yields the correct answer 55.

Consider another example of a negative value, minus 59. Its bit representation in two's complement is:

REGISTER	EVEN	ODD
Binary value:	0011	1011 (plus 59)
Reverse bits:	1100	0100
Add 'one':	1100	0101 (minus 59)

The even register contains the sign, a minus, in the leftmost bit. CVD converts the contents of the even register to −4. (Depict 4 in binary, reverse the bits, and add 1 to check that the two's complement of −4 is 1100.) Multiplying −4 by 16 gives −64. The odd register containing 0101 when converted to decimal yields +5. And −64 + 5 gives the correct answer, −59.

But a problem arises if the odd register contains a 1 in its leftmost bit, because CVD treats the value as negative. Assume the value in the double-register is +40, or 0010 1000. Converting the even register to decimal yields +2. Multiplying +2 by 16 gives +32. CVD converts the odd register to −8, and the sum of +32 and −8, which is 24, is incorrect.

We can use LTR to test the leftmost sign bit in the odd register. If there is a 0-bit, the nonminus condition code is set; the conversion may proceed as already described. If, however, the odd register sign is a 1-bit, the condition code is minus. The following procedure produces the correct answer for the same example of 0010 1000:

— The odd register is "minus". Add 1 to the even register, giving 0011 1000.
— Converting the even register to decimal gives +3. Multiplying +3 by 16 yields +48.
— Converting the odd register to decimal gives −8. 48 plus −8 gives the correct answer, 40.

This additional step of testing if the odd register is "minus" and adding 1 to the even register provides the correct answer in all cases. Note that the incorrect answer was 24 instead of 40, a difference of 16. But the addition of 1 was equivalent to incrementing the double-precision value by 2^4, or 16. Figure 9-13 gives the programming for this procedure, in which multiplication of binary values produces a two-register product.

```
 8            DS    0D
 9  DATA1     DC    PL8'0123456'
10  DATA2     DC    PL8'-456789'
11  DBLWD     DS    D
12  PRODPK    DC    PL16'0'
13  CONSTANT  DC    P'4294967296'
14  *                               REG-6 HEX  REG-7 HEX    DECIMAL      +
                                    ---------  ---------    -------
15  E10DOUBL  CVB   6,DATA1         0001E240
16            CVB   7,DATA2         0001E240   FF8907AB
17            MR    6,6             FFFFFFF2   DEB1E0C0
18            LTR   7,7
19            BNM   E20
20            AH    6,=H'1'         FFFFFFF3   DEB1E0C0

22  E20       CVD   6,PRODPK+8      PRODPK:                      013-
23            MP    PRODPK,CONSTANT PRODPK:      55,834,574,848-
24            CVD   7,DBLWD         DBLWD :         558,767,936-
25            AP    PRODPK,DBLWD    PRODPK:      56,393,342,784-
```

FIGURE 9-13   Conversion of double-precision binary to packed.

The two fields, DATA1 and DATA2, are converted into binary format in registers of 6 and 7. When the registers are multiplied, the product exceeds the capacity of register-7. Since register-7 contains a "minus value", 1 is added to register-6. Register-6 is converted to decimal format into PRODPK. The constant now used to multiply is not 2^4 but 2^{32}, or 4,294,967,296. Register-7 is next converted to decimal format in DBLWD, and PRODPK is added to it. The final product is correct: 56,393,342,784−.

SAMPLE PARTIAL PROGRAM—FINANCE CHARGE REBATES

For some types of loans, finance charges are precomputed; that is, the amount of interest is precalculated for the term of the loan and added to the amount of the loan. For example, $500.00 is borrowed for a term of 6 months with precomputed finance charge of $30.00. The sum of $530.00 is repayable in 6 equal instalments of $88.33. A borrower who repays the full amount of the balance remaining before the end of the term is entitled to a partial rebate on the precomputed finance charge. The rebate can be calculated by the "sum of digits" formula.

$$t = \text{original term in months} \qquad F = \text{pre-computed finance charge}$$
$$r = \text{remaining term in months} \qquad R = \text{rebate}$$

$$R = \frac{\dfrac{r^2+r}{2}}{\dfrac{t^2+t}{2}} \times F = \frac{r^2+r}{t^2+t} \times F$$

Example:

$$t = 6, \ r = 5, \ f = \$30.00$$
$$\frac{5^2+5}{6^2+6} \times \$30.00 = \frac{30}{42} \times \$30.00 = \$21.42$$

Figure 9-14 gives the programming that calculates the rebate. The program also checks for minimum finance charge of $10.00. That is, finance charge less rebate must equal at least $10.00. *Example:* $30.00 − $21.42 = $8.58. Since $8.58 is less than $10.00, the rebate is $30.00 − $10.00 = $20.00.

DEBUGGING TIPS

The instructions introduced in this chapter provide an additional dimension of error possibilities:

```
003806 0000
003808 00000006          8 ORIGTERM DC     F'06'
00380C 00000005          9 REMGTERM DC     F'05'
003810 00000BB8         10 FINCHGE  DC     F'03000'        030.00
003814                  11 REBATE   DS     F               XXX.XX
                        12 *                               REG:   DECIMAL FORMAT:
                        13 * CALCULATE R SQUARED + R :
003818 5890 300A        14 CALCREB  L      9,REMGTERM      9: 05
00381C 1879             15          LR     7,9
00381E 1C69             16          MR     6,9             7: 25
003820 1A79             17          AR     7,9             7: 30

                        19 * MULTIPLY BY FINANCE CHARGE :
003822 5880 300E        20          L      8,FINCHGE       8: 030.00
003826 1C68             21          MR     6,8             7: 900.00
003828 5C60 3176        22          M      6,=F'100'       7: 900.0000   SHIFT LEFT

                        24 * CALCULATE T SQUARED + T :
00382C 5890 3006        25          L      9,ORIGTERM      9: 06
003830 1859             26          LR     5,9             5: 06
003832 1C49             27          MR     4,9             5: 36
003834 1A59             28          AR     5,9             5: 42

                        30 * DIVIDE TO CALCULATE REBATE:
003836 1D65             31          DR     6,5             7: 21.4285
003838 4A70 3182        32          AH     7,=H'50'        7: 21.4335    ROUND
00383C 1B66             33          SR     6,6                           CLEAR REMAINDER
00383E 5D60 3176        34          D      6,=F'100'       7: 21.43      SHIFT RIGHT

                        36 * CHECK FOR $10.00 MINIMUM CHARGE :
003842 1898             37          LR     9,8             9: 30.00
003844 1B87             38          SR     8,7             8: 08.57
003846 5980 317A        39          C      8,=F'1000'
00384A 47B0 3052        40          BNL    B1ONOTLO
00384E 5B90 317A        41          S      9,=F'1000'      9: 20.00
003852 1879             42          LR     7,9             7: 20.00

003854 5070 3012        44 B1ONOTLO ST     7,REBATE        7: 20.00
```

FIGURE 9-14   Calculation of finance charge rebate.

—Operand-2 of CVD and CVB must be a doubleword.

— For many operations, the selection of the correct instruction is critical. Consider the following similar-looking instructions that assemble with no error but may produce unexpected results:

LR 7,4	Loads contents of register-4 into register-7.
L 7,4	Loads contents of storage locations 4, 5, 6, 7 into register-7.
LH 7,4	Loads contents of storage locations 4 and 5 into register-7.
LA 7,4	Loads the displacement value 4 into register-7.

— Binary division causes more problems than multiplication because the even register should be initialized with the same sign as the odd one.

— Binary calculations may unexpectedly generate a large value that exceeds the capacity of one register.

PROBLEMS

9-1. Add the following as 5-bit binary numbers:

$$
\begin{array}{ccccc}
6 & 9 & 8 & 7 & -9 \\
\underline{+5} & \underline{+4} & \underline{-5} & \underline{+(-4)} & \underline{-8} \\
11 & 13 & 3 & 3 & -17
\end{array}
$$

9-2. Explain halfword, fullword, and doubleword alignment, and the significance of alignment on the 360 and the 370.

9-3. Given the following declaratives, explain concisely what each of the following unrelated operations does. Check for possible coding errors.

```
BINA   DC   F'285'
BINB   DC   F'394'
BINC   DS   D
```

(a)	L	6,BINA	(e)	L	6,BINA	(i)	MVC	BINA,BINB
(b)	CVB	6,=P'500'	(f)	LM	6,7,BINA	(j)	CVD	6,BINC
(c)	LR	9,5	(g)	LH	8,=H'25'	(k)	ST	12,BINB
(d)	LA	12,5000	(h)	ZAP	12,=P'5'	(l)	LH	8,BINA

9-4. Use the same declaratives as in the previous problem to explain the following unrelated problems. Check for coding errors.

(a)	SH	8,=H'9'	(e)	C	9,BINB	(i)	MH	8,=H'9'
(b)	S	8,BINA	(f)	SH	8,BINB	(j)	MR	8,9
(c)	SR	8,9	(g)	S	8,=F'9'	(k)	SRA	8,9
(d)	CR	8,9	(h)	M	8,BINA	(l)	SLDA	8,9

9-5. Revise Problem 5-5 (Multiply Packed) to perform binary multiplication. Use the same constants and store the final product in decimal format in PROD.

9-6. Explain the effect of the following related operations. BINA refers to 9-3.

(a)	SR 4,4	(b)	ACCUM DS PL3	(c)	L 5,BINA
	L 5,=F'15'		LA 6,ACCUM		SLA 5,2
	MR 4,5		AP 0(3,6),0(3,6)		ST 5,BINA

9-7. Follow the same requirements as for Problems 9-3 and 9-4:

(a) D 8,BINA   (b) DR 8,9   (c) DR 8,8

9-8. Revise Problem 5-6 (Divide Packed) to perform binary division. Use the same constants and store the final quotient in binary format in QUOT.

9-9. Code the following routine. There are two binary values: BINAM contains a value to be raised to a power n, called EXPON. Perform repetitious binary multiplying of BINAM n times to compute $BINAM^n$. Program for a double-precision result, and print the final answer. Both BINAM and EXPON may be defined as DC H with constant values.

CHAPTER 10

EXPLICIT USE OF BASE REGISTERS

In many previous examples, we coded the length explicitly to override the implicit length of the field, such as: MVC P+30(2),=C'**'. In a similar fashion *a base register may explicitly override the assigned base register.* This chapter uses base registers explicitly to permit the use of such operations as EDMK and COMRG, and to modify an address for table look-up. We may use a base register explicitly in any operand that references storage, with a reference to a base register (B1 or B2). Since a base register contains the address of an area of storage, we may override the program's normal base register with another register containing an address of some other area.

Figure 10-1 is illustrative only and not intended to be realistic. BALR initializes register-4 with X'3002'. The examples show three different ways to move a field (ASTERS) to the print area.

ASSGN1 shows a conventional move operation, with both operands subject implicitly to base register-4. The assembled object code for operand-1 (PRINT+60), is 4056, or base register-4, displacement X'056'. The effective address is X'3002' plus X'056', or X'3058'.

ASSGN2 explicitly uses a base register. The address of PRINT+60 (X'3058') is loaded into register-8. MVC explicitly uses the contents of register-8. Since the format

```
 LOC   OBJECT CODE      ADDR1 ADDR2   STMT      SOURCE STATEMENT

003000                                  3 PRCG10    START X'3000'
003000 0540                             4          EALR  4,0
                              03002      5          USING *,4

                                         8 *                IMPLICIT BASE REGISTER:
003002 D201 4056 4093 03058 03095        9 ASSGN1   MVC   PRINT+60(2),ASTERS

                                        12 *                EXPLICIT BASE REGISTER:
003008 5880 4096            03098       13 ASSGN2   L     8,=A(PRINT+60)
00300C D201 8000 4093 00000 03095       14          MVC   0(2,8),ASTERS

                                        17 *                EXPLICIT BASE/DISPLACEMENT:
003012 5880 409A            0309C       18 ASSGN3   L     8,=A(PRINT)
003016 D201 803C 4093 0003C 03095       19          MVC   60(2,8),ASTERS
                                        20 *          .
                                        21 *          .
                                        22 *          .
00301C 4040404040404040               23 PRINT    DC    CL121' '
003095 5C5C                             24 ASTERS   DC    C'**'
003098                                  25          LTORG
003098 00003058                         26                =A(PRINT+60)
00309C 0000301C                         27                =A(PRINT)
```

FIGURE 10-1   Base register assignment and explicit use of a base register.

for MVC is D1(L,B1),D2(B2), we code the first operand explicitly with zero displacement, a length of 2, and base register-8, or 0(2,8). The assembled object code for operand-1 is 8000, or base register-8, displacement zero. The effective address is X'3058'.

ASSGN3 illustrates both explicit base register and displacement. The address of PRINT (X'301C') is loaded into register-8. Since the move operation is to reference PRINT+60, we need a displacement of 60. The first operand is expressed as 60(2,8). The assembled object code for operand-1 is 803C, or base register-8 plus displacement X'03C'. The effective address is X'301C' plus X'03C', or X'3058'. Note how the Assembler generates the same effective address in each case:

	ASSGN1	ASSGN2	ASSGN3
Base	X'3002'	X'3058'	X'301C'
Displacement	X'0056'	X'0000'	X'003C'
Effective address	X'3058'	X'3058'	X'3058'

EDIT AND MARK—EDMK.   On printed checks and customer bills, it is usually desirable to print the dollar sign to the immediate left of the first significant digit of the amount. If a field provides for seven digits, and only five are significant, the resulting edited field could appear as $bbb123.45. We may use EDMK to print the amount as $123.45.

NAME	OPERATION	OPERAND
[symbol]	EDMK	S1,S2 or D1(L1,B1),D2(B2)

EDMK is identical to ED except that it inserts into *register-1 the address of the first significant digit* in the edited field. We may then decrement register-1 by one since the dollar sign must be printed one position to the left. We then use register-1 as an explicit base register to move a dollar sign.

Note: If the significance start character (X'21') forces a zero digit to be printed, the address is not stored in register-1. Therefore, we should ensure against this possibility by initially loading into register-1 the address of the significance starter plus one. After the EDMK operation, we deduct one from register-1; if the significance starter forced the first printed digit, then register-1 will contain the address of the significance starter, where the dollar sign should appear.

In Figure 10-2, the editword is moved into P+30, and the address of the X'21' is P+33. We load the address of P+34 into register-1. After EDMK, register-1 contains the address of the first significant digit at P+33. Decrementing register-1 causes it to contain the address of P+32, where MVI inserts the $.

```
                        32  *        --------------------
                        33  *        EDMK   EDIT & MARK
                        34  *        --------------------
0030A0 4110 40E2        35           LA     1,P+34              LOAD ADDRESS OF SIGNIFICANT
                                                            *    START CHARACTER +1
0030A4 D206 40DE 40B6   36           MVC    P+30(7),EDWORD      |40|20|20|21|4B|20|20|
0030AA DFC6 40DE 4CBD   37           EDMK   P+30(7),AMOUNT      |40|40|40|F3|4B|F5|F2|
0030B0 4B10 413E        38           SH     1,=H'1'             DECREMENT REG1 (OR BCTR 1,0)
0030B4 925B 1000        39           MVI    0(1),C'$'           |40|40|5B|F3|4B|F5|F2|
                        40  *         •                          $   3  .   5   2
                        41  *         •
                        42  *         •                              ↑
0030B8 4C202021482020   43 EDWORD    DC     X'40202021482020'        └─P+32
0030BF 00352C           44 AMOUNT    DC     P'003.52'           WILL EDIT AS $3.52
0030C2 4C4C4C4040404040 45 P         DC     CL121' '
```

FIGURE 10-2   Sample edit and mark operation.

OPERATIONS EXPLICITLY USING BASE REGISTERS

Some operations involve explicit use of base registers. These include Assembler instructions EDMK, SRP, MVCL, and CLCL and IBM macros COMRG and TIME.

THE COMRG AND TIME MACROS.   The communication region is a storage area in the Supervisor. The first eight bytes contain the date as initialized each day by the computer operator. The format for the date, including the slashes, is: dd/mm/yy or mm/dd/yy.* Although we do not know the address of the communication region, under DOS we can use COMRG to ask the Supervisor for the address. *The Supervisor places the address of the communications region in register-1.* We then can use register-1 explicitly to address the communications region:

```
DATE    DS      CL8'DD/MM/YY'     Area to store date
        COMRG                     Locate address of comm'n region
        MVC     DATE,0(1)         Move date from comm'n region
```

The OS macro is called TIME. It returns the date in packed format in register-1, as /00/YY/DD/DC/. The day (D) is Julian, the day of the year. C is a sign digit. Also, the time is stored in register-0.

```
FULLWD  DS      F                 Fullword area
DATE    DS      CL7               Area for date 00YYDDD
        TIME    DEC               OS  TIME  macro,  packs  date  in
                                  register-1
        ST      1,FULLWD          Store packed date in FULLWD
        UNPL    DATE,FULLWD       Unpack date in DATE
```

SHIFT AND ROUND PACKED—SRP.   The 370 instruction, SRP, permits rounding, and shifting of packed digits either left or right. SRP can therefore replace MVO and AP in decimal multiply and divide, and replace MP where used to shift the dividend to the left.

NAME	OPERATION	OPERAND
[symbol]	SRP	S1,S2 or D1(L,B1),D2(B2),I3

Although SS-format, SRP has three operands. Operand-1 denotes the field containing packed data to be shifted and optionally rounded. Operand-2 is a base/displacement reference that indicates the number of digits to be shifted. The maximum shift is 31 digits. Operand-3 provides the value 0–9 to be used for rounding: a left shift will normally have a 0 to indicate no rounding, and a right shift usually rounds with 5. SRP sets the condition code for zero, minus, and plus.

LEFT SHIFT.   A positive value as the shift factor indicates a left shift. For example, +2 means shift left two digits (digits, not bytes). We may load the shift factor in a

---

*The communications region contains other fields that may be of interest to the advanced programmer. See the IBM Supervisor manual for your installation. The 370 also contains a different area called "input/output communications area."

register, and then reference the register explicitly with the SRP, as shown by SHIFL2A in Figure 10-3. More conveniently, we may code the shift factor as an explicit displacement using base register-0 (that is, no base register), as in SHIFL2B and SHIFL2C. Shifting a significant digit (1–9) off the left sets the decimal overflow condition but does not cause termination, so we can use Branch Overflow to test if a significant digit was lost.

```
*                  HEX REPRESENTATION:
AMOUNT    DC       PL5'1234567'               00 12 34 56 7C

*         SHIFT LEFT 2 DIGITS:               RESULT IN AMOUNT:
SHIFL2A   LH       14,=H'2'
          SRP      AMOUNT,0(14),0             12 34 56 70 0C

SHIFL2B   SRP      AMOUNT,2(0),0             12 34 56 70 0C

SHIFL2C   SRP      AMOUNT,2,0               12 34 56 70 0C

*         SHIFT RIGHT 2 DIGITS (AND ROUND):
SHIFR2A   LH       14,=H'-2'
          SRP      AMOUNT,0(14),5             00 00 12 34 6C

SHIFR2B   SRP      AMOUNT,X'3E',5           00 00 12 34 6C

SHIFR2C   SRP      AMOUNT,62,5              00 00 12 34 6C
```

FIGURE 10-3   Use of SRP—shift and round packed.

RIGHT SHIFT.   A negative value as the shift factor indicates a right shift. We may load the negative value into a register and reference the register with the SRP, as shown by SHIFR2A. Although it is more convenient to code the shift factor as a displacement rather than load a base register, we cannot code such a right shift as SRP AMOUNT,−2,5; the Assembler does not accept negative "displacements" [that is, −2(0) for $D_2(B_2)$]. Now, we can solve the problem by *representing* the −2 as a hexadecimal value. Since SRP can shift only up to 31 digits, we can express the shift factor with six bits (5 data bits plus a "sign" bit: 011111 = 31). The value 2 as six binary digits is 00 0010, and −2 in two's complement is 11 1110. The hex representation of this number is X'3E', which we can use directly as a shift factor as in SHIFR2B in Figure 10-3. Similarly, the decimal equivalent of X'3E' is 62, which we may code as a shift factor, as shown in SHIFR2C.

Note that other right shifts include: 1 = X'3F' or 63, 3 = X'3D' or 61, and 4 = X'3C' or 60, up to a shift of 31 digits.

MOVE LONG AND COMPARE LONG—MVCL AND CLCL.   Move Long (MVCL) and Compare Logical Long (CLCL) are available only on the 370. MVCL will move fields and records that exceed 256 positions. One major use is to clear storage. CLCL compares fields and records that exceed 256 positions. The instruction has an additional attribute: if the two fields are unequal, CLCL makes the address of the unequal byte available.

NAME	OPERATION	OPERAND
[symbol]	MVCL	R1,R2
	CLCL	R1,R2

MVCL and CLCL require the use of four registers. Operand-1 and -2 both reference the even-numbered register of an even-odd pair. The complexity of MVCL and CLCL rather limits their practical use; see the IBM Principles of Operation manual for details.

TABLES

Many programs require the use of tables (or arrays) in storage for the following purposes: (1) To provide additional information, such as the tax rate for an income tax table; and (2) To provide storage by categories as data is processed, such as accumulating sales according to inventory number.

A simple example of a table is one that stores the numeric and the alphabetic month. The numeric month from an input record is used to locate the alphabetic month in the table, used to print on the report heading. In tabular form, the table appears as:

```
01JANUARY
02FEBRUARY
      .
      .
      .
12DECEMBER
```

TERMINOLOGY.   In the preceding example, the numeric month on the input record used to search through the table is called the *search argument*. Each entry in the table in storage consists of a *table argument* (the numeric month against which the search argument is compared), and a *function* (the alphabetic month, which is the item for which we are searching). The function may contain more than one field. Each table argument in the table is the same length and format, and each function is the same length and format. The search argument is the same length and format (such as character or packed) as the table argument. Further, the table arguments normally are defined in an ascending sequence.

TYPES OF TABLES.   There are two common types of tables used in business programming. The preceding table of months consists of discrete entries in which the table argument must exactly equal the search argument. Another example of this type could be an Inventory table containing Stock numbers as arguments and Stock prices as functions. Also, a second field in the function could be used to accumulate total

Stock issues by Stock number. The Stock numbers in the table are *sequential* but not necessarily *consecutive,* because not all Stock numbers are used. If the search argument does not equal one of the table arguments, then a possible error condition exists. The table could appear as:

STOCK NUMBER (TABLE ARGUMENT)	PRICE (FUNCTION)	
121	5.25	
135	3.10	
137	4.00	etc . . .

The second common type of table consists of table arguments that provide ranges or segments, such as the sequential steps of taxable income in an income tax table. In this case, the search argument will fall *within* one of the segments. The function is the tax rate for the segment. The table could appear as:

TAXABLE INCOME (TABLE ARGUMENT)	TAX RATE (FUNCTION)
6,000.00	8.0%
8,000.00 etc. . . .	10.0% etc. . . .

In the table, all taxable income up to $6,000 is taxed at 8.0%, and taxable income from $6,000.01 through $8,000 is at 10%.

We may define and store tables one of two ways:

1. The table arguments and functions are defined by DC's as constants. This method is useful when the arguments and functions do not change very often.
2. The area for the table is defined, but the contents of the table, the argument and function, are read sequentially as data at the start of the program and stored in the table. This method is useful when the arguments or functions are subject to frequent change. This method permits changes to the table without reassembling the program.

TABLE LOOK-UP. A table search requires repetitive processing. We initialize the search by loading the address of the table into a register, which the program uses explicitly as a base register. The search argument is compared against the first table argument. To compare against successive table arguments, the address in the register is incremented by the length of the argument/function entries in the table. When we compare the search argument to a table argument, there are three possibilities:

1. *The Search Argument Is Equal.* In this case the required function has been found, and the search is terminated.
2. *The Search Argument Is High.* We must continue the search by examining the next entry in the table.
3. *The Search Argument Is Low.* The action depends on the type of table. If the table contains *segments* such as a tax table, then the required function has been found; the tax rate is in this step. If, however, the table contains *discrete entries* (such as

nonconsecutive inventory stock numbers), then the required table argument does not exist. This latter condition is a common situation that must be checked for in this type of table.

TERMINATION OF THE LOOP. We must ensure that the search can be terminated. If no provision is made to end the loop, then the program may compare a very high search argument against all the entries in the table and against the area following the table. Several means may force termination:

1. We may assign the last table argument with *the highest possible value,* such as packed nines for packed fields, and hex F's for character or hex fields. Because the search argument cannot exceed this value, there will always occur a branch on equal (found), or low (found or nonexistent argument depending on the type of table). Figure 10-4 gives an example.
2. If we know the *number of entries* in the table, the program may count each time it compares to an entry. When the count exceeds the number of entries, the search is terminated. Figure 10-5 gives an example.
3. If we know the *address of the last table argument,* the program can compare the address being modified against this address. If the modified address exceeds the address of the last argument, then the table argument does not exist. Figure 10-6 gives an example.
4. If we know the *value of the highest table argument,* the program may compare the value of the search argument to this value. If the value of the search argument exceeds the known value, then the table argument does not exist, and the search does not have to be performed.

TABLE LOOK-UP WITH HIGH ARGUMENT. Figure 10-4 provides the coding for the table look-up of the numeric and alphabetic month discussed earlier, explained as follows:

— The table consists of a 2-character numeric month and a 9-character alphabetic month. (The longest month, September, is nine characters.) The last table argument contains hex F's.
— Initialization: The address of the table, MONTAB (at location X'300C'), is loaded into register-8, to be used explicitly as a base register. (*Note:* LA loads the address of the table, not its contents.)
— At C10LOOP, operand-2 of the CLC has the form D2(B2), and the coding 0(8) references base register-8 and zero displacement, giving the address X'300C'. The CLC compares the 2-character search argument, MONIN, against the first two bytes of the table, 01 at X'300C'.
— If the condition is equal, the month is found, and the program branches to C20EQUAL.
— If the condition is low, the month is not in the table, and the program branches to an error routine. This error could occur if the search argument invalidly contained a value either less than 01 or greater than 12. All search arguments will be lower than hex F's at the end of the table, so a low condition is always an error.

```
C0300C FCF1C1C1D5E4C1D9    10 MONTAB    DC    C'01JANUARY  '    TABLE OF NUMERIC AND ALPHA
003017 F0F2C6C5C2D9E4C1    11          DC    C'02FEBRUARY '    *    MONTHS
003022 FCF3D4C1D9C3C840    12          DC    C'03MARCH    '    *
00302D F0F4C1D7D9C9D340    13          DC    C'04APRIL    '    *
003038 F0F5D4C1E8404040    14          DC    C'05MAY      '    *
003043 F0F6D1E4D5C54040    15          DC    C'06JUNE     '    *
00304E FCF7C1E4D3E84040    16          DC    C'07JULY     '    *
003059 F0F8C1E4C7E4E2E3    17          DC    C'08AUGUST   '    *
003064 FCF9E2C5D7E3C5D4    18          DC    C'09SEPTEMBER'    *
00306F F1F0D6C3E3D6C2C5    19          DC    C'10OCTOBER  '    *
00307A F1F1D5D6E5C5D4C2    20          DC    C'11NOVEMBER '    *
003085 F1F2C4C5C3C5D4C2    21          DC    C'12DECEMBER '    *
003090 FFFF                22          DC    X'FFFF'           *    END OF TABLE

003092                     24 MONIN     DS    CL2               SEARCH ARGUMENT
003094 4040404040404040    25 PRINT     DC    CL121' '          PRINT AREA
                           26 *         .
                           27 *         .
00310D 00
00310E 4180 400A           28           LA    8,MONTAB          INITIALIZE ADDRESS OF TABLE

003112 D501 4090 8000 0.   30 C10LOOP   CLC   MONIN,0(8)        INPUT MONTH : TABLE MONTH?
003118 4780 4126       0   31           BE    C20EQUAL          *    EQUAL - FOUND
00311C 4740 50A4       0   32           BL    R10INV            *    LOW  - NOT IN TABLE
003120 4A80 42A6           33           AH    8,=H'11'          INCREMENT BY 11 FOR NEXT ENTRY
003124 47FC 4110       0   34           B     C10LOOP           *    IN THE TABLE

003128 D208 40F6 8002 0    36 C20EQUAL  MVC   PRINT+100(9),2(8) MOVE ALPHABETIC MONTH TO PRINT
```

FIGURE 10-4   Table look-up with hex F's as last argument.

— If the condition is high, it is necessary to examine the next table argument. We increment base register-8 by 11, the length of each entry. The base register now contains X'300D', where table argument 02 resides. The program then branches back to C10LOOP which compares the search argument against table argument 02.

— At C20EQUAL, the found function, the alphabetic month, is moved to the print area. Operand-1 indicates that nine bytes are to be moved. Operand-2 references base register-8 which contains the address of the found table argument. The displacement is two bytes because the function is two bytes from the first position of the table argument (the address in register-8).

TABLE LOOK-UP USING A COUNT: BCT, BCTR, BXLE, BXH.   This section examines two ways of performing a table search using the techniques for loop termination described earlier. The following instructions may be used to decrement a count and to test termination of a loop. The condition code is not changed.

NAME	OPERATION	OPERAND
	BCT	R1,X2 or R1,D2(X2,B2)
	BCTR	R1,R2
[symbol]	BXLE	R1,S2 or R1,R3,D2(B2)
	BXH	R1,S2 or R1,R3,D2(B2)

BRANCH ON COUNT—BCT AND BCTR.   Before using these instructions, we normally load a count in a register, such as the number of entries in the table. The routine may then use Branch on Count in the loop to decrement the count by 1 and to check if the count has been reduced to zero. The rules are:

1. Operand-1 specifies any register, which contains a count.
2. Operand-2 references an address in storage if BCT, or a register containing an address if BCTR. On execution, the computer decrements the contents of the operand-1 register by 1. If the contents are not zero, the program branches to the operand-2 address. If the contents are zero, the operation continues with the next sequential instruction. Since the operation performs no other checking, we must ensure that the count is initialized with a positive, nonzero amount.
3. For BCTR, if operand-2 specifies register-0, 1 is decremented from the operand-1 register, but no test is made and no branch taken. This use of BCTR is a convenient way of decrementing by 1 the value in any register. For example, assume that register-7 contains a positive value:

BCT 7,K50	means decrement register-7 by 1, and if nonzero branch to the address K50.
LA 9,K50	
BCTR 7,9	means decrement register-7 by 1, and if nonzero, branch to the address in register-9 (K50).
BCTR 11,0	means decrement register-11 by 1 and continue with the next instruction.

Figure 10-5 depicts a table search using two registers and BCT. The search argument is a 3-character field called JOBNO. The table, called JOBTABLE, contains 60 5-byte entries, a 3-character Job number as the table argument, and a 2-byte

```
00312E                        41 JOBNO    DS    CL3          JOB NUMBER - SEARCH ARGUMENT
003131                        42 RATE     DS    PL2          RATE FOR STORING FOUND FUNCTION

003133 F0F0F6585C             44 JOBTABLE DC    C'006',P'5.85'   *  JOB NO. 3 BYTES, RATE 2 BYTES
003138 F0F1F2715C             45          DC    C'012',P'7.15'   *
00313D FCF1F5830C             46          CC    C'015',P'8.30'   *
003142                        47          DS    57CL5            *    REST OF TABLE
                              48 *             .
                              49 *             .
                              50 *             .

00325F 0C
003260 4160 4131              52          LA    6,JOBTABLE   LOAD ADDRESS OF JOB TABLE
003264 4190 003C              53          LA    9,60         LOAD NO. OF ENTRIES

003268 D502 412C 6000         55 K10LOOP  CLC   JOBNO,0(6)   INPUT JOB# : TABLE JOB# ?
00326E 4780 427C              56          BE    K20EQUAL     *    EQUAL - FOUND
003272 4160 6005              57          LA    6,5(0,6)     INCREMENT BY 5 FOR NEXT ENTRY
003276 4690 4266              58          BCT   9,K10LOOP    DECR REG 9 BY 1. NOT ZERO? - LOOP
00327A 47F0 50A4              59          B     R10INV       *    ZERO? - NOT IN TABLE, ERROR

00327E FE11 412F 6003         61 K20EQUAL ZAP   RATE,3(2,6)  STORE RATE FROM TABLE
```

FIGURE 10-5   Table look-up using a count and BCT operation.

packed rate as the function. The function when found is to be stored in a field called RATE. The example loads the number of entries in the table, 60, into a register. BCT is used to decrement this count. If the loop is performed 60 times, the count is reduced to zero, and the required argument is known to be not in the table. An advantage of this approach is that Job numbers need not be in ascending sequence, so that the most commonly referenced Job numbers could be first in the table.

BRANCH ON INDEX LOW OR EQUAL—BXLE.   This instruction requires the use of three registers, two of which are an even-odd pair. BXLE does not directly reference the odd-numbered register. Before executing the BXLE we must ensure that all three registers are properly initialized. BXLE is an RS format instruction with three operands. The rules are:

1. Operand-1 specifies a register containing generally a count or an address.
2. Operand-2 normally denotes the even-numbered register of an even-odd pair such as 10 and 11. It contains a value used to increment or decrement the operand-1 register. All 31 bits are added in normal binary addition. The odd-numbered register is not directly referenced. It contains the limit or address against which operand-1 is compared.
3. Operand-3 references a storage address, the branch point for low/equal conditions.

On execution, BXLE adds the operand-2 even register constant to the operand-1 register. Operand-1 is then compared to the unreferenced odd register. If the operand-1 contents are low or equal, the program branches to the address in operand-3. If the contents are high, the program continues with the next sequential instruction.

Note: If the register in operand-2 is odd rather than even, the comparison is made to the operand-2 odd register rather than to the next register. Therefore, the operand-2 register is both the increment (decrement), and the limit.

Figure 10-6 illustrates a table search using three registers and the BXLE instruction. The table, JOBTABLE, is defined in Figure 10-5. This example loads the length of each entry (5) and the address of the last entry into the even-odd registers, 8 and 9. BXLE increments the address of base register-6 by the constant 5 in register-8. If the base register exceeds the address of the last entry, the program has stepped through the table without locating the required argument.

BRANCH ON INDEX HIGH—BXH.   BXH is similar to BXLE except that whereas BXLE branches if not high (low or equal), BXH branches if high. BXH is used to search through tables from the high argument through the low argument, that is a "reverse scan".

```
66 *           -----------------------------------
67 *           BXLE  BRANCH CN INDEX LOW OR EQUAL
68 *           -----------------------------------
69             LA    6,JOBTABLE          LOAD ADDRESS OF JOB TABLE
70             LA    8,5                 LOAD LENGTH OF EACH ENTRY
71             LA    9,JOBTABLE+59*5     LOAC ADDRESS OF LAST ENTRY

73 L1OLOOP     CLC   JOBNC,0(6)          INPUT JOB# : TABLE JOB# ?
74             BE    L20ECUAL            *    EQUAL - FOUND
75             BXLE  6,8,L1OLOOP         INCR REG 6 BY 5, CCMP REG 6 : 9
76 *                                     *    LO/EQ? - BRANCH TO L1OLOOP
77             B     R1CINV              *    HIGH? - NOT IN TABLE

79 L20EQUAL    ZAP   RATE,3(2,6)         STORE RATE FROM TABLE
```

FIGURE 10-6   Table look-up using BXLE.

SUMMARY.   The preceding examples give some of the common methods of terminating a table search. The commonest and simplest method is to define the last table argument with a high value, such as hex F's for character and nines for packed format. The methods using BCT and BXLE are efficient if enough registers are available. We should use whatever method is efficient and clearly understood.

Problems 10-1, 10-2, and 10-3 should now be attempted.

DIRECT TABLE ADDRESSING

Table arguments are normally arranged sequentially, but are not necessarily consecutive. Consider a table composed of discrete arguments, such as Job numbers or inventory Stock numbers. If the table is *both* sequential and consecutive, such as 10,11,12, . . . , then we do not require table arguments or a table look-up. To locate the required function, we can by *direct table addressing* calculate its *relative position* in the table. For example, the function for Stock item 0010 would be the tenth entry in the table. Direct table addressing is an extremely efficient way of locating functions, because no repetitive looping and comparing are required.

Refer to the table of numeric and alphabetic months in Figure 10-4. The table contains arguments of numeric months from 01 through 12 that are both sequential and consecutive. Figure 10-7 omits the arguments and finds the function by direct table addressing. Assume that the search argument, MONIN, contains 04 for April. The month is tested and found valid. It is converted into a register and decremented by 1, giving 3. Since each table entry is 9 long, the 3 is multiplied by 9, giving 27 or hex '1B'. Since the address of MONTABLE is X'4000', when added to X'1B' we get X'401B', the correct address for 'APRIL'.

Note: We must ensure that the search argument is valid. For example, if the search argument is incorrectly punched as 14, then the program will calculate an address that is outside the bounds of the table.

```
004000 D1C1C5E4C1D9E840    88 MONTABLE DC    C'JANUARY   '    TABLE OF 12 9-CHARACTER
004009 C6C5C2D9E4C1D9E8    89          DC    C'FEBRUARY  '    *    ALPHABETIC MONTHS
004012 D4C1D9C3C8404040    90          DC    C'MARCH     '    *
00401B C1D7D9C9D3404040    91          DC    C'APRIL     '    *
004024 D4C1E84040404040    92          DC    C'MAY       '    *
00402D D1E4D5C540404040    93.         DC    C'JUNE      '    *
004036 D1E4D3E840404040    94          DC    C'JULY      '    *
00403F C1E4C7E4E2E34040    95          DC    C'AUGUST    '    *
004048 E2C5D7E3C5D4C2C5    96          DC    C'SEPTEMBER'     *
004051 D6C3E3D6C2C5D940    97          DC    C'OCTOBER   '    *
00405A D5D6E5C5D4C2C5D9    98          DC    C'NOVEMBER  '    *
004063 C4C5C3C5D4C2C5D9    99          DC    C'DECEMBER  '    *

00406C 00004000          101 ADDRTAB DC    A(MONTABLE)        ADDRESS OF TABLE
004070                   102 DBLEWORD DS    D                 DOUBLE WORD FOR SEARCH ARG
                         103 *          •
                         104 *          •
00407E F271 506E 4C90    105          PACK  DBLEWORD,MONIN    PACK MONTH IN DOUBLE WORD
00407E F970 506E 50AA    106          CP    DBLEWORD,=P'1'    IS MONTH < 1 ?
004084 4740 50A4         107          BL    R50LOW                YES - ERROR

004088 F971 506E 50A6    109          CP    DBLEWORD,=P'12'   IS MONTH > 12 ?
00408E 4720 50A4         110          BH    R60HIGH               YES - ERROR

004092 4F7C 506E         112          CVB   7,DBLEWORD        CONVERT MONTH TO BINARY
C04096 0670              113          BCTR  7,0               DECREMENT MONTH BY 1
0040C8 4C70 50A8         114          MH    7,=H'9'           MULTIPLY MONTH BY LENGTH
00409C 5A70 506A         115          A     7,ADDRTAB         ADD TABLE ADDRESS
0040A0 D2C8 40F6 7C00    116          MVC   PRINT+100(9),0(7) MOVE ALPHABETIC MONTH
```

FIGURE 10-7   Direct table addressing.

CALCULATION OF THE DIRECT ADDRESS.   Assume the following:

A(F) = the address of the required function

A(T) = the address of the table

SA   = the value of the search argument

L   = the length of each function

N   = the value of the table argument representing the first, or lowest, function in the table. SA ≥ N.

The function is located by the formula: $A(F) = A(T) + [(SA-N) \times L]$. In the example program, $A(T) = X'4000'$, $L = 9$, and $N = 01$ (for January). Given search arguments of respectively 01, 02, and 12, the calculation of A(F) is as follows:

SA: Calculation of A(F):

01   $X'4000' + [(01-1) \times 9] = X'4000'$

02   $X'4000' + [(02-1) \times 9] = X'4009'$

12   $X'4000' + [(12-1) \times 9] = X'4063'$

Check the logic of the formula and the calculations of A(F) against the table in Figure 10-7.

SORTING DATA IN STORAGE

Computer manufacturers supply package "utility" programs for such operations as sorting. These programs are used to sort disk and tape *records* according to some user-specified sequence. Records are read by the sort program into main storage, sorted into the new sequence, and written on another disk or tape. More records are read, sorted, and eventually merged with the previously sorted records on disk or tape. Finally, the entire file is processed and the file is fully sorted.

Occasionally a program must be written to sort *data*. This problem should not be confused with the sorting of *records* on disk or tape. To sort data we must write our own routine. Data to be sorted typically is in the form of a table. The table is arranged in sequence of the argument; generally it is to be rearranged in sequence of the function.

In the example in Figure 10-5, the argument was the Job number and the function was the rate-of-pay. Assume that we are to sort the table by the rate-of-pay in order to print a report as ascending rate-of-pay with Job number. Figure 10-8 gives the coding for the sort, one of many techniques.

```
002802 416C 3057        7 S10SORT  LA    6,JOBTABLE          REG6: ADDRESS OF 1ST ENTRY
002806 4170 317E        8          LA    7,JOBTABLE+59*5     REG7: ADDRESS OF LAST ENTRY
00280A 4180 3179        9          LA    8,JOBTABLE+58*5     REG8: ADDRESS OF NEXT-TO-LAST

00280E 419C 6005       11 S20       LA    9,5(0,6)           REG9: ADDRESS OF REG-6 + 5

002812 F911 6003 90C3  13 S30       CP    3(2,6),3(2,9)      COMPARE FUNCTIONS (RATE-OF-PAY)
00281E 47DC 303E       14          BNH   S40                *    NOT HIGH - BYPASS EXCHANGE
00281C D202 3C54 6C00  15          MVC   SAVE3,0(6)         EXCHANGE
002822 D202 6000 9C00  16          MVC   0(3,6),0(9)        *    JOB NUMBERS
002828 D202 9000 3054  17          MVC   0(3,9),SAVE3       *
00282E F811 3052 6003  18          ZAP   SAVE2,3(2,6)       EXCHANGE
002834 FE11 6003 9003  19          ZAP   3(2,6),3(2,9)      *    RATES-OF-PAY
00283A FE11 9003 3052  20          ZAP   3(2,9),SAVE2       *

00284C 419C 9005       22 S40       LA    9,5(C,9)           INCREMENT REG9 BY ENTRY-LENGTH
002844 1997            23          CR    9,7                ADDR IN REG 9 : ADDR LAST ENTRY
002846 47DC 3010       24          BNH   S30                *    NOT HIGH - CONTINUE SORT

00284A 416C 6005       26          LA    6,5(0,6)           INCREMENT REG6 BY ENTRY-LENGTH
00284E 1968            27          CR    6,8                ADDR IN REG 6:ADDR NEXT-LAST
002850 47DC 300C       28          BNH   S20                *    NOT HIGH - CONTINUE SORT
                       29 *         .
                       30 *         .                       END OF SORT
                       31 *         .
002854                 32 SAVE2     DS    PL2
002856                 33 SAVE3     DS    CL3

002859 FCF0F2999C      35 JOBTABLE  DC    C'002',P'9.99'     JOB NO. & RATE-OF-PAY
00285E F0F0F6876C      36          DC    C'006',P'8.76'     *
0C28E3 FCF1F2715C      37          CC    C'012',P'7.15'     *
002868 F0F2F6585C      38          DC    C'026',P'5.85'     *
00286D F1F2F3450C      39          DC    C'123',P'4.50'     *
                       40 *         DC    .                  REST
                       41 *         DC    .                  OF
                       42 *         DC    .                  TABLE ENTRIES
```

FIGURE 10-8   Program to sort table functions in ascending sequence.

This routine works as follows: Function-1 (the first rate of pay) is compared against function-2. If function-1 is higher, the two entries are exchanged. Function-1 is next compared against function-3. If function-1 is higher, they are exchanged. Function-1 is compared successively against each other function, until eventually the *lowest entry* is stored in entry-1. Function-2 is then compared against function-3, function-4, etc., until the second lowest entry is stored in entry-2. The remaining functions are compared against the higher functions as in the preceding steps, exchanging entries where necessary. Once the next-to-last function compares to the last function, the sort is ended.

BINARY SEARCH

For long tables that do not lend themselves to direct addressing, it is often more efficient to use a *binary search* rather than a regular sequential table look-up. The search uses an approach of successive halving. It starts at the midpoint of the table— if the search argument is higher than the mid entry, we compare to the midpoint of the upper half of the table; if lower than the mid entry, we compare to the midpoint of the lower half. The search continues in this fashion until the argument is found or determined as not in the table. The following routine uses the same table as in Figure 10-8, the sort.

Note that COUNT initially contains a value of one more than the number of arguments in JOBTABLE (i.e., if JOBTABLE has 50 arguments, then COUNT contains 51). The routine initializes register-6 with 1 for the low entry-point, and loads COUNT in register-10 for the initial high entry-point. It uses these two values to calculate the midpoint (initially $[1 + 51] \div 2$ would give entry 26 as the middle). Since the length of each entry is five bytes, the routine multiplies this midpoint value by 5 to calculate a displacement, and adds the starting address of JOBTABLE (actually JOBTABLE-5) for the direct address of the midpoint. Use JOBTABLE as defined in Figure 10-8 with five arguments, and work through the binary search routine in Figure 10-9 to locate each of the five arguments.

SAMPLE PROGRAM—CALCULATE STOCK VALUE

The flowchart in Figure 10-10 and the program in Figure 10-11 illustrate the use of subroutines and many features in the last two chapters. The objective is to calculate the cost of inventory Stock on hand. There is one type of input record containing:

Column	3–4	Branch number
	5–8	Stock number
	11–13	Quantity

The program reads each input record and checks sequence on Branch/Stock number:

```
COUNT      DS      F                       NUMBER OF ENTRIES IN TABLE + 1
SEARCH     DS      CL3                     SEARCH ARGUMENT

           LA      6,1                     LOAD INITIAL LOW ENTRY
           L       10,COUNT                LOAD INITIAL HIGH ENTRY
           LA      8,0                     CLEAR MID-POINT

C10LOOP    LR      9,6                     LOAD LOW ENTRY IN CALC'N REGISTER
           AR      9,10                    ADD HIGH ENTRY TO CALC'N REGISTER
           SRA     9,1                     MID = 1/2 SUM
           CR      8,9                     COMPARE NEW MID TO PREV. MID
           BE      R10ERR                  ERROR IF EQUAL - ENTRY NOT IN TABLE

           LR      8,9                     MID NEW MID INTO PREVIOUS
           LA      5,JOBTABLE-5            LOAD ADDR OF TAB MINUS ENTRY LENGTH
           MH      9,=H'5'                 DISPLACEMENT = MID X ENTRY LENGTH
           AR      5,9                     ADD DISPLACEMENT TO ADDRESS
           CLC     SEARCH,0(5)             COMPARE SEARCH TO TABLE
           BE      D10FOUND                *    EQUAL - FOUND
           BL      C20LOW                  *    LOW

           LR      6,8                     *    HIGH - LOAD MID INTO LOW
           B       C10LOOP

C20LOW     LR      10,8                    *    LOW  - LOAD MID INTO HIGH
           B       C10LOOP

D10FOUND   ...                             ROUTINE FOR FOUND CONDITION
R10ERR     ...                             ROUTINE FOR NOT FOUND

REGISTER USAGE:
           5        FOR CALCULATION OF THE TABLE ADDRESS.
           6        LOW ENTRY NUMBER FOR THE TABLE.  INITIALIZED TO 1.
           8        MID-POINT NUMBER FOR THE TABLE.
           9        FOR CALCULATION OF THE TABLE DISPLACEMENT.
           10       HIGH ENTRY NO. FOR TABLE.  INITIALIZED WITH NO. OF ENTRIES + 1
```

FIGURE 10-9   Binary search.

Low — Error routine for out-of-sequence input.

Equal — Add the quantity on the record to the accumulated quantity for that stock number.

High — Use the Stock number for the previously stored stock to search a table. The table contains Stock number, unit cost, and description. If the item is found, the routine calculates cost = quantity × unit cost. If not found, this is an error.

The program prints totals of cost by Stock number (minor), Branch number (intermediate), and final total (major). It is organized as follows:

Initialization Section initializes the base register, opens the reader and print files, and sets the line counter to a high value to force an initial page overflow.

Main Logic Section reads input records and sequence-checks by Branch/Stock number. At the end of file, *A40END,* the program prints Stock, Branch, and Final totals.

Process Receipts Subroutine, E10RECT, adds the quantity received to Stock quantity.

Cost Calculation Subroutine, G10CALC, is performed for a new Stock number and

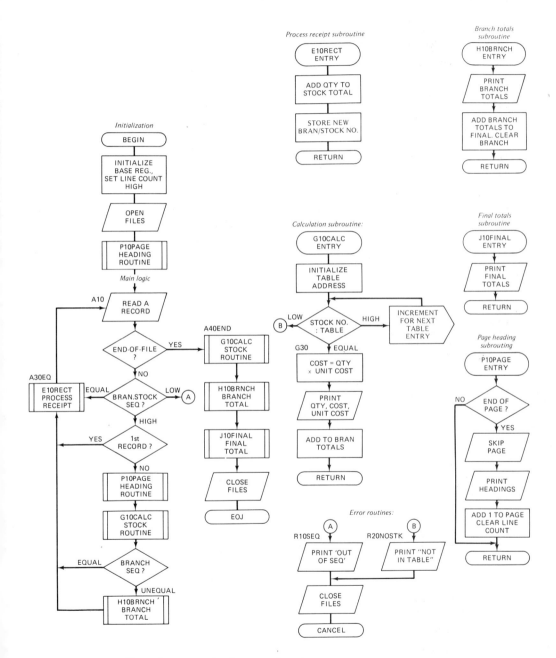

FIGURE 10-10   Flowchart to calculate stock values.

```
*                I N I T I A L I Z A T I O N
*                ---------------------------
PROG10   START  0
         SAVE   (14,12)
         BALR   3,0                      INITIALIZE BASE REGISTER
         USING  *,3
         ST     13,SAVEAREA+4
         LA     13,SAVEAREA
         OPEN   (FILEIN,(INPUT),PRTR,(OUTPUT))
         LH     10,=H'55'                SET LINE COUNT PAST MAXIMUM
         BAL    9,P10PAGE                PRINT HEADING FOR PAGE 1

*                M A I N   L O G I C
*                -------------------
A10READ  GET    FILEIN,INAREA
         CLC    CTLIN,PREVCTL            NEW BRANCH/STOCK : PREVIOUS?
         BE     A30EQ                    *    EQUAL - PROCESS RECEIPT
         BL     R10SEQ                   *    LOW   - OUT-OF-SEQUENCE
*                                        *    HIGH  - NEW STOCK NO.
         CLI    PREVCTL,X'00'            FIRST RECORD OF FILE?
         BE     A30EQ                    *    YES - PROCESS RECORD
         BAL    9,P10PAGE                CHECK FOR PAGE OVERFLOW
         BAL    9,G10CALC                CALC. & PRINT UNIT COST

         CLC    BRANCHIN,PREVBR          NEW BRANCH = PREV BRANCH?
         BE     A30EQ                    *    YES - PROCESS RECORD
         BAL    9,H10BRNCH               *    NO  - PRINT BRANCH TOTAL

A30EQ    BAL    9,E10RECT                PROCESS RECEIPT RECORD
         B      A10READ

*                E N D - O F - F I L E
*                ---------------------
A40END   BAL    9,G10CALC                EOF - CALC & PRINT UNIT COST
         BAL    9,H10BRNCH               *      PRINT BRANCH TOTAL
         BAL    9,J10FINAL               *      PRINT FINAL TOTAL
         CLOSE  (FILEIN,,PRTR)
         L      13,SAVEAREA+4
         RETURN (14,12)

*                P R O C E S S   R E C E I P T   S U B R O U T I N E
*                ----------------------------------------------------
E10RECT  PACK   QTYPK,QTYRECIN
         AP     QTYPKDW,QTYPK            ADD QUANTITY RECEIVED TO STOCK
         MVC    PREVCTL,CTLIN            STORE BRANCH-STOCK IN PREV
         BR     9

*                C O S T   C A L C U L ' N   S U B R O U T I N E
*                -----------------------------------------------
G10CALC  LA     2,COSTABLE               INITIALIZE TABLE SEARCH
G20      CLC    PREVSTK,0(2)             INPUT STOCK# : TABLE STOCK#?
         BE     G30                      *    EQUAL - FOUND
         BL     R20NOSTK                 *    LOW   - NOT IN TABLE
         AH     2,=H'14'                 *    HIGH  - TEST NEXT ENTRY
         B      G20

G30      ZAP    COSTPKDW,4(3,2)          EXTRACT UNIT COST FROM TABLE
         CVB    1,COSTPKDW               CONVERT UNIT COST TO BINARY
         CVB    0,QTYPKDW                CONVERT QUANTITY  TO BINARY
         MR     0,0                      MULT UNIT COST BY QUANTITY
         CVD    1,COSTPKDW               CONVERT COST TO PACKED

         MVC    COSTPR,EDCOS             EDIT:
         ED     COSTPR,COSTPKDW+4        *    STOCK COST
         MVC    UNCOSPR,EDUNIT
         ED     UNCOSPR,4(2)             *    UNIT COST (FROM TABLE)
         MVC    QTYPR,EDQTY
         ED     QTYPR,QTYPKDW+5          *    QUANTITY
```

FIGURE 10-11

230

```
          MVC     DESCRIPR,7(2)           MOVE DESCRIPTION (FROM TABLE)
          MVC     STOCKPR,PREVSTK         *    STOCK NO.
          MVC     BRANPR,PREVBR           *     BRANCH NO.
          BAL     11,M10WSP1              PRINT STOCK INFORMATION
          AP      BRCOSTPK,COSTFKDW+4(4)  ADD COST TO BRANCH TOTAL
          ZAP     QTYPKDW,=P'0'           CLEAR STOCK QUANTITY
          BR      9                       RETURN


*                 B R A N C H   T O T A L   S U B R O U T I N E
*                 ------------------------------------------------
H10BRNCH  BAL     11,M50SPC1              SPACE 1 LINE
          MVC     COSTPR(L'EDCOS+1),EDCOS
          ED      COSTPR,BRCOSTPK
          MVC     DESCRIPR(12),=C'BRANCH TOTAL'
          BAL     11,M20WSP2              PRINT BRANCH TOTAL

          AP      FINCOSPK,BRCOSTPK       ADD BRANCH COST TO FINAL
          ZAP     BRCOSTPK,=P'0'          CLEAR BRANCH COST
          BR      9                       RETURN


*                 F I N A L   T O T A L   S U B R O U T I N E
*                 ------------------------------------------------
J10FINAL  LA      1,P+69                  ADDRESS OF SIGNIF. START + 1
          MVC     COSTPR(L'EDCOS+2),EDCOS EDIT FINAL TOTAL COST
          EDMK    COSTPR,FINCOSPK         *    WITH FLOATING $ SIGN
          SH      1,=H'1'                 *    DECREMENT REGISTER-1
          MVI     0(1),C'$'               *    INSERT $ SIGN
          MVC     DESCRIPR(12),=C'FINAL  TOTAL'
          BAL     11,M10WSP1              PRINT FINAL TOTAL
          BR      9                       RETURN


*                 P R I N T   S U B R O U T I N E
*                 ------------------------------------
M00SKIP   MVI     P,X'8B'                 SKIP TO PAGE
          SR      10,10                   CLEAR LINE COUNT
          B       M90PRINT
M10WSP1   MVI     P,X'09'                 WRITE, SPACE 1
          AH      10,=H'1'                ADD 1 TO LINE COUNT
          B       M90PRINT
M20WSP2   MVI     P,X'11'                 WRITE, SPACE 2
          AH      10,=H'2'                ADD 2 TO LINE COUNT
          B       M90PRINT
M50SPC1   MVI     P,X'0B'                 SPACE, NO WRITE
          AH      10,=H'1'                ADD 1 TO LINE COUNT

M90PRINT  PUT     PRTR,PRINT
          MVC     PRINT,BLANK
          BR      11

*                 P A G E   H E A D I N G   S U B R O U T I N E
*                 ----------------------------------------------
P10PAGE   CH      10,=H'55'               END OF PAGE?
          BL      P20                     *    NO - BYPASS PAGE OVERFLOW
          BAL     11,M00SKIP              SKIP TO A NEW PAGE
          MVC     PRINT,PRHEAD1
          BAL     11,M20WSP2              PRINT REPORT HEADING-1
          MVC     PAGEPR,EDPAGE           SET UP
          ED      PAGEPR,PAGEPK           *    PAGE NO.
          MVC     PRINT,PRHEAD2
          BAL     11,M20WSP2              PRINT REPORT HEADING-2
          AP      PAGEPK,=P'1'            INCREMENT PAGE COUNT
P20       BR      9                       RETURN
```

FIGURE 10-11 (*Continued*)

231

```
*                 E R R O R   R O U T I N E S
*                 -------------------------
R10SEQ    MVC    P+41(L'ERRSEQ),ERRSEQ    OUT OF SEQUENCE BRANCH-STOCK
          B      R80

R20NOSTK  MVC    P+41(L'ERRSTK),ERRSTK    STOCK ITEM NOT IN TABLE
          SPACE
R80       MVC    STOCKPR,PREVSTK
          MVC    BRANPR,PREVBR
          BAL    11,M20WSP2               PRINT ERROR MESSAGE
          CLOSE  (FILEIN,,PRTR)
          ABEND  09,DUMP


*                 D E C L A R A T I V E S
*                 -------------------------

FILEIN    DCB    BLKSIZE=80,              DEFINE THE INPUT FILE        +
                 DDNAME=SYSIN,                                         +
                 DEVD=DA,                                              +
                 DSORG=PS,                                             +
                 EODAD=A40END,                                         +
                 MACRF=(GM)

PRTR      DCB    BLKSIZE=133,             DEFINE THE PRINTER FILE      +
                 DDNAME=SYSPRINT,                                      +
                 DEVD=DA,                                              +
                 DSORG=PS,                                             +
                 MACRF=(PM),                                           +
                 RECFM=FM

SAVEAREA  DS     18F                      REGISTER SAVE AREA
          DS     0D                       PACKED - ALIGNED DOUBLEWORD:
COSTPKDW  DC     PL8'0'                   *
QTYPKDW   DC     PL8'0'                   *

QTYPK     DC     PL2'0'                   NORMAL PACKED DECLARES:
BRCOSTPK  DC     PL4'0'                   *
FINCOSPK  DC     PL4'0'                   *
PAGEPK    DC     PL2'1'                   *

ERRSEQ    DC     C'RECORD OUT OF SEQUENCE ON BRANCH/STOCK'
ERRSTK    DC     C'STOCK ITEM NOT IN TABLE'

PREVCTL   DS     0CL6                     PREVIOUS CONTROL WORD
PREVBR    DC     XL2'00'                  *     BRANCH NO.
PREVSTK   DC     XL4'00'                  *     STOCK NO.

EDCOS     DC     X'4020206B2020214B2020C3D9',C'**'
EDUNIT    DC     X'402020214B2020'
EDQTY     DC     X'402020202020C3D9'
EDPAGE    DC     X'40202020'
*                                         STOCK TABLE:
COSTABLE  DC     C'1234',P'001.00',C'GIDGETS'  STOCK NO., COST, DESCR'N
          DC     C'2468',P'015.25',C'WIDGETS'  *
          DC     C'2470',P'100.17',C'MIDGETS'  *
          DC     C'2844',P'020.00',C'FIDGETS'  *
          DC     4X'FF',PL3'0',C'INVALID'      *  END OF TABLE

INAREA    DS     0CL80                    INPUT RECORD:
CODEIN    DS     CL2                      01-02 RECORD CODE
CTLIN     DS     0CL6                     BRANCH/STOCK CONTROL WORD
BRANCHIN  DS     CL2                      03-04 BRANCH
STOCKIN   DS     CL4                      05-08 STOCK NO.
          DS     CL2                      09-10 UNUSED
QTYRECIN  DS     ZL3                      11-13 QUANTITY
          DS     CL67                     14-80 UNUSED
```

FIGURE 10-11 (*Continued*)

232

```
PRHEAD1   DS    0CL133                      HEADING-1 AREA:
          DC    CL29' '                     *
          DC    CL104'I N V E N T O R Y  U N I T  C O S T  R E P O R T'

PRHEAD2   DS    0CL133                      HEADING-2 AREA
          DC    CL15' '                     *
          DC    CL29'BRANCH STOCK'          *
          DC    CL42'QUANTITY UNITCOST    COST'
          DC    CL09'     PAGE'             *
PAGEPR    DS    CL04                        *
          DC    CL34' '                     *


BLANK     DC    C' '                        BLANK FOR CLEARING PRINT AREA
PRINT     DS    0CL133                      REPORT PRINT AREA
P         DS    CL01                        *
          DC    CL16' '                     *
BRANPR    DS    CL02                        *   BRANCH NO.
          DC    CL03' '                     *
STOCKPR   DS    CL04                        *   STOCK NO.
          DC    CL02' '                     *
DESCRIPR  DS    CL07                        *   DESCRIPTION
          DC    CL09' '                     *
QTYPR     DS    ZL08                        *   QUANTITY
          DC    CL01' '                     *
UNCOSPR   DS    ZL07                        *   UNIT COST
          DC    CL01' '                     *
COSTPR    DS    ZL12                        *   COST
          DC    CL60' '                     *

          END   PROG10
```

TEST INPUT DATA:

DEPT	STOCK	QTY
03	1234	125
03	2844	086
03	2844	086
05	2470	035
05	2470	035


```
        I N V E N T O R Y   U N I T   C O S T   R E P O R T

BRANCH STOCK                    QUANTITY UNITCOST       COST                    PAGE    1

  03    1234   GIDGETS            125      1.00       125.00
  03    2844   FIDGETS            172     20.00     3,440.00

               BRANCH TOTAL                           3,565.00  *

  05    2470   MIDGETS             70    100.17     7,011.90

               BRANCH TOTAL                           7,011.90  *

               FINAL   TOTAL                        $10,576.90  **
```

FIGURE 10-11 *(Continued)*

233

for end-of-file. The routine includes a table look-up, binary multiplication, and printing of the Stock detail line. It also adds Stock cost to Branch cost.

Branch Total Subroutine, H10BRNCH, is performed on a change of Branch and at the end-of-file. It prints Branch cost and adds to Final cost.

Final Total Subroutine, J10FINAL, performed at the end-of-file, prints total Final cost.

Page Heading Subroutine, P10PAGE, is performed at the start of the program and whenever the end of a page is reached.

Error Routines process out-of-sequence records and Stock items not in the table.

Register Usage:

0,1	Calculation of binary cost
1	EDMK
2	Table look-up on the Stock Cost Table
3	Base register for program addressing
9	Subroutine linkage
10	Line count for page overflow

DEBUGGING TIPS

Among the many common errors that programmers tend to make when using tables are the following:

— There are arguments missing from the table, or the functions are incorrect. Argument/function also may not be consistently the same length.
— The increment value for stepping through the table is incorrect.
— There is no way to ensure termination of the search, so that a CLC, for example, may continue frantically checking right through main storage.
— The branch instruction that returns to perform the next compare goes instead to the preceding instruction that initializes the search:

```
W30SRCH   LA    9,TABLE
          CLC
          . . .
          B     W30SRCH
```

The program loops endlessly—an error more popular with programmers than with operators.
— Sophisticated routines such as direct addressing, binary search, and sorting can generate spectacular errors. Most programmers code these so carefully they execute perfectly the first time (but everything else blows up!).

This chapter completes comments on debugging. At this point you are far enough advanced and your programs so complex that your best debugging aids are carefulness, detective skills, hex storage dumps, and access to an experienced systems programmer.

PROBLEMS

10-1. Given the contents of registers: 7 = X'3000', 8 = '4500', and 9 = X'4000', what is the result in register-6 for LA 6,7(8,9)?

10-2. What is the effect of the following AP?

```
TOTAL        DS  PL5
AMOUNT       DS  PL4
             LA  8,TOTAL
             LA  9,AMOUNT
             AP  6(5,8),0(4,9)
```

10-3. Provide the code to extract today's date from your computer system. Assume any necessary declaratives.

10-4. What are the various ways an Assembler program may use to force termination of a table look-up? What may be the result if some provision is not made to force termination if the argument is (a) packed; or (b) character?

10-5. Assume that register-4 is initialized to zero in each case. Given declaratives BIN1 and BIN2, explain the code and determine the contents of register-4 in each case.

```
            (a)                              (b)
BIN1 DC F'20'        L    6,BIN1         LA    5,100
BIN2 DC F'200'  A15  A    4,=F'2'        LM    8,9,BIN1
                     BCT  6,A15     B15  A     4,=F'3'
                                         BXLE  5,8,B15
```

10-6. What does the following accomplish?

```
LA   6,W30
LA   5,10
BCTR 5,6
```

10-7. Define the table required to calculate the current federal income tax. Use a field called TAXINC for taxable income to locate the required rate. Calculate TAX based on this rate.

10-8. *Direct table addressing.* Assume a payroll table, with consecutive job numbers from 031 through 055. Each job number has an associated rate-of-pay (xx.xx) as the function. The following declaratives are given:

```
JOBNO DS CL3
HOURS DS P'00.0'
WAGES DS P'0000.00'
```

Code the declaratives for the payroll rate table, called JOBTAB. Write the routine to use JOBNO to locate the correct rate in the table. Multiply HOURS by the rate, round the result to two decimals, and store it in WAGES.

10-9. CUSTOMER BILLING FOR ELECTRIC CONSUMPTION.

Required: A program that reads customer billing records containing previous and present electric reading, and calculates consumption and the billing amount.

Input: Customer billing records containing:

	BILLING MASTER	CONSUMPTION CARD
Record code	1–2 (31)	1–2 (32)
Region	3–4	3–4
Customer number	5–9	5–9
Customer name and address	10–69	

Previous reading:	Day/month/year		10–15 (dd/mm/yy)
	Meter reading		16–20
Present reading:	Day/month/year		21–26 (dd/mm/yy)
	Meter reading.		27–31

Procedure:

— Check for valid record codes, and sequence-check the file according to region-customer number. Within a region, customer numbers are in ascending sequence. Each customer has one billing master card (31) followed by one consumption card (32).

— Calculate electric consumption in kilowatt-hours = present reading − previous reading and calculate the billing amount based on the electric billing schedule for your community.

— Print the detail for each customer, and print total consumption and billing amount for each region and for the final total.

— Use subroutines extensively.

CHAPTER 11

LOGICAL OPERATIONS AND BIT MANIPULATION

Certain logical operations, such as CLC, CLI, MVC, and LA treat data as "logical". The operations assume that the fields contain no sign, and act nonalgebraically on each byte as a string of eight bits. Similarly, certain binary operations process binary data as logical by treating all 32 bits of the binary fullword as unsigned data. The first section discusses the logical operations that add, subtract, compare, and shift. These instructions are useful if arithmetic fields are of such magnitude that they require *double precision,* a 63-bit field plus a sign bit. Such a field requires two registers: the left one contains the sign and the leftmost 31 data bits; the right register contains the rightmost 32 data bits.

Of greater use are the other logical operations: Test Under Mask, Translate, and Translate and Test. Although technically a branch operation, Execute is also included. These instructions provide a repertoire of powerful techniques to manipulate bits, to translate bits to other codes, and to handle variable length records. Logical operations are also used to translate binary (fixed-point) to floating-point format.

LOGICAL OPERATIONS

ADD AND SUBTRACT LOGICAL—AL, ALR, SL, SLR. These instructions treat binary fields as unsigned logical data.

NAME	OPERATION	OPERAND
[symbol]	AL	R1,X2 or R1,D2(X2,B2)
	ALR	R1,R2
	SL	R1,X2 or R1,D2(X2,B2)
	SLR	R1,R2

AL, ALR, SL, and SLR are similar to A, AR, S, and SR, with the following differences: (1) Since the field is treated as logical data there is no sign; all 32 bits are added or subtracted; (2) There may be a carry out of the leftmost bit (bit 0). For subtract, if the carry out of bit 0 differs from bit 1, an overflow occurs; (3) The condition code is set as follows:

CODE	ADD	SUBTRACT
0	Zero sum	Zero difference
1	Nonzero sum	Minus
2	Zero sum, with carry	Plus
3	Nonzero sum, carry	Overflow

DOUBLE PRECISION ADDITION.   Double precision binary fields contain a sign bit and 63 data bits. We must give such fields special programming consideration, because a register can handle only 32 bits.

Assume two 64-bit fields, called DBL1 and DBL2, are to be added, and the result stored in DBL1. Figure 11-1 gives the coding. It is necessary to split each field into two 32-bit fields. DBL1 is loaded into register-6 (the leftmost 32 bits) and register-7 (the rightmost 32 bits). The sign is the left bit of register-6. The rightmost 32 bits of DBL2 are added to register-7. We use a logical add because register-7 has no sign bit. If an overflow occurs, a bit has been lost; adding '1' to register-6 remedies this situation. Then the leftmost 32 bits of DBL2 are added to register-6. The example shows two 5-bit registers for ease of understanding. Check the binary values for each step.

```
 6 *                              REG-6: REG-7:
 7 DBL1      DS    D              00101 11010   ASSUME 10-BIT FIELD 186
 8 DBL2      DS    D              00011 10110   ASSUME 10-BIT FIELD 118

10           L     6,DBL1         00101         LOAD LEFTMOST  32 BITS
11           L     7,DBL1+4       00101 11010   LOAD RIGHTMOST 32 BITS
12           AL    7,DBL2+4       00101 10000   ADD   RIGHTMOST 32 BITS
13           BC    12,NOFLOW      BRANCH IF COND CODE 0 OR 1
14 *                              NO BRANCH IF CARRY SUM OR
15 *                              NON-ZERO SUM.
16           AH    6,=H'1'        00110 10000   ADD 1 TO LEFTMOST FIELD
17 NOFLOW    A     6,DBL2         01001 10000   ADD LEFTMOST 32 BITS
18           ST    6,DBL1                       STORE LEFTMOST  32 BITS
19           ST    7,DBL1+4                     STORE RIGHTMOST 32 BITS
```

FIGURE 11-1   Addition of double precision binary fields.

COMPARE LOGICAL—CL, CLR.

NAME	OPERATION	OPERAND
[symbol]	CL CLR	R1,X2 or R1,D2(X2,B2) R1,R2

These instructions are similar to C and CR. However, CL and CLR compare logically all 32 bits from left to right regardless of sign. An unequal compare terminates the operation. The usual condition code is set: Equal (0), Low (1), High (2).

SHIFT LOGICAL—SRL, SLL, SRDL, SLDL. These instructions shift bits right or left logically regardless of sign, and treat the entire 32 or 64 bits as a single unsigned field. Operand-1 of SRDL and SLDL references the even register of an even-odd pair.

NAME	OPERATION	OPERAND
[symbol]	SRL SLL SRDL SLDL	R1,S2 or R1,D2(B2) R1,S2 or R1,D2(B2) R1,S2 or R1,D2(B2) R1,S2 or R1,D2(B2)

The rules for SRL, SLL, SRDL, and SLDL are similar to those for SRA, SLA, SRDA, and SLDA except that: (1) All 32 or 64 bits shift; (2) Zero bits replace bits shifted off the left or right; (3) The condition code is *not* set and no overflow occurs.

BINARY DATA PACKING AND UNPACKING. The following routine illustrates shifting of logical data in registers. Frequently a file consists of thousands or hundreds of thousands of records stored on tape or disk. One way to conserve storage is to "pack" fields in binary format. Assume an electric utility with part of each Customer record in character format.

	NUMBER OF CHARACTERS	NUMBER OF BITS FOR BINARY REPRESENTATION
District	3	10
Account	5	17
Rate Code	1	1
Service Code	1	2
	10 bytes	30 bits or 4 bytes

We can store the contents of District in 3 characters or alternatively in a 10-bit binary field, which can store a value up to 1023. Similarly, Account, with a maximum value of 99999, can be stored in a 17-bit binary field. Rate Code requires only a 1-bit field: 0 for domestic or 1 for commercial rate. Service Code can contain 4 possibilities requiring two bits:

	CODE	BITS		CODE	BITS
None	0	00	Meter rental	2	10
Budget	1	01	Both	3	11

Character format requires 10 bytes to store the data. Binary format requires only 30 bits or one fullword of 4 bytes. If there are 400,000 records kept on a disk or tape file, then we have saved 400,000 × 6 = 2,400,000 bytes of disk or tape storage (not main storage). We have to condense or compress these fields into one binary fullword prior to writing the data on disk or tape. Figure 11-2 illustrates coding that performs this condensing. Because there are no signs, we can use logical shift operations. The "packed" binary format is to be:

	BITS			BITS
Unused	0-1		Rate	29-29
District	2-11		Service	30-31
Account	12-28			

```
145 *                      ASSUMED VALUES- CHAR:  BINARY:
146 DISTRICT DC      CL3'838'           838    1101000110
147 ACCOUNT  DC      CL5'17683'         17683  00100010100010011
148 RATE     DC      CL1'1'             1      1
149 SERVICE  DC      CL1'2'             2      10
150 DOUBWORD DS      D
151 FULLWORD DS      F
152 *                            REG:       BINARY FORMAT:
153 BINPACK  PACK    DOUBWORD,DISTRICT
154          CVB     6,DOUBWORD          6: --    --22ZEROS--       --1101000110

156          PACK    DOUBWORD,ACCOUNT
157          CVB     7,DOUBWORD          7: -- 15ZEROS --  00100010100010011
158          SLL     7,15               7: 00100010100010011--  15ZEROS  --
159          SLDL    6,17               6: 000001101000110001000101000010011

161          PACK    DOUBWORD,RATE
162          CVB     7,DOUBWORD          7: ----     --31ZEROS--       ---1
163          SLL     7,31               7: 1---     --31ZEROS--       ----
164          SLDL    6,1                6: 0000110100011000100010100010011

166          PACK    DOUBWORD,SERVICE
167          CVB     7,DOUBWORD          7: ----     --30ZEROS--       --10
168          SLL     7,30               7: 10 -     --30ZEROS--       ---
169          SLDL    6,2                6: 00110100011000100010100010011110
170          ST      6,FULLWORD
```

FIGURE 11-2 Binary data packing.

Problem 11-1 should now be attempted.

BOOLEAN LOGIC

Boolean logic was devised by George Boole (1815–1864). Practical applications have been in switches for telephone circuits and in the design of electronic computers. Boolean logic uses only digits 0 and 1 and has two arithmetic functions—addition and multiplication:

ADDITION					MULTIPLICATION			
0	0	1	1		0	0	1	1
+0	+1	+0	+1		×0	×1	×0	×1
0	1	1	1		0	0	0	1

Assembler language uses Boolean logic for the logical functions AND, OR, and Exclusive OR (XOR) to perform bit manipulation. For each of the three logical functions there are four instructions, in RR, RX, SI, and SS format (not available on some smaller models).

AND:	OR:	XOR:	Instruction Format:
NR	OR	XR	RR
N	O	X	RX or R1,D2(X2,B2)
NI	OI	XI	SI or D1(B1),S2
NC	OC	XC	SS or D1(L,B1),D2,(B2)

For all twelve instructions, operand-1 is called the *target* field and operand-2 is the *mask*. The operations compare the bits in the mask against those in the target, one at a time from left to right. The target bits are modified to 0 or 1 according to the bit contents and the logical operation. The condition code is set as follows:

0 if all target bits are set to 0.   Test with BZ or BNZ.
1 if any target bit is set to 1.   Test with BM or BNM.

The following shows two 4-bit fields, called MASK and TARGET. The three unrelated cases illustrate AND, OR, and XOR. Each case sets the condition code to 1.

Field:	AND	OR	XOR
MASK	0011	0011	0011
TARGET	0101	0101	0101
Result	0001	0111	0110

AND.   The logical function AND is equivalent to Boolean multiplication. If both the mask AND and the target bit are 1, then the target bit is set to 1. All other cases set the target bit to zero. In Figure 11-3, NR ANDs the contents of register-8 (the mask) with that of register-9 (the target). N ANDs the contents of MASK in storage (a fullword aligned) with the target in register-8. NI, an immediate operation, ANDs the single immediate byte with the first byte of TARGET. NC ANDs the first two bytes of MASK and TARGET.

OR.   The logical function OR is equivalent to Boolean addition. If either or both the mask or the target bit is 1, then the target bit is set to 1. Where both bits are zero, the target bit is set to zero. Figure 11-3 illustrates the four OR operations.

EXCLUSIVE OR (XOR).   If either the mask *or* the target bit (but not both) is 1, then

```
23                DS    0F                         FORCE FULLWORD ALIGNMENT
24 MASK           DC    B'0011011100101001111000011001101'
25 TARGET         DC    B'0101010111001001100001110011110'
26 *                    --------------------
27 *              AND - NR, N, NI, NC
28 *                    --------------------
29 AND            L     8,MASK                      LOAD MASK VALUE
30                L     9,TARGET                    LOAD TARGET VALUE
31                NR    9,8                         'AND' TARGET WITH MASK

33                L     8,TARGET                    LOAD TARGET VALUE
34                N     8,MASK                      'AND' TARGET WITH MASK

36                NI    TARGET,B'01010101'          'AND' FIRST BYTE OF TARGET

38                NC    TARGET(2),MASK              'AND' FIRST 2 BYTES OF TARGET

40 *                    --------------------
41 *              OR  - OR, C, OI, OC
42 *                    --------------------
43 OR             L     8,MASK                      LOAD MASK VALUE
44                L     9,TARGET                    LOAD TARGET VALUE
45                OR    9,8                         'OR'  TARGET WITH MASK

47                L     8,TARGET                    LOAD TARGET VALUE
48                O     8,MASK                      'OR'  TARGET WITH MASK

50                OI    TARGET,B'01010101'          'OR'  FIRST BYTE OF TARGET

52                OC    TARGET(2),MASK              'OR'  FIRST 2 BYTES OF TARGET

54 *                    ------------------------------
55 *              EXCLUSIVE OR - XR, X, XI, XC
56 *                    ------------------------------
57 XOR            L     8,MASK                      LOAD MASK VALUE
58                L     9,TARGET                    LOAD TARGET VALUE
59                XR    9,8                         'XOR' TARGET WITH MASK

61                L     8,TARGET                    LOAD TARGET VALUE
62                X     8,MASK                      'XOR' TARGET WITH MASK

64                XI    TARGET,B'01010101'          'XOR' FIRST BYTE OF TARGET

66                XC    TARGET(2),MASK              'XOR' FIRST 2 BYTES OF TARGET
```

FIGURE 11-3   Boolean operations: AND, OR, EXCLUSIVE OR.

XOR sets the target bit to 1. Where both are zero or 1, the target is set to zero. Figure 11-3 illustrates the four XOR operations.

COMMON USES FOR BOOLEAN OPERATIONS. Figure 11-4 shows several applications of Boolean operations. In CLEAR, the Exclusive OR clears an area to hex zeros. Since both mask and target contain the same bits, Exclusive OR sets all bits to zero. The example clears a binary field to X'00's, all binary zeros. Some programmers use XC to clear the print area, as XC PRINT,PRINT.

```
70 FULLWD    DS    F                          BINARY FULLWORD
71 PAGENO    DC    PL2'1'                      PAGE COUNTER

73 *               CLEAR A FIELD TO HEX ZEROS:                           +
                   --------------------------
74 CLEAR     XC    FULLWD,FULLWD               CLEAR BINARY VALUE

76 *               CORRECT SIGN FOR PRINTING:                            +
                   --------------------------
77 SIGN      UNPK  PRINT+91(3),PAGENO          UNPACK PAGE COUNTER
78           OI    PRINT+93,X'F0'              FORCE F-SIGN WITH OR OPERATOR

80 *               EXCHANGE 2 REGISTERS:       7: 1010   8: 1001         +
                   --------------------
81 REVERSE   XR    7,8                         7: 0011   8: 1001
82           XR    8,7                         7: 0011   8: 1010
83           XR    7,8                         7: 1001   8: 1010

85 *               CHANGE NOP TO BRANCH                                  +
                   --------------------
86 SWITCH    NOP   CHANGE                      INSTRUCTION DEFINED AS NO-OP
87 *          .
88 *          .
89           OI    SWITCH+1,X'F0'              CHANGE SWITCH MASK TO
90 *                                           X'F' (B)
91 *          .
92           B     SWITCH
93 CHANGE    NI    SWITCH+1,X'0F'              CHANGE SWITCH MASK TO
94 *                                           X'0' (NOP)
95 *          .

97 *               TEST BITS ON FOR CUSTOMER CODE:                       +
                   -------------------------------
98 CODES     MVC   TEST,CODE                   MOVE CODE TO TEST
99           NI    TEST,B'11100000'            'AND' FIRST 3 BITS
100 *        BNZ   ...                         BRANCH IF ANY BIT IS ON
101 *         .
102 *         .
103 CODE     DS    BL1
104 TEST     DS    BL1

106 *              TEST CHARACTERS FOR F-ZONE                            +
                   --------------------------
107 ZONES    MVC   STORE,FIELD                 MOVE CHARACTER FIELD TO STORE
108          NC    STORE,=X'F0F0F0F0F0'        'AND' WITH X'F0'S
109          CLC   STORE,=X'F0F0F0F0F0'        IF UNEQUAL, SOME BYTE HAS
110 *        BNE   ...                         NO F-ZONE
111 *         .
112 *         .
113 FIELD    DS    CL5
114 STORE    DS    CL5
```

FIGURE 11-4   Sample use of Boolean operators.

SIGN corrects the sign in an unpacked field. Earlier we saw that a packed field such as /23/4C/ when unpacked becomes /F2/F3/C4/. This amount prints incorrectly as 23D. The solution used MVZ to insert an "F"-sign in place of the C-sign, /F2/F3/F4/. This example unpacks a page counter, PAGENO, in the print area. OI forces all four sign bits to be turned on, thereby adjusting the sign to X'F'. For example, C4 OR'd with F0 gives F4.

REVERSE shows how XR may interchange two registers without the use of an intermediary register. The 4-bit areas illustrate how the example works.

SWITCH illustrates switching. We may manipulate the mask in the Branch on Condition (BC) instruction to change the program flow. BC 15 (unconditional branch) is commonly written as B. BC 0 is a no-operation condition which performs no branch at all; the extended mnemonic is NOP. The mask is in bits 8–11 of the object code. The example switches the mask from X'0' to X'F' (NOP becomes B) and vice versa. Clever, but not good programming practice.

CODES uses bits that represent yes or no conditions for customers. In the example, a utility company customer has an 8-bit code designed as follows:

Bit 0 - Electric account   Bit 4 - Electric heating
Bit 1 - Gas account   Bit 5 - 30 days delinquent
Bit 2 - Budget account   Bit 6 - Rented meter
Bit 3 - Industrial   Bit 7 - Not used

A 1-bit means the condition exists, and more than one bit may be validly on. The example tests if the customer has *any* of the conditions: electric, gas, budget. The NI operation tests bits 0, 1, and 2; any equal bits set the condition code to 1.

ZONES tests for F-zones in a character field. This is a useful check for validity of input data, such as date, account number, and amounts (except the units portion of minus amounts, such as F1F2F3F4D5).

The TM instruction in the next section may more effectively test bits.

OTHER OPERATIONS

TEST UNDER MASK—TM.   The previous section used bits as switches or indicators. An efficient instruction to test bit conditions is TM, Test Under Mask.

NAME	OPERATION	OPERAND
[symbol]	TM	S1,I2 or D1(B1),I2

TM is an immediate instruction (like MVI) with two operands: Operand-1 refers to one byte in storage, containing the bits to be tested; operand-2 is the 8-bit mask in immediate format. One-bits in the mask indicate which bits to test in operand-1. TM compares the 1-bits in the mask against the selected bits in operand-1, bit for bit. For example, if the immediate operand is B'01001100', then TM tests only bits 1, 4, and 5 of operand-1. Operand-1 is unchanged. The condition code is set as follows:

SELECTED BITS IN OPERAND-1	CONDITION CODE	TEST USING
All selected bits are 0	0	BZ Branch Zeros or BNZ not Zeros
Bits are mixed—some are 1, some are 0	1	BM Branch Mixed or BNM Branch not Mixed
All selected bits are 1	3	BO Branch Ones or BNO Branch not Ones

TM tests only the bit position of the mask that contains a 1 and ignores zero mask positions. (Boolean operators, however, process all bit positions regardless of 0 or 1.) The extended mnemonics for testing the condition code are the same—BZ, BM, and BO, but for TM are described differently. Branch Minus is called Branch Mixed and Branch Overflow becomes Branch Ones.

In the example CODES in the previous section, an 8-bit code represented yes or no conditions for utility customers. The next three examples in Figure 11-5 test this code for BZ, BM, and BO.

```
 6 *          --------------------
 7 *          TM    TEST UNDER MASK
 8 *          --------------------
 9 CODE       DC    B'11100100'

11 TESTZERO TM    CODE,B'00010010'   ALL SELECTED BITS ARE ZERO
12 *          BZ    ...              BRANCH ON ZEROS

14 TESTMIX  TM    CODE,B'10001100'   ALL SELECTED BITS ARE MIXED
15 *          BM    ...              BRANCH ON MIXED

17 TESTONES TM    CODE,B'11100000'   ALL SELECTED BITS ARE CNES
18 *          BO    ...              BRANCH ON ONES
```

FIGURE 11-5   Sample uses of test under mask—TM.

To test if the customer has an industrial account with a rented meter, we test bits 3 and 6 of CODE. In the example TESTZERO, the selected bits in CODE are both 0. Because the condition code is set to 0, BZ causes a branch. To test if the customer has an electric account, electric heating, and is 30 days delinquent in paying his bill, we test bits 0, 4, and 5 of CODE. In the example TESTMIX, the selected bits are: bit 0 is on, bit 4 is off, bit 5 is on. Because the bits are mixed off and on, the condition code is set to 1. BM causes a branch. To test if the customer has electric, gas, and budget, we test bits 0, 1, and 2. In the example TESTONES, the selected bits in CODE all contain 1. The condition code is set to 3, and BO causes a branch.

INSERT CHARACTER AND STORE CHARACTER—IC AND STC. IC moves a single byte (8 bits) from storage into a register, and STC moves a byte from a register into storage.

NAME	OPERATION	OPERAND	
[symbol]	IC	R1,X2 or	R1,D2(X2,B2)
	STC	R1,X2 or	R1,D2(X2,B2)

For both instructions, operand-1 references the rightmost 8 bits of a register (bits 24–31). Operand-2 references one byte of storage. IC, like LH, transfers data from operand-2 (storage) to operand-1 (register). STC, like STH, transfers data from operand-1 (register) to operand-2 (storage). However, the IC and STC operations do not affect the other bits (0–23) of the register. Further, operand-2 can specify any storage position, odd or even.

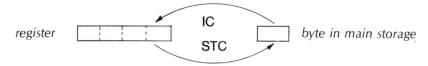

EXTENDED IC AND STC EXAMPLE. Figure 11-6 illustrates both IC and STC and introduces variable length fields. This example reads a record from an input device. The record, called NAMEADDR, consists of two fields, name and address, both of which may be any length. The length of each field is defined by a 1-byte binary number preceding the field, as shown:

```
118 *          -----------------------
119 *      IC      INSERT CHARACTER
120 *      STC     STORE CHARACTER
121 *          -----------------------
122        XR      1,1             CLEAR REG 1
123        LA      9,NAMADDR       ADDRESS OF 1ST LENGTH INDICATOR
124        IC      1,0(0,9)        LENGTH OF NAME IN REG 1
125        LR      8,1             LOAD REG 1 INTO REG 8
126        BCTR    1,0             DECREMENT REG 1 BY 1

128        STC     1,M1OMOVE+1     STORE DECREMENTED LENGTH
129        LA      9,1(0,9)        INCREMENT FOR NAME FIELD
130 M1OMOVE MVC    PRINT+20(0),0(9) MOVE NAME TO PRINT
131        AR      9,8             ADDRESS OF NAME + LENGTH FOR    *
                                   2ND LENGTH INDICATOR
132        IC      1,0(C,9)        LENGTH OF ADDRESS IN REG 1
133        BCTR    1,0             DECREMENT REG 1 BY 1
134        STC     1,M20MOVE+1     STORE DECREMENTED LENGTH
135,       LA      9,1(0,9)        INCREMENT FOR ADDRESS FIELD
136 M2OMOVE MVC    PRINT+50(0),0(9) MOVE ADDRESS TO PRINT
137 *      •
138 *      •
139 NAMADDR DS     CL42            VARIABLE NAME & ADDRESS
140 PRINT   DC     CL121' '        PRINT AREA
```

FIGURE 11-6 Moving variable name and address fields using IC and STC.

name   *address*

0A	ADAM SMITH	0C	423 JONES ST

hex   character   hex   character

The name is 10 characters long. Therefore X'0A' is stored as a length indicator before the name. Because the address is 12 characters long, X'0C' is stored before the address. The entire record consists of $1+10+1+12 = 24$ bytes. Other records would vary in length accordingly. The maximum record length is assumed to be 42 bytes. The purpose is to move the name and the address separately to the print area. IC extracts the length indicator, and STC inserts the length indicator (minus 1) into the second byte, the length, of the MVC instruction. (At execute-time, the computer adds 1 to the instruction length.) Carefully check each instruction. The next section uses the EX instruction for the same example.

print area: **ADAM SMITH   423 JONES ST**

↑   ↑

PRINT+20   PRINT+50

Problems 11-2, 11-3 and 11-4 should now be done.

EXECUTE—EX. Although generally we keep declaratives separate from instructions, under certain unique circumstances an instruction may be coded within the declaratives, or at least outside of the normal execute flow. This is called a *"subject instruction"* and may be executed by means of the EX (Execute) operation.

NAME	OPERATION	OPERAND
[symbol]	EX	R1,X2 or R1,D2(X2,B2)

The ability of EX to modify the second byte of the subject instruction gives us the power, depending on the instruction format, to change the register reference, the immediate operand, or the operand lengths. The second byte (in machine object code) that is subject to change is underlined:

FORMAT	OPERANDS	
RR	R1,R2	
RS	R1,R3,D2(B2)	
RX	R1,D2(X2,B2)	
SI	D1(B1),I2	
SS (1)	D1(L,B1),D2(B2)	(one length)
SS (2)	D1(L1,B1),D2(L2,B2)	(two lengths)

The rules for EX are: (1) Operand-1 designates a register containing some value used to modify the second byte of the subject instruction; (2) operand-2 refers to the subject instruction, defined somewhere in storage, to be executed by EX. Any instruction except another EX may be subject to EX; (3) EX ORs bits 8–15 (byte 2) of the subject instruction with bits 24–31 (the rightmost byte) of the operand-1 register. The subject instruction, however, is not actually changed in storage. Exception: If register-0 is specified, no modification is done. After executing the subject instruction, the program either returns to the next sequential instruction following the EX or, if the subject instruction is a branch, to where the branch is directed.

Figure 11-7 depicts each instruction format subject to EX. (In practice, the contents of the operand-1 register would generally be a result of a calculation.) In each case the second byte of the subject instruction (ADDREG, STOREGS, etc.) is defined as zero because the byte is to be ORed. These examples are intended to illustrate how EX works, but not how we would use it in practice.

EXRR inserts X'14' into register-5 and ORs byte 2 of ADDREG with X'14'. This process causes the second byte of ADDREG to reference temporarily registers 1 and 4. ADDREG executes out-of-line as: add the contents of register-4 to register-1. EXRS ORs the second byte of STOREGS with X'DF'. This process causes byte 2 of STOREGS to reference registers 13 and 15. STOREGS executes out-of-line as: store the contents of registers 13, 14, and 15 in SAVEREGS.

```
                         6 *              ---------------
                         7 *              EX    EXECUTE
                         8 *              ---------------
003802 435C 43EE         9 EXRR     IC    5,=X'14'        INSERT X'14' IN REG 5
003806 4450 40C0        10          EX    5,ADDREG        ADD CONTENTS OF REG 4 TO REG 1

00380A 436C 43EF        12 EXRS     IC    6,=X'DF'        INSERT X'DF' IN REG 6
00380E 4460 40C2        13          EX    6,STOREGS       STORE CONTENTS OF REGS 13,14,15

003812 4370 43F0        15 EXRX     IC    7,=X'20'        INSERT X'20' IN REG 7
00381C 447C 40C6        16          EX    7,STORCH        STORE RIGHTMOST BYTE OF REG 2

00381A 438C 43F1        18 EXSI     IC    8,=X'58'        INSERT X'58' IN REG 8
00381E 4480 40CA        19          EX    8,MOVIMM        MOVE $ TO PRINT AREA

003822 4390 43F2        21 EXSSL    IC    9,=X'02'        INSERT X'02' IN REG 9
003826 4490 40CE        22          EX    9,MOVECHAR      MOVE *** TO PRINT AREA

00382A 43A0 43F3        24 EXSSLL   IC    10,=X'32'       INSERT X'32' IN REG 10
00382E 44AC 40D4        25          EX    10,ADDPK        ADD FLD2 TO FLD1
                        26 *              .
                        27 *              .

003834                  29 SAVEREGS DS    3F              3 FULLWORDS
003840                  30 SAVEBYTE DS    C               ONE BYTE
003841 4C40404040404040 31 PRINT    DC    CL121' '        PRINT AREA
0038EA                  32 FLD1     DS    PL4
0038BE                  33 FLD2     DS    PL3

                        35 *              SUBJECT INSTRUCTIONS FOR EX:
0038C1 00
0038C2 1A00             36 ADDREG   AR    0,0             ADD REGISTERS        RR
0038C4 9000 4032        37 STOREGS  STM   0,0,SAVEREGS    STORE REGISTERS      RS
0038C8 4200 403E        38 STORCH   STC   0,SAVEBYTE      STORE CHARACTER      RX
0038CC 9200 4053        39 MOVIMM   MVI   PRINT+20,X'00'  MOVE IMMEDIATE       SI
0038D0 D200 405D 43F4   40 MOVECHAR MVC   PRINT+30(0),=C'***'  MOVE ASTERISKS  SS
0038D6 FA00 4088 408C   41 ADDPK    AP    FLD1(0),FLD2(0) ADD PACKED FIELDS    SS
```

FIGURE 11-7　Sample operations using EX.

EXRX ORs the second byte of STORCH with X'20'. This process causes byte 2 of STORCH to reference base register-2 and index register-0. STORCH executes as: store the rightmost 8 bits of register-2 in SAVEBYTE. EXSI ORs the second byte of MOVIMM with X'5B'($). This process causes byte 2 of MOVIMM to "contain" X'5B'. (Remember that the subject instruction is not physically changed.) MOVIMM then moves X'5B' to P+20, and the instruction can thus move any immediate value.

EXSSL and EXSSLL both modify operand lengths. Remember that when executing an SS instruction, the computer adds 1 to the operand length. EXSSL uses MOVECHAR to move a specified number of asterisks (up to three) to the print area, and could be used to print one, two, or three asterisks to denote the total level. EXSSLL executes an AP operation in which byte-2 contains both length codes.

EXTENDED EX EXAMPLE.   Figure 11-6 illustrated variable length move operations. Figure 11-8 in this section uses EX to code the same example. Carefully compare the two examples to see how EX is used. A later section uses the same example to illustrate the TRT instruction.

```
22              XR      1,1                 CLEAR REG 1
23              LA      9,NAMADDR           ADDRESS OF 1ST LENGTH INDICATOR
24              IC      1,0(0,9)            LENGTH OF NAME IN REG 1
25              LR      8,1                 SAVE LENGTH IN REG 8

27              BCTR    1,0                 DECREMENT REG 1 BY 1
28              LA      9,1(0,9)            INCREMENT FOR NAME FIELD
29              EX      1,M30MOVE           EXECUTE M30MOVE INSTRUCTION
30              AR      9,8                 ADDRESS OF NAME + LENGTH FOR    +
                                            2ND LENGTH INDICATOR
31              IC      1,0(0,9)            LENGTH OF ADDRESS IN REG 1
32              BCTR    1,0                 DECREMENT REG 1 BY 1
33              LA      9,1(0,9)            INCREMENT FOR ADDRESS FIELD
34              EX      1,M40MOVE           EXECUTE M40MOVE INSTRUCTION
35 *                  .
36 *                  .
37 *                  .
38 NAMADDR      DS      CL42                VARIABLE NAME & ADDRESS
39 PRINT        DC      CL121' '            PRINT AREA

41 M30MOVE      MVC     PRINT+20(0),0(9)    MOVE NAME TO PRINT
42 M40MOVE      MVC     PRINT+50(0),0(9)    MOVE ADDRESS TO PRINT
```

FIGURE 11-8   Moving variable name and address fields using EX.

TRANSLATE—TR.   At times data introduced into a program is not in the required EBCDIC code. (EBCDIC is the standard 360/370 8-bit code.) Or, it may be necessary to translate certain EBCDIC characters into some other characters. Examples of the need to translate code include:

— Some systems use ASCII mode (American Standard Code for Information Interchange). If delivered as input to the 360 or 370 (by magnetic tape or teleprocessing), ASCII must be translated to EBCDIC.

— Card columns may be punched with invalid characters in amount fields that are to be packed. For example, a column punched with 12-6-8 punches is read as X'4E'. When packed, the byte becomes X'E4'. Because the byte is not in valid packed format, operations such as AP or SP cause a program interrupt.

— Source programs on other computers may have similar but not identical codes. The 360 or 370 may have to translate the different codes to EBCDIC in order to list a program source deck.

— Alphabetic letters are normally recorded in upper-case format. It may be required to translate and print in lower-case on either the console typewriter or a special print device.

The instruction that translates code from one format to another is Translate, TR. The rules for TR are: (1) Operand-1 references the address of the *argument*—the byte or bytes to be translated. TR may translate a field or record up to 256 bytes long (such as a record coded in ASCII). (2) Operand-2 references a *table of functions,* which contains the required new code (such as the correct EBCDIC code). The definition of the table is the key to the use of TR (and TRT following).

NAME	OPERATION	OPERAND
[symbol]	TR	S1,S2 or D1(L,B1),D2(B2)

   TR starts with the leftmost byte of the argument. A byte can contain any value X'00' — X'FF', and TR adds this value to the address of the table, giving a range of addresses from table+X'00' through table+X'FF'. The contents of the table address is the *function* that TR uses to replace the argument byte. The operation continues then with the next argument, proceeding from left to right one byte at a time until completing the argument length.

   Figure 11-9 translates hex numbers to alphabetic characters. Assume that the number one (X'01') is to be translated to the first character "A" (X'C1'), 10 or X'0A' to the tenth character 'J', 19 or X'13' to the 19th character 'S', etc. The only valid expected values are 0 through 26 (X'1A'). The table is defined as TABLE, with a blank followed by the letters A through Z. Assume that the argument, ARGUMENT, contains X'0104010D'. The example works as shown on page 251:

```
45 *          ------------------
46 *      TR      TRANSLATE
47 *          ------------------
48 ARGUMENT DS     CL4                        ASSUME CONTAINS X'0104010D'
49 TABLE    DC     C' ABCDEFGHIJKLMNOPQRSTUVWXYZ'

51        TR     ARGUMENT,TABLE              TRANSLATE ARGUMENT
```

FIGURE 11-9 Translation of argument using TR.

ARGUMENT before TR: 01 04 01 0D

Contents of TABLE: b A B C D E F G H I J K L M N . . . Z

ARGUMENT after TR: A D A M

— TR adds the first byte of ARGUMENT containing X'01' to the address of TABLE. At TABLE+1 is the letter 'A' (X'C1'). 'A' replaces X'01' in ARGUMENT.
— TR adds the second byte of ARGUMENT containing X'04' to the address of TABLE. At TABLE+4 is the letter 'D' which replaces X'04' in ARGUMENT.
— TR adds the third byte of ARGUMENT containing X'01' to TABLE. The letter 'A' replaces X'01' in ARGUMENT.
— TR adds the fourth and last byte of ARGUMENT containing X'0D' to TABLE. At TABLE+13 is the letter 'M' which replaces the X'0D'. ARGUMENT is now correctly translated to 'ADAM'.

Question: Why does TABLE begin with a blank byte rather than the letter 'A'? *Warning:* An argument may be invalid with respect to the table of functions. For example, assume that ARGUMENT contains X'28', or decimal value 40. TR will access the address TABLE+40, which yields a "function" that is outside the bounds of the table. Preediting the argument for validity prior to the TR is recommended. For many types of translations where almost any argument is valid, it is necessary to define a table with all possible 256 EBCDIC codes, as illustrated in the next section.

EXTENDED TR EXAMPLE. Figure 11-10 depicts an example discussed earlier which translates bytes in an input amount field that may contain invalid characters. When read in character format, these bytes should contain only the values:

−0 through −9, represented by X'D0' through X'D9'
and
+0 through +9, represented by X'F0' through X'F9'

```
55  *                                      POSITION:
56  TABLE2   DC    208X'F0'                000-207  208 BYTES INVALID
57           DC    X'D0D1D2D3D4D5D6D7D8D9'  208-217   10 BYTES -0 THRU -9
58           DC    22X'F0'                 218-239   22 BYTES INVALID
59           DC    X'F0F1F2F3F4F5F6F7F8F9'  240-249   10 BYTES +0 THRU +9
60           DC    6X'F0'                  250-255    6 BYTES INVALID

62  INAREA   DS    CL80                    INPUT AREA
63  AMTPK    DS    PL4                     PACK AREA

65           TR    INAREA+10(6),TABLE2     TRANSLATE INPUT AREA
66           PACK  AMTPK,INAREA+10(6)      PACK VALIDATED FIELD
```

FIGURE 11-10   Translate invalid bytes for packing using TR.

These valid values are to stay the same, whereas all other hex values are to translate arbitrarily to X'F0'. We therefore define all possible keypunch codes in a table of functions that "translates" valid argument bytes to the same value, and translates invalid bytes to X'F0'. Note the positioning of the table functions:

TABLE FUNCTIONS			HEX VALUE	DEC. VAL.	TRANSLATES TO
First	208	Invalid hex arguments	X'00'–X'CF'	0–207	X'F0'
Next	10	Valid characters −0 through −9	X'D0'–X'D9'	208–217	not changed
Next	22	Invalid	X'DA'–X'EF'	218–239	X'F0'
Next	10	Valid characters +0 through +9	X'F0'–X'F9'	240–249	not changed
Last	6	Invalid	X'FA'–X'FF'	250–255	X'F0'

The example shows how invalid bytes in INAREA, assumed to be an amount field, are translated to X'F0'. Devise some examples of valid and invalid data to check the operation. Another approach translates a field to check if all bytes are numeric. The following translates all numeric (0–9) bytes to asterisks, and checks if the TR changed every one to an asterisk. (Checking if the rightmost byte could contain a minus overpunch will require special treatment.)

```
TEST    DS  CL6       MVC  TEST,INAMOUNT    Move numeric amount
TABLE   DC  240X'00'  TR   TEST,TABLE       Translate numerics to *
        DC  10C'*'     CLC  TEST,=6C'*'      Test all asterisks?
        DC  6X'00'     BNE  error           No—perform error routine
```

If it is necessary to know *which* record positions contain an invalid character and to print a warning message, we can use the TRT instruction covered next.

TRANSLATE AND TEST—TRT.   It is sometimes necessary to *scan* a record in order to detect an invalid character (as in the previous example under TR), or to detect an unique character, such as a "delimiter" that terminates a variable length record. Translate and test, TRT, conveniently serves this purpose.

NAME	OPERATION	OPERAND
[symbol]	TRT	S1,S2 or D1(L,B1),D2(B2)

TRT is similar to TR in that: (1) Operand-1 references the address of the argument, up to 256 bytes in length; (2) operand-2 references a table of functions containing the required new code; (3) the operation begins with the first byte of the argument, and processes one byte at a time. TRT adds the value of each argument byte to the address of the table to find each function in the table.

TRT differs from TR in that: (1) If the value of the table function is *zero*, TRT continues with the next argument byte; (2) if the value of the function is *nonzero,*

TRT inserts into register-1 the address of the argument in bits 8–31 (bits 0–7 are unchanged), and inserts into register-2 the contents of the function in bits 24–31 (bits 0–23 are unchanged); (3) *the argument byte is unchanged*—there is no translation. In effect, TRT is a *scan* operation; (4) TRT terminates on finding a nonzero function or on reaching the end of the argument; (5) the condition code is set as follows:

CODE	CAUSED BY	TEST WITH
0	All functions found were zero	BZ, BNZ
1	A nonzero function found, but not yet at the end of the argument	BM, BNM
2	A nonzero function found at the end of the argument	BP, BNP

The three examples in Figure 11-11 illustrate the condition codes set by TRT. Each example assumes the same argument, ARG. For SCAN1, each byte (pair of hex digits) of ARG is scanned. For instance, X'02' is directed to TABLEA+2, etc. All function bytes are found to be zero. Therefore, the condition code is set to zero and registers 1 and 2 remain unchanged, as shown in comments to the right.

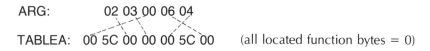

ARG: 02 03 00 06 04

TABLEA: 00 5C 00 00 00 5C 00   (all located function bytes = 0)

```
70  *        --------------------------
71  *        TRT    TRANSLATE & TEST
72  *        --------------------------
73  ARG      DC     X'0203000604'
74  *                                     REG-1:       REG-2:     CODE:

75  SCAN1    TRT    ARG,TABLEA            UNCHANGED    UNCHANGED    0
76  TABLEA   DC     X'005C0000005C00'

78  SCAN2    TRT    ARG,TABLEB           A(ARG+3)     X'5C'        1
79  TABLEB   DC     X'004B000000048 5C'

81  SCAN3    TRT    ARG,TABLEC           A(ARG+4)     X'5B'        2
82  TABLEC   DC     X'004B00005B5C00'
```

FIGURE 11-11   Sample translate and test TRT operations.

For SCAN2, X'02', X'03', and X'00' in ARG direct the operation to zero functions in TABLEB. X'06' in ARG, however, directs the operation to TABLEB+6, which contains X'5C'. Therefore TRT does the following: (1) Inserts the address of ARG+3 in register-1; (2) inserts the table function X'5C' in register-2; and (3) sets the condition code to 1.

For SCAN3, the first four bytes of ARG locate zero functions in TABLEC. The last byte, X'04', however, directs the operation to TABLEC+4, which contains X'5B'.

TRT does the following: (1) Inserts the address of ARG+4 in register-1; (2) inserts the table function X'5B' in register-2; and (3) because the last byte of ARG was processed, sets the condition code to 2.

EXTENDED TRT EXAMPLE. The next example for variable length fields is similar to those for IC, STC, and EX in Figures 11-6 and 11-8. This example has no length indicator preceding the name and address. Instead, a "delimiter" character, in this case an *, indicates the end of the variable length field:

ADAM SMITH*423 JONES ST*

In Figure 11-12 TRT scans the record to find the delimiter. We then use the address of the delimiter to calculate the length of the name and the address, and to determine the address of the next field. The program uses two TRT and two EX operations to move the name and address to the print area. The table, TABSCAN, contains only a nonzero function for the X'5C' (*) position, and zero functions for all other codes. The example assumes, perhaps unwisely, that a delimiter always follows both name and address.

Further examples of EX, TRT, and variable length records are in the next chapter.

```
                             86 *                            POSITION:
003A91 0000000000000000      87 TABSCAN  DC   92X'00'        000-091   92 ZERO FUNCTIONS
003AED 5C                     88         DC   X'5C'          092-092    1 ASTERISK *
003AEE 000000000000000000     89         DC   163X'00'       093-255  163 ZERO FUNCTIONS

003B91                        91 NAMADD   DS   CL42           VARIABLE NAME & ADDRESS

003BBB 00
003BBC 1B11                   93         SR   1,1            CLEAR REG 1
003BBE 4190 438F              94         LA   9,NAMADD       LOAD ADDRESS OF VARIABLE RECORD
003BC2 DD14 9000 428F         95         TRT  0(21,9),TABSCAN SCAN FOR NAME DELIMITER
                             96 *         BZ   ...           *    NOT FOUND, ERROR

003BC8 1871                   98         LR   7,1            SAVE ADDRESS OF DELIMITER
003BCA 1B19                   99         SR   1,9            CALCULATE LENGTH OF NAME
003BCC 0610                  100         BCTR 1,0            DECREMENT LENGTH BY 1
003BCE 4410 43E2             101         EX   1,M50MOVE      EXECUTE M50MOVE INSTRUCTION
003BD2 4190 7001             102         LA   9,1(0,7)       INCREMENT FOR ADDRESS FIELD

003BD6 DD14 9000 428F        104         TRT  0(21,9),TABSCAN SCAN FOR ADDRESS DELIMITER
                            105 *         BZ   ...           *    NOT FOUND, ERROR
003BDC 1B19                  106         SR   1,9            CALCULATE LENGTH OF ADDRESS
003BDE 0610                  107         BCTR 1,0            DECREMENT LENGTH BY 1
003BE0 4410 43E8             108         EX   1,M60MOVE      EXECUTE M60MOVE INSTRUCTION
                            109 *         .
                            110 *         .

                            112 *        SUBJECT INSTRUCTIONS FOR EX:
003BE4 D200 4053 9000       113 M50MOVE  MVC  PRINT+20(0),0(9) MOVE NAME TO PRINT
003BEA D200 4071 9000       114 M60MOVE  MVC  PRINT+50(0),0(9) MOVE ADDRESS TO PRINT
```

FIGURE 11-12 Moving variable name and address fields using TRT.

BINARY OPERATIONS—SUMMARY

Most arithmetic can be performed adequately with packed data and decimal arithmetic. Since input data on cards is normally in character format, an additional step is required to translate into packed format. To convert the packed data to binary requires yet another step. However, the following reasons often determine the need for binary format:

— Explicit use of base registers for address modification.
— Faster processing *if* there are many repetitive arithmetic operations.
— Certain operations can only be accomplished with binary operations.
— Data may be stored efficiently in binary format on disk and tape, and read into storage in this format.

PROBLEMS

11-1. Figure 11-2 "packs" four fields into one binary fullword. Assume that the fullword has been read from tape into a storage field called FULLWORD DS FL4. Write the coding to "unpack" the fullword into four individual character fields called DIST, ACCOUNT, RATE, SERVICE.

11-2. STC stores the rightmost 8 bits of a register into a field called BYTE. Use Boolean operations to (a) force the leftmost 4 bits of BYTE to be zeros; (b) force the leftmost 4 bits of BYTE to be ones; (c) reverse all 8 bits, zeros to ones and vice versa.

11-3. Figure 11-5 shows how to test bit values. Code the instruction to test if the customer has both gas and industrial account.

11-4. Figure 11-6 illustrates variable length name and address. Change NAMADDR to 63 bytes, allowing for a *third* variable field, city. Revise the coding to move this field to P+80. Also, recode the routine as a *loop* so that there is one set of instructions executed three times, one for each field. HINT: Change operand-1 of the MVC to explicit register format. Expand the code to include a read and print, then test the program.

11-5. Recode Figure 11-8 using one EX for the same changes required in Problem 11-4.

11-6. Design a table for TR to translate upper case letters (A–Z) to lower case (a–z). Leave unchanged characters 0–9, comma, and period. Convert all other characters to X'40'.

11-7. ASCII code is given in IBM S/370 Reference Summary card. Design two tables of functions to translate (a)ASCII to EBCDIC and (b)EBCDIC to ASCII.

11-8. In Figure 11-10 TR translated invalid bytes on a card to character zero. Change the example so that the program prints the card column where the invalid code occurred. A card may contain more than one invalid column.

11-9. Translate hex into character format. Each four bits (hex digit) of register-9 is to print as a single character (as is done by dumping the contents of storage). Hex zero should print as character zero, X'9' as character 9, X'A' as character A, etc. Since register-9 contains 32 bits, eight characters are required, printing from P+11 to P+18. Suggestion: Shift the four leftmost bits of register-9 into register-8. Store these in a one-byte field and use TR to translate from hex to character. Repeat the loop eight times. The table can be defined as quite short.

11-10. Recode Figure 11-12 using one TRT for the same changes required in Problem 11-4.

PART IV

EXTERNAL STORAGE

CHAPTER 12

MAGNETIC TAPE

Up to this chapter, the only input/output devices have been the card reader and the printer. This chapter and the next cover two other common devices that store data—magnetic tape and disk storage. Tape, like punched cards, stores data as *records*. It may help to think of a reel of tape records as a series of "punched card" records. The reel is "loaded" onto a tape drive in much the same manner as a conventional tape recorder. The data records are then read into the computer's main storage as a card file would be.

We write data on tape and disk over the old data, much as a tape recorder records a new sound over the previous. The data may be reread and rewritten, almost indefinitely. Tape and disks are used for both input and output. Normally a tape reel designated as input to a program is only read, and not written on until its contents are obsolete, and a reel designated as output is written on, to be read later. The data on the reel is saved for a predetermined time as an "audit trail" or "backup" if jobs must be rerun. Recent developments in disk storage devices have permitted storing large files on disks. Disk storage gives the advantage of processing records both sequentially and directly. Most installations now use disk to store large files.

259

USES OF MAGNETIC TAPE

Magnetic tape is not only a means of rapid input/output. It also acts as a medium to store large quantities of condensed, easily filed data. Like cards, tape is used to store master and transaction files. It also acts as intermediary storage, for example as output from a program, storing data to be used in a subsequent program. Many department store chains and utility companies maintain customer records on magnetic tape. Their records are many in number, long in length, and are stored sequentially. Among the advantages of magnetic tape over punched cards are:

— Tape input/output is considerably faster.
— Tape files require much less storage space.
— Tape records when sorted (by an IBM tape library program) are virtually assured of being in the correct sequence. (Physical handling makes punched card sequence unreliable.)
— Tape stores data not only in character format but also in packed and binary, permitting more condensed records.
— Tape may be reused almost indefinitely.
— Tape permits records of virtually any length.
— Tape is an inexpensive, convenient way to mail large volumes of data.

Among the disadvantages are:

— Magnetic tape devices are relatively expensive.
— Usually the system requires at least three or four drives to operate (where there are no disk drives available).
— The complex input/output operations require more program storage, although a trivial consideration in these days of low-cost main storage.

MAGNETIC TAPE CHARACTERISTICS

This chapter limits discussion to IBM magnetic tape units, although tape units of other manufacturers have similar features. The tape consists of a thin ferromagnetic coating on flexible plastic, ½-inch wide. A full reel is 2400 feet long, with shorter lengths available such as 1200 and 600 feet.

TAPE DENSITY.   Tape density is expressed in bytes-per-inch (bpi), such as 800 and 1600 bpi. A 2400-foot reel (28,800″) contains a maximum storage of about 23 million bytes with 800 bpi, and 46 million bytes with 1600 bpi tape.

TAPE SPEED.   Tape read/write speed varies considerably by tape drive model. At 125 inches per second (ips), a tape drive could read a 2400-foot reel, with very little time for processing, in about 230 seconds. For example, IBM 3420 Magnetic Tape units are available in the following models, with tape densities of 800, 1600, and 6250 bpi. (Another density, 556 bpi, provides compatibility with second generation equipment.)

IBM 3420	MODEL 3	MODEL 4	MODEL 5	MODEL 6	MODEL 7	MODEL 8
Tape speed (ips)	75	75	125	125	200	200
Data rate (KB/sec):						
At 800 bpi	60		100		160	
At 1600 bpi	120	120	200	200	320	320
At 6250 bpi		470		780		1250

CODE STRUCTURE.   Tape records data using a 9-bit code similar to the byte in storage: eight bits for data and one bit for odd parity, arranged vertically on the tape. (A 7-bit code is also accepted to provide compatibility with earlier tape models.)

TAPE MARKERS.   Near both ends of the reel is an aluminum strip called a tape marker that is sensed by a photoelectric device on the tape drive:

— *The load point marker* is a strip about ten feet from the start of the reel to provide space for the initial threading of the tape. Reading or writing begins after this point.

— *The end-of-tape marker* is a strip about 14 feet from the end of the reel. When tape is being written, the marker warns the system that the end of the tape is near. Four feet provides space to finish writing data after the marker, and ten feet permits threading of the tape.

TAPE READ/WRITE.   The operator loads the reel to be processed onto the tape drive and initializes the tape at the load point marker. The drive contains an empty reel to take up the processed tape. The tape passes a read/write head. For *input* each byte is read, then reread, to ensure the read was performed correctly. For *output* an erase operation prior to the write clears old data from the tape. The write operation magnetizes small areas within the tracks. A byte written is reread to check its validity. These validity checks are entirely automatic. When the tape has been completely processed, there are two alternatives:

1. Most often the tape is rewound onto the original reel. The operator may then unload it from the tape drive or leave it for further processing.
2. The tape may be reprocessed by reading it *backwards*. Although the tape runs backwards, data from each record reads into storage in the normal sequence. IBM library tape sort programs and occasionally programmers use this feature.

TAPE FORMATS.   A *block* of data written on tape consists of one or more records. The minimum block length is about 18 bytes. The maximum is subject to available storage in programs using the tape file and the operating system used. IOCS reads a tape block into, and writes from, an input/output area (or buffer) in storage. Blocks consisting of one record only are *unblocked*. Blocks having more than one record are *blocked*. The *blocking factor* specifies the number of records in a block. The program that initially writes (or creates) the tape file defines the record length and block length. All other programs that read the file must designate the same record and block lengths. After each block, the tape drive automatically generates a space of about 0.6 inch. On tape with density of 6250 bytes per inch, the IBG is about 0.3 inch. This space, called an *interblock gap (IBG),* has two functions:

1. The IBG clearly defines the beginning and end of a block of data. A tape read starts with the first byte of data in a block. The IBG terminates the read operation.
2. The IBG allows space for the tape drive to slow down after a read or write, and to restart with the next read/write (stop/start time).

FIXED AND VARIABLE LENGTHS.   Records and blocks may be *fixed* in length (each has the same length throughout the entire file), or *variable* (the length of each record and the blocking factor are not predetermined). There are five distinct tape formats:

1. *Fixed, unblocked*—one record of fixed length per block.
2. *Fixed, blocked*—more than one fixed length record per block.
3. *Variable, unblocked*—one variable length record per block.
4. *Variable, blocked*—more than one variable length record per block.
5. *Undefined*—not all operating systems support this format; see the IBM Supervisor manuals for details.

Figure 12-1 depicts the first two formats. A later section describes variable length records.

Problems 12-1, 12-2, and 12-3 should now be done.

DOS TAPE PROGRAMMING EXAMPLE—CREATING A TAPE FILE

The DOS file definition macro that defines a magnetic tape file is DTFMT (OS uses DCB). We specify one DTFMT entry with a unique name for each tape input or output file that the program processes. The entries are similar to the DTFCD, DTFPR, and DTFDI macros covered earlier. We use the same imperative macros: OPEN, CLOSE, GET, and PUT. As explained later, IOCS handles all label processing, blocking and deblocking.

Fixed unblocked

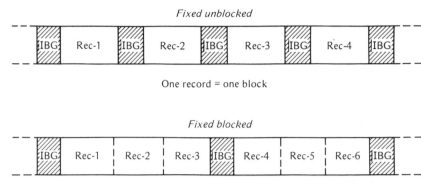

One record = one block

Fixed blocked

Three records = one block

FIGURE 12-1   Tape formats for fixed unblocked and blocked.

Figure 12-2 illustrates reading cards and writing them on tape. The cards are read into CARDIN. Required fields are transferred to the tape workarea called TAPEWORK. This workarea is then "PUT" to the tape output file called FILEOTP. IOCS blocks four records before physically writing the block onto tape. Therefore, for every four cards read, IOCS writes one tape block onto tape. The DTFMT entries are described next:

BLKSIZE=360 means that each block to be written from the 1OAREA is 360 bytes long (4 records × 90 bytes).

DEVADDR=SYS025 denotes the logical address of the tape device that will write the file. The operator assigns one of the system's tape drives with this (or some other) logical device name, as required by the installation.

FILABL=STD indicates that the tape file contains "standard labels", as discussed in a later section.

IOAREA1 and IOAREA2 are the two IOCS buffers, similar to those for card and printer files. We define the two IOAREAs as the same length as BLKSIZE, 360 bytes. Some programmers omit defining a second buffer in order to reduce program size, especially if the blocked record area is large.

RECFORM=FIXBLK specifies that output records are to be fixed in length, and blocked (tape records may also be variable length or unblocked).

RECSIZE=90 means that each fixed-length record is 90 bytes in length, the same as the workarea.

TYPEFLE=OUTPUT stipulates that the type of file is output: the file is for writing tape, not reading.

WORKA=YES means that we are to process output records in a workarea. In this program, TAPEWORK is the workarea, and is the same length as RECSIZE, 90 bytes. (Alternatively, we may code IOREG, just as for card and printer files, and use the macro PUT FILEOTP with no workarea coded.)

Magnetic tape input requires a DTFMT entry EOFADDR=address to denote the

```
 5 *              I N I T I A L I Z A T I O N

 7 PROG12A  START X'3850'             X'3800' + X'50' FOR LBLTYP TAPE
 8          BALR  3,0                 INITIALIZE BASE REGISTER
 9          USING *,3
10          OPEN  FILEICD,FILEOTP     ACTIVATE FILES

20 ***           M A I N   P R O C E S S I N G

22 A10READ  GET   FILEICD,CARDIN      READ RECORD
28          MVC   ACCTTPO,ACCTIN      MOVE CARD FIELDS TO TAPE
29          MVC   NAMETPO,NAMEIN      *     WORK AREA
30          MVC   ADDRTPO,ADDRIN      *
31          PACK  BALNTPO,BALNIN      *
32          MVC   DATETPO,DATEIN      *
33          PUT   FILEOTP,TAPEWORK    WRITE WORK AREA ONTO TAPE
39          B     A10READ

41 *             E N D - O F - F I L E

43 X10EOFCD CLOSE FILEICD,FILEOTP     DE-ACTIVATE FILES
52          EOJ                       NORMAL END-OF-JOB

56 *             D E C L A R A T I V E S

58 CARDIN   DS    0CL80               CARD INPUT AREA:
59 CODEIN   DS    CL2                 01-02   CARD CODE
60 ACCTIN   DS    CL6                 03-08   ACCOUNT NO.
61 NAMEIN   DS    CL20                09-28   NAME
62 ADDRIN   DS    CL40                29-68   ADDRESS
63 BALNIN   DS    ZL6'0000.00'        69-74   BALANCE
64 DATEIN   DS    CL6'CDMMYY'         75-80   DATE


67 TAPEWORK DS    0CL90               TAPE WORK AREA:
68 ACCTTPO  DS    CL6                 01-06   ACCOUNT NO.
69 NAMETPO  DS    CL20                07-26   NAME
70 ADDRTPO  DS    CL40                27-66   ADDRESS
71 BALNTPO  DS    PL4                 67-70   BALANCE
72 DATETPO  DS    CL6                 71-76   DATE
73          DC    CL14' '             77-90   RESERVED FOR EXPANSION

75 FILEICD  DTFCD DEVADDR=SYSIPT,     CARD INPUT FILE DECLARATION  +
                  IOAREA1=IOARCDI1,                                +
                  IOAREA2=IOARCDI2,                                +
                  BLKSIZE=80,                                      +
                  DEVICE=2501,                                     +
                  EOFADDR=X10EOFCD,                                +
                  TYPEFLE=INPUT,                                   +
                  WORKA=YES

117 IOARCDI1 DS   CL80                IOCS CARD BUFFER-1
118 IOARCDI2 DS   CL80                IOCS CARD BUFFER-2

120 FILEOTP  DTFMT BLKSIZE=360,       TAPE OUTPUT FILE DECLARATION +
                   DEVADDR=SYS025,                                 +
                   FILABL=STD,                                     +
                   IOAREA1=IOARTPO1,                               +
                   IOAREA2=IOARTPO2,                               +
                   RECFORM=FIXBLK,                                 +
                   RECSIZE=90,                                     +
                   TYPEFLE=OUTPUT,                                 +
                   WORKA=YES

157 IOARTPO1 DS   CL360               IOCS TAPE BUFFER-1
158 IOARTPO2 DS   CL360               IOCS TAPE BUFFER-2

160          END   PROG12A
```

FIGURE 12-2 Writing a tape file under DOS.

name of our routine where IOCS branches when it reaches the end of the tape file. The next chapter illustrates tape input. Further information on DTFMT is in the IBM Supervisor manuals.

OS CODING FOR MAGNETIC TAPE

For OS, there are several additional entries that the DCB requires for magnetic tape. The entry DEN specifies tape density: DEN=2 is for 800 bytes per inch and DEN=3 is 1600, and must agree with the actual tape drive setting. LRECL (logical record length) designates the length of each record, if fixed-length. RECFM indicates the "record format": F (Fixed), FB (Fixed Blocked), V (Variable), and VB (Variable Blocked).

The program in Figure 12-3 is a revision of the preceding DOS example that reads records and writes them on tape. The DD (Data Definition) job cards appear first. Note that the example illustrates a common practice: BLKSIZE, RECFM, and DEN are coded in the tape DD entry instead of the DCB, enabling a user to change the entries without reassembling the program.

Tape and disk records may be processed directly in the buffers, using Locate Mode. The DCB requires MACRF=(GL) for input and (PL) for output.

Another DCB entry, EROPT, provides for specifying the action if an input operation encounters problems. The options are:

=ACC   Accept the possibly erroneous data block.
=SKP   Skip the data block entirely and continue with the next one.
=ABE   Abend—abnormal end of program execution, the normal default if the entry is omitted.

ACC and SKP can use a SYNAD entry for printing an error message and continue processing. If the error routine is called R20ERROR, the DCB coding could be:

```
EROPT=SKP,
SYNAD=R20ERROR
```

Use of ACC and SKP may cause invalid results, so it may be preferable to use ABE (or allow it to default) for important production jobs. Be sure to examine the OS Supervisor manuals for other DCB options.

TAPE FILE ORGANIZATION

Tape files are typically stored in ascending sequence by control field, such as Customer number. Files ("data sets" under OS) may be organized according to how much tape space they require. For compatibility with disks, a reel of tape is called a *volume*. The simplest case is a *one-volume file*, in which one file is entirely and exclusively stored on one reel (volume). This storage is common where the file is medium-sized.

```
//GO.TAPEOT  DD DSNAME=TRFILE,DISP=(NEW,PASS),UNIT=3420,     X  |DD for tape data
               DCB=(BLKSIZE=360,RECFM=FB,DEN=3)                 } set output

//GO.CARD    DD *                                             DD for input


*                 I N I T I A L I Z A T I O N

PROG12B   START
          SAVE   (14,12)
          BALR   3,0
          USING  *,3
          ST     13,SAVEAREA+4
          LA     13,SAVEAREA
          OPEN   (FILEIN,(INPUT),FILEOTP,(OUTPUT))

***               M A I N   P R O C E S S I N G

A10READ   GET    FILEIN,RECRDIN
          MVC    ACCTTPO,ACCTIN          MOVE CARD FIELDS TO TAPE
          MVC    NAMETPO,NAMEIN         *      WORK AREA
          MVC    ADDRTPO,ADDRIN        *
          PACK   BALNTPO,BALNIN        *
          MVC    DATETPO,DATEIN        *
          PUT    FILEOTP,TAPEWCRK       WRITE WORK AREA ONTO TAPE
          B      A10READ

*                 E N D - O F - F I L E

X10EOF    CLOSE  (FILEIN,,FILEOTP)
          L      13,SAVEAREA+4
          RETURN (14,12)


*                 D E C L A R A T I V E S

RECRDIN   DS     0CL80                  CARD INPUT AREA:
CODEIN    DS     CL2                    01-02  CARD CODE
ACCTIN    DS     CL6                    03-08  ACCOUNT NO.
NAMEIN    DS     CL20                   09-28  NAME
ADDRIN    DS     CL40                   29-68  ADDRESS
BALNIN    DS     ZL6'0000.00'           69-74  BALANCE
DATEIN    DS     CL6'DDMMYY'            75-80  DATE

TAPEWORK  DS     0CL90                  TAPE WORK AREA:
ACCTTPO   DS     CL6                    01-06  ACCOUNT NO.
NAMETPO   DS     CL20                   07-26  NAME
ADDRTPO   DS     CL40                   27-66  ADDRESS
BALNTPO   DS     PL4                    67-70  BALANCE
DATETPO   DS     CL6                    71-76  DATE
          DC     CL14'                  77-90  RESERVED FOR EXPANSION

FILEIN    DCB    DDNAME=CARD,           DCB FOR INPUT DATA SET        +
                 DEVD=DA,                                            +
                 DSORG=PS,                                           +
                 EODAD=X10EOF,                                       +
                 MACRF=(GM)

FILEOTP   DCB    DDNAME=TAPEOT,         CCB FOR TAPE DATA SET         +
                 DSORG=PS,                                           +
                 LRECL=90,                                           +
                 MACRF=(PM)

SAVEAREA  DS     18F                    REGISTER SAVE AREA
          LTORG  ,
          END    PROG12B
```

FIGURE 12-3 Writing a tape file under OS.

An extremely large file (such as department store accounts receivable) uses a *multivolume file* which requires more than one volume for the file. Many small files can be stored in a *multifile volume,* one after the other on one volume.

IOCS and job control handle the complexities of such file organization, requiring no special programming effort.

STANDARD LABELS.   Under the various operating systems, tapes require unique identification. Each reel and each file on a reel contains certain descriptive *standard labels* supported by IOCS for the following reasons:

— To uniquely identify the reel and the file for each program.
— To provide compatibility with disk storage devices (to facilitate device independence).
— To provide compatibility with other IBM systems and those of other manufacturers.

Most installations use standard labels. Nonstandard labels and unlabeled tapes are permitted but are not covered in this text. There are two kinds of standard labels: *volume* and *file labels.* Figure 12-4 illustrates standard tape labels for the cases: one

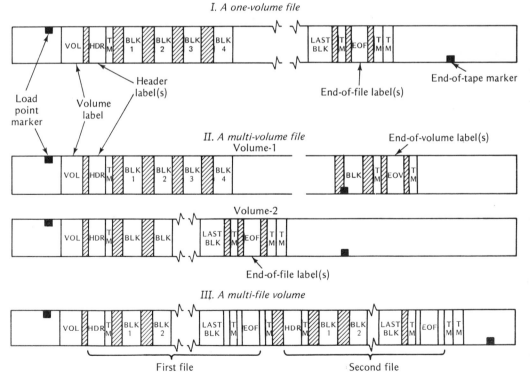

FIGURE 12-4   Magnetic tape standard labels.

file on a volume, a multivolume file, and a multifile volume. IBG's are denoted by striped lines. TM, meaning tape mark, is discussed in a later section, IOCS.

VOLUME LABELS.   The volume label is the first record after the load point marker. The label describes the volume (reel). The first three bytes contain the identification VOL. Although some systems support more than one volume label, this text describes only the common situation of one label.

On receipt of a new tape reel, we use an IBM utility program to write the volume label and a temporary file label ("header"). In all programs that process the reel, IOCS expects the volume label to be the first record. It checks the tape serial number against the number supplied by the special tape job control card TLBL or under OS, DD (Data Definition). The following describes each field of the 80-byte standard volume label:

POSITIONS	NAME	DESCRIPTION
01–03	Label Identifier	Contains VOL to identify the label.
04–04	Volume Label Number	Some systems permit more than one volume label; this field contains the numeric sequence of the volume label.
05–10	Volume Serial Number	The permanent unique number usually assigned when the reel is received. (The number also becomes the File Serial number in the Header label.)
11–11	Volume Security	A special security code, supported by OS.
12–41		Not used, reserved.
42–51	Owner Name and Address Code	May be used under OS to identify the owner of the reel.
52–80		Reserved for future expansion.

STANDARD FILE LABELS.   A tape volume contains a file of data, part of a file, or more than one file. Each file is uniquely identified to ensure, for example, that the correct file is being processed and that the tape we are using to write on is obsolete. To provide such identification there are two file labels for each file for each reel: the *header label* and the *trailer label*.

1. HEADER LABEL. There is a header label at the start of the file. If the file requires more than one volume (multivolume file) then there is one header for each of the volumes, each numbered consecutively from one. If there is more than one file on a volume (multifile volume) then a header label begins each file.

The header label contains HDR in the first three bytes, the file identification (such as ACCTS RECEIVABLE), the date the file may be deleted, etc. IOCS expects the header label to be the first record of the file, immediately following the volume label. IOCS checks the file identification, date, etc., against information supplied by the tape job control card, TLBL or DD.

OS supports two header labels, HDR1 and HDR2, plus two trailer labels. The second label is also 80 bytes and immediately follows the first. It contains such data as record format (fixed, variable, or undefined), the block length, record length, and density in which the tape is written.

2. TRAILER LABEL. There is a trailer label at the end of each file (EOF). For a multivolume file, there is also a trailer at the end of each volume (EOV). (OS requires a second trailer label.) If the trailer label is the end of the *file* (the file may require more than one volume), then the first three bytes of the label contain EOF. If the file requires more than one volume, then the first three bytes of the trailer label at the end of each volume contain EOV. The trailer label is otherwise identical to the header label with one exception: a block count field. IOCS counts the blocks as they are written and writes the total in the trailer label. Remember that IOCS fully performs label processing for standard labels.

The following describes each field of the 80-byte standard file label, for both the header and the trailer.

POSITIONS	NAME	DESCRIPTION
01–03	Label Identifier	Contains HDR if Header label, EOF if end of a data file, or EOV if end of volume (reel).
04–04	File Label Number	Some systems permit more than one file label; this field specifies the sequence of the file label. OS supports two labels each for HDR, EOF and EOV.
05–21	File Identifier	Unique name to describe the file, such as INVENTORY MASTER.
22–27	File Serial Number	Same as the volume serial number of the first or only volume of the file. For a multivolume file, all file serial numbers are the same as the first one.
28–31	Volume Sequence Number	For multivolume files, this gives the sequence of volume numbers. The first or only volume contains 0001, the second 0002, etc.
32–35	File Sequence Number	For a multifile volume, this gives the sequence of the file. The first file on a volume contains 0001, the second 0002, etc.
36–39	Generation Number	Each time the file is rewritten, IOCS increments the generation number by 1 to identify the edition of the file.
40–41	Version Number of Generation	Specifies the version of the generation of the file.
42–47	Creation Date	Provides the year and the day when the file was written. For example, January 17, 1984 is stored as b84017.

POSITION

1	Not used
2–3	Year
4–6	Day of year

POSITIONS	NAME	DESCRIPTION
48–53	Expiration Date	The year and day when the file may be erased and re-written. Same format as creation date.
54–54	File Security	A special security code used by OS.
55–60	Block Count	Used in trailer labels to store the number of blocks since the previous header label.
61–73	System Code	Identifies the programming system.
74–80		Reserved.

IOCS FOR MAGNETIC TAPE

Assuming standard labels, IOCS (Data Management) performs the following functions for output and for input.

OUTPUT.   If the file is being written, processing is as follows:

1. *Processing the Volume Label.* Through the OPEN macro, IOCS checks that the first record is a volume label (VOL). It compares the volume serial number against the serial number (if any) on the tape job control card (TLBL or DD).
2. *Processing the Header Label.* After the volume label, IOCS reads the header label. It checks the expiration date against the date in the communications region. If the expiry date has passed, IOCS backspaces the tape and writes a new header (HDR1) over the old header, using data from the tape job card. (Under OS, a second header (HDR2) is written next.) Then IOCS writes a *tape mark,* a special block that it recognizes.
3. *Writing Records.* The PUT macro uses either a workarea or an IOREG. If the records are unblocked (one record per block), processing is similar to printing. If records are to be blocked, however, IOCS performs the required blocking. For example, assume two IOAREAs (buffers), three records per block, and a workarea. We format the record to be printed in the workarea. The first PUT executed writes the workarea record into the first record of IOAREA1:

There is *no physical writing of tape* at this time. The second PUT writes the workarea record in the second record of IOAREA1, and the third PUT writes in the third record:

WORKAREA $\boxed{\text{Rec-3}}$

IOAREA1 $\boxed{\text{Rec-1} \mid \text{Rec-2} \mid \text{Rec-3}}$ IOAREA2 $\boxed{ \mid \mid }$

At this time, IOCS physically writes the contents of IOAREA1 onto tape, and while this is happening, *internal processing continues*. The fourth PUT writes the work-area in the first record of IOAREA2, the fifth in the second record of IOAREA2, and the sixth in the third record. At this time, IOCS physically writes IOAREA2 onto tape. The seventh PUT resumes writing the workarea in the first record of IOAREA1. Records blocked in three require three PUT commands before a block is physically written.

4. *End-of-Volume.* If the system detects the reflective marker near the end of the reel, IOCS writes an EOV trailer label similar to the header label. The EOV label includes a block count of all blocks written. Next, IOCS writes a tape mark. If an alternate tape drive is assigned, IOCS OPENs the alternate volume, processes its labels, and resumes writing of the file. It rewinds the old reel if required.

5. *End-of-File.* When all data is processed, we CLOSE the tape file. IOCS writes the last block of data (if any). The last block may contain fewer records than the blocking factor specifies. IOCS then writes a tape mark and an EOF trailer label with a block count. Finally, IOCS writes two tape marks and deactivates the file from further processing.

INPUT. This section briefly outlines the IOCS functions for tape input. When an input file is opened, IOCS checks the header and volume labels. The file identification in the header must agree with that on the TLBL job control card to ensure that the correct file is being read. For input, IOCS does not check the expiration date or write a new header. The GET macro reads records, specifying either a workarea or IOREG. If the tape records are unblocked, processing is similar to reading cards. If records are blocked, IOCS performs the required "deblocking."

Assume again two IOAREAs, three records per block, and a workarea. The first GET executed reads a tape block containing records 1, 2, and 3, into IOAREA1, filling it with three records. IOCS then transfers the first record to the workarea, and reads the second tape block, containing records 4, 5, and 6, into IOAREA2:

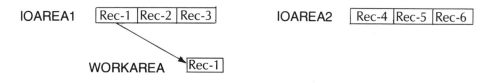

IOAREA1 $\boxed{\text{Rec-1} \mid \text{Rec-2} \mid \text{Rec-3}}$ IOAREA2 $\boxed{\text{Rec-4} \mid \text{Rec-5} \mid \text{Rec-6}}$

WORKAREA $\boxed{\text{Rec-1}}$

If IOCS encounters the end-of-volume label before the end of file (meaning that the file is continued on another reel), IOCS checks that the block count is correct.

The reel is rewound, an alternate tape drive is opened, labels are checked, and reading of the next reel resumes.

END-OF-FILE.   Each GET operation causes IOCS to transfer a record to our work-area. Once every record has been transferred, and we attempt to read the end-of-file label into the workarea, this means there are no more records to be read. They have all been processed. IOCS then checks the block count and rewinds the reel. Control is transferred to our end-of-file address designated in the DTFMT or DCB macros. We should now CLOSE the file and attempt no further reading of it.

Problems 12-4 through 12-7 should now be done.

VARIABLE LENGTH RECORDS

Tape and disk files provide for variable length records, both unblocked and blocked. The use of variable length reduces the amount of unused tape or disk storage, but a disadvantage is in additional programming steps. A record may be variable length because it contains one or more variable length fields or a variable number of fixed length fields:

1. *Variable Length Fields.* Some fields, such as name and address, may vary considerably in length. In the normal fixed-length format, we define the length as that of the longest possible content. It is possible to store only the significant characters of the field. For example, an address such as 123 W. 35TH ST. requires only 15 characters, whereas an address such as 1234 SOUTH HOLLINGSWORTH DRIVE requires 30 characters.
2. *Variable Number of Fields.* Certain applications require some data fields for one customer and not for another. For example, a utility company sells both electricity and gas, and customers may adopt paying by budget. For any given customer, the *basic* subrecord could be customer number, name, address, and balance owing. Optionally, the customer may have an *electric* subrecord (containing rate and history of consumptions), a *gas* subrecord (containing rate and history of consumptions), and a *budget* subrecord (containing payment record). Customers may have any combination of these subrecords, but their record need not provide space for all possibilities. If the customer buys only electricity and does not pay by budget, then only the basic subrecord and electric subrecord are stored.

VARIABLE UNBLOCKED AND BLOCKED RECORDS.   IOCS processes variable length records similar to its processing of fixed length records. However, both IOCS and the programmer must know the length of each *record* that is being read or written. Therefore, immediately preceding each record we define a 4-byte *record control word* containing the length of the record. For example, if the record is 310 bytes long, then the record control word contains 314 (310 plus 4 bytes required by the record control word itself). Further, IOCS must know the length of each *block*.

Therefore, immediately preceding each block is a 4-byte *block control word* containing the length of the block. We calculate and store the record length; IOCS calculates and stores the block length.

Figure 12-5 illustrates both variable unblocked and blocked records. For *variable unblocked* note the following: (1) The first record (Rec-1) is 310 bytes long and the record control word contains '314'. The block control word contains '318', which is the length of the entire block. (IOCS generates a block control word even for unblocked records.) (2) The second record (Rec-2) is 260 bytes long. The record control word contains '264', and the block control word contains '268'.

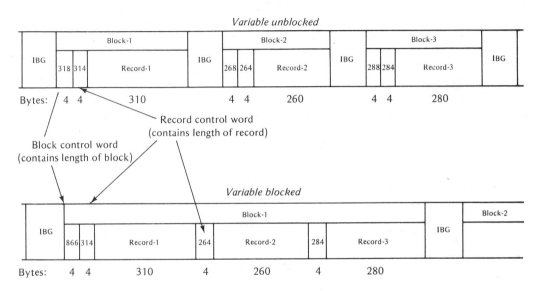

FIGURE 12-5   Variable unblocked and blocked record formats.

For *variable blocked* the example shows three records stored in the first block. A record control word precedes each record, and a block control word (containing '866') precedes the block. IOCS calculates the length in the block control word as:

$$
\begin{aligned}
\text{Length of record-1: } 310 + 4 &= 314 \text{ bytes}\\
\text{Length of record-2: } 260 + 4 &= 264\\
\text{Length of record-3: } 280 + 4 &= \underline{284}\\
&\ 862 \text{ bytes}\\
\text{Add length of block control word: } &\ \underline{4}\\
\text{Total length of block: } &\ \underline{866} \text{ bytes}
\end{aligned}
$$

We designate a maximum block length in the DTF entry BLKSIZE, and IOCS fits as many records into this block as possible. For example, the block length may have been defined as (maximum) 900. If it had been defined as 800, only the first two records would have fit in this block and IOCS would begin the next block with the third record. Although records are blocked, the block length and the number of records per block will vary depending on the lengths of the records.

VARIABLE TAPE PROGRAMMING.   Although IOCS performs most of the processing required for variable length records, we must provide the record length. The additional programming steps are concerned with record and block length:

1. *Record Length.* As with fixed-length records, the program may process variable records in a workarea or in the I/O areas (buffers). We define the workarea as the *length of the largest possible record,* including the 4-byte record control word. When creating the record, we calculate and store the record length in the record control word field. This field must be four bytes in binary format, aligned on a halfword boundary (DOS uses only the first two bytes).
2. *Block Length.* We define the I/O area as the *length of the largest desired block,* including the 4-byte block control word. On output, IOCS stores as many complete records in the block as will fit. IOCS performs all blocking and calculating of the block length. On input, IOCS deblocks the records similar to its deblocking of fixed-length records.

EXAMPLE: READ AND PRINT VARIABLE LENGTH RECORDS.   Assume a file of tape records that contains variable length name and address, with fields defined as:

1–4 Record length   5–9 Account number   10–82 Variable name and address

The name is immediately followed by a "delimiter", in this case a '+' (12-8-6 punch, or X'4E'), to denote the end of the name. A '+' delimiter also terminates the next field, the house address, and another terminates the city:

JP PROGRAMMER+1327 NORTH 37TH STREET+KINGSTOWN+

Figure 12-6 illustrates a simple program that reads and prints the variable length records. Devise several records and trace the logic of this routine carefully, step by step. Note that DTFMT specifies RECFORM=VARBLK (record form = variable blocked). The program reads each record and uses TRT and a loop to scan each of the three variable length fields for the record delimiter. The length of the field is calculated, and EX moves each field to the print area. The program also checks for the absence of a delimiter.

> *Note:*   RECSIZE is omitted, because IOCS needs to know only the maximum block length. For OS, the DCB entry for variable, blocked record format is RECFM=VB.

```
 5 *                       I N I T I A L I Z A T I O N
 6 PROG12C   START  X'3850'                 X'3800' + X'50' FOR LBLTYP TAPE
 7          BALR   3,0                      INITIALIZE BASE REGISTER
 8          USING  *,3
 9          OPEN   FILEITP,FILEOPR           ACTIVATE FILES

19 ***                     M A I N   P R O C E S S I N G
20 A10GET    GET    FILEITP,TAPEWORK         READ TAPE RECORD
26          LA     6,IDENTPIN               ESTAB. ADDRESS OF INPUT IDENT
27          LR     7,6                      ESTABLISH ADDRESS OF
28          AH     7,RECLEN                       END OF RECORD
29          SH     7,=H'9'
30          MVC    P+10(5),ACCTTPIN         MOVE ACCOUNT NO. TO PRINT

32 A20SCAN   TRT    0(73,6),SCANTAB          SCAN FOR DELIMITER
33          BZ     A30                      *    NO DELIMITER FOUND
34          LR     4,1                      SAVE ADDRESS OF DELIMITER
35          SR     1,6                      CALC. LENGTH OF FIELD
36          BCTR   1,0                      DECREMENT LENGTH BY 1
37          EX     1,M10MOVE                MOVE VARIABLE LENGTH FIELD
38          MVI    CTLCHAR,WSP1
39          PUT    FILEOPR,PRINT            PRINT, SPACE 1
45          XC     PRINT,PRINT              CLEAR PRINT AREA
46          LA     6,1(0,4)                 INCREMENT FOR NEXT FIELD
47          CR     6,7                      PAST END OF RECORD?
48          BL     A20SCAN                  *    NO  - SCAN NEXT FIELD
49 A30       MVI    CTLCHAR,WSP2             *    YES - END
50          PUT    FILEOPR,PRINT            PRINT, SPACE 2
56          B      A10GET

58 M10MOVE   MVC    P+20(0),0(6)            MOVE VARIABLE FIELD TO PRINT

60 *                       E N D - O F - F I L E
61 X10EOF    CLOSE  FILEITP,FILEOPR          DE-ACTIVATE FILES
70          EOJ                             NORMAL END-OF-JOB

74 *                       D E C L A R A T I V E S
75 SCANTAB   DC     78X'00'                 TRT TABLE:
76          DC     X'4E'                    *  DELIMITER POSITION
77          DC     177X'00'                 *  REST OF TABLE
78 *                                        TAPE RECORD WORKAREA:
79          DS     0H                       *  ALIGN ON EVEN BOUNDARY
80 TAPEWORK  DS     0CL82                    *  TOTAL MAX. RECORD + LENGTH
81 RECLEN    DS     H                        *  2-BYTE RECORD LENGTH
82          DC     H'0'                     *  2 BYTES UNUSED IN DOS
83 ACCTTPIN  DS     CL5                      *  ACCOUNT NUMBER
84 IDENTPIN  DS     CL73                     *  AREA FOR VAR. NAME|ADDRESS

86 FILEITP   DTFMT  BLKSIZE=300,             TAPE INPUT FILE DECLARATION    +
                    DEVADDR=SYS025,                                         +
                    EOFADDR=X10EOF,                                         +
                    FILABL=STD,                                             +
                    IOAREA1=IOARTPI1,                                       +
                    IOAREA2=IOARTPI2,                                       +
                    RECFORM=VARBLK,                                         +
                    TYPEFLE=INPUT,                                          +
                    WORKA=YES
126          DS     0H                       ALIGN ON EVEN BOUNDARY
127 IOARTPI1 DS     CL300                    BUFFER-1 TAPE FILE
128 IOARTPI2 DS     CL300                    BUFFER-2 TAPE FILE

130 WSP1     EQU    X'09'                    CTL CHAR: PRINT, SPACE 1
131 WSP2     EQU    X'13'                    *          PRINT, SPACE 2

133 PRINT    DS     0CL121                   PRINT AREA
134 CTLCHAR  DS     0CL1                     *
135 P        DS     0CL1                     *
136          DC     CL121' '                 *

138 FILEOPR  DTFPR  BLKSIZE=121,             PRINTER FILE DECLARATION       +
                    CTLCHR=YES,                                             +
                    DEVADDR=SYSLST,                                         +
                    DEVICE=1403,                                            +
                    IOAREA1=IOARPRO1,                                       +
                    IOAREA2=IOARPRO2,                                       +
                    WORKA=YES
159 IOARPRO1 DS     CL121                    BUFFER-1 PRINT FILE
160 IOARPRO2 DS     CL121                    BUFFER-2 PRINT FILE
162          END    PROG12C
```

FIGURE 12-6 Printing variable length records.

PROBLEMS

12-1. Name seven advantages that magnetic tape has over punched cards. What are some disadvantages?

12-2. Explain the following: (a) tape density; (b) tape markers; (c) IBG; (d) blocking factor; (e) fixed and variable length.

12-3. Give an advantage and a disadvantage of increasing the blocking factor.

12-4. What is the purpose of (a) volume label; (b) header label; (c) trailer label?

12-5. Distinguish between (a) EOV and EOF on the trailer label; (b) a multifile volume and a multivolume file; (c) volume sequence number and file sequence number.

12-6. Revise the program in Figure 12-2 or 12-3 for the following: 6 records per block, locate mode. Change file identification to your own name. Assemble and test the program.

12-7. Revise any previous card program so that the input data is on magnetic tape. Provide for fixed, blocked records.

12-8. Assume a variable tape file, with six records whose lengths respectively are 326, 414, 502, 384, 293, and 504. Maximum block length is 1200 bytes. Depict the records showing all block and record lengths.

12-9. Write a program that creates a Supplier Master File.

— Input fields are: Supplier number (7 bytes); Amount payable (7 digits to be stored in packed format); Name (20 bytes); Street (24 bytes); City (24 bytes); Date of last purchase (ddmmyy).

— Name, street, and city are to be stored as variable length fields, with hex 'FF' as a delimiter after each field.

— Next, write a program that updates the file with two tape files: (1) purchase entries (supplier number, amount, date); and (2) miscellaneous changes to name and address records.

CHAPTER 13

DIRECT ACCESS STORAGE

Every installation has its own unique file organization and processing requirements. Also, its budget constraint limits the size of main storage and the type and number of devices. For one installation, the optimum configuration is a simple small diskette system, whereas for another it is a combination of magnetic tapes, direct access storage devices, and teleprocessing terminals. Direct Access Storage devices (DASD) have a significant advantage not provided by other devices: *DASD permits the organization and processing of files not only in sequence (as for cards and tape), but also directly (randomly).* On tape, to access a particular record, we must process every preceding record; under DASD, however, we may directly access any record on the file.

This capability of direct accessing is particularly useful for *"on-line"* processing. For example, a department store keeps its accounts receivable on a DASD. When customers present their credit cards for a purchase, the cashier submits the customer credit number through a terminal to the computer center. A computer program uses this credit number to directly access the customer number in the file, determines the customer's credit rating, and signals the rating to the cashier. The cashier is informed almost immediately whether the customer can have more credit, or has exceeded the limit, or possibly that the card was reported lost.

DASD's are also commonly used for storing on-line the installation's operating system, the various support programs, and catalogued macros and subroutines. The DASD then, like tape, acts as both an input/output device and external storage. There are many types of direct access storage devices, of which the more common ones include:

— Drives with removable disk packs: 2311, 2314, 3330, and 3340.
— Drives with nonremovable storage: 2305, 3344, and 3350.

Each type of device has unique physical differences. However, the programming for each device is similar. Each record stored on a device has a specific location with a unique address and has a control field ("key") for identification.

DASD CHARACTERISTICS

Certain of the DASD's, such as the 2311, 3344, and 3330, have disks for recording data. These disks, made of metal coated with magnetic oxide, are similar to phonograph record surfaces. But a record has tracks that spiral inward, whereas the DASD tracks are concentric—each track makes a unique circle, as shown in Figure 13-1.

The track contains the data, generally recorded bit-by-bit, with records and blocks stored just as on magnetic tape. Similarly, data may be written and rewritten on the same track for permanent or temporary records. Although innermost tracks are shorter in circumference, all tracks contain the same number of bytes. On a 2311, for example, the disk surface has 200 *primary tracks* plus 3 *alternate tracks* used if any of the primary tracks become defective. The number of tracks on a disk surface and their capacity varies by device.

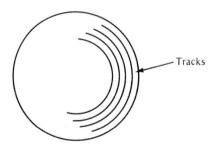

Tracks

FIGURE 13-1   Disk tracks.

A *disk pack* consists of a number of rotating disks on a vertical shaft. Except for the top and bottom disk, the surfaces are recorded on both sides. Figure 13-2 shows the access arms that move horizontally to position at any track. Each arm has two read/write heads—one for the upper surface and one for the lower. Only one head at a time reads and writes. To read a record, for example, on the outermost track, all the access arms position there. The record to be read is on one of the surfaces—only the

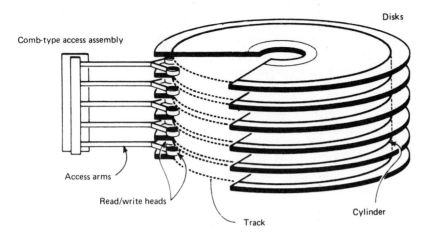

FIGURE 13-2   Disk storage device mechanism.

head for that surface is activated to read the record. As the disk rotates, the read occurs when the data record reaches the head. Figure 13-3 lists the number of tracks and their capacity. The 3330, for example, has 19 surfaces, giving a total of 100 million bytes of storage (certain of this space is required for nondata records and gaps).

TIMING.   There is some delay from the time a read/write instruction is executed until the data is actually received. As shown in Figure 13-3, the time varies considerably by device, but includes:

Access Motion. The more often and further that the access arm moves, the more time is taken. The section Cylinder Concept explains how data is organized to minimize this seek time.

Device	Capacity				Speed		
	Bytes per track	Tracks per cylinder	Number of cylinders	Total bytes	Ave. seek time (ms)	Ave. rot'l delay (ms)	Data rate KB/ sec.
2311	3625	10	200	7,250,000	75	12.5	156
3340–1	8368	12	348	35,000,000	} 25	10.1	885
3340–2	8368	12	696	70,000,000			
3344	8368	12	4 × 696	280,000,000			
3330–1	13030	19	404	100,000,000	} 30	8.4	806
3330–11	13030	19	808	200,000,000			
3350	19069	30	555	317,000,000	25	8.4	1200

FIGURE 13-3   IBM direct access devices.

Rotational Delay. As the disk rotates, time is required for the data to reach the read/write head. The average rotational delay ("latency") is half a rotation.

Data Transfer Rate. The device's rotation speed and density of data affect the time to transfer data between the device and main storage.

CYLINDER CONCEPT.   Data is organized to minimize arm movement. The DASD does not store data on a surface starting with the outermost track through to the inner tracks of the same surface. Such a storage method would require considerable access arm movement back and forth across surfaces. Rather, *the DASD stores data downwards beginning with the outermost track of the top surface through to the outermost track of the bottom surface.* This series of vertical tracks is called a *cylinder,* and the outermost one is cylinder-0.

The tracks for a cylinder are numbered beginning with 0, so that cylinder-0, track-0 is the outermost track of the top surface, and cylinder-0, track-1 is the next one below it. When all cylinder-0 is filled with data, the DASD stores next on cylinder-1 (the next inner series of tracks), beginning at cylinder-1, track-0. (The cylinder concept may be clearer if you imagine a series of different size tin cans, with no top or bottom lids, one inside the other. Each can is a "cylinder," with data stored in grooves around the sides.)

When the DASD reads sequentially, it positions the heads at cylinder-0. Head-0 begins reading from cylinder-0, track-0. When all track-0 records are read, the device selects head-1 to read from track-1—no access motion is required. The device then continues reading down through to the last track on cylinder-0. Next, the access arm moves (for the first time) to cylinder-1, where it processes successively from track-0 through to the last track of cylinder-1.

TRACK FORMAT.   Every track contains certain information about its address and condition. Between the different records on the track are gaps; these vary by device and their location on the track. The basic format for a track is:

(a) *The Index Point* tells the read/write device that this point is the physical beginning of the track—data is recorded following the Index Point.

(b) *The Home Address* tells the system the address of the track (the cylinder and head, or surface, number) and whether the track is a primary or alternate track, or defective.

(c) *The Track Descriptor Record (R0)* immediately follows the Home Address. The system stores information about the track in this record. There are two separate fields: a *Count Area* and a *Data Area.* The Count Area contains '0' for record number and '8' for data length. It is otherwise similar to the Count Area described next for Data Record under item (d). The Data Area contains eight bytes of information used by the system. The Track Descriptor Record is not normally accessible to the programmer.

(d) *Data Record Formats (R1 through Rn).* Following the Track Descriptor (R0) record is one or more of our data records, each consisting of the following:

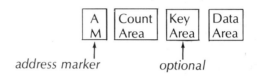

Address Marker. The I/O control unit stores a two-byte Address Marker prior to each block of data. When reading records, the control unit uses the Address Marker to locate the beginning of data.

Count Area. This is a field that the system also stores and uses. Included are:
An Identifier field gives the cylinder/head number (similar to that in the Home Address), and the sequential record number (0–255) in binary, representing R0 through R255. (The Track Descriptor Record, R0, contains zero for record number.)
The Key Length field is explained in the next section, Key area.
The Data Length is a binary value 0 through 65,535 that specifies the number of bytes in the Data Area field (the length of our block of data). For the end-of-file, the system generates a last ("dummy") record containing a length of zero in this field. When the system reads the file, this zero length indicates that there are no more records.

Key Area. Under DASD, the *key* is the control field for the records in the file, such as customer or inventory number. The key, if stored in this separate Key Area, can facilitate locating of records. The key area is *optional.* If omitted, then the file is called *formatted without keys (Count-Data-Format).* The key length in the Count Area contains zero. If the file is *formatted with keys (Count-Key-Data-Format),* then the Key Length contains the length of the Key area.

Data Area. We store our data blocks in this area in any format—unblocked or blocked, fixed length or variable, just as on magnetic tape.

Under normal circumstances, the programmer is not concerned with the Home Address and Track Descriptor record, nor with the Address Marker, Count Area, and Key Area portions of the Data Record field. The system completely handles the processing of these fields. As shown in the following example programs, it is simply necessary to specify appropriate entries in the DTF or DCB and job control statements. We can then read and write sequential disk records much like cards and tape.

The system stores as many records on the track as possible. Usually, records are stored completely (intact) on a track. A *record overflow* feature permits records to overlap from one track to the next.

FILE ORGANIZATION

There are several ways to organize a DASD file. The choice of method is a systems, not a programming, problem, and therefore this text gives a limited description of organization methods. The four main methods of DASD file organization are:

1. *Sequential Organization.* In this method, also used by cards and magnetic tape, each record follows another successively according to a predetermined key (control field). We would adopt sequential if we do not require on-line processing, and if most records are processed when the file is read. The DOS organization method is Sequential Access Method (SAM), and we use the macro DTFSD (Define The File Sequential Disk). Advantage: sequential provides simplest design and programming, and minimizes DASD storage space. Disadvantage: it is difficult to locate a unique record and to insert a new record without rewriting the file.

2. *Direct (Random) Organization.* This method stores records based on a relationship between the key (control field) and the track address where the DASD record is stored. Our program performs a calculation on the key number to locate the address of the record. The DOS method is Direct Access Method (DAM), and we use DTFDA (Direct Access). Advantage: Direct Access provides fast and efficient use of DASD storage for directly accessing any record. Disadvantages: (1) The file keys must lend themselves to such a calculation. (2) A calculation for more than one key may generate the same track address ("synonyms"). (3) The file may be arranged in a sequence other than sequential, and require special programming to produce sequential reports. (4) We must provide special programming to locate the record.

3. *Indexed Sequential Organization.* Records are stored *sequentially,* permitting normal sequential processing. In addition, this method has *indexes* related to the file; we may use these indexes to locate records *directly.* The DOS method is Indexed Sequential Access Method (ISAM), and we use DTFIS (Indexed Sequential). Advantage: Indexed Sequential permits both sequential and direct processing of files with little special programming effort. Disadvantage: IS may use more DASD storage and process more slowly.

4. *Virtual Storage Access Method.* VSAM is a more recent development for the 370 systems, and permits both sequential and direct processing.

This text covers programming for Sequential and Indexed Sequential organization.

Problems 13-1 through 13-5 should now be attempted.

DOS PROGRAMMING EXAMPLE—CREATING A SEQUENTIAL DISK FILE

Programming for sequential disk is similar to that for magnetic tape. The program in Figure 13-4 creates a sequential disk file. The input is the tape file created in Chapter 12, Figure 12-2. A later section describes the disk job control entries, DLBL and

```
 6  *                    I N I T I A L I Z A T I O N
 7  PROG13A   START  X'3850'                  X'3800' + X'50' FOR LBLTYP TAPE
 8           BALR   3,0                       INITIALIZE BASE REGISTER
 9           USING  *,3
10           OPEN   TAPE,SDISK                ACTIVATE FILES

20  *                    M A I N   P R O C E S S I N G
21  A10GET    GET    TAPE                      READ 1 TAPE RECORD
26           MVC    TAPEIN,0(5)               MOVE FROM TAPE BUFFER
27           MVC    ACCTDKO,ACCTIN            MOVE TAPE FIELDS TO DISK
28           MVC    NAMEDKO,NAMEIN            *    WORK AREA
29           MVC    ADDRDKO,ADDRIN           *
30           ZAP    BALNDKO,BALNIN           *
31           MVC    DATEDKO,DATEIN           *
32           PUT    SDISK,DISKWORK            WRITE WORK AREA ONTO DISK
38           B      A10GET

40  *                    E N D - O F - F I L E
41  P10END    CLOSE  TAPE,SDISK                DE-ACTIVATE FILES
50           EOJ                               NORMAL END-OF-JOB

54  *                    D E C L A R A T I V E S
55  TAPEIN    DS     0CL90                     TAPE INPUT AREA
56  ACCTIN    DS     CL6                      *   ACCOUNT NO.
57  NAMEIN    DS     CL20                     *   NAME
58  ADDRIN    DS     CL40                     *   ADDRESS
59  BALNIN    DS     PL4                      *   BALANCE
60  DATEIN    DS     CL6'DDMMYY'              *   DATE
61           DS     CL14                     *   UNUSED

63  DISKWORK  DS     0CL90                     DISK WORK AREA
64  ACCTDKO   DS     CL6                      *   ACCOUNT NO.
65  NAMEDKO   DS     CL20                     *   NAME
66  ADDRDKO   DS     CL40                     *   ADDRESS
67  BALNDKO   DS     PL4                      *   BALANCE
68  DATEDKO   DS     CL6                      *   DATE
69           DC     CL14' '                  *   RESERVED FOR EXPANSION

71  TAPE      DTFMT  BLKSIZE=360,              TAPE INPUT FILE DECLARATION  +
                    DEVADDR=SYS025,                                         +
                    EOFADDR=P10END,                                         +
                    ERROPT=IGNORE,                                          +
                    FILABL=STD,                                             +
                    IOAREA1=IOARTPI1,                                       +
                    IOREG=(5),                                              +
                    RECFORM=FIXBLK,                                         +
                    RECSIZE=090,                                            +
                    TYPEFLE=INPUT
109 IOARTPI1  DS     CL360                     IOCS INPUT TAPE BUFFER-1
```
```
111 SDISK     DTFSD  BLKSIZE=368,              DISK OUTPUT FILE DECLARATION  +
                    DEVADDR=SYS015,                                          +
                    DEVICE=3340,                                             +
                    IOAREA1=IOARDKO1,                                        +
                    RECFORM=FIXBLK,                                          +
                    RECSIZE=90,                                              +
                    TYPEFLE=OUTPUT,                                          +
                    VERIFY=YES,                                              +
                    WORKA=YES
162 IOARDKO1  DS     CL368                     IOCS DISK BUFFER-1
```
```
164           END    PROG13A
// LBLTYP TAPE
// EXEC LNKEDT
// TLBL    TAPE,'CUST REC TP',0,100236
// ASSGN   SYS015,X'162'
// DLBL    SDISK,'CUSTOMER RECORDS SD',0,SD
// EXTENT  SYS015,222222,1,0,0700,10
```

FIGURE 13-4 Sequential disk processing under DOS.

283

EXTENT (bottom of the figure). Entries for the DTFSD macro are similar to those for DTFMT.

Note that there is no FILABL entry because DASD labels must be standard.

BLKSIZE=368 means that the blocksize for output is 360 bytes (4 × 90) plus 8 bytes for IOCS to construct a count field. The IOAREAs are also 368 bytes. We provide for these extra 8 bytes only for output; for input the entry is 360.

DEVICE=3340 means that for this program, records are written on a 3340 DASD.

VERIFY=YES tells the system to reread each output record to check its validity.

This example creates a sequential disk file. In a later section, this file becomes input to create ("load") an indexed sequential file. It is also possible to update an SD file directly (rewrite a record over the previous one); this chapter does not cover this practice.

Note: DEVADDR may be omitted (the system uses the SYSnnn from the job control entry).

OS PROGRAM EXAMPLE

The example OS coding in Figure 13-5 is a revision of the previous DOS example that reads tape records and copies them onto disk. The DD job control cards contain some of the DCB entries: for tape input, BLKSIZE, RECFM, and DEN, and for disk output, BLKSIZE, and RECFM.

For a disk DCB, an entry MACRF=(GM,PM) means the program can both read and write the same file.

DISK LABELS

Disks, like magnetic tape, use labels to identify the volume and the file. This text describes the IBM standard labels as supported by IOCS. Cylinder-0, track-0 is reserved for labels, as depicted in Figure 13-6:

Record-0—the Track Descriptor, R(0).

Record-1 and 2—Certain devices, if the disk is SYSRES (containing the operating system), reserve R(1) and R(2) for the IPL (Initial Program Load) routine. For all other cases, R(1) and R(2) contain zeros.

Record-3—the VOL1 label. (There may actually be more than one volume label, from R(3) through R(10), not supported by DOS.)

Record-4 through the end of the track—This is the standard location for the *Volume Table Of Contents (VTOC)*. The VTOC contains the file label(s) for the files on the DASD.

```
//GO.TAPEIN   DD DSNAME=TRFILE,DISP=(OLD,PASS),UNIT=3420,              X
              DCB=(BLKSIZE=360,RECFM=FB,DEN=3)
```
```
//GO.DISKOT   DD DSNAME=&TEMPDSK,DISP=(NEW,PASS),UNIT=3340,SPACE=(TRK,10),  X
              DCB=(BLKSIZE=360,RECFM=FB)
```

```
***                 I N I T I A L I Z A T I C N

PROG13B    START  0
           SAVE   (14,12)
           BALR   3,0
           USING  *,3
           ST     13,SAVEAREA+4
           LA     13,SAVEAREA
           OPEN   (TAPE,(INPUT),SDISK,(OUTPUT))

***                 M A I N   P R O C E S S I N G
A10GET     GET    TAPE                      READ 1 TAPE RECORD
           MVC    TAPEIN,0(1)               MOVE FROM TAPE BUFFER

           MVC    ACCTDKO,ACCTIN            MOVE TAPE FIELDS TO DISK
           MVC    NAMEDKO,NAMEIN            *     WORK AREA
           MVC    ADDRDKO,ADDRIN           *

           ZAP    BALNDKO,BALNIN           *
           MVC    DATEDKO,DATEIN           *
           PUT    SDISK,DISKWORK            WRITE WORK AREA ONTO DISK
           B      A10GET

***                 E N D - O F - F I L E

P10END     CLOSE  (TAPE,,SDISK)
           L      13,SAVEAREA+4
           RETURN (14,12)

***                 D E C L A R A T I V E S

TAPEIN     DS     0CL90                     TAPE INPUT AREA
ACCTIN     DS     CL6                      *   ACCOUNT NO.
NAMEIN     DS     CL20                     *   NAME
ADDRIN     DS     CL40                     *   ADDRESS
BALNIN     DS     PL4                      *   BALANCE
DATEIN     DS     CL6'DDMMYY'              *   DATE
           DS     CL14                     *   UNUSED

DISKWORK   DS     0CL90                     DISK WORK AREA
ACCTDKO    DS     CL6                      *   ACCOUNT NO.
NAMEDKO    DS     CL20                     *   NAME
ADDRDKO    DS     CL40                     *   ADDRESS
BALNDKO    DS     PL4                      *   BALANCE
DATEDKO    DS     CL6                      *   DATE
           DC     CL14' '                  *   RESERVED FOR EXPANSION

TAPE       DCB    DDNAME=TAPEIN,            TAPE INPUT DATA SET         +
                  DSORG=PS,                                            +
                  EODAD=P10END,                                        +
                  LRECL=90,                                            +
                  MACRF=(GL)
```
```
SDISK      DCB    DDNAME=DISKOT,            DISK OUTPUT DATA SET        +
                  DSORG=PS,                                            +
                  LRECL=90,                                            +
                  MACRF=(PM)
```
```
SAVEAREA   DS     18F                       REGISTER SAVE AREA
           LTORG  ,
           END    PROG13B
```

FIGURE 13-5   Sequential disk processing under OS.

285

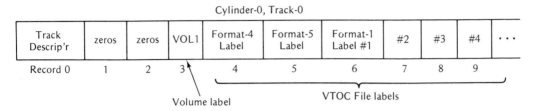

Cylinder-0, Track-0

FIGURE 13-6   Disk volume layout.

VOLUME LABELS.   The standard Volume label uniquely identifies the DASD volume. A 4-byte key area immediately precedes the 80-byte volume data area. The Volume label is the fourth record (R3) on cylinder-0. The 80 bytes are arranged similarly to a tape volume label with one exception: positions 12–21 are the "Data File Directory", containing the starting address of the VTOC.

FILE LABELS.   File labels identify and describe a file (data set) on a volume. The file label is 140 bytes long, consisting of a 44-byte key area and a 96-byte file data area. Each file on a volume requires a file label for identification. In Figure 13-6 all file labels for the volume are stored together in the Volume Table Of Contents (VTOC). Although we may place the VTOC in any cylinder, its standard location is cylinder-0, track-0. There are four types of file labels:

1. The *Format-1 label* is equivalent to the magnetic tape file label. The Format-1 label differs, however, in that it defines the actual cylinder-track addresses of the start and end of the file—the "*extent*". Further, a file may be stored intact in an extent or in several extents on the same volume. Format-1 permits up to three extents on a volume. (Format-3 is used if the file is scattered over more than three extents.)
2. The *Format-2 label* is used for indexed sequential files.
3. The *Format-3 label* is stored if the file occupies more than three extents.
4. The *Format-4 label* is the first record in the VTOC, and defines the VTOC for the system.

The *Format-1 File Label* contains the following:

POSITIONS	NAME	DESCRIPTION
01–44	File Identification	An unique identification consisting of File-ID. Generation number.Version Number (we may use simply File-ID).
45–45	Format Identifier	'1' for Format-1.
46–51	File Serial Number	The Volume Serial number from the volume label.
52–53	Volume Sequence Number	The file may require more than one volume— this is the sequence number.
54–56	Creation Date	ydd (Binary) y = year (0–99),
57–59	Expiration Date	dd = day (1–366)

POSITIONS	NAME	DESCRIPTION
60–60	Extent Count No.	Number of extents for this file on this volume.
61–61	Bytes Used in Last Block of Directory	Used by OS only.
62–62		Reserved.
63–75	System Code	Contains the name of the operating system.
76–82		Reserved.
83–84	File Type	Contains a code to identify if SD, DA, or IS type of organization.
85–85	Record Format	Used by OS only.
86–86	Option Codes	IS only—to indicate if file contains Master index and type of overflow areas.
87–88	Block Length	IS only—the length of each block.
89–90	Record Length	IS only—the length of each record.
91–91	Key Length	IS only—the length of the key area for data records.
92–93	Key Location	IS only—the leftmost position of the key field within the record.
94–94	Data Set Indicators	SD only—indicates if this is the last volume.
95–98		OS only.
99–103	Last Record Pointer	OS only.
104–105		Reserved.
106–106	Extent Type	⎫
107–107	Extent Sequence No.	⎬ Descriptors for the first or only extent for the file.
108–111	Extent Lower Limit	⎪
112–115	Extent Upper Limit	⎭
116–125		Descriptors for the second extent, if any.
126–135		Descriptors for the third extent, if any.
136–140	Pointer	Address of the next label. For IS, the format-2 label; for SD and DA, the format-3 label if any.

Note: In the above example, IS means Indexed Sequential and OS means Operating System.

Problems 13-6 through 13-9 should now be attempted.

INDEXED SEQUENTIAL FILE ORGANIZATION

This chapter covers mainly the concepts and the more important features of Indexed Sequential File Organization; more details are available in the Supervisor manuals. DOS sequential files for card, tape, and disk use the Sequential Access Method (SAM). DOS Indexed sequential files use *Indexed Sequential Access Method (ISAM)*. ISAM provides the facilities to process disks both sequentially and directly. Before examining the programming requirements, we should first see how an indexed sequential file is organized. In addition to our data records in a *"prime data area,"* there are *indexes* that assist ISAM to locate our record.

THE PRIME DATA AREA.   ISAM writes ("loads") our records on tracks in the
"prime data area." These records are written *with keys,* in key sequence, and may be
unblocked or blocked. Preceding our data records in the track is the Home Address
(HA). See Figure 13-7: Under the Prime Data Area, for cylinder-0/track-1, the first key
is 0001 and the highest is 0021. The last record on the ISAM file is on track-n (the
number of surfaces varies by device) and contains the highest key on the cylinder,
0825.

THE TRACK INDEX.   When creating the file, ISAM establishes a *"track index"* in
track-0 of each cylinder used. The track index contains an entry for the highest key
for each track on the cylinder. See Figure 13-7: For the track index for cylinder-0, the
first entry is the Home Address. Next is the "Cylinder Overflow Control Record"
(COCR), covered later. Next is an entry "key 0021, cylinder-0/track-1," which
means that the highest key on cylinder-0/track-1 is 0021. The last entry is key 0825
on cylinder-0/track-n. This entry is followed by a "dummy entry" to indicate the end
of the index. The dummy entry contains the highest possible value in the key, X'F's.

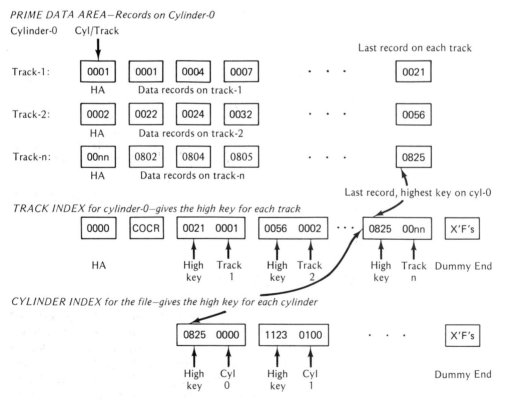

FIGURE 13-7   Index sequential organization.

Therefore, we should never use X'F's as our own key. (Figure 13-7 is intentionally simplified. There are actually two entries for each track: a *normal entry* (shown) and an *"overflow entry"* (not shown).)

THE CYLINDER INDEX.   ISAM creates a *"cylinder index"* for the file on a separate cylinder (or on a separate volume). The cylinder index contains an entry for the highest key for each cylinder—the home address. In Figure 13-7, the first entry is "key 0825, cylinder-0," meaning that the highest key on cylinder-0 is 0825. The cylinder index is also terminated by a dummy record containing X'F's in the key. We tell ISAM where to store the cylinder index. At execute-time, ISAM can load the cylinder index into main storage for faster reference during the run, thereby reducing disk access and processing time.

The program may access an ISAM file either sequentially or directly. Sequential processing involves the use of the GET and PUT macros, as GET filename,workarea. Direct processing uses READ and WRITE; to access a record directly, we code READ filename, key and ISAM uses our key to locate the disk record. Assume that the key is 0024 and the program is accessing directly:

— ISAM searches the cylinder index to locate the *cylinder* where the required record is stored. The first entry in the index is high key 0825, cylinder-0. Since our key 0024 is lower than 0825, our record must be on cylinder-0.
— Having located the cylinder, ISAM accesses cylinder-0/track-0 for the track index to locate the *track* where the record is stored. The first index entry is high key 0021, track-1. Our key is greater, so the record is not on track-1. The second entry is key 0056, track-2; record 0024 is on cylinder-0/track-2.
— ISAM has now located the correct cylinder/track, so it accesses track-2, reads record 0024, and transfers it to the program's input area.

THE MASTER INDEX.   If the cylinder index occupies more than four tracks, it may be more efficient to have an optional higher level of index, a "master index." The master index immediately precedes the cylinder index and contains one entry for each track of the cylinder index—the highest key and the track. The system can first search the master index to locate the track where the required cylinder index is stored.

OVERFLOW AREAS.   When we update a file we often have to insert new records, such as new employees and customers. Under sequential processing we rewrite the file, inserting the new records. But ISAM permits us to insert new records without rewriting the entire file. ISAM writes the new records as unblocked in an *overflow area,* and stores an overflow entry in the track index to point to the overflow record. There are two types of overflow areas; either or both may be used:

1. *Cylinder Overflow Area.* The EXTENT card defines the number of tracks in each cylinder for ISAM to insert added records. The cylinder overflow area is in the

prime area and stores all overflow records for that cylinder. The Cylinder Overflow Control Record (COCR) in Figure 13-7 stores the address of the last overflow record in the track and the number of unused bytes in the overflow area.

2. *Independent Overflow Area.* We may define the number and location of cylinders used exclusively for new added records. Our job control extent statement at execute-time tells ISAM where to store records in the independent overflow area.

3. *Use of Both Areas.* If we specify both types of overflow areas, ISAM places all new records first in the cylinder overflow area. When any cylinder is full, ISAM places excess overflow records for that cylinder in the independent overflow area.

ISAM handles all overflow records and the linkage from the prime area to the overflow area. As the overflow areas become full, more processing time is required to access records. We may periodically use a special utility program to "reorganize" the file. The program rewrites the file, and merges the overflow records in with the prime area records.

There are four approaches to programming ISAM:

1. *Load or Extend an ISAM File.* The initial creation of an ISAM file is called "loading." Once the file is loaded, it is possible to include higher-key records at the end of the file—"extending".

2. *Adding Records to an ISAM File.* New records have keys that do not exist on the file. Special programming is required to insert or "add" these records within the file.

3. *Random Retrieval of an ISAM File.* New data requires that the file be updated at regular intervals. We can read the new data (such as sales records), use the key to randomly locate the ISAM master record, and rewrite the updated ISAM master.

4. *Sequential Processing of an ISAM File.* If there are many records to update and the new detail records are in sequence, then we can sequentially read and rewrite the ISAM master.

PROCESSING DOS INDEXED SEQUENTIAL FILES

The following illustrates required imperative macros and the DTFIS file definition macro for indexed sequential under DOS. The DOS Supervisor and I/O Macros manual supplies additional useful information.

LOAD OR EXTEND AN ISAM FILE UNDER DOS.   Figure 13-8 creates an ISAM file. The input is sequential disk (SD) records created in Figure 13-4. This program writes these records onto an indexed sequential (IS) file called DISKIS. The new instructions are macros SETFL, WRITE, ENDFL, and DTFIS. The job control entries also vary for ISAM: (1) The DLBL card entry for 'codes' contains ISC, meaning Indexed Sequential Create (Load), and (2) there is an EXTENT card for both the cylinder index and for the data area. In addition, ISAM requires that we check the *status condition* caused by each macro (covered later).

```
  6  *                  I N I T I A L I Z A T I O N
  7  PROG13C   START X'3850'                 X'3800' + X'50' FOR LBLTYP NSD
  8            BALR  3,0                      INITIALIZE BASE REGISTER
  9            USING *,3
 10            OPEN  DISKSD,DISKIS            ACTIVATE FILES
 19            SETFL DISKIS                   SET ISAM LIMITS
 25            TM    DISKISC,B'10011000'      ANY SETFL ERRORS?
 26            BO    R10ERR                       YES - ERROR ROUTINE

 28  *                  M A I N   P R O C E S S I N G
 29  A10GET    GET   DISKSD,SDISKIN           GET SEQUENTIAL DISK RECORD
 35            MVC   KEYNO,ACCTIN             SET UP KEY NUMBER
 36            MVC   RECORD,SDISKIN           SET UP ISAM DISK RECORD
 37            WRITE DISKIS,NEWKEY            WRITE ISAM RECORD
 42            TM    DISKISC,B'11111110'      ANY WRITE ERRORS?
 43            BO    R10ERR                       YES - ERROR ROUTINE
 44            B     A10GET                       NO  - CONTINUE

 46  *                  E N D - O F - F I L E
 47  P10END    ENDFL DISKIS                   END ISAM FILE LIMITS
 59            TM    DISKISC,B'11000001'      ANY ENDFL ERRORS?
 60            BO    R10ERR                       YES - ERROR ROUTINE
 61  P20       CLOSE DISKSD,DISKIS            DE-ACTIVATE FILES
 70            EOJ                            NORMAL END-OF-JOB

 74  *                  D A S D   E R R O R   R O U T I N E S
 75  R10ERR    EQU   *                        DASD ERROR
 76  *             .                           RECOVERY ROUTINES
 77            B     P20

 79  *                  D E C L A R A T I V E S
 80  SDISKIN   DS    0CL90                    SEQ'L DISK INPUT AREA
 81  ACCTIN    DS    CL6                      *     KEY
 82            DS    CL84                     *     REST OF RECORD

 84  DISKSD    DTFSD BLKSIZE=360,             SEQUENTIAL DISK INPUT          +
                     DEVADDR=SYS015,                                         +
                     EOFADDR=P10END,                                         +
                     DEVICE=3340,                                            +
                     IOAREA1=IOARSD1,                                        +
                     RECFORM=FIXBLK,                                         +
                     RECSIZE=90,                                             +
                     TYPEFLE=INPUT,                                          +
                     WORKA=YES
130  IOARSD1   DS    CL360                    SEQ'L DISK BUFFER-1
```

```
132  DISKIS    DTFIS CYLOFL=1,                INDEXED SEQUENTIAL DISK LOAD   +
                     DEVICE=3340,                                            +
                     DSKXTNT=2,                                              +
                     IOAREAL=IOARISAM,                                       +
                     IOROUT=LOAD,                                            +
                     KEYLEN=6,                                               +
                     NRECDS=1,                                               +
                     RECFORM=FIXUNB,                                         +
                     RECSIZE=90,                                             +
                     VERIFY=YES,                                             +
                     WORKL=ISAMOUT
182  IOARISAM  DS    CL104                    ISAM OUTPUT AREA
```

```
184  ISAMOUT   DS    0CL96                    ISAM WORKAREA
185  KEYNO     DS    CL6                      *     KEY LOCATION
186  RECORD    DS    CL90                     *     DATA AREA

188            END   PROG13C
```

FIGURE 13-8   Creating (loading) a DOS ISAM file.

ISAM MACROS FOR LOAD AND EXTEND.   We code the usual OPEN and CLOSE to activate and deactivate the files. The new macros are:

SETFL	filename
WRITE	filename, NEWKEY
ENDFL	filename

SETFL (Set File Load Mode). When we load or extend a file, SETFL initializes the ISAM file by preformatting the last track of each track index. The operand references the DTFIS name of the ISAM file to be loaded.

WRITE. The macro WRITE loads a record onto the ISAM file. The filename is our DTFIS name. Operand-2 is the word NEWKEY. We store the key and data area in a workarea (called ISAMOUT in Figure 13-8). DTFIS knows this area through the entry WORKL=ISAMOUT. For the WRITE statement, ISAM checks that the new key is in ascending sequence. Then ISAM transfers the key and data area to an I/O area (this is IOARISAM in the program, known to DTFIS by IOAREAL=IOARISAM). Here ISAM constructs the count area:

ENDFL (End File Load Mode). After all records are written, ENDFL performs the following: (1) writes the last block of data (if any); (2) writes an end-of-file record; and (3) writes any required index entries.

THE DTFIS MACRO.   The maximum length for an ISAM filename is seven. In Figure 13-8, the DTFIS entries for the file to be loaded are:

CYLOFL=1 gives the number of tracks on each cylinder to be reserved for each cylinder overflow area (if any). The maximum depends on the device.

DEVICE=3340 is the DASD unit containing the prime data area or overflow area for the file.

DSKXTNT=2 designates the number of extents that the file uses. The number consists of one for each data extent and one for each index area and independent overflow area extent. This program has one extent for the prime data area and one for the cylinder index.

IOAREAL=IOARISAM provides the name, IOARISAM, of the ISAM load I/O area. Our symbolic name IOARISAM references our DS output area. For loading unblocked records, the IOAREAL field length is calculated as:

Count Area (8) ı Key Length (6) + Record Length (90)

IOROUT=LOAD tells the Assembler that the program is to load an ISAM file.

KEYLEN=6 provides the length of our key area.

NRECDS=1 gives the number of records per block for this file (unblocked).

RECFORM=FIXUNB means that the records are to be fixed-length and unblocked.

RECSIZE=90 is the length of each record's data area.

VERIFY=YES tells the system to check the parity of each record as it is written.

WORKL=ISAMOUT gives the name, ISAMOUT, of our load workarea (the DS for the workarea is defined elsewhere in the program). For unblocked records, this length is calculated as:

Key Length (6) + Data Area (90)

STATUS CONDITION.   ISAM macros may generate certain error conditions, and the system allows us to test them. After each I/O macro operation, ISAM places the "*status*" in a 1-byte field called *filenameC*. For example, if our DTFIS name is DISKIS, then ISAM calls the status byte DISKISC. Following is a list of the eight bits in *filenameC* that the system may set when a program loads an ISAM file:

BIT	LOAD STATUS ERROR CONDITION
0	Any uncorrectable DASD error except wrong length record.
1	Wrong length record detected during output.
2	The prime data area is full.
3	The cylinder index is full, discovered by SETFL.
4	The master index is full, discovered by SETFL.
5	Duplicate record—the current key is the same as the one previously loaded.
6	Sequence check—the current key is lower than the one previously loaded.
7	The prime data area is full and there is no space for ENDFL to store the end-of-file record.

In Figure 13-8, TM operations test DISKIS after the macros SETFL, WRITE, and ENDFL. After SETFL, for example, the TM instruction tests if bits 0, 3, and 4 are on. If any of the conditions exist, the program branches to an error routine (not coded). There, special programming action may isolate the error, print an error message, and possibly terminate the job.

RANDOM RETRIEVAL OF AN ISAM FILE.   Figure 13-9 randomly retrieves an ISAM file. The DLBL job card has one difference: the entry for 'codes' contains ISE, used to indicate any load extension, add, or retrieve. The program reads detail cards in random sequence, with changes to the ISAM master file. The ISAM master is the one loaded in the previous example. For each card, the program uses the account number (key) to locate the correct ISAM record. The program then rewrites the updated record on the ISAM file.

```
 6 *                 I N I T I A L I Z A T I O N
 7 PROG13D  START  X'3850'                   X'3800' + X'50' FOR LBLTYP NSD
 8          BALR   3,0                        INITIALIZE BASE REGISTER
 9          USING  *,3
10          OPEN   CARD,DISKIS                ACTIVATE FILES

20 *                 M A I N   P R O C E S S I N G
21 A10GET   GET    CARD,CARDIN                READ INPUT RECORD
27          MVC    KEYNO,ACCTIN               SET UP KEY NUMBER
28          READ   DISKIS,KEY                 READ ISAM RANDOMLY
33          TM     DISKISC,B'11010101'        ANY READ ERROR?
34          BO     R10ERR                          YES - ERROR ROUTINE
35          WAITF  DISKIS                     COMPLETE READ OPERATION
40          MVC    ACCTDKO,ACCTIN             MOVE CARD FIELDS TO DISK
41          MVC    NAMEDKO,NAMEIN             *     WORK AREA
42          MVC    ADDRDKO,ADDRIN             *
43          PACK   BALNDKO,BALNIN             *
44          MVC    DATEDKO,DATEIN             *
45          WRITE  DISKIS,KEY                 WRITE NEW ISAM RECORD
50          TM     DISKISC,B'11000000'        ANY WRITE ERROR?
51          BO     R10ERR                          YES - ERROR ROUTINE
52          B      A10GET                          NO  - CONTINUE

54 *                 E N D - O F - F I L E
55 P10END   CLOSE  CARD,DISKIS                DE-ACTIVATE FILES
64          EOJ                               NORMAL END-OF-JOB

68 *                 D A S D   E R R O R   R O U T I N E S
69 R10ERR   EQU    *                          DASD ERROR
70 *               .                          RECOVERY ROUTINES
71          B      P10END
```

FIGURE 13-9   Random retrieval of a DOS ISAM file.

ISAM MACROS FOR RANDOM RETRIEVAL.   The new macros are:

READ	filename,KEY
WAITF	filename
WRITE	filename,KEY

READ. The READ macro causes ISAM to access the required record from the file. Operand-1 contains the DTFIS filename, and operand-2 contains the word KEY. We must store our key in the field referenced by the DTFIS entry KEYARG. In this program KEYARG=KEYNO. For each card read, the program transfers the account key number to KEYNO.

WAITF. The WAITF macro allows a READ or WRITE operation to be completed before another is attempted. In a random retrieval we are reading and rewriting the same records, and we must ensure that the operation is finished. We may code WAITF anywhere following a READ/WRITE, and preceding the next READ/WRITE.

WRITE. The WRITE macro rewrites the ISAM record. Operand-1 is the DTFIS filename, and operand-2 is the word KEY. KEY refers to our entry in KEYARG.

THE DTFIS MACRO.   DTFIS differences for random retrieval include:

```
 73 *                    D E C L A R A T I V E S
 74 CARD         DTFCD DEVADDR=SYSIPT.              CARD INPUT FILE DECLARATION      +
                       IOAREA1=IOARCDI1,                                            +
                       IOAREA2=IOARCDI2,                                            +
                       BLKSIZE=80,                                                  +
                       DEVICE=2501,                                                 +
                       EOFADDR=P10END,                                              +
                       TYPEFLE=INPUT,                                               +
                       WORKA=YES
115 IOARCDI1 DS        CL80                         IOCS CARD BUFFER 1
116 IOARCDI2 DS        CL80                         IOCS CARD BUFFER 2

118 CARDIN   DS        OCL80                        CARD INPUT AREA
119 CODEIN   DS        CL2                          *   CARD CODE '01'
120 ACCTIN   DS        CL6                          *   ACCOUNT NO.
121 NAMEIN   DS        CL20                         *   NAME
122 ADDRIN   DS        CL40                         *   ADDRESS
123 BALNIN   DS        ZL6'0000.00'                 *   BALANCE
124 DATEIN   DS        CL6'DDMMYY'                  *   DATE

126 DISKIS   DTFIS CYLOFL=1.                        ISAM RANDOM RETRIEVAL           +
                       DEVICE=3340,                                                 +
                       DSKXTNT=2,                                                   +
                       IOAREAR=IOARISAM,                                            +
                       IOROUT=RETRVE,                                               +
                       KEYARG=KEYNO,                                                +
                       KEYLEN=6,                                                    +
                       NRECDS=1,                                                    +
                       RECFORM=FIXUNB,                                              +
                       RECSIZE=90,                                                  +
                       TYPEFLE=RANDOM,                                              +
                       VERIFY=YES,                                                  +
                       WORKR=ISAMOUT

209 IOARISAM DS        CL106                        KEY LEN + 10 + REC LENGTH

211 ISAMOUT  DS        OCL96                        ISAM WORKAREA
212 KEYNO    DS        CL6                          KEY AREA
213 RECORD   DS        OCL90                        DATA AREA
214 ACCTDKO  DS        CL6                          *   ACCOUNT NO.
215 NAMEDKC  DS        CL20                         *   NAME
216 ADDRDKO  DS        CL40                         *   ADDRESS
217 BALNDKO  DS        PL4                          *   BALANCE
218 DATEDKO  DS        CL6                          *   DATE
219              DC    CL14' '                      *   RESERVED FOR EXPANSION

221              END   PROG13D
```

FIGURE 13-9 (Continued)

IOAREAR=IOARISAM gives the name, IOARISAM, to the ISAM retrieve I/O area. Our symbolic name IOARISAM references the DS area for retrieving unblocked records. The IOAREAR field length is: Key length (6) + "Sequence Link field" (10) + Record length (90.)

TYPEFLE=RANDOM means that we are to retrieve records randomly, by key. Other entries are SEQNTL for sequential processing, and RANSEQ for both random and sequential.

WORKR=ISAMOUT is the name of our retrieval work area.

STATUS CONDITION.   The status condition byte for Add and Retrieve is different from Load. The following is a list of the bits:

BIT	ADD AND RETRIEVE CONDITION
0	Any uncorrectable DASD error except wrong length record.
1	Wrong length record detected during an I/O operation.
2	End-of-file during sequential retrieval (*not an error!*).
3	The record to be retrieved is not in the data file.
4	The ID specified to the SETL in SEQNTL is outside the prime data limits.
5	An attempt to add a record to the file for which the key already exists.
6	The cylinder overflow area is full.
7	A retrieval function is trying to process an overflow record.

Figure 13-9 tests for various conditions after the ISAM macros. Once again, the program would normally isolate the error, print a message, and perhaps terminate the job.

SEQUENTIAL READING OF AN ISAM FILE.   Sequential reading of a DOS ISAM file involves use of the macros SETL, GET, and ESETL. SETL (Set Low) establishes the starting point for the first record to be processed. SETL options include:

SETL   filename,BOF   Set start at 1st record of the file.
SETL   filename,KEY   Set start at the record with the key in the field defined by the DTFIS KEYARG entry.

SETL   filename,GKEY   Set start at 1st record within a required group. The KEYARG field could contain, for example, "A340000" to indicate all records with keys beginning with A34.

The ESETL macro terminates sequential mode, and is coded as ESETL,filename. DTFIS entries include:

IOROUT=RETRVE
TYPEFLE=SEQNTL   or   RANSEQ
KEYLOC=n   (to indicate the 1st byte of the key in the record, if processing begins with a specified key or group of keys, and records are blocked)

PROCESSING OS INDEXED SEQUENTIAL FILES

Processing ISAM files under OS is similar to, but not identical to, DOS processing. (Fortunately, DOS coding for VSAM has been designed to be more compatible with OS.) Under OS, ISAM provides for a "delete code"—if the first byte of the record contains X'FF', ISAM will automatically delete the record where required. The following provides some features of OS ISAM processing.

LOAD AN ISAM FILE UNDER OS. The OS imperative macros concerned with creating an indexed sequential file are the conventional OPEN, PUT, and CLOSE. DCB entries are:

DDNAME = name of the data set
DSORG   = IS for indexed sequential
MACRF   = (PM) or (PL)
BLKSIZE = length of each block
CYLOFL = number of overflow tracks per cylinder
KEYLEN = length of the key area
LRECL   = length of each record
NTM   = number of tracks for master index, if any
OPTCD   = options required. For example, MYLRU:
     M   establishes a master index (or omit M)
     Y & R control use of cylinder overflow and independent areas
     L   is delete code to cause bypassing records with X'FF' in first byte
     U   (for fixed length only) establishes track index in main storage
RECFM   = record format for fixed/variable and unblocked/blocked:
      F, FB, V, VB

SEQUENTIAL RETRIEVAL AND UPDATE. Under OS, sequential retrieval and update involves the OPEN, SETL, GET, PUTX, ESETL, and CLOSE macros. Once the data set has been created with standard labels, many DCB entries are no longer required. DDNAME and DSORG=IS are still used, and the following are applicable:

MACRF=(entry)   (GM) or (GL) for input only. (PM) or (PL) for output only.
                         (GM,SK,PU) if read and rewrite in place: S = use of SETL, K
                         = Key or Key class used, PU = use of PUTX macro.
EODAD=eofaddress   For input, if reading to end-of-file.
SYNAD=address   Optional error checking.

THE SETL MACRO. SETL (Set Low address) establishes the first sequential record to be processed, used because the programmer may want to start anywhere in the data set.

SETL   dcb-name,start-position,address

The "start-position" operand has a number of options:

B = Begin with first record in the data set. (Omit operand-3 for B or BD.)
K = Begin with the record with the key in the operand-3 address.
KC = Begin with the 1st record of the "Key class" in operand-3. If the first record is "deleted," begin with the next nondeleted record. A Key class is any group of keys beginning with a common value, such as all keys 287XXXX.
I = Begin with the record at the actual device address in operand-3.

BD, KD, KDH, KCD, and ID cause retrieval of only the data portion of the record.

Following are some examples of SETL to set the first record in an ISAM file called DISKIS, using a 6-character key:

	SETL DISKIS,B	Begin with the 1st record of the data set
	SETL DISKIS,K,KEYADD1	Begin with key 012644 in data set
	SETL DISKIS,KC,KEYADD2	Begin with 1st record that begins with key 012
KEYADD1 DC	C'012644'	6-character key
KEYADD2 DC	C'012',XL3'00'	3-character key followed by 3 bytes of hex zeros

The ESETL macro, used as ESETL dcb-name, terminates sequential retrieval. If there is more than one SETL, ESETL must precede each additional one.

In Figure 13-10, the program sequentially reads an ISAM file. The objective is to insert a delete code (X'FF') in any record that is more than five years old. The standard date from the TIME macro is packed 00yyddd+, and the date in the records in positions 26–28 is in the same format. The PUTX macro rewrites any such old record, with the delete byte.

There are many other features and macros associated with OS. Check especially the IBM OS Data Management Services Guide and Data Management Macro Instructions manuals.

```
PROG13     START
           SAVE    (14,12)
           BALR    3,0
           USING   *,3
           ST      13,SAVEAREA+4
           LA      13,SAVEAREA
           OPEN    (ISFILE)
           SETL    ISFILE,B              START 1ST RECORD OF DATA SET
           TIME
           ST      1,TODAY
           SP      TODAY,=P'5000'        CALC DATE 5 YEARS AGO

A10GET     GET     ISFILE
           CP      26(3,1),TODAY         5 YEARS OR OLDER?
           BNL     A10GET                *    NO  - BYPASS
           MVI     0(1),X'FF'            *    YES - SET DELETE CODE
           PUTX    ISFILE                *    RE-WRITE RECORD
           B       A10GET

A90END     ESETL   ISFILE
           CLOSE   (ISFILE)
           L       13,SAVEAREA+4
           RETURN  (14,12)

SAVEAREA   DS      18F
TODAY      DS      F                     TODAY'S DATE: 00YYDDD+
IOAREA     DS      CL100                 DISK IO AREA
ISFILE     DCB     DDNAME=INDEXDD,DSORG=IS,EODAD=A90END,MACRF=(GL,S,PU)
           END     PROG13
```

FIGURE 13-10   Sequential retrieval of an OS ISAM file.

PROBLEMS

13-1. What is the advantage of DASDs compared with magnetic tape?

13-2. Based on Figure 13-3, how many bytes can be stored in a *cylinder* for each device listed?

13-3. Why does a DASD store data by *cylinder* rather than by tracks across a surface?

13-4. What is the purpose of (a) Home Address? (b) Track Descriptor Record? (c) Key Area?

13-5. Distinguish the differences amongst Sequential, Direct, and Indexed Sequential processing.

13-6. Revise the file definition macro entries and I/O areas in Figure 13-4 or 13-5 for the following. Input: 6 records per block, each 90 bytes long. Output: 3 records per block, to be run on a 3330 as SYS017. Assemble and test.

13-7. What is the purpose, location and contents of the VTOC?

13-8. What is the DASD equivalent to the magnetic tape header label—what is its location and how does it differ?

13-9. Revise the job control for Figure 13-4 or 13-5 for the following: filename = DISKOUT, file-ID = ACCTS RECEIVABLE, retain for 30 days, run on SYS017, serial no. 123456, using a 2311 on cylinder-15 track-0 for 15 tracks.

13-10. For ISAM, what is the purpose of (a) Master index? (b) Cylinder index? (c) Track index?

13-11. What are the different ways to process an ISAM file? What is the difference between extending and adding records?

13-12. Revise Figure 13-7 for the input as revised in Problem 13-6, and for new ISAM output: 3 records per block and both a cylinder and independent overflow area. You will have to review the Supervisor manual for this. Assemble and test.

13-13. Revise, assemble, and test Figure 13-8 according to the changes in the previous problem.

PART V

ADVANCED TOPICS

CHAPTER 14

MACRO WRITING

The Greek word *makros* means "long." In programming, macro means a "long" instruction, one that causes the generation of several or many instructions. For each macro, the Assembler generates one or more instructions. We generally suppress the generated code, but in this chapter print it by means of PRINT GEN. There are two sources of macros:

1. *Manufacturer-supplied Macros.* IBM macros facilitate the complex Supervisor and input/output operations, and include OPEN, GET, EOF, DTF's, and DCB's. These macros simplify much difficult but repetitive coding. They are catalogued in the system library for assembling with source programs.
2. *User-defined Macros.* We may code as our own macro any routine commonly used in a program or in other programs. We may then include it with the program source deck at assembly-time or assemble and catalogue it in the system library. Common examples include multiply, divide, program and base register initialization, and table look-up.

MACROS AND SUBROUTINES. Subroutines covered earlier have a significantly different use from macros. In a subroutine, the program branches out of the main logic into a separately coded routine. This routine is performed identically each time

303

it is executed. A macro, however, generates Assembler instructions wherever it is coded. Depending on how the macro is coded, the generated instructions each time may be identical or different.

We must assess which technique is more efficient for any given situation. Subroutines are more easily coded and use less storage. Macros, however, are more versatile. High-level languages such as COBOL and PL/I use both subroutines and macros in converting the Assembler language.

WRITING MACROS

There are three basic types of macros:

1. *Positional Macros.* For these, we code the entries or *parameters* in a predetermined sequence. An example is PUT PRTR,PRINT. Depending on the way the macro has been defined, in some cases a parameter may be omitted, as PUT PRTR. Figure 14-1 illustrates a positional macro.
2. *Keyword Macros.* For these we code the entries in any sequence. The Assembler recognizes the presence of the parameter, followed by an equal sign (=). A familiar example is:

CARD DTFCD TYPEFLE=INPUT, +
WORKA=YES,   +   etc...

TYPEFLE and WORKA may be in any sequence, and are recognized as keywords by the Assembler. In some cases we may omit keywords; the Assembler then assumes default values. Figure 14-3 depicts a keyword macro.
3. *Mixed.* A macro definition may combine both positional and keyword. Positional entries are specified first, in sequence. Figure 14-9 illustrates mixed types.

Certain rules govern writing and assembling macros. Figure 14-1 is a simple packed divide positional macro, and shows the basic terminology for a *macro definition:*

```
                                    symbolic parameters
(a)  Header        3    MACRO
(b)  Prototype     4    DIVID  &QUOT,&DIVDEND,&DIVISOR
     Model         5    ZAP    &QUOT,&DIVDEND          MOVE DIVIDEND TO QUOT
(c)    Statements  6    DP     &QUOT,&DIVISOR          DIVIDE BY DIVISOR
(d)  Trailer       7    MEND
```

FIGURE 14-1   Definition of positional divide macro DIVID.

(a) The first statement of the macro definition is the *header* statement, containing the operation MACRO. This instruction tells the Assembler that a macro is being defined next.
(b) The *prototype* statement informs the Assembler the name of the macro (in this example DIVID), and how the macro-instruction will be coded. The operand

contains three *symbolic parameters* (a name preceded by an ampersand &) for quotient, dividend, and divisor.

(c) The *model statements* are instructions that the Assembler uses to generate Assembler instructions. (There may also be comments and *Conditional Assembly* instructions, covered later.)

(d) The *trailer* statement, MEND, terminates the macro definition.

In the partial program in Figure 14-2, DIVID is the *macro-instruction* coded once for execution. DIVID was the only instruction coded; the ZAP and DP instructions are *generated code* or the *macro expansion.* The Assembler inserts a plus sign (+) beside the statement number in all the instructions that it generates. The Assembler generated these instructions based on (1) the macro definition, and (2) the operands coded in the macro-instruction.

```
14          DIVID  MILEAGE,MILES,GALS      MACRO-INSTRUCTION
15+         ZAP    MILEAGE,MILES           MOVE DIVIDEND TO QUOT
16+         DP     MILEAGE,GALS            DIVIDE BY DIVISOR
17 *          .
18 *          .
19 MILEAGE  DS     PL6                     QUOTIENT - MILES/GAL
20 MILES    DS     PL3                     DIVIDEND - MILES
21 GALS     DS     PL3                     DIVISOR  - GALLONS
```

FIGURE 14-2   Use of DIVID macro-instruction.

There are three entries in the macro-instruction operand, MILEAGE, MILES, and GALS, for each of the three parameters in the prototype, &QUOT, &DIVDEND, and &DIVISOR. For a positional macro, the macro-instruction operands correspond exactly with the prototype. The Assembler replaces each parameter in the macro definition:

MACRO-INSTRUCTION		MACRO DEFINITION
MILEAGE	replaces	&QUOT
MILES		&DIVDEND
GALS		&DIVISOR

MILEAGE, MILES, and GALS are defined in the source program. The Assembler uses their addresses and lengths when producing the generated code (see the ZAP and DP instructions generated).

We insert macro definitions before the main source program. Only comments and Assembler control instructions EJECT, PRINT, SPACE, TITLE, ICTL, and ISEQ may precede the header. We may define more than one macro, one after another, but we may not define a macro within another macro. Also, a macro may be separately assembled and catalogued for use in other programs.

Within the program we may use the macro-instruction any number of times, using either the same labels or labels of any other valid fields. However, there is no automatic checking for validity. For example, if the macro-instruction is wrongly coded with character instead of packed operands, the Assembler generates character operands. To check for validity, we use *Conditional Assembly instructions,* covered later.

VARIABLE SYMBOLS.   In a macro definition, a variable symbol begins with an ampersand (&) followed by 1 to 7 letters or digits, the first of which must be a letter. Examples are &NAME and &DIVISOR. There are three types of variable symbols.

1. *Symbolic Parameters.* We may use these in the macro definition name field and operand. In the prototype DIVID, one symbolic parameter is &QUOT. In the macro-instruction we coded a value MILEAGE that the Assembler assigned to the symbolic parameter &QUOT.
2. *System Variable Symbols.* The Assembler automatically assigns values to these special symbols. There are three: &SYSECT, &SYSLIST, and &SYSNDX, covered later.
3. *Set Symbols.* These permit us to define temporary storage and work areas to be used within the macro definition. They are defined and processed by Conditional Assembly instructions, covered later.

EXPLANATION OF THE MACRO DEFINITION.   The general format for macro definition is as follows:

	NAME	OPERATION	OPERAND
Header:	blank	MACRO	blank
Prototype:	Symbolic parameter or blank	symbol	Symbolic parameter(s)
Model Statements:	Ordinary, sequence or variable symbol, or blank	Instruction or variable symbol	Ordinary or variable symbols
Trailer:	Sequence symbol or blank	MEND	blank

HEADER.   The MACRO header statement is blank in the name or operand fields. It tells the Assembler that a macro is to be defined.

PROTOTYPE.   The *name field* may be blank, as in Figure 14-1, or it may contain a symbolic parameter (a name preceded by an ampersand [&] as explained earlier). The operation is a unique symbolic name, such as DIVID, that is not the name of another macro or Assembler instruction. The *operand* may contain zero to 100 symbolic parameters separated by commas. OS permits up to 200 parameters.

MODEL STATEMENTS.   These statements define the Assembler statements that are to be generated. There may be none or many model statements. We indicate continuation in column 72 with any character. The *name field* may be blank (as in Figure 14-1), or it may contain an ordinary symbol, a variable symbol, or a sequence symbol (a name preceded by a period, explained later). The *operation* may contain an Assembler instruction, a macro-instruction or a variable symbol. The *operand* may contain ordinary symbols (such as AMTPK) or variable symbols (such as &QUOT).

TRAILER.   MEND is a required entry to terminate the macro-definition. The name may be blank or may contain a sequence symbol (a name preceded by a period).

COMMENTS.   Comments may begin anywhere after a blank following the operand. In Figure 14-1, model statement comments begin in column 41. Also, an entire line may be coded as a comment. We may include comment lines anywhere in the macro definition following the prototype statement. There are two ways: (1) An asterisk (*) in column 1 causes the Assembler to print the comment along with the generated code (see Figure 14-5 and 14-6); (2) A period in column 1 followed by an asterisk (.*) tells the Assembler not to print the comment with the generated code (see Figures 14-5 and 14-6).

KEYWORD MACROS.   Keyword macros have two advantages over positional macros: (1) We may code keyword parameters in *any sequence;* (2) the symbolic parameters in the prototype statement may contain *standard values* allowing us to omit the parameter when using the macro-instruction. Other than the prototype statement, keyword macros are defined the same as positional macros. The parameters of the keyword prototype are immediately followed by an equal sign (=) and an optional standard value.

The macro in Figure 14-3 is similar to the one in Figure 14-1. The prototype is keyword, and is coded as DIVID &QUOT=QUOTIENT,&DIVDEND=,&DIVISOR=. Figure 14-4 uses the macro twice, depicting two ways to code keyword macros. The first operand, &QUOT=, is followed by a standard value, QUOTIENT. When using the macro-instruction, we may omit the parameter &QUOT. In this case, the Assembler assumes that the name to be used by &QUOT is always QUOTIENT (see B10DIV in Figure 14-4). Alternatively, we may override the standard value by coding a different label, such as QUOT=SPEED (see B20DIV in Figure 14-4).

```
1          MACRO
2          DIVID  &QUOT=QUOTIENT,&DIVDEND=,&DIVISOR=
3          ZAP    &QUOT,&DIVDEND          MOVE DIVIDEND TO QUOT
4          DP     &QUOT,&DIVISOR          DIVIDE BY DIVISOR
5          MEND
```

FIGURE 14-3   Definition of keyword divide macro DIVID.

The other prototype parameters, &DIVDEND and &DIVISOR have no standard values. We must code the name to be used in the macro-instruction as DIVDEND=DIST, etc. (See Figure 14-4. Note that in B20DIV the operands are not coded in sequence.)

Except for operands that have standard values, keyword macros require coding the keyword each time they are used. Unless there are a number of standard values, a keyword macro-instruction could cause more coding for the programmer.

```
12 B10DIV    DIVID  DIVDEND=DIST,DIVISOR=TIME
13+          ZAP    QUOTIENT,DIST            MOVE DIVIDEND TO QUOT
14+          DP     QUOTIENT,TIME            DIVIDE BY DIVISOR

16 B20DIV    DIVID  DIVISOR=TIME,DIVDEND=DIST,QUOT=SPEED
17+          ZAP    SPEED,DIST               MOVE DIVIDEND TO QUOT
18+          DP     SPEED,TIME               DIVIDE BY DIVISOR
19 *            .
20 *            .
21 QUOTIENT  DS     PL7                      QUOTIENT
22 DIST      DS     PL4                      DIVIDEND - DISTANCE
23 TIME      DS     PL3                      DIVISOR  - TIME
24 SPEED     DS     PL7                      QUOTIENT - SPEED
```

FIGURE 14-4   Use of keyword DIVID macro-instruction.

CONCATENATION.   Concatenation means linking together, as a chain. In model statements it is possible to concatenate a symbolic parameter with another symbolic parameter or with characters.

1. *Concatenate Symbolic Parameters.* Figure 14-5 codes a load operation that varies according to the type of data to be loaded. We code L concatenated with a symbolic parameter, called here &TYPE, as L&TYPE. If &TYPE contains blank, H, E, or D, the Assembler generates L, LH, LE, or LD.
2. *Concatenate Characters.* If a symbolic parameter is concatenated with digits, letters, left bracket, or a period, there must be a period joining the two fields. Assume a symbolic parameter &AREA. If it references a label called FIELD, then &AREA.A results in generated code FIELDA. Figure 14-5 illustrates concatenation with a bracket &PRIN.(&LEN) to permit different length codes.

The macro in Figure 14-5 multiplies both binary fullword or halfword fields and illustrates symbolic parameters, comments and concatenation. The prototype, MPY,

```
1             MACRO
2  &LABEL1    MPY    &REG1,&REG2,&MULTCAN,&MULTPLR,&TYP,&LEN,&PRIN
3  .*                LOAD REGISTERS WITH MULTIPLICAND & MULTIPLIER
4  &LABEL1    L&TYP  &REG2,&MULTCAN            LOAD MULTIPLICAND
5             L&TYP  &REG1,&MULTPLR           LOAD MULTIPLIER
6  *                 MULTIPLY TWO REGISTERS
7             MR     &REG1,&REG1              MULTIPLY REGISTERS
8  .*                CONVERT PRODUCT TO DECIMAL
9             CVD    &REG2,DBLEWORD           STORE PRODUCT
10            UNPK   &PRIN.(&LEN),DBLEWORD    UNPACK IN PRINT AREA
11            MEND
```

FIGURE 14-5   Definition of multiply macro MPY with concatenation.

contains a symbolic parameter &LABEL1 in the name field. When using MPY as a macro-instruction we may code a label such as M10MULT, which the Assembler includes in the generated code. The symbolic parameters in the prototype operand are:

&REG1	the even-numbered register of an even-odd pair.
&REG2	the odd-numbered register.
&MULTCAN	the multiplicand field, full or halfword.
&MULTPLR	the multiplier field, full or halfword.
&TYP	the type of operation—blank for fullword and H for halfword.
&LEN	the length in the print area where the product is unpacked.
&PRIN	the name of the print area.

The first model statement contains the same symbolic parameter &LABEL1 as the prototype, because the Assembler is to generate this label for this statement. The operation loads the full or halfword multiplicand into the odd register. The second model statement loads the full or halfword multiplier into the even register. The third model statement multiplies the contents of the two registers. (Operand-1 of MR is the even register of an even-odd pair.)

The fourth statement converts the product in the odd register to decimal format in DBLEWORD, defined in the main source program. Finally, the decimal product is unpacked in the print area. Note the concatenation to append the length code in operand-1.

The program in Figure 14-6 tests the macro-instruction twice. M10MULT designates H in the &TYP position. Note that LH is generated for L&TYP. M20MULT

```
19 M10MULT  MPY    8,9,FIELDH1,FIELDH2,H,6,PRINT+10
20+M10MULT  LH     9,FIELDH1              LOAD MULTIPLICAND
21+         LH     8,FIELDH2              LOAD MULTIPLIER
22+*               MULTIPLY TWO REGISTERS
23+         MR     8,8                    MULTIPLY REGISTERS
24+         CVD    9,DBLEWORD             STORE PRODUCT
25+         UNPK   PRINT+10(6),DBLEWORD    UNPACK IN PRINT AREA


27 M20MULT  MPY    0,1,FIELDF1,FIELDF2,,10,PRINT+25
28+M20MULT  L      1,FIELDF1             LOAD MULTIPLICAND
29+         L      0,FIELDF2             LOAD MULTIPLIER
30+*               MULTIPLY TWO REGISTERS
31+         MR     0,0                    MULTIPLY REGISTERS
32+         CVD    1,DBLEWORD             STORE PRODUCT
33+         UNPK   PRINT+25(10),DBLEWORD   UNPACK IN PRINT AREA
34 *           .
35 *           .
36 DBLEWORD DS    D                      DOUBLEWORD PRODUCT
37 FIELDH1  DS    H                      HALFWORD MULTIPLICAND
38 FIELDH2  DS    H                      HALFWORD MULTIPLIER
39 FIELDF1  DS    F                      FULLWORD MULTIPLICAND
40 FIELDF2  DS    F                      FULLWORD MULTIPLIER
41 PRINT    DC    CL121' '               PRINT AREA
```

FIGURE 14-6   Use of MPY macro-instruction.

omits the &TYP position by means of two commas. The instruction L is generated for L&TYP.

This example is still relatively simple. The Conditional Assembly instructions in the next section test for validity and permit more variations.

Problems 14-1, 14-2, and 14-3 should now be attempted.

CONDITIONAL ASSEMBLY INSTRUCTIONS

Conditional Assembly instructions permit us to test such attributes as data format, value, field length, and to define fields and change values. They do not generate any code in themselves; rather, they help determine which Assembler instructions are generated. There are two main groups:

1. *Branching and Testing.* AGO, ANOP, AIF, and ACTR permit testing attributes and branching to different locations within the macro definition.
2. *Defining Symbols (SET Symbols) and Varying Their Values.* Local set symbols, LCLA, LCLB, and LCLC, provide defining within a macro expansion. Global set symbols, GBLA, GBLB, and GBLC, enable symbols to be known in other macro expansions. The values in the SET symbols are modified by SETA, SETB, and SETC instructions.

ATTRIBUTES. For each Assembler constant or instruction, the Assembler assigns attributes such as field length and packed format. We may reference these attributes by Conditional Assembly instructions. There are six kinds of attributes:

ATTRIBUTE		NOTATION
L'	Length	Length of symbolic parameter.
I'	Integer	Integer attribute of fixed-point, float, or decimal number.
S'	Scaling	Scale attribute of fixed-point, float, or decimal number.
K'	Count	Number of characters in a macro instruction operand.
N'	Number	Number of operands coded in the macro-instruction.
T'	Type	Type of DC or DS, such as P, C, X, F, etc.

LENGTH. Only AIF, SETA, and SETB statements may reference the length of a variable symbol. For example &X SETA L'&Y means store the length of &Y in the field defined by the SET symbol &X.

INTEGER AND SCALING. The macro may check the defined integer and scaling attributes of fixed-point (binary), floating-point, and decimal numbers with AIF, SETA, and SETB. In the statement AMT DC P'1234.56' the integer attribute is 4 (4 digits left of the decimal point), and the scale is 2 (2 digits right of the decimal point). Integer and scaling are not further covered.

COUNT AND NUMBER.   The count attribute refers to the number of characters in a macro-instruction operand. The number attribute refers to the number of operands in a macro-instruction. They may be referenced with AIF, SETA, and SETB. For example: DIVID MPG,MILES,GALS. The count attribute of GALS, having four characters, is four. The number attribute of the macro, having three operands, is three. Count and number are not further covered.

TYPE.   The type attribute refers to the type of DC, DS, or instruction. Among the types are:

A	A-type address	F	Fullword	P	Packed
B	Binary	H	Halfword	V	V-type address
C	Character	I	Machine instruction	X	Hexadecimal
D	Long float	L	Extended float	Y	Y-type address
E	Short float	O	Omitted operand	Z	Zoned

The type may be referenced by AIF, SETC, and SETB. The next section under AIF and Figure 14-7 give examples.

```
 1              MACRO
 2 &LABEL2  DIVID  &QUOT,&DIVDEND,&DIVISOR
 3 .*              TEST IF DIVIDEND & DIVISOR BOTH DEFINED PACKED
 4              AIF   (T'&DIVISOR NE T'&DIVISOR).NOTPAK
 5              AIF   (T'&DIVDEND NE 'P').NOTPAK
 6 .*              TEST IF QUOTIENT LENGTH ADEQUATE
 7              AIF   (L'&DIVDEND+L'&DIVISOR GT L'&QUOT).WRONLN
 8              AGO   .DIVE               VALID PACKED FIELDS
 9 .NOTPAK  MNOTE 'PARAMETER NOT DEFINED AS PACKED'
10           MEXIT
11 .WRONLN  MNOTE 'LENGTH OF DIVIDEND + DIVISOR GREATER THAN QUOTIENT'
12           MEXIT
13 .*              PERFORM DIVISION
14 .DIVE    ANOP
15 &LABEL2  ZAP   &QUOT,&DIVDEND          MOVE DIVIDEND TO QUOTIENT
16           DP    &QUOT,&DIVISOR         DIVIDE BY DIVISOR
17           MEND
```

FIGURE 14-7   Definition of divide macro DIVID with validity tests.

BRANCHING & TESTING—AGO, AIF.   These instructions make use of *sequence symbols*. A sequence symbol begins with a period (.) followed by one to seven letters or digits, the first of which is a letter. Examples are .B25, .AROUND, and .P. Since a name field of a model statement may contain a sequence symbol, it is possible to branch to different statements. Branching is done by the following:

NAME	OPERATION	OPERAND
Sequence symbol or blank	AGO	Sequence symbol
Sequence symbol or blank	AIF	(logical expression) sequence symbol

AGO—UNCONDITIONAL BRANCH.   AGO branches unconditionally to a statement with a sequence symbol for its name, as:

```
            AGO     .B25
              .
              .
              .
      .B25    MVC     P+25(8),DATE
```

AIF—CONDITIONAL BRANCH.   AIF means "ask if". The operand consists of two parts: (1) A *logical expression* in brackets; and (2) Immediately following, a sequence symbol. The AIF logical expression may use *relational operators:*

EQ   equal   NE   not equal
LT   less than   LE   less than or equal
GT   greater than   GE   greater than or equal

The following are five AIF examples:

1. **AIF (T'&AMT EQ 'P').B25PAK** (If the type of &AMT equals packed, then branch to .B25PAK.)
2. **AIF (L'&AMT GT 16).E35ERR** (If the length of &AMT is greater than 16, then branch to .E35ERR.)
3. **AIF (T'&LINK NE 'I').R45ERR** (If the type of &LINK does not equal an instruction, branch to .R45ERR.)
     This testing occurs when the Assembler converts the macro to generated code. The first example tests if &AMT is *defined* as packed, not what the field actually contains. (This macro may be catalogued for use by other programmers.) The Assembler cannot test the contents of a field at execution-time.
     Logical operators AND, OR, and NOT combine terms in a logical expression:
4. **AIF ('&TAB' EQ '' AND T'&ARG EQ 'O').R65** (If *contents* of &TAB are blank and &ARG is omitted, branch to .R65. The latter is a way of checking if a macro-instruction operand is omitted—intentionally or accidentally.)
     Finally, *arithmetic operators,* +(add), −(subtract), *(multiply), and /(divide) may combine terms of an expression:
5. **AIF (L'PROD GE (L'&MULTCD+L'&MPR+1)).VALID** (If the length of product is greater than or equal to the length of &MULTCD plus &MPR plus 1, branch to .VALID. This test ensures that the defined product area is large enough for an MP operation.)

     Examine the AGO and AIF instructions in Figure 14-7. This example is similar to Figure 14-1, with the additional checks that the dividend and divisor are defined as packed, and that the quotient area is at least as large as the dividend plus divisor. Figure 14-8 tests the macro. D10DIV shows valid operands that generate the correct instructions. D20DIV and D30DIV illustrate invalid operands that generate error messages.

```
24 D10DIV     DIVID MILEAGE,MILES,GALS        VALID DIVISION
25+D1CDIV     ZAP   MILEAGE,MILES             MOVE DIVIDEND TO QUOTIENT
26+           DP    MILEAGE,GALS              DIVIDE BY DIVISOR

28 D20DIV     DIVID MILEAGE,MILES,PRINT       INVALID DIVISION
29+PARAMETER NOT DEFINED AS PACKED

31 D30DIV     DIVID MILES,MILEAGE,GALS        INVALID DIVISION
32+LENGTH OF DIVIDEND + DIVISOR GREATER THAN QUOTIENT
33 *            •
34 *            •
35 MILES     DS    PL3                        DIVIDEND - MILES
36 GALS      DS    PL3                        DIVISOR  - GALLONS
37 MILEAGE   DS    PL6                        QUOTIENT - MILES PER GAL
```

FIGURE 14-8   Use of DIVID macro-instruction.

OTHER INSTRUCTIONS

There are as well three instructions not yet covered: ANOP, MNOTE, and MEXIT.

ANOP—NO OPERATION.   ANOP is a convenience instruction. AGO and AIF require a sequence symbol as a branch operand. But AGO or AIF may require branching to an instruction whose name is an ordinary or variable symbol. If so, then AGO and AIF must branch to an ANOP immediately before the statement.

NAME	OPERATION	OPERAND
A Sequence Symbol	ANOP	blank

Figure 14-7 illustrates the use of ANOP, where AGO has to branch to &LABEL2. Since AGO cannot branch to a variable symbol, it goes to .MULT containing the ANOP operation, and immediately preceding &LABEL2.

MNOTE AND MEXIT.   We use these operations to print error messages and to exit from the macro.

NAME	OPERATION	OPERAND
Sequence symbol, variable symbol, or blank	MNOTE	any message, within apostrophes
Sequence symbol or blank	MEXIT	blank

MNOTE—MACRO ERROR MESSAGE.   MNOTE is used to print programmer macro messages at assembly-time. The message is enclosed in apostrophes. In order to print an ampersand or an apostrophe as part of the message, we must code two adjacent ampersands or apostrophes. For example: MNOTE 'CAIN && ABEL''S'. Two MNOTE messages in Figure 14-7 warn that the dividend or divisor are not packed format and that the quotient length is too short. In Figure 14-8 when the error condition occurs, the Assembler statements are not generated. Before program execution, we should first check for and correct any assembly errors.

MEXIT—MACRO DEFINITION EXIT.   MEXIT provides a convenient way to terminate processing of a macro. It acts like MEND, although MEND must be the last statement of the macro definition. Figure 14-7 shows exit and termination of the macro. The MEXIT could have been alternatively coded as:

```
              MNOTE   'message'
              AGO       .FINISH (or any sequence symbol)
              ·
              ·
              ·
      .FINISH   MEND
```

Problem 14-4 should now be attempted.

SET SYMBOLS

SET symbols are variable symbols that define and assign values. We may then use them to test values and to build instructions. SET symbols are assigned values when we code SETA, SETB, or SETC Conditional Assembly instructions. They must first have been defined by an LCL or GBL instruction. Local or global instructions may define and assign an initial value. GBL's, and then LCL's, must be coded in the macro definition immediately following the prototype statement.

NAME	OPERATION	OPERAND
blank	LCLA LCLB LCLC	One or more variable (SET) symbols, separated by commas

LCLA is used to define a SETA symbol. It creates a 32-bit field initialized with zero. LCLB defines a SETB symbol that creates a 1-bit field initialized with zero. LCLC defines a SETC symbol that creates a "null character value"—that is, a field with no length defined.

GBLA, GBLB, and GBLC similarly define SET symbols, for values that are to be known in other macro expansions in the same assembly. They are briefly discussed later.

LCL instructions merely define and initialize SET symbols. The SET operations, SETA, SETB, and SETC, then assign values to SET symbols.

SETA—SET ARITHMETIC.   SETA assigns an arithmetic value to a SETA symbol.

NAME	OPERATION	OPERAND
A SETA symbol	SETA	an arithmetic expression

The maximum and minimum values of the expression are $+2^{31}-1$ and -2^{31}. An expression consists of a term or an arithmetic combination of terms. Valid terms are:

— *Self-defining terms.* Such a term has an inherent value, one that is not assigned a value by the Assembler. These may be decimal (as 11), hexadecimal (as X'B'), and binary (as B'1011').
— *Variable symbols,* such as &AMT.
— *Attributes for count, integer, length, number, and scale.* Examples of SETA arithmetic are:

```
          LCLA    &FLD1,&FLD2
&FLD1     SETA    15
&FLD2     SETA    &FLD1+L'&AMT+25
```

LCLA defines &FLD1 and &FLD2 as SETA symbols.
    &FLD1: the value 15 (a self-defining term) is assigned to &FLD1.
    &FLD2: the expression contains an arithmetic combination of terms. Assume that &AMT is defined elsewhere with a length of 6. The Assembler calculates the expression as:

TERM		VALUE
&FLD1	(variable symbol)	15
L'&AMT	(length attribute)	6
25	(self-defining term)	25
Value assigned to &FLD2		46

The maximum number of terms in the expression is 16. Also, brackets may contain terms in the expression, such as (&COUNT−X'1B')*3.

    Figure 14-9 illustrates LCLA and SETA. In this mixed-type macro, the first two parameters are positional whereas the third and fourth are keyword. This macro prints a heading line containing a heading title, page number, and the date. The macro centers the heading title on the page.

PARAMETER	SPECIFIES	LENGTH IN BYTES
&HEAD	Heading	Up to 90 characters
&PAGE	Page number	2 Packed bytes
&DAT	Date	Not defined
&PRT	Print area	121

```
 3                 MACRO
 4 &NAME           HEDNG  &HEAD,&PAGE,&CAT=DATE,&PRT=PRINT
 5                 LCLA   &LEN,&MID                    LENGTH & MID-POINT
 6                 LCLC   &LIT,&L1,&L2                 AREA FOR CHARS.
 7 .*                     TEST VALIDITY OF PARAMETERS
 8                 AIF    (T'&PAGE NE 'P').ERRPACK
 9                 AIF    (T'&HEAD NE 'C').ERRCHAR
10                 AIF    (L'&HEAD GT 90).ERRSIZE   HEADING > 90 CHARS?
11 .*                     SET VALUES
12 &LEN            SETA   L'&HEAD                   LENGTH OF HEADING
13 &MID            SETA   (120-&LEN)/2              CENTER HEADING
14 &LIT            SETC   '=C''PAGE'''              LITERAL FOR 'PAGE'
15 &L1             SETC   'L'''                     LENGTH CODE
16 &L2             SETC   '&CAT'                    DATE
17 .*
18 &NAME           UNPK   &PRT+115(3),&PAGE         UNPK PAGE CTR.
19                 OI     &PRT+117,X'F0'            CLEAR UNITS ZONE
20                 MVC    &PRT+110(4),&LIT          MOVE PAGE LITERAL
21                 MVC    &PRT+&MID.(&LEN),&HEAD    MOVE HEADING
22                 MVC    &PRT+1(&L1&L2),&DAT       MOVE DATE
23                 MEXIT
24 .*                     ERROR MESSAGES
25 .ERRPACK        MNOTE  'PAGE COUNT NOT DEFINED AS PACKED'
26                 MEXIT
27 .ERRCHAR        MNOTE  'HEADING NOT DEFINED AS CHARACTER'
28                 MEXIT
29 .ERRSIZE        MNOTE  'LENGTH OF HEADING EXCEEDS PRINT AREA'
30                 MEND
```

FIGURE 14-9   Definition of heading macro HEDNG with conditional assembly instructions.

&LEN and &MID define two SETA symbols. AIF checks that the length of heading does not exceed 90 bytes. (Assume 120 print positions with space for date and page.) SETA assigns the length of &HEAD to &LEN. The title is centered by calculating the first print position of &HEAD. For example:

L'&HEAD	EXPRESSION	1ST POSITION
23	$(120-23)/2 = 97/2 =$	48
16	$(120-16)/2 = 104/2 =$	52
11	$(120-11)/2 = 109/2 =$	54

These lengths are used in Figure 14-10. Check that they cause centering of the heading and that the correct code is generated.

Figure 14-10 also illustrates the SETC symbol, covered next.

SETC—SET CHARACTER.   SETC assigns a character value to a SETC symbol, up to eight characters enclosed in apostrophes. The operand generally defines a character expression.

NAME	OPERATION	OPERAND
A SETC symbol	SETC	one character operand

```
39 P10HED    HEDNG  HEADG1,PAGEPK
40+P10HED    UNPK   PRINT+115(3),PAGEPK    UNPK PAGE CTR.
41+          OI     PRINT+117,X'F0'        CLEAR UNITS ZONE
42+          MVC    PRINT+110(4),=C'PAGE'  MOVE PAGE LITERAL
43+          MVC    PRINT+48(23),HEADG1    MOVE HEADING
44+          MVC    PRINT+1(L'DATE),DATE   MOVE DATE

46 P20HED    HEDNG  HEADG2,PAGEPK,DAT=DATOT
47+P20HED    UNPK   PRINT+115(3),PAGEPK    UNPK PAGE CTR.
48+          OI     PRINT+117,X'F0'        CLEAR UNITS ZONE
49+          MVC    PRINT+110(4),=C'PAGE'  MOVE PAGE LITERAL
50+          MVC    PRINT+52(16),HEADG2    MOVE HEADING
51+          MVC    PRINT+1(L'DATOT),DATOT MOVE DATE

53 P30HED    HEDNG  HEADG3,PAGEPK,PRT=OUTAREA,DAT=DATOT
54+P30HED    UNPK   OUTAREA+115(3),PAGEPK  UNPK PAGE CTR.
55+          OI     OUTAREA+117,X'F0'      CLEAR UNITS ZONE
56+          MVC    OUTAREA+110(4),=C'PAGE' MOVE PAGE LITERAL
57+          MVC    OUTAREA+54(11),HEADG3  MOVE HEADING
58+          MVC    OUTAREA+1(L'DATOT),DATOT MOVE DATE

60 P40HED    HEDNG  HEADG4,PAGEPK
61+LENGTH OF HEADING EXCEEDS PRINT AREA

63 *            .
64 *            .
65 PRINT     DC     CL121' '              PRINT AREA
66 OUTAREA   DC     CL121' '              PRINT AREA
67 PAGEPK    DC     PL2'0'                PAGE COUNTER
68 HEADG1    DC     CL23'HOTROD CUSTOM IMPORTERS'
69 HEADG2    DC     CL16'ABC DISTRIBUTORS'
70 HEADG3    DC     CL11'BAKER CORP.'
71 HEADG4    DS     CL100                 LONG HEADING
72 DATE      DS     CL12                  DATE AREA
73 DATOT     DS     CL12                  DATE AREA
```

FIGURE 14-10   Use of HEDNG macro-instruction.

Examples of SETC character operations:

```
             LCLC  &CHAR1,&CHAR2,&CHAR3
      &CHAR1 SETC  'SAM''S'
      &CHAR2 SETC  '&TYPE.A'
      &CHAR3 SETC  'L''FLOAT'
```

LCLC defines three SETC symbols.

&CHAR1: the character value SAM'S is assigned to the SETC symbol &CHAR1. Two apostrophes within the expression denote a single apostrophe.

&CHAR2: Assume that &TYPE contains the value FIELD. The expression concatenates FIELD with A and assigns FIELDA to &CHAR2.

&CHAR3: the value L'FLOAT is assigned to the SETC symbol &CHAR3.

In Figure 14-9 SETC defines three symbols, &LIT, &L1, and &L2. One SETC assigns &LIT with a character expression to be used as a literal. Note the literal, =C'PAGE', in the generated code in Figure 14-10. Instead of using &LIT in the macro-definition, we could have coded the literal itself: MVC

&PRT+110(4),=C'PAGE'. &L1 and &L2 are used to create a symbolic length reference for moving the date to the print area. Note the macro-definition and generated code for this example.

We have now covered all the features used in the macro HEDNG. Some remaining items, SETB symbols, system variable symbols, and global SET symbols, are covered next.

SETB—SET BINARY.   SETB assigns the binary value 0 or 1 to a SETB symbol. SETB determines if a condition is false (0) or true (1). SETB is commonly used as a switch indicator in the macro definition.

NAME	OPERATION	OPERAND
A SETB symbol	SETB	0 or 1, or (0) or (1), or (a logical expression)

A logical expression, enclosed in brackets, consists of one term (arithmetic relationship, character relationship, or SETB symbol), or a logical combination of terms (connected by AND, OR, or NOT). Assume that &SYM1 is format C containing the value 6, &SYM2 is format C, and &SYM3 contains the word YES in the following examples of SETB binary operations:

```
        LCLB    &B1,&B2,&B3,&B4
&B1     SETB    1
&B2     SETB    (&SYM1 LT 7)
&B3     SETB    ('&SYM3' EQ 'NO')
&B4     SETB    ('&SYM3' EQ 'YES' AND T'&SYM1 NE T'&SYM2)
```

LCLB defines four SETB symbols.

&B1: an arithmetic term (1 = true) is assigned to &B1.

&B2: the arithmetic relationship is true, so 1 is assigned to &B2.

&B3: the character relationship is false, so 0 is assigned to &B3.

&B4: the logical combination of terms is false, so 0 is assigned to &B4.

In Figure 14-11, SETB is a switch &ERRB that determines if any errors have been encountered in the macro-instruction. If an error is found, the Assembler prints the appropriate message, and the switch is set. The macro then continues with the next test. Only after *all* validity testing does the macro terminate processing. In this way, we fully test the macro-instruction each time it is used.

Note: SETB symbols such as &ERRB can contain only 0 or 1. In an instruction AIF (&ERRB).A30, AIF tests if &ERRB contains 1, and if so, branches to A30.

```
 1              MACRO
 2 &LOOK       LOOKP  &TABLE,                      ADDRESS OF TABLE                  +
                      &SERARG,                     ADDRESS OF SEARCH ARGUMENT        +
                      &FUNCTN,                     ADDRESS TO STORE FUNCTION         +
                      &NOTFND                      ADDRESS IF ARG'T NOT FOUND
 3              GBLB   &SAVIND                      SAVE AREA INDICATOR
 4              LCLA   &LSER,&LENTRY                LENGTH OF SEARCH & ENTRY
 5              LCLB   &ERRB                        ERROR SWITCH INDICATOR
 6              LCLC   &H,&HALF                     HALFWORD LITERAL
 7 &ERRB       SETB   (1)                          SET ERROR INDICATOR TO 1
 8 .*                 TEST FOR VALIDITY
 9              AIF    (T'&NOTFND EQ 'I').A10       IS NOTFND A VALID ADDRESS?
10              MNOTE  'ADDRESS FOR NOTFOUND IS INVALID'
11 &ERRB       SETB   (0)                          SET ERROR INDICATOR TO 0
12 .A10        AIF    (T'&TABLE EQ 'C' AND T'&SERARG EQ 'C').A20
13              AIF    (T'&TABLE EQ 'P' AND T'&SERARG EQ 'P').A20
14              MNOTE  'TABLE && SEARCH NOT BOTH CHAR OR PACKED'
15 &ERRB       SETB   (0)                          SET ERROR INDICATOR TO 0
16 .A20        AIF    (&ERRB).A30                  IS ERROR INDICATOR = 1?
17              MNOTE  'MACRO CANNOT BE RESOLVED - TERMINATED'
18              MEXIT
19 .*                 SET VALUES
20 .A30        ANOP
21 &LSER       SETA   L'&SERARG                    LENGTH OF SEARCH ARGUMENT
22 &LENTRY     SETA   &LSER+L'&FUNCTN              LENGTH OF SEARCH + FUNCTION
23 &H          SETC   '=H'                         SET UP HALFWORD
24 &HALF       SETC   '''&LENTRY'''                *  CONSTANT
25 &LOOK       ST     10,SAVREG                    SAVE REGISTER-10
26              LA     10,&TABLE                    LOAD ADDRESS OF TABLE
27              AIF    (T'&TABLE EQ 'P').B10        IS TABLE DEFINED AS PACKED?
28 .*                 COMPARE SEARCH TO TABLE ARGUMENT
29 R&SYSNDX CLC       &SERARG,0(10)                COMPARE CHARACTER
30              AGO    .B20
31 .B10        ANOP
32 R&SYSNDX CP        &SERARG,0(&LSER,10)          COMPARE PACKED
33 .B20        BE     T&SYSNDX                     *  EQUAL - FOUND
34              BL     S&SYSNDX                     *  LOW  - NOT IN TABLE
35              AH     10,&H&HALF                   INCREMENT NEXT ENTRY
36              B      R&SYSNDX
37 .*                 DEFINE SAVEAREA FIRST TIME ONLY
38              AIF    (&SAVIND).B30                HAS SAVIND BEEN DEFINED?
39 SAVREG      DS     F                            REGISTER SAVE AREA
40 &SAVIND     SETB   (1)                          SET INDICATOR ON (1)
41 .B30        ANOP
42 .*                 ARGUMENT NOT FOUND
43 S&SYSNDX L        10,SAVREG                     RESTORE REG-10
44              B      &NOTFND                      GO TO ERROR ROUTINE
45 .*                 ARGUMENT FOUND
46 T&SYSNDX MVC      &FUNCTN,&LSER.(10)            MOVE FUNCTION FROM TABLE
47              L      10,SAVREG                    RESTORE REG-10
48              MEND
```

FIGURE 14-11 Definition of table look-up macro LOOKP.

SYSTEM VARIABLE SYMBOLS

The Assembler automatically assigns values to the three local system variable symbols, &SYSECT, &SYSLIST, and &SYSNDX. Because of its limited use &SYSECT is not covered.

&SYSLIST—MACRO INSTRUCTION OPERAND.   We may use &SYSLIST as an alternative way of referencing a positional macro operand. In the HEDNG macro in Figure 14-9, we could have coded the UNPK instruction as UNPK &PRT+115(3),&SYSLIST(2). The subscript (2) refers to the second parameter in the prototype (&PAGE).

&SYSNDX—MACRO INSTRUCTION INDEX.   For the first macro-instruction processed in an assembly, the Assembler initializes &SYSNDX with 0001. For each succeeding macro-instruction, the Assembler increments &SYSNDX by 1. In Figure 14-10 the macro HEDNG is used four times. Since this is the only macro-instruction in the assembly, at P10HED, &SYSNDX is set to 0001; at P20HED, &SYSNDX is set to 0002, etc.

&SYSNDX can prevent a macro from generating duplicate labels. This situation did not occur in any examples up to this point. However, in Figure 14-11, the macro LOOKP requires that the macro generate several labels. If the macro-instruction is coded more than once, the macro generates labels with the same name, causing Assembler error messages. To avoid this, the macro uses labels such as R&SYSNDX. In the generated code in Figure 14-12, this label becomes R0001 for L10LK, and R0002 for L20LK.

Problems 14-5, 14-6, and 14-7 should now be attempted.

GLOBAL SET SYMBOLS

LCLA, LCLB, and LCLC define local SET symbols for use within the same macro-definition. GBLA, GBLB, and GBLC define Global SET symbols for communicating values between different macro-definitions.

NAME	OPERATION	OPERAND
blank	GBLA GBLB GBLC	One or more variable (SET) symbols, separated by commas

Global operations define the same initial values as do local operations. However, they are initialized only once, the first time the Assembler encounters the GBLA, GBLB, or GBLC. We define global instructions immediately after the prototype statement. Figure 14-11 gives an example. GBLB defines and initializes &SAVIND to zero, and prevents SAVREG DS F from being defined more than once. The macro tests if &SAVIND contains zero. If so, it permits SAVREG to be defined and sets &SAVIND to 1. &SAVIND is now permanently set to 1, through all succeeding macro-instructions, and the Assembler, through the AIF statement, bypasses generating more than one DS for SAVREG. (Consider how &SYSNDX could achieve the same result.)

```
55 L10LK     LOOKP JOBTABPK,JOBNOPK,RATEPK,R10NOFND
56+L10LK     ST    10,SAVREG         SAVE REGISTER-10
57+          LA    10,JOBTABPK       LOAD ADDRESS OF TABLE
58+R0001     CP    JOBNOPK,0(4,10)   COMPARE PACKED
59+          BE    T0001           *   EQUAL - FOUND
60+          BL    S0001           *   LOW   - NOT IN TABLE
61+          AH    10,=H'7'          INCREMENT NEXT ENTRY
62+          B     R0001
63+SAVREG    DS    F                 REGISTER SAVE AREA
64+S0001     L     10,SAVREG         RESTORE REG-10
65+          B     R10NOFND          GO TO ERROR ROUTINE
66+T0001     MVC   RATEPK,4(10)      MOVE FUNCTION FROM TABLE
67+          L     10,SAVREG         RESTORE REG-10


69 L20LK     LOOKP JOBTABCH,JOBNOCH,RATECH,R10NOFND
70+L20LK     ST    10,SAVREG         SAVE REGISTER-10
71+          LA    10,JOBTABCH       LOAD ADDRESS OF TABLE
72+R0002     CLC   JOBNOCH,0(10)     COMPARE CHARACTER
73+          BE    T0002           *   EQUAL - FOUND
74+          BL    S0002           *   LOW   - NOT IN TABLE
75+          AH    10,=H'9'          INCREMENT NEXT ENTRY
76+          B     R0002
77+S0002     L     10,SAVREG         RESTORE REG-10
78+          B     R10NOFND          GO TO ERROR ROUTINE
79+T0002     MVC   RATECH,5(10)      MOVE FUNCTION FROM TABLE
80+          L     10,SAVREG         RESTORE REG-10


82 L30LK     LOOKP JOBTABPK,JOBNCCH,RATEPK,R20NOFND
83+ADDRESS FOR NOTFOUND IS INVALID
84+TABLE & SEARCH NOT BOTH CHAR OR PACKED
85+MACRO CANNOT BE RESOLVED - TERMINATED

87 R10NOFND MVC   PRINT+10(21),=C'ARGUMENT NOT IN TABLE'
88 *            .
89 *            .
90 PRINT     DC    CL121' '          PRINT AREA
91 JOBTABPK  DS    25PL7             TABLE OF PACK JOBS & RATES
92 JOBNOPK   DS    PL4               SEARCH ARG - JOB NUMBER
93 RATEPK    DS    PL3               TO STORE FOUND TABLE RATE

95 JOBTABCH  DS    15CL9             TABLE OF CHAR JOBS & RATES
96 JOBNOCH   DS    CL5               SEARCH ARG - JOB NUMBER
97 RATECH    DS    CL4               TO STORE FOUND TABLE RATE
```

FIGURE 14-12   Use of LOOKP macro-instruction.

EXTENDED EXAMPLE—TABLE LOOK-UP MACRO

The table look-up macro, LOOKP, is defined in Figure 14-11 and used in Figure 14-12. LOOKP permits us to code in one statement a table look-up routine that:

— Initializes a register with the table address.
— Compares a search argument to the table argument.
— If equal, branches to an address where the table function is extracted.
— If low, branches to the address of an error routine.
— If high, increments for the next argument and returns to the compare.

The macro allows for either character or packed arguments. It requires that the table contain discrete arguments (unique numbers such as Job or Stock numbers, rather than table ranges as in income tax), in ascending sequence. The comments beside each parameter explain the symbolic parameters in the prototype operand. We must code as the fourth parameter in the macro-instruction the address to which the look-up routine branches if the search argument cannot be found. The program must contain the address of this error routine. The routine should provide usual error handling, such as the printing of a message.

The remaining problems should now be done.

PROBLEMS

14-1. Distinguish between a positional and a keyword macro.

14-2. What is the difference between the use of a variable symbol and a sequence symbol?

14-3. Revise Figures 14-5 and 14-6 so that the operation is DR (Divide Register). Changes the names to suit.

14-4. Revise Figures 14-7 and 14-8 as in the previous problem.

14-5. Revise Figures 14-9 and 14-10 for the following: Print area = 133 positions—change other lengths accordingly; Add '1' to the page counter; Edit (ED) the page counter.

14-6. Write a macro that provides for MP with round and shift to two decimal places.

14-7. Expand the macro in the previous problem to provide as well for M and MH.

14-8. Write a macro to initialize a program with three base registers.

14-9. Write a macro to test given character fields for blank positions. (Assume that the fields are input fields, to be packed.) Replace any blank position with a zero.

CHAPTER 15

SUBPROGRAMS AND OVERLAYS

This chapter covers the concept of writing and assembling programs as separate subprograms. This chapter uses the general term subprogram to mean a section of coding that comprises a separate part of the program, such as a control section (CSECT) or a phase. The link edit step combines the separate subprograms into a single executable program. We may want to code a program in more than one subprogram for the following reasons:

— Several programmers can work separately on subprograms.
— Breaking the program into logical components simplifies the problem.
— It is easier to debug smaller sections.
— There may not be enough base registers available for a large program.
— Main storage may be too small for the entire program. The use of "Virtual Storage," however, provides automatic program sectioning and overlays, and to a large degree reduces the need for programmers to design such programs.

CSECT—CONTROL SECTION

Chapter 6 introduced the term *control section* (CSECT). A CSECT is *a block of coding that can be relocated without affecting the operating logic of the program*. Both the Assembler and Linkage Editor process control sections, not programs. We may code

323

CSECTs as separate assemblies, each with its own unique base registers. Then we link edit the CSECTs into one or more phases, the Linkage Editor output. A program may consist of one or more phases, and a phase may consist of one or more control sections. Among the ways to section a program into subprograms are:

1. The program may consist of a single phase—one or more control sections. The CSECTs are assembled separately or together, and link edited into a single phase. For execution, the system loads the entire phase into storage.
2. The program may consist of more than one phase, each with one or more CSECT. Each phase is separately assembled, then link edited together. At execution-time, the system loads the first (*root*) phase into storage. The root phase loads (*overlays*) the other phases into storage as required.

There are two main problems associated with the use of subprograms:

1. Some data is common to more than one subprogram. But data is defined in only one subprogram. Because subprograms are assembled separately, the Assembler treats each subprogram as a completely different program. Data defined in one subprogram is not therefore known in another. Among the ways of making data known between subprograms are the use of "DSECTs" and "passing parameters".
2. A subprogram must be able to link to another subprogram, its register contents must be saved (especially base registers), and there must be some means of returning and restoring the register contents. The Assembler macros that provide this linkage are CALL, SAVE, and RETURN. The Assembler requires a standard savearea for registers and a standard linkage convention.

We will first examine a simple case of how a DSECT works. Then we will see how to assemble and link together two CSECTs for execution. The last example combines three separately assembled phases into one program—a root phase and two overlay phases.

DSECT—DUMMY SECTION

We may want to *describe* a data area without actually reserving any storage. For example, the main subprogram, SUBPROGA, contains the main data and certain other coding, including instructions to link to SUBPROGB. SUBPROGB is a separately assembled control section. Within SUBPROGB we want to reference the main data that is defined and exists in SUBPROGA. We may describe this main data in SUBPROGB so that when assembling SUBPROGB, the Assembler knows the names, lengths, formats, and relative position of each field in SUBPROGA. For this purpose we may use a special Assembler instruction, DSECT, Dummy Section.

NAME	OPERATION	OPERAND
Name	DSECT	blank

The name of the DSECT refers to the first (leftmost) byte of the section. DSECT reserves no storage. Instead, it gives the Assembler a mask or image of data defined elsewhere. Figure 15-1 illustrates a DSECT defined within a CSECT. The partial program reads card records with two buffers and no workarea (IOREG=5). Rather than transfer the current buffer to a workarea with MVC CARDIN,0(5), we want to process input records directly in the buffer, and we want the fields defined.

Note the following: The DSECT, called DATAIN, generates no object code. The fields defined within the DSECT tell the Assembler the names and formats. USING DATAIN,5 assigns register-5 as a base register for DATAIN. This is because the CARD buffers are under register-5 (IOREG=5). Register-5 acts as a base register with respect

```
 LOC   OEJECT CODE      STMT    SOURCE STATEMENT

000000                      4 TESTA     CSECT .              CONTROL SECTION
000000 0530                 5           BALR  3,0            INITIALIZE BASE REG
                            6           USING *,3
                            7           USING DATAIN,5

                            9           OPEN  CARD            ACTIVATE FILE
                           17           GET   CARD            READ A RECORD
00001E D501 5000 3132      22           CLC   CODEIN,=C'03'   IS IT VALID RECORD?
000024 4770 302C           23           BNE   R10CODE       *   NO - ERROR

000028 D205 303E 5002      25           MVC   PREV,ACCTIN
                           26 *               .
                           27 *               .
                           28 R10CODE   EQU   *               ERROR ROUTINE

                           30 Z10END    CLOSE CARD
                           38           EOJ

000040 0C0000000000        42 PREV      DC    XL6'00'         PREVIOUS ACCOUNT NO.

                           44 CARD      DTFCD BLKSIZE=80,                        +
                                              DEVADDR=SYSIPT,                    +
                                              DEVICE=3504,                       +
                                              EOFADDR=Z10END,                    +
                                              IOAREA1=CARBUFF1,                  +
                                              IOAREA2=CARBUFF2,                  +
                                              RECFORM=FIXUNB,                    +
                                              TYPEFLE=INPUT,                     +
                                              IOREG=(5)

00007A                     67 CARBUFF1 DS    CL80            INPUT BUFFER-1
0000CA                     68 CARBUFF2 DS    CL80            INPUT BUFFER-2

000000                     70 DATAIN    DSECT .              DATA DUMMY SECTION
000000                     71 CARDIN    DS    OCL80         *   CARD RECORD
000000                     72 CODEIN    DS    CL2           *   CARD CODE
000002                     73 ACCTIN    DS    CL6           *   ACCOUNT NO.
000008                     74           DS    CL72          *   REST OF RECORD
                           75           DROP  5

00011A                     77 TESTA     CSECT .              RESUME CONTROL SECTION
000120                     78           LTORG
000120 5E5BC2D6D7C5D540    79                 =C'$$BOPEN '
000128 5B5BC2C3D3D6E2C5    80                 =C'$$BCLOSE'
000130 00000048            81                 =A(CARD)
000134 F0F3                82                 =C'03'
                           83           END   TESTA
```

FIGURE 15-1   Example CSECT and DSECT.

to DATAIN. When we code CLC CODEIN,=C'03', the Assembler treats CODEIN as under register-5. The operand for CODEIN in object code is 5000 (base register-5, no displacement, because CODEIN is the first byte within DATAIN). Assume IOCS has loaded register-5 with the address of buffer-1 (CARBUFF1) for the first card record. Since register-5 contains the address of CARBUFF1, then a reference to CODEIN is to the first two bytes of CARBUFF1. On the next read operation, IOCS loads the address of CARBUFF2 into register-5, and CODEIN references that area.

We want base register-5 to apply only to the fields in the DSECT. The statement DROP 5 tells the Assembler to discontinue applying base register-5. The Assembler resumes addressing with base register-3. The CSECT following DROP terminates the DSECT, and because the CSECT is named TESTA, tells the Assembler to resume with the initial CSECT called TESTA.

Under OS, Locate Mode involves register-1. The changes necessary to convert from the DOS DSECT example would be:

— OS linkage for initialization and return to the Supervisor.
— A DCB specifying MACRF=(GL).
— After the GET, load the contents of register-1 into register-5, as in the example:

```
GET   INCARD
LR    5,1
```

It is also possible to use register-1 as the DSECT base register, provided the program executes no macro that destroys the base address while it is still required.

Problems 15-1 through 15-4 should now be attempted.

SUBPROGRAM LINKAGE

We may use DSECTs to make data known between separately assembled subprograms. Additionally, we use standard linkage and saveareas to link between subprograms and to save the contents of registers.

LINKAGE REGISTERS. The standard linkage registers are 0, 1, 13, 14, and 15:

REGISTER	USE
0 & 1	Parameter registers, used by the CALL macro to pass "parameters" (i.e., addresses of data) to the called program.
13	Savearea register—contains the address of the calling program's savearea, to be stored by the called program.
14	Return register—contains the address of the calling program, to which the called program is to return.

15   Entry point register—contains the address of the called program's entry point, where we want to link to begin executing.

THE STANDARD SAVEAREA. Each calling program requires definition of a savearea to preserve the contents of its registers. The savearea contains 18 fullwords (or 9 doublewords), aligned on a doubleword boundary. The savearea provides for an additional condition—one subprogram may call another subprogram, which in turn may call yet another subprogram. Figure 15-2 gives the savearea format.

Word	Displace- ment	Contents of each fullword
1	0	Used by PL/I programs.
2	4	Address of the savearea of the calling program. The called program saves this in its own savearea.
3	8	*Address of the savearea of the called program.
4	12	*Contents of register-14, return address to the calling program.
5	16	*Contents of register-15, the address of the entry point to the called program.
6	20	*Contents of register-0.
7–18	24	*Contents of registers-1 through 12.

*Called program stores these in calling program's savearea.

FIGURE 15-2   Standard savearea words.

LINKAGE MACROS.   The following macros link between subprograms:

NAME	OPERATION	OPERAND
[name]	CALL	entrypoint[,(parameter, . . .)]
	SAVE	(r1,r2)
	RETURN	(r1,r2)

Assume that SUBPROGA is the main subprogram, loaded in storage and being executed. SUBPROGA *calls* SUBPROGB for execution (SUBPROGB must also be in storage). SUBPROGA is the *calling* program, and SUBPROGB is the *called* program.

THE CALL MACRO.   We use CALL in the calling program to link to the called program. The operand 'entrypoint' is the name of the first executable instruction of the called program. (Following entrypoint is an optional parameter list. Parameters are symbolic addresses that we want known in the called program.) CALL loads the address of the next sequential instruction in register-14 and branches to the called program.

```
 LOC   OBJECT CODE       STMT    SOURCE STATEMENT

000000                  4 PROGA    CSECT  .              MAIN CONTROL SECTION
                        5 *               COMMON DECLARATIVES
000000                  6 DATA     DS     OCL1           DATA AREA
000000 120C             7 HRSPK    DC     PL2'12.0'      |XX|.XC|
000002 300C             8 RATEPK   DC     PL2'3.00'      |X.X|XC|
000004                  9 WAGEPK   DS     PL4

000008 0530            11 BEGINA   BALR   3,0            INITIALIZE BASE REGISTER-3
                       12          USING  *,3
                       13          USING  DATA,4         ASSIGN BASE REG-4 TO DATA
00000A 5840 307E       14          L      4,=A(DATA)     LOAD BASE REGISTER-4
                       15 *          .
                       16 *          .
00000E F831 4004       17          ZAP    WAGEPK,HRSPK   SET UP MULTIPLICAND IN PROD
                       18 *          .
                       19 *          .
000014 41D0 3026       20          LA     13,SAVEA       LOAD ADDRESS OF SAVE AREA
                       21          CALL   PROGB          LINK TO PROGB
                       25 A10RTN   EQU    *              ANY VALID INSTRUCTION HERE
                       26 *          .
                       27 *          .
                       28 *          .
                       29          PDUMP  DATA,BEGINA
                       34          EOJ


000030                 38 SAVEA    DS     9D             PROGA REGISTER SAVEAREA
000078                 39          LTORG
000078 5B5BC2D7C4E4D4D7 40                =CL8'$$BPDUMP'
000080 0000000000000008 41                =A(DATA,BEGINA)
000088 00000000         42                =A(DATA)
00008C 00000000         43                =V(PROGB)

                       45          END    BEGINA

// EXEC ASSEMBLY

000000                  3 DATAB    DSECT  .              PROGB COMMON DATA AREA
000000 000C             4 HRSPK    DC     PL2'0'         |XX|.XC|
000002 000C             5 RATEPK   DC     PL2'0'         |X.X|XC|
000004                  6 WAGEPK   DS     PL4

000000                  8 PROGB    CSECT
                        9          SAVE   (14,12)        SAVE REGISTERS 14 - 12
000004 0590            12          BALR   9,0            INITIALIZE BASE REGISTER-9
                       13          USING  *,9
                       14          USING  DATAB,4        ASSIGN BASE REGISTER-4
                                                            TO DATAB
000006 50D0 9022       16          ST     13,SAVEB+4     SAVE ADDRESS OF SAVEA
00000A 18CD            17          LR     12,13
00000C 41D0 901E       18          LA     13,SAVEB
000010 50DC 0008       19          ST     13,8(12)       STORE ADDRESS OF SAVEB
                       20 *          .
                       21 *          .
                       22 *          .
000014 FC31 4004       23          MP     WAGEPK,RATEPK  MULT HOURS X RATE
                       24 *          .
                       25 *          .
00001A 58D0 9022       26          L      13,SAVEB+4     LOAD ADDRESS OF SAVEA
                       27          RETURN (14,12)        RETURN TO A10RTN IN PROGA

000024                 32 SAVEB    DS     18F            PROGB SAVEAREA

                       34          END    PROGB
```

FIGURE 15-3 Linkage between main and subprogram.

THE SAVE MACRO.   When we link to the called program, we must save the contents of the registers of the calling program. The calling program defines the standard savearea for this purpose. Before issuing the CALL macro, we first load the address of the savearea in register-13. At the beginning of the called program we code SAVE (14,12) to save the contents of the registers, except 13.

THE RETURN MACRO.   In order to return to the calling program, we code RETURN (14,12) to restore the original contents of the calling program's registers and to return to the calling program.

Next we examine the generated code for the macros and the additional instructions needed to complete the linkage.

LINKING TWO CONTROL SECTIONS

Figure 15-3 gives skeleton coding for two separately assembled CSECTs—a calling subprogram, PROGA, and a called subprogram, PROGB. The savearea in PROGA is called SAVEA, and that in PROGB is SAVEB. PROGA defines common data under DATA (immediately at the start). DATA is subject to base register-4, and the rest of the program following BEGINA is under base register-3. Before calling PROGB we load register-13 with the address of our savearea, SAVEA. For the macro CALL PROGB, the Assembler generates:

```
L      15,=V(PROGB)      Load address of PROGB in register-15
BALR   14,15             Load next instruction address in register-14 and branch
                         to PROGB
```

The literal =V(PROGB) is an *external address constant.* Since the Assembler does not know the address of PROGB, we tell it that this address is external to this assembly. The Assembler inserts an address of X'0000', and the Linkage Editor inserts the correct address. BALR loads the address of the next instruction, A10RTN, in register-14 and branches to PROGB. Immediately PROGB saves PROGA's registers. The SAVE macro here generates STM 14,12,12(13). In effect, SAVE stores registers 14 through 12 beginning at SAVEA+12 (word 4 through 18)—check this to Figure 15-2.

Next, PROGB initializes base register-9. It could be any available register, but not register-4. Register-4 still contains the address of DATA (the common data area) as loaded in PROGA. We still need this address in order to reference these fields, called DATAB in PROGB. Since register-4 is already loaded, we need only tell the Assembler to assign base register-4 with USING DATAB,4. The Assembler will use register-4 for any reference to the fields in the DATAB DSECT.

PROGB must now save the contents of register-13, which contains the address of PROGA's savearea. We store the contents of register-13 in SAVEB+4 (word 2) because, before returning, we must reload PROGA's registers. The next three instructions store the address of SAVEB in SAVEA+8 (word 3). This is done because if there are many subprograms, we can refer to this field for debugging and tracing if the program does not work correctly. The linkage routine has now stored the following:

SAVEA				SAVEB		
Word	Displ't	Contents		Word	Displ't	Contents
1	0			1	0	
2	4			2	4	A(SAVEA)
3	8	A(SAVEB)		3	8	
4	12	A(A10RTN)		4	12	
5	16	A(PROGB)		5	16	
6–18	20	Contents of registers 0–12		6–18	20	

Now PROGB may perform required processing, and reference the fields defined in the DATAB DSECT (actually DATA in PROGA). In order to return to the calling program, PROGA, we simply reload register-13 with SAVEB+4, the address of SAVEA.

The RETURN macro next generates:

```
LM   14,12,12(13)    Reload registers 14-12 starting with SAVEA+12 (Word 4)
BR   14              Branch to A10RTN in PROGA.
```

RETURN restores the original SAVEA registers (14 through 12). Since register-14 now contains the return address (A10RTN), BR branches to this address. We now resume normal processing in PROGA, with base registers reinitialized.

The question may arise: Why doesn't PROGA save its own registers in SAVEA before linking to PROGB? Assume that this is done, and PROGB then initializes its own register values. When PROGB returns to PROGA, PROGA's base registers are not loaded—and without a base register PROGA has no way to reload its own registers.

In this example, SAVEB does not require a full save area. This is the way we would define SAVEB if PROGB were to link to another subprogram. If so, then the called program would store PROGB's registers, linkage address, and savearea in SAVEB.

TECHNICAL NOTE ON USING.   One rule of the Assembler is "in calculating the base register to be used, the Assembler always uses the available register giving the smallest displacement". This rule sometimes causes the Assembler to override a DROP or another USING. Suppose, for example, that the program uses two base registers (3 and 4). The common data is under register-5 and is defined toward the end of the CSECT:

```
            BALR    3,0
            USING   *,3,4         3 & 4 are base registers for program
            USING   DATA,5        5 is base register for common data
            .
            .
            .

DATA   DS      0C               common data area
            .
            .
```

Depending on the size of the program preceding DATA, the Assembler may apply register-4 to DATA rather than the specified register-5. For this reason, the program defines the common data before the BALR/USING where the Assembler is sure to apply the correct base register.

Problems 15-5 through 15-8 should now be attempted.

PASSING PARAMETERS

Another way to make data known between subprograms is through the use of "passing parameters." The CALL statement contains a parameter list of the address(es) to be passed to the called program:

CALL   subprogram,(parameter-list)

Each parameter generates a fullword address, one after the other. CALL loads into register-1 the address of the first parameter in the list. Since the parameter is itself an address, register-1 will contain the address of the first address. The called program can load the address of the first parameter into an available register.

Figure 15-4 provides the same simple example as the previous one, converted to parameters. In the calling program, the instruction

CALL   PROGB,(WAGEPK)

loads the address of WAGEPK's address into register-1 and links to PROGB. The code that the CALL generates is (in part) the following:

```
L       15,=V(PROGB)      Load address of PROGB in register-15.
LA      14,*+10           Load return address in register-14
BALR    1,15              Load address of WAGEPK address in register-1,
DC      A(WAGEPK)            and link to PROGB
```

The called program uses this address to load the actual address of WAGEPK into

```
LCC    OEJECT CODE     STMT    SOURCE STATEMENT

C00000                   5 PROGA      CSECT
000000 0530              6            BALR    3.0
                         7            USING   *.3
                         8 *           .
                         9 *           .
000002 F831 3C68 3066   10            ZAP     WAGEPK.HRSPK    SET UP MULTIPLICAND
                        11 *           .
                        12 *           .
000008 41D0 301E        13            LA      13.SAVEA        LOAD ADDRESS OF SAVE AREA
                        14            CALL    PROGB.(WAGEPK)  LINK TO PROGB
                        24 *           .
                        25 *           .
                        26            EOJ
000020                  29 SAVEA      DS      18F             PROGA REGISTER SAVEAREA
000068 120C             30 HRSPK      DC      PL2'12.0'       |xx|.xc|
00006A                  31 WAGEPK     DS      PL4
00006E 600C             32 RATEPK     DC      PL2'6.00'       |x.x|xc|
000070                  33            LTORG
000070 00000000         34                    =V(PROGB)
                        35            END     PROGA

// EXEC ASSEMBLY.SIZE=64K


000000                   3 PROGB      CSECT
                         4            SAVE    (14,12)         SAVE REGISTERS 14 - 12
C00004 0590              7            BALR    9,0             INITIALIZE BASE REG-9
                         8            USING   *.9
0000C6 50D0 9026         9            ST      13,SAVEB+4      SAVE ADDRESS OF SAVEA
00000A 18CD             10            LR      12,13
C0000C 41D0 9022        11            LA      13,SAVEB
000010 5CDC 0008        12            ST      13,8(12)
000014 5E80 1000        13            L       8,0(0.1)        LOAD ADDRESS OF WAGEPK
000018 FC31 8000 8004   14            MP      0(4,8),4(2,8)   MULTIPLY HOURS X RATE
                        15 *           .
                        16 *           .
00001E 58D0 9026        17            L       13,SAVEB+4      LOAD ADDRESS OF SAVEA
                        18            RETURN  (14,12)         RETURN TO PROGA

000028                  23 SAVEB      DS      18F             PROGB SAVEAREA

                        25            END     PROGB
```

FIGURE 15-4   Passing parameters.

register-8: L 8,0(0,1). The program can use this address explicitly as a base address reference. In the instruction

$$MP \quad 0(4,8),4(2,8)$$

operand-1 references WAGEPK (containing hours), and operand-2 references the next field in storage, RATEPK.

The example provides standard program linkage, although there are shortcut methods. For example, PROGB could assume register-15 as a base register, since it contains the starting address of PROGB. We could omit the standard BALR/USING and code USING *,15 at its start. Also, we need not store the contents of register-13 in the save area and reload it on return. These practices may be shortsighted, because any input/output or CALL executed in PROGB will destroy the contents of registers 13 and 15, causing a subsequent execution error.

Problem 15-9 should now be attempted.

LINKING PHASES

We may assemble and link edit one or more control sections, and may arrange the assembly so that the Linkage Editor output is one or more *phases*. Up to now our programs consist of only one phase. The Linkage Editor writes the object code phase into the Core Image or Load library. The job card // EXEC causes the first or only phase to load into main storage and to begin execution. If we have organized the program into additional phases, the system does not load them into storage. We use the LOAD or FETCH macros to load subsequent phases. The purposes of organizing a program into phases are:

1. Some phases may be separately assembled and catalogued. A useful example is data common to many programs—file declarations and record definitions. We need not reassemble these phases each time we need them; we can use the INCLUDE statement to link edit them into our program.
2. The entire program may not fit into main storage. We may arrange the program into separate logical phases.

The main (*root*) phase is first, followed by as many additional (*overlay*) phases as required. After the link edit, the // EXEC card loads the root phase into storage and begins its execution. The root phase generally contains the common data and the main program logic. It may load (with LOAD or FETCH) the various phases as they are required. (The system loads phases, not programs or CSECTs.) Such phases are called *overlays*—when they load into storage they may overlay previously loaded phases. The root phase generally remains intact and is not overlaid.

THE PHASE CONTROL STATEMENT.   Linkage Editor control statements include the cards PHASE, INCLUDE, ENTRY, and ACTION. The PHASE card tells the Linkage Editor that a section of coding is to link edit as a separate phase. If the code is to be assembled, we insert the PHASE card ahead of // EXEC ASSEMBLY.

NAME	OPERATION	OPERAND
blank	PHASE	name,origin

The *name* gives the symbolic name of the phase, up to 8 characters. If the program consists of more than one phase, then the first four characters of each phase name must be identical. The *origin* gives the address of where the phase is to load at execute-time. Among the commonly used entries are:

```
// OPTION LINK,NOXREF,LOG
         ACTION MAP
         PHASE PHASA,ROOT
// EXEC ASSEMBLY,SIZE=64K


  LOC   OBJECT CODE      STMT    SOURCE STATEMENT

000000                    4 PROGA     CSECT
000000                    5 DATA      DS      0CL1            COMMON DATA AREA
000000 120C               6 HRSPK     DC      PL2'12.0'       |XX|.XC|
000002 300C               7 RATEPK    DC      PL2'3.00'       |X.X|XC|
000004                    8 WAGEPK    DS      PL4

000008 0530              10 BEGINA    BALR    3,0
                         11           USING   *,3
                         12           USING   DATA,4
00000A 5840 31E6         13           L       4,=A(DATA)      DATA BASE REGISTER
                         14           OPEN    PRTR
                         22           LOAD    PHASB           LOAD PHASB INTO STORAGE
000026 5010 309A         28           ST      1,ADDRESB       SAVE ENTRY POINT TO PHASB
                         29 *           .
00002A F831 4004 4000    30           ZAP     WAGEPK,HRSPK    SET UP MULTIPLICAND IN PROD
                         31 *           .
000030 41D0 3052         32           LA      13,SAVEA        LOAD ADDRESS OF SAVEAREA
000034 58F0 309A         33           L       15,ADDRESB      LOAD ADDRESS OF PHASB
                         34           CALL    (15)            LINK TO PHASB ENTRY POINT
                         37 *           .
                         38 *           .
                         39 *           .
                         40           LOAD    PHASC           LOAD PHASC INTO STORAGE
000042 18F1              46           LR      15,1            LOAD PHASC ENTRY POINT
000044 41D0 3052         47           LA      13,SAVEA        LOAD ADDRESS OF SAVEAREA
                         48           CALL    (15)            LINK TO PHASC ENTRY POINT
                         51 *           .
                         52 *           .
                         53           CLOSE   PRTR
                         61           EOJ

00005C                   65 SAVEA     DS      18F             SAVE AREA FOR THIS PHASE
0000A4                   66 ADDRESB   DS      F               ADDRESS OF PHASB ENTRY

                         68 PRTR      DTFPR   BLKSIZE=121,                        +
                                              CTLCHR=YES,                         +
                                              DEVADDR=SYSLST,                     +
                                              DEVICE=1403,                        +
                                              IOAREA1=IOARPRT1,                   +
                                              IOAREA2=IOARPRT2,                   +
                                              RECFORM=FIXUNB,                     +
                                              IOREG=(5)

0000D8                   90 IOARPRT1  DS      CL121           BUFFER-1 PRINTER FILE
000151                   91 IOARPRT2  DS      CL121           BUFFER-2 PRINTER FILE
                         92           ENTRY   PRTR
0001D0                   93           LTORG
0001D0 5B5BC2D6D7C5D540  94                   =C'$$BOPEN '
0001D8 D7C8C1E2C2404040  95                   =CL8'PHASB'
0001E0 D7C8C1E2C3404040  96                   =CL8'PHASC'
0001E8 5E5BC2C3D3D6E2C5  97                   =C'$$BCLOSE'
0001F0 00000000          98                   =A(DATA)
                         99           END     BEGINA
```

FIGURE 15-5 Linkage between three phases.

```
                   PHASE PHASB,*
// EXEC ASSEMBLY

000000                          2 DATAB    DSECT  .               COMMON DATA
000000 000C                     3 HRSPK    DC    PL2'0'           |xx|.xc|
000002 000C                     4 RATEPK   DC    PL2'0'           |x.x|xc|
000004                          5 WAGEPK.  DS    PL4

000000                          7 PROGB    CSECT
                                8 BEGINB   SAVE  (14,12)          SAVE REGISTERS IN SAVEA
000004 0530                    11          BALR  3,0              INITIALIZE PROGB BASE REG
                               12          USING *,3
                               13          USING DATAB,4

000006 50D0 3022               15          ST    13,SAVEB+4       SAVE ADDRESS OF SAVEA
00000A 18CD                    16          LR    12,13
00000C 41D0 301E               17          LA    13,SAVEB
000010 50DC 0008               18          ST    13,8(12)         STORE ADDRESS OF SAVEB
                               19 *         .
000014 FC31 4004 4002          20          MP    WAGEPK,RATEPK    MULT HOURS X RATE
                               21 *         .
                               22 *         .
00001A 58D0 3022               23          L     13,SAVEB+4       LOAD ADDRESS OF SAVEA
                               24          RETURN (14,12)         RETURN TO PROGA

000024                         29 SAVEB    DS    18F              PROGB SAVEAREA
                               30          END   BEGINB
                   PHASE PHASC,PHASB
// EXEC ASSEMBLY

C00060                          2 DATAC    DSECT  .               CCMMON DATA AREA
000000 000C                     3 HRSPK    DC    PL2'0'           |xx|.xc|
000002 000C                     4 RATEPK   DC    PL2'0'           |x.x|xc|
000004                          5 WAGEPK   DS    PL4

00000C                          7 PROGC    CSECT
                                8 BEGINC   SAVE  (14,12)          SAVE REGISTERS IN SAVEA
000004 0530                    11          BALR  3,0              INITIALIZE PROGC BASE REG
                               12          USING *,3
                               13          USING DATAC,4

000006 50D0 303E               15          ST    13,SAVEC+4       SAVE ADDRESS OF SAVEA
00000A 18CD                    16          LR    12,13
00000C 41D0 303A               17          LA    13,SAVEC
000010 50DC 0008               18          ST    13,8(12)         STORE ADDRESS OF SAVEC
                               19 *         .
                               20 *         .
000014 9209 3082               21          MVI   PRINT,X'09'
000018 D2C9 308C 3106          22          MVC   PRINT+10(10),=X'40202021204B20202060'
00001E DE09 308C 4004          23          ED    PRINT+10(10),WAGEPK
000024 D278 5000 3082          24          MVC   0(121,5),PRINT
                               25          PUT   PRTR             PRINT WAGE
                               30 *         .
0C0036 58D0 303E               31          L     13,SAVEC+4       LOAD ADDRESS OF SAVEA
                               32          RETURN (14,12)         RETURN TO PROGA

000040                         37 SAVEC    DS    18F              PROGC SAVEAREA
000088 4040404040404040        38 PRINT    DC    CL121' '

                               40          EXTRN PRTR
0001C8                         41          LTORG
000108 00000000                42                =A(PRTR)
00010C 4020202120482020        43                =X'40202021204B20202060'

        00000                  45          END   BEGINC
```

FIGURE 15-5 (*Continued*)

```
// EXEC LNKEDT                                                    Relocation factor
                                                                         ↓
          PHASE   XFR-AD  LOCORE  HICORE  DSK-AD   ESD TYPE  LABEL    LOADED   REL-FR
ROOT    ( PHASA )  0CA080  0DA078  0DA2CF  001 05 01 CSECT  ( PROGA )  0DA078  0DA078
                                                      ENTRY  PRTR      0DA120

                                                     CSECT   IJDFYZIZ  0DA270  0DA270

       ( PHASB )  0DA2D0  0DA2D0  0DA33B  001 05 02 CSECT  ( PROGB )  0DA2D0  0DA2D0

       ( PHASC )  0CA2D0  0CA2D0  0DA3E5  001 05 03 CSECT  ( PROGC )  0DA2D0  0DA2D0
```

FIGURE 15-5 (*Continued*)

PHASE name,ROOT: The name phase is the root phase, to be always in storage during execution of the program. Only the *first* phase may be ROOT. Under a simple operating system, the root phase begins at a doubleword address immediately following the Supervisor. In a multiprogramming system, the root phase loads at the beginning of a partition.

PHASE name,*: The * references the Linkage Editor location counter (similar to that of the Assembler). If not the first phase, the Linkage Editor assigns it to begin at a doubleword address following the previous phase. If the first phase, it is assigned a starting location like the root phase.

PHASE name,symbol: We may instruct the Linkage Editor that at execute-time this phase is to be overlaid in storage beginning at the same address as a previously defined phase.

In Figure 15-5 there are three phases. They are organized as follows:

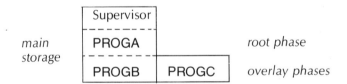

main storage

Supervisor	
PROGA		→ *root phase*
PROGB	PROGC	→ *overlay phases*

The PHASE cards are:

PHASE PROGA, ROOT defines PROGA as the root phase, always in storage during execution.

PHASE PROGB,* tells the Linkage Editor to begin the phase PROGB following the previous phase (PROGA).

PHASE PROGC,PROGB tells the Linkage Editor to assign the phase PROGC to begin at the same storage location as PROGB (an overlay).

THE LOAD AND FETCH MACROS.   These macros are used to load a phase into storage during program execution.

NAME	OPERATION	OPERAND
[name]	LOAD	phasename or (1)
[name]	FETCH	phasename or (1)

THE LOAD MACRO.   The operand contains the name of the phase to be loaded. We may use the phase name or load the phase name into register-1. LOAD causes the phase to load into storage and returns control to the calling phase. LOAD also stores in register-1 the entry point address of the called phase. This address is required because we later use it to CALL the overlay phase for execution. LOAD should be placed so that the overlay phase does not erase it.

THE FETCH MACRO.   The operand contains the name of the phase to be loaded. We may use the phase name or load the phase name into register-1. FETCH loads the phase into storage and branches to its entry point address. In effect, FETCH acts as a combined LOAD and CALL, but with no automatic return.

THE LINKAGE EDITOR MAP.   In Figure 15-5, each phase name begins with the same first four characters, PROG. At the end of the sample program is the *Linkage Editor Map.* We cause this map to print with the DOS control statement ACTION MAP. The map lists the starting address of each phase and CSECT in the program. In large programs, the map is a useful debugging and tracing device.

   The CSECT beginning IJD in the Linkage Editor Map represents the module that IOCS generated for the DTFPR macro for the file PRTR in the program. The module is called PRMOD. Details are in the IBM Supervisor and I/O Macro manual. Other DOS modules include the following:

DEVICE	DTF MACRO	IBM MODULE	
Card	DTFCD	CDMOD	IJCxxxxx
Printer	DTFPR	PRMOD	IJDxxxxx
Magnetic Tape	DTFMT	MTMOD	IJFxxxxx
Sequential Disk	DTFSD	SDMOD	IJGxxxxx
Indexed Seq'l	DTFIS	ISMOD	IJHxxxxx
Direct Access	DTFDA	DAMOD	IJIxxxxx

OVERLAY PROGRAM.   Figure 15-5 illustrates a simple overlay program that links three phases. The first phase initializes hours (HRSPK) in a product field (WAGEPK) and links to the second phase. This phase multiplies hours by rate-of-pay (RATEPK) to calculate wage, and returns to phase-1. Next, phase-1 loads phase-3 over phase-2, and links to phase-3, which prints the wage.

DETAILED EXPLANATION.   After assembly and link edit, the // EXEC card loads the first phase, PHASEA, into storage. The first statements define the common data area. At BEGINA, base register-3 for the program and register-4 for the common data area are loaded. Then LOAD causes PHASB, the second phase, to load into storage, following PHASA. LOAD also places in register-1 the address of the entry point to PHASB. The program stores this entry point in ADDRESB for later use. The program then initializes WAGEPK with HRSPK, and links to PHASB.

PHASB saves the registers of PHASA and initializes its own registers. Then it multiplies WAGEPK by RATEPK (DSECT entries, defined in PHASA), and returns to PHASA.

PHASA next loads and links to PHASC, which saves the registers, prints WAGEPK, and returns to PHASA. At this point, PHASA, and the program, terminate.

> *Note:*   PHASA contains definition of the DTFPR macro, PRTR, which PHASC also uses. The Assembler instruction ENTRY PRTR makes PRTR known outside PHASA. In PHASC, EXTRN PRTR tells the Assembler that PRTR is defined outside this phase. The Link Editor completes the address linkage.

Under OS, the relative location of each CSECT appears in the "CROSS REFERENCE TABLE" following the last assembled CSECT. Look for "CONTROL SECTION" that could appear with such entries as:

CONTROL NAME	SECTION ORIGIN	LENGTH
PHASA	00	. . .
PHASB	6D8	. . .
PHASC	6D8	. . .

If the entry-point addresss (EPA) of the first CSECT, PHASA, is 99080, then the entry-point of both PHASB and PHASC in this case is:

EPA of PHASA	99080
Origin of PHASB & PHASC	6D8
EPA of PHASB & PHASC	99758

Any field can be found in a storage dump through use of the EPA plus the contents of the location counter (LOC) on the program printout.

Note also that execution diagnostics show the contents of the registers under "SA" (save area) in the same 18 fullword format as explained in this chapter.

OVERLAY CONSIDERATIONS

LOAD brings a phase into storage, where it remains until overlaid by another phase. Therefore, *once we LOAD a phase, we may CALL it any number of times.* To load and immediately execute a phase once, we may use FETCH. If there is insufficient storage, large programs may require loading and reloading phases as needed. A common use of overlays is the following:

1. The ROOT phase contains all common declaratives and basic main logic. It loads (or fetches) the initialize phase.
2. The initialize phase contains routines executed only once, such as OPEN files, handle date card, and extract the date from the communications region.
3. The ROOT phase then overlays the initialize phase with the general processing phase, which includes calculations, and input/output. (Storage restrictions may require overlaying some of these phases as required.)
4. At the end of the run, the ROOT phase overlays the general processing phase with an end-of-file phase. This phase includes final totals and CLOSEs the files.

There are countless ways to handle program overlays. However, in all programming problems, *the simplest way is generally the best way.* And simpler may include dividing a problem not into phases but into completely separate programs.

The remaining problems should now be attempted.

PROBLEMS

15-1. For what reasons would it be useful to organize a program into subprograms?

15-2. What is the difference (if any) between a CSECT and a DSECT?

15-3. USING tells the Assembler to apply a base register to a particular section of code. What instruction tells it to discontinue applying the base register?

15-4. Recode and test a previous program using Locate Mode for input and output, with buffers defined under a DSECT.

15-5. Why is it an especially dangerous practice to use register-13 as a base register?

15-6. For subprogram linkage, what is the purpose of registers 0, 1, 13, 14, and 15?

15-7. What are the three macros, and their purpose, required to link to another subprogram, to preserve register contents and to return?

15-8. Revise and test any previous program into two separately assembled CSECTS. Use a DSECT for common data.

15-9. Revise problem 15-8, changing the common data from a DSECT to passing parameters.

15-10. What is the difference between the LOAD and CALL macros? Between LOAD and FETCH?

15-11. Revise any previously written program into 4 phases. Phase-1 (ROOT) calls Phase-2 for initialization and OPEN. Phase-1 then overlays Phase-2 with Phase-3 for processing. At end-of-job, Phase-1 overlays Phase-3 with Phase-4 for final processing.

CHAPTER 16

OPERATING SYSTEMS

The topic of operating systems is large and complex. This chapter introduces material that is useful for advanced Assembler programming. The first section examines general operating systems and its various support programs, including the Assembler and the Linkage Editor. The following sections examine the functions of the Supervisor, the Program Status Word, and the interrupt system. Finally, there is a discussion of channels, Physical IOCS, the channel program, and the input/output system.

A knowledge of these features can be a useful asset when serious bugs occur and where the solution requires a more intimate knowledge of the system. For the serious student, these topics are a useful introduction to *systems programming* and the relationship between the computer hardware and manufacturer-supplied software.

OPERATING SYSTEMS

IBM supplies various programs ("software") to support the computer system. These include language translators such as Assembler, COBOL, and PL/I, and "utility" programs to facilitate disk and tape processing. The levels of programming support depend on the size of the CPU and the needs of the user. Among the categories of support are Basic Programming Support (BPS) for the minimum card, tape and disk installations, and *operating systems*.

On earlier and on smaller computers the operators were very much involved in operating the computer. For example, to assemble and execute a program, the operator would have done the following:

— Load the Assembler translator program into storage.
— Load the source program into storage for translation into machine language object code onto punched cards.
— Load the punched object program into the computer storage.
— Load the data into storage for the object program to execute.

Each step is separate, time-consuming and prone to errors. In a large system such operator intervention is too costly. Therefore, *operating systems* were devised to minimize operator intervention in the processing of programs. An operating system is a collection of related programs that provides for the preparation and execution of our programs. The operating system is stored on disk or tape, and part of it, the Supervisor program, is kept in the lower part of main storage. Under a typical operating system we provide *job control cards* to tell the system what we want it to do. For example, we may want to assemble and execute a program. In simple terms the operating system could work as in Figure 16-1.

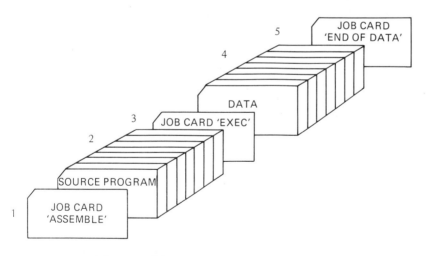

FIGURE 16-1   Job control for an operating system.

1. Preceding the job is a job control card that tells the operating system to assemble a program. The Assembler program is stored (catalogued) in a library on disk. The system loads the Assembler program from the disk library into storage.

2. The Assembler reads and translates the source program. It writes the object program onto another library on disk.
3. Following the source program is a job control card telling the system to execute the assembled object program. The system then loads the object program from the disk library into storage.
4. The program executes the data.
5. Following the data is a job card telling the system that there is no more data. The operating system is now ready to process the next job.

An operating system involves little manual operating, but a complex system is required to perform the preceding and other necessary tasks. There are various operating systems, depending on the user's requirements. They differ in services offered and the amount of main storage they require. The systems include:

SYSTEM		TYPICAL USER
Basic Operating System	BOS	Smaller systems
Disk Processing System	DPS	Smaller systems with disk
Tape Operating System	TOS	Medium systems with tape
Disk Operating System	DOS	Medium systems with disk
Disk Operating System	DOS/VS	Medium systems with "virtual storage"
360 Operating System	OS/MFT	Large 360, "Fixed number of Tasks"
360 Operating System	OS/MVT	Large 360, "Variable number of Tasks"
370 Operating System	OS/VS1	Large 370, equivalent to OS/MFT
370 Operating System	OS/VS2	Large 370, equivalent to OS/MVT

The computer central processing unit (CPU), main storage, and input/output devices are called the *hardware*. IBM "customer engineers" install the hardware and service breakdowns. The operating system is a group of IBM-supplied programs, and is called *software*. IBM "system engineers" help install and maintain the software. Large installations have their own "systems programmers" who are responsible for maintaining these complex operating systems. An operating system is composed of several interrelated parts. Disk Operating System (DOS), on which this text is mostly based, is organized as in Figure 16-2. The three main parts are *Control Program, System Service Programs, and Processing Programs.*

CONTROL PROGRAM.   The control program controls all other programs that are processed. It consists of the Supervisor, Job Control, and Initial Program Load. Under OS, the functions are Data Management, Job Management, and Task Management.

The Supervisor is the nucleus of the operating system. At all times part of the Supervisor resides in lower storage. The system loads user programs (ours) in storage after the Supervisor area. Therefore there are always two (or more) stored programs in storage: the Supervisor program and our program(s). Only one is executed at one time, but control passes between them. The Supervisor's functions include the han-

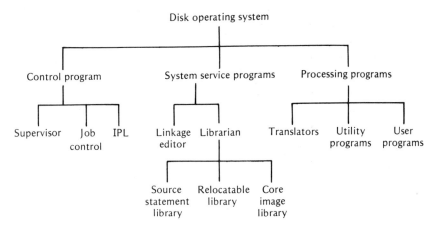

FIGURE 16-2   Disk operating system organization.

dling of "interrupts" (such as our program asking to use an input or output device), fetching required routines from the program library, and handling program execution errors. An important part of the Supervisor is the *Input/Output Control System (IOCS)* to handle the complex input/output. IOCS handles such items as checking for valid tape and disk files, and data transfer between I/O units and storage. A later section covers the Supervisor in detail.

Storage:

```
IBM
Supervisor
Program
- - - - - - - -
User
Program(s)
```

Job Control handles the transition between jobs run in the system. When required, the Supervisor loads job control into storage. We provide job control cards with our job to tell the system what we want to do next.

Initial Program Load (IPL) is a program that the operator uses to load the Supervisor into storage (done daily or whenever required).

SYSTEM SERVICE PROGRAMS.   These include the *Linkage Editor* and the *Librarian*.

THE LINKAGE EDITOR.   The Linkage Editor has two main functions:

1. IOCS is composed of complex input/output routines. We store (catalogue) these in the library (covered next). We do not code a program with the complete input/output operations. The Linkage Editor includes the required IOCS routines after the program is assembled.
2. We may code a program in more than one section, and then assemble each section separately. These assembled sections may then be link-edited into one program. The Linkage Editor links the programs together and enables data in one section to be recognized in another section (covered in Chapter 15).

THE LIBRARIAN.   The operating system contains libraries on disk or tape to store or catalogue IBM and our own commonly used programs and routines. Under the Disk Operating System (DOS), there are three libraries:

1. The *Source Statement Library (SSL)* catalogues any program or routine still in source code. We use instructions, such as COPY, to include the catalogued source code into our program for subsequent assembling.
2. The *Relocatable Library (RL)* catalogues frequently used routines such as IOCS. The routines are stored in assembled format not yet ready for execution. We use the instruction INCLUDE to tell the Linkage Editor to include such routines in with our assembled program.
3. The *Core Image Library (CIL)* contains programs and routines in executable format, ready for execution. The CIL contains, for example, Assembler, PL/I, COBOL, and other translator programs, and the various utility programs such as Sort. We use the job control card EXEC to request the Supervisor to load a program from this library into main storage for execution.

The OS libraries equivalent to DOS Source Statement, Relocatable, and Core Image libraries are Source Library, Object library, and Load library.

PROCESSING PROGRAMS.   Processing programs are stored (catalogued) on disk or tape. They are classified into three groups:

1. *Language Translators* supplied by IBM with the system include Assembler, PL/I, Fortran, COBOL, RPG, and ALGOL.
2. *Utility Programs* supplied by IBM include various utility and special purpose programs, such as copy disk to printer, disk initialization, and various sort/merge programs.
3. *User-Written Programs* are written by the user (us) and are not maintained or supported by IBM. All examples in this text are user-written programs.

THE SUPERVISOR

The size of the operating system and of the Supervisor vary considerably according to their complexity and functions they must perform. A medium-sized Supervisor under

DOS typically requires some 10,000 bytes of main storage, whereas under a large system the Supervisor often requires over 100,000 bytes.

Although the Supervisor program resides permanently in lower main storage, the first section up to X'200' is allocated for use by the CPU. These "Fixed Storage Locations" are listed in Figure 16-3. Some of the locations are explained in the later section, Program Status Word.

FIXED STORAGE LOCATIONS

Area, dec.	Hex addr	EC only	Function
0- 7	0		Initial program loading PSW, restart new PSW
8- 15	8		Initial program loading CCW1, restart old PSW
16- 23	10		Initial program loading CCW2
24- 31	18		External old PSW
32- 39	20		Supervisor Call old PSW
40- 47	28		Program old PSW
48- 55	30		Machine-check old PSW
56- 63	38		Input/output old PSW
64- 71	40		Channel status word (see diagram)
72- 75	48		Channel address word [0-3 key, 4-7 zeros, 8-31 CCW address]
80- 83	50		Interval timer
88- 95	58		External new PSW
96-103	60		Supervisor Call new PSW
104-111	68		Program new PSW
112-119	70		Machine-check new PSW
120-127	78		Input/output new PSW
132-133	84		CPU address assoc'd with external interruption, or unchanged
132-133	84	X	CPU address assoc'd with external interruption, or zeros
134-135	86	X	External interruption code
136-139	88	X	SVC interruption [0-12 zeros, 13-14 ILC, 15:0, 16-31 code]
140-143	8C	X	Program interrupt. [0-12 zeros, 13-14 ILC, 15:0, 16-31 code]
144-147	90	X	Translation exception address [0-7 zeros, 8-31 address]
148-149	94		Monitor class [0-7 zeros, 8-15 class number]
150-151	96	X	PER interruption code [0-3 code, 4-15 zeros]
152-155	98	X	PER address [0-7 zeros, 8-31 address]
156-159	9C		Monitor code [0-7 zeros, 8-31 monitor code]
168-171	A8		Channel ID [0-3 type, 4-15 model, 16-31 max. IOEL length]
172-175	AC		I/O extended logout address [0-7 unused, 8-31 address]
176-179	B0		Limited channel logout (see diagram)
185-187	B9	X	I/O address [0-7 zeros, 8-23 address]
216-223	D8		CPU timer save area
224-231	E0		Clock comparator save area
232-239	E8		Machine-check interruption code (see diagram)
248-251	F8		Failing processor storage address [0-7 zeros, 8-31 address]
252-255	FC		Region code*
256-351	100		Fixed logout area*
352-383	160		Floating-point register save area
384-447	180		General register save area
448-511	1C0		Control register save area
512†	200		CPU extended logout area (size varies)

*May vary among models; see system library manuals for specific model.
†Location may be changed by programming (bits 8-28 of CR 15 specify address).

FIGURE 16-3   Fixed storage locations.

The Supervisor loads operating system routines stored on disk (usually) into main storage as required. The section of storage that the Supervisor uses for temporary routines is the *"transient area"*. Figure 16-4 illustrates the layout of the Supervisor in main storage (not an exact representation).

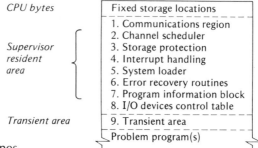

CPU bytes

Supervisor resident area

Transient area

Fixed storage locations
1. Communications region
2. Channel scheduler
3. Storage protection
4. Interrupt handling
5. System loader
6. Error recovery routines
7. Program information block
8. I/O devices control table
9. Transient area
Problem program(s)

FIGURE 16-4   Supervisor routines.

1. *Communication Region.* This area contains the current date as well as other fields shown in the diagram. (There is one Communication region for each partition under multiprogramming.)

Date Mo/Day/Yr or Day/Mo/Yr	Reserved	User Area – set to zero when JOB statement is read. (Communication within a job step or between job steps)	Program Switches (UPSI)	Job Name (Entered from Job Control)	Address: Uppermost Byte of Problem Program Area	Address: Uppermost Byte of Current Problem Program Phase	Address: Uppermost Byte of phase with highest ending address	Length of Problem Program Label Area
0 7	8 11	12 22	23	24 31	32 35	36 39	40 43	44 45

Bytes →

2. *Channel Scheduler.* The channels provide a path between main storage and the input/output devices, and permit overlapping of program execution with I/O operations. The Channel Scheduler routine handles all I/O. If the requested channel, control unit, and device are available, the channel operation begins. If busy, the Channel Scheduler places its request in a queue to wait until the device is available. The channel notifies the Channel Scheduler when the I/O operation is complete, or that an error has occurred (these are "I/O interrupts").

3. *Storage Protection.* Storage Protection is an optional feature that prevents the problem program from erroneously moving data into the Supervisor area and destroying it. Under a multiprogramming system, storage protection is required to prevent a program in one partition from erasing a program in another partition.

4. *Interrupt Handling.* An interrupt is a signal that informs the system that special action is required, to interrupt the program currently being executed, and to give control to the appropriate Supervisor routine. This topic is covered in detail in the next section, PSW.

5. *System Loader.* This routine is responsible for loading programs into main storage for execution.

6. *Error Recovery.* For each I/O device (or class of devices) there is a special routine to handle device error-recovery. When an error is sensed, the Channel Scheduler invokes the required routine which attempts to correct the error.

7. *Program Information Block (PIB).* The PIB contains information tables required by the Supervisor about the current program(s) in storage.

8. *I/O Devices Control Table.* This area contains the table of I/O devices that relate physical unit addresses (X'nnn') with logical units (SYSxxx).

9. *Transient Area.* This area provides temporary storage for routines that the Supervisor loads as required: OPEN/CLOSE, DUMP, computer operator messages, end-of-job handling, some error recovery, and "checkpoint" routines.

THE PROGRAM STATUS WORD—PSW

The PSW is a doubleword of data stored in the control section of the CPU. (On small models, the PSW is only a fullword in length, and its format differs from that described here; its functions, however, are similar.) The PSW controls an executing program and indicates its status. There are two PSW modes that provide control and status information: *Basic Control (BC) mode* and *Extended Control (EC) mode.* Both the 360 and 370 use BC mode, and the mode is indicated by a 0 in the PSW bit-12. EC mode is available only on the 370 for "virtual storage", with the "extended-control" facility. When in EC mode, PSW bit-12 contains a 1. For each mode the PSW format is the same in only certain positions. The charts next show the two modes (bits are numbered from left to right zero through 63):

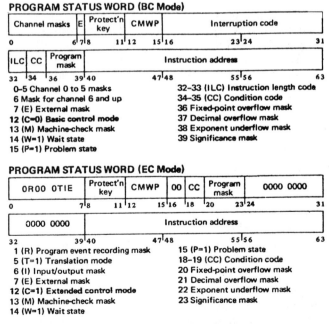

Fields that programmers may find useful include:

Bit 15: State. In both modes, 0 = Supervisor state and 1 = Problem state (the computer always functions in one or the other state). When the computer is executing the Supervisor program, the bit is 0, and all instructions are valid. When in the Problem state, the bit is 1, and certain *privileged* instructions (such as Start IO and Load PSW) cannot be executed.

Bits 16–31: Program Interrupt Code (BC mode only). The computer sets these bits according to the type of program interrupt when one occurs. The following list of interrupt codes shows the hex representation of the 16-bit code:

PROGRAM INTERRUPTION CODES

Code	Description	Code	Description
0001	Operation exception	000C	Exponent overflow excp
0002	Privileged operation excp	000D	Exponent underflow excp
0003	Execute exception	000E	Significance exception
0004	Protection exception	000F	Floating-point divide excp
0005	Addressing exception	0010	Segment translation excp
0006	Specification exception	0011	Page translation exception
0007	Data exception	0012	Translation specification excp
0008	Fixed-point overflow excp	0013	Special operation exception
0009	Fixed-point divide excp	0040	Monitor event
000A	Decimal overflow exception	0080	Program event (code may be
000B	Decimal divide exception		combined with another code)

Bits 34–35: Condition Code (BC mode only. Under EC mode, the Condition code is in bits 18–19). Certain arithmetic and logical instructions set this code.

Bits 40–63: Instruction Address (both modes). This area contains the address of the next instruction to be executed. The CPU accesses the designated instruction from main storage, decodes it in the control section, and then executes it in the arithmetic/logical section. The first two bits of every machine code instruction indicate its length. Assume an RR-format instruction, two bytes long; when executing the RR instruction, the CPU increments the instruction address in the PSW by two, and this now indicates the address of the next instruction. In the case of a "branch" instruction, the branch address may replace the PSW instruction address.

INTERRUPTS

An interrupt occurs when it is necessary for the Supervisor to perform some special task. There are six main classes of interrupts:

1. *Program Interrupt.* This is caused by an operation that the computer cannot execute, such as an attempt to perform arithmetic on invalid arithmetic data. This is the common type of interrupt when a program terminates abnormally (sometimes called "bombing"). Appendix B lists the various types of program interrupts that can occur during execution.

2. *Supervisor Call Interrupt.* A transfer from the Problem program to the Supervisor requires a "Supervisor Call" (SVC) operation and causes an interrupt. For example, our program may issue a request for input/output or to terminate processing. Control is passed to the Supervisor by means of a Supervisor Call (SVC).

3. *External Interrupt.* An external device may need attention. For example, the computer operator may press the request key on the console typewriter, or there may be a request for telecommunications.

4. *Machine Check Interrupt.* The machine-checking circuits may detect a hardware error, such as a byte not containing an odd number of bits (odd parity).

5. *Input/Output Interrupt.* Completion of an I/O operation making the unit available or malfunction of an I/O device (such as damaged tape) cause this interrupt.

6. *Restart Interrupt* on the 370 permits the operator or another CPU to invoke execution of a program.

For every interrupt, the system alters the PSW as required, and stores the PSW in a Fixed Storage Location, where it is available to any program for testing.

The PSW referenced to this point is often called the "current" PSW. When an interrupt occurs, the computer stores the current PSW and loads a "new" PSW that controls the new program (usually the Supervisor Program). The current PSW is in the control section of the CPU, but the "old" and "new" PSW's are stored in main storage.

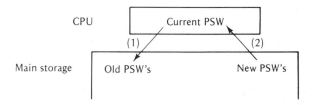

The interrupt replaces the current PSW: (1) It stores the current PSW into main storage as the "old" PSW, and (2) It fetches a "new" PSW from main storage, to become the "current" PSW. (The old PSW will therefore contain in its instruction address the location following the instruction that caused the interrupt.) The computer stores PSW's in 12 doubleword locations in Fixed Storage; six are for "old" PSW's and six for "new" PSW's, depending on the class of interrupt:

	OLD PSW	NEW PSW		OLD PSW	NEW PSW
Restart	0008	0000	Program	0040	0104
External	0024	0088	Machine	0048	0112
Supervisor	0032	0096	Input/Output	0056	0120

The following illustrates the sequence of events following a Supervisor interrupt. Assume that the Supervisor has stored in each of the six *new* PSW's the address of each of its interrupt routines (the old PSW's are not yet required). Remember also that when any instruction executes, the computer updates the current PSW—the Instruction Address, and the Condition Code as required.

1. Assume that our program requests input from disk. The input macro-instruction, GET or READ, contains a Supervisor Call to link to the Supervisor for I/O. This is a *Supervisor interrupt.*

2. The Instruction Address in the current PSW contains the address in our program immediately following the SVC that caused the interrupt. The CPU stores this current PSW in the *old* PSW for Supervisor interrupt, location 32. The *new* PSW for Supervisor interrupt, location 96, contains Supervisor state bit = 0 and the address of the Supervisor Interrupt routine. The CPU moves this new PSW to the current PSW, and is now in Supervisor state.

3. The PSW Instruction Address contains the address of the Supervisor I/O routine, which now executes. The Channel Scheduler requests the channel for disk input.

4. To return to our program, the Supervisor loads the old PSW from location 32 back into the current PSW. The instruction "goes to" the PSW instruction address, which is the address in our program following the original SVC that caused the interrupt. The system switches from Supervisor back to Problem state.

In the case of a *program check interrupt,* the computer sets the cause of the program check in PSW bits 16–31, the Program Interrupt code. If the Problem program attempts arithmetic on invalid data, the computer senses a "Data Exception," and stores X'0007' in PSW bits 16–31 (i.e., B'111' in bits 29–31). The computer then stores the current PSW in old PSW location 0040, and loads the new PSW from 0104 into the current PSW. This PSW contains the address of the Supervisor's Program Check routine, which tests the old PSW to determine which type of program check caused the interrupt.

The Supervisor prints the contents of the old PSW in hexadecimal and the cause of the program check, "DATA EXCEPTION", "flushes" the interrupted program, and begins processing the next job. Suppose that the invalid operation is an MP at location X'6A320'. Since MP is six bytes long, the instruction address in the PSW and the one printed will be X'6A326'. We can tell from the Supervisor diagnostic message first, that the error is a "Data Exception", and second, that the invalid operation immediately precedes the instruction at X'6A326'.

CHANNELS

On the 360/370, channels direct data between devices and main storage. A channel is a component that functions as a separate computer operated by "channel commands" to control input/output devices. Channels permit attaching a great variety of I/O devices. There are two types of channels:

1. *The multiplexor channel* is designed to handle low-speed devices, such as card, printer, and terminals. It permits simultaneous operation of more than one device. There is typically only one multiplexor channel on a system, although some 370's have more than one.

2. *The selector channel* is designed to handle high-speed devices, such as magnetic tape and disk. However, data can be transferred from only one device at a time (burst mode). Depending on the model, there may be up to six selector channels.

Each channel has a four-bit address:

CHANNEL	ADDRESS	TYPE	CHANNEL	ADDRESS	TYPE
0	0000	Multiplexor	4	0100 ⎫	Selector
1	0001 ⎫		5	0101 ⎬	channels
2	0010 ⎬	Selector	6	0110 ⎭	
3	0011 ⎭	channels			

To interface a device with a channel requires a *control unit*. Since many devices may be attached, the control unit is specific to the device. For example, a magnetic tape control unit connects tape drives with a selector channel. The control unit also has a 4-bit address. Further, each *device* has a 4-bit address, and is known to the system by a *physical address*—a 12-bit code that specifies channel/control unit/device, as 0CCC UUUU DDDD (C = channel, U = control unit, D = device). This physical address permits the attaching of 2^8 or 256 devices. Figure 16-5 illustrates one possible configuration.

For example, a printer device number is 1110, and is attached to channel 0, control unit 1. To the system, the physical address of the printer is 0000 0001 1110,

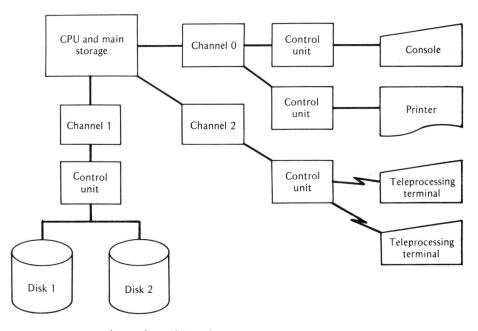

FIGURE 16-5   Channels and I/O devices.

or X'01E'. Assume that the two disk devices are numbered 0000 and 0001; if they are both attached to channel 1, control unit 9, their physical addresses are respectively X'190' and X'191'.

SYMBOLIC ASSIGNMENTS. Although the Supervisor references I/O devices by their physical numbers, our programs use symbolic names. We can assign a symbolic name "permanently" or temporarily to any device, and a device may have assigned more than one symbolic name. The system control program uses certain names, called *system logical units,* including the following:

SYSIPT The card reader, tape, or disk device used as input for programs.

SYSRDR The card reader, tape, or disk device used as input for job control for the system.

SYSIN The system name to assign both SYSIPT and SYSRDR to the same card reader, tape, or disk device.

SYSLST The printer, tape, or disk used as the main output device for the system.

SYSPCH The card punch, tape, or disk used as the main device for "punching."

SYSOUT The system name to assign both SYSLST and SYSPCH to the same tape device.

SYSLNK The disk area used as input for the Linkage Editor.

SYSLOG The console typewriter (or printer) used by the system to log operator messages and job control statements.

SYSRES The disk or tape device where the operating system resides.

SYSRLB The devices for the relocatable and system libraries.
and
SYSSLB

In addition, there are *programmer logical units,* SYS000 − SYSnnn. A user may assign any valid symbolic name to a device, such as assigning a disk drive, physical address X'160', with a logical address SYS002. The Supervisor stores these physical and logical addresses in a table in order to relate them. The table is called I/O Devices Control Table, and in simplified form could contain the following:

I/O DEVICE	PHYSICAL ADDRESS	LOGICAL UNIT(S)
card reader	X'00C'	SYSIPT, SYSRDR
printer	X'00E'	SYSLST
disk drive	X'160'	SYSLNK, SYSRES, SYS002
tape drive	X'280'	SYS026, SYS035

For example, a reference to SYSLST is to the printer, and the disk device, X'160', is known as SYSLNK, SYSRES, and SYS002, depending on its particular use. We may assign a logical address permanently or temporarily, and may change logical addresses from job to job. For instance, we could use an ASSGN job control statement to reassign SYS035 from tape output for a program to disk output on X'160'.

PHYSICAL IOCS

The basic level of IOCS provides for channel scheduling, error recovery, and interrupt handling. We must write the "channel program" (the Channel Command Word), and synchronize the program with completion of the I/O operation. We must also provide for testing the Command Control Block for certain errors, checking wrong-length records, switching between I/O areas where two are used, and, if records are blocked, for blocking and deblocking. PIOCS macros include CCW, CCB, EXCP, and WAIT.

[name]	CCW	Command code, Data address, Flags, Count field
Blockname	CCB	SYSnnn, Command-list-name
[name]	EXCP	Blockname or (1)
[name]	WAIT	Blockname or (1)

CHANNEL COMMAND WORD—CCW. The CCW instruction causes the Assembler to construct an 8-byte Channel Command Word that defines the I/O command to be executed.

Command code—Defines the operation to be performed, such as 1 = Write, 2 = Read, X'09' = Print, and space one line.

Data address—The storage address of the first byte where data is to be read or written.

Flags—When the channel completes an operation defined in a CCW, it determines its next action from these flag bits, and we can set flag bits to '1' to vary the channel's operation (explained in detail later).

Count field—An expression that defines the number of bytes in the data block that is to be processed.

COMMAND CONTROL BLOCK—CCB. There must be a CCB for each I/O device that PIOCS macros reference. The CCB comprises the first 16 bytes of most generated DTF tables. The CCB communicates information to PIOCS to cause required I/O operations, and receives status information after the operation.

Blockname—The symbolic name associated with this CCB, used as an operand for the EXCP and WAIT macros.

SYSnnn—The symbolic name of the I/O device associated with this CCB.

Command-list name—The symbolic name of the first CCW used with the CCB.

THE EXECUTE CHANNEL PROGRAM (EXCP) AND WAIT MACROS.   The operand of both EXCP and WAIT gives the symbolic name of the CCB macro to be referenced. The EXCP macro requests Physical IOCS to start an I/O operation, and PIOCS relates the blockname to the CCB to determine the device. When the channel and the device become available, the channel program is started. Program control then returns to our program. The WAIT macro synchronizes program execution with completion of an I/O operation, since the program normally requires its completion before it can continue execution. For example, we have issued EXCP to read a data block—we must now WAIT for delivery of the entire data block before we can begin processing it. (When bit-0 of byte-2 of the CCB for the file is set to '1', the WAIT is completed and processing continues.)

EXAMPLE PHYSICAL IOCS PROGRAM.   Figure 16-6 simply generates and prints the sum of the digits from 1 through 10, i.e., $1 + 2 + 3 + \ldots + 10$. The program prints successively 1, then 3, then 6, etc., and terminates after the tenth calculation with 55. Note that the operands of both EXCP and WAIT specify PRTR, the name of the CCB. Operand-2 of the CCB designates PRCOMWD, the name of the CCW.

```
PHYSIO     START  0
           BALR   3,0
           USING  *,3
           LA     8,10                ESTABLISH COUNT OF 10

A10LOOP    AP     SUM,DIGIT           ADD DIGIT TO SUM
           AP     DIGIT,=P'1'         INCREMENT DIGIT BY 1
           UNPK   PRINT+21(3),SUM     UNPACK SUM INTO PRINT
           OI     PRINT+23,X'F0'      SET ZONE SIGN TO X'F'

           EXCP   PRTR                EXECUTE PRINT COMMAND
           WAIT   PRTR                WAIT FOR COMPLETION

           BCT    8,A10LOOP           DECREMENT COUNT, LOOP IF NON-ZERO
           EOJ                        TERMINATE IF ZERO
***        DECLARATIVES       ***
PRINT      DC     CL120' '            PRINT AREA
PRTR       CCB    SYSLST,PRCOMWD      COMMAND CONTROL BLOCK

PRCOMWD    CCW    X'09',PRINT,X'20',120   CHANNEL COMMAND WORD

DIGIT      DC     PL2'1'
SUM        DC     PL2'0'              SUM-OF-DIGITS ACCUMULATOR

           END    PHYSIO
```

FIGURE 16-6   Example physical IOCS program.

CCW FLAG BITS.   The flag bits in the CCW may be set and used as follows:

Bit 32 "Chain Data flag", set by X'80'. This bit specifies "data chaining". When the CCW has processed the number of bytes defined in its Count field, the I/O operation does not terminate if this flag bit is set. The operation continues with the *next* CCW in storage. We can use data chaining to read or write data into or out of storage areas that are not necessarily adjacent. In the following three CCW's, the first two specify data chaining with X'80' in the Flag bits, operand-3. An EXCP and CCB may then reference the *first* CCW, and as a result, the chain of three CCW's causes the contents of an 80-byte input record to be read into three separate areas in storage—20 bytes in NAME, 30 in ADDRESS, and 30 in CITY.

DATACHAIN	CCW 2,NAME,X'80',20	Read 20 bytes into NAME, then chain.
	CCW ,ADDRESS,X'80',30	Read 30 bytes into ADDRESS, then chain.
	CCW ,CITY,X'00',30	Read 30 bytes into CITY, no chain (stop).

Bit 33, "Chain Command flag", set by X'40'. This bit specifies "command chaining" to enable the channel to execute more than one CCW before terminating the I/O operation. Each CCW applies to a *separate I/O record*. The following set of CCW's could provide for reading three input blocks, each 100 bytes long.

COMCHAIN	CCW 2,INAREA,X'40',100	Read record-1 into INAREA, then chain.
	CCW 2,INAREA+100,X'40',100	Read record-2 into INAREA+100, chain.
	CCW 2,INAREA+200,X'00',100	Read record-3 into INAREA+200, stop.

Bit 34, "Suppress Length Indication flag", set by X'20', is used to suppress an error indication that occurs when the number of bytes transmitted differs from the count in the CCW.

Bit 35, "Skip flag", set by X'10', is used to suppress transmission of input data. The device actually reads the data, but the channel does not transmit the record.

Bit 36, "Program Controlled Interrupt flag", set by X'08', causes an interrupt when this CCW's operation is complete (used when one Supervisor SIO instruction executes more than one CCW).

Bit 37, "Indirect Data Address flag". This flag as well as other features about Physical IOCS are covered in the IBM Principles of Operation manual and in the appropriate Supervisor manual.

PROBLEMS

16-1. What is the purpose (if any) of an operating system?

16-2. Where is the Supervisor program located?

16-3. What are the two main features of the Linkage Editor?

16-4. What do the first 512 bytes of main storage contain?

16-5. What is the purpose and contents of the Supervisor "transient area"?

16-6. What are the two modes of the PSW? The two states?

16-7. Where in the PSW (the name and bit positions) is the next sequential instruction located?

16-8. What are the classes of interrupts and their causes?

16-9. What is the purpose of channels? What are the two types and their differences?

16-10. A printer, number 1101, is attached to control unit 0010 and a multiplexor channel. What is the printer's physical address in hex?

16-11. Distinguish between physical address and logical address.

16-12. What are system logical units and programmer logical units?

16-13. Revise some simple program and substitute Physical IOCS for input/output.

CHAPTER 17

FLOATING-POINT OPERATIONS

The preceding chapters discussed arithmetic data in two formats: packed decimal and binary, or fixed-point. There are two disadvantages that may derive from performing arithmetic in these formats: (1) The maximum and minimum values may be inadequate for the calculation being performed; and (2) the programmer is fully responsible for maintaining decimal and binary point precision. Assembler floating-point format has its own unique set of instructions designed to overcome these disadvantages. (On many smaller models, floating-point is optional.) Its most common use is for calculations such as in astronomy or in nuclear physics that require extremely high or low values. Most programs requiring floating-point arithmetic are written in high-level languages such as FORTRAN and PL/I. These languages replace much of the tedious detail that Assembler programming requires. Studying the Assembler floating-point instructions gives better understanding of the high-level languages and results in better programming performance. However, be warned that the problem in Assembler of translating between binary and floating-point is formidable.

FLOATING-POINT FORMATS

BASE 10 FLOATING-POINT. Floating-point can be best explained in terms of decimal (base 10) values. Any decimal value can be expressed by the formula $N = 10^e \times f$, where:

357

N = the decimal value

e = exponent, or power, to which the base 10 is raised

f = fraction

Consider the following decimal values:

Decimal value N = $10^e \times f$

123.45	= 10^3	× .12345 =	1000	× .12345
1.2345	= 10^1	× .12345 =	10	× .12345
0.12345	= 10^0	× .12345 =	1	× .12345
0.0012345	= 10^{-2}	× .12345 =	0.01	× .12345

A floating-point value omits the base (10) and stores only the exponent (e) and the fraction (f). As a fullword, the floating-point value could be stored as

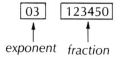

meaning $10^3 \times 0.123450$.

CONVERTING BASE 10 TO BASE 16.   The 360 and 370 store floating-point values in base 16. The following technique converts decimal values into hexadecimal. Assume a decimal value of 123.45:

1. Use the decimal-to-hexadecimal conversion table in Appendix A to convert the integer portion 123 to base 16 = 7B.0000.
2. Convert the fraction portion as:

7B.0000

```
    0.45
  × 16      Multiply by 16
= 7.20      Extract the 7        =   .7000

    0.20
  × 16      Multiply by 16
= 3.20      Extract the 3        =   .0300

    0.20
  × 16      Multiply by 16
= 3.20      Extract the 3        =   .0030
```

$$
\begin{array}{l}
 0.20 \\
\underline{\times\ 16} \quad \text{Multiply by 16} \\
=\ \underline{3.20} \quad \text{Extract the 3} \qquad\qquad =\ .0003
\end{array}
$$

$$\text{Hexadecimal value} \qquad\qquad 7B.7333$$

Float numbers are stored as 6 digits in single-precision, or 14 digits in double-precision. The value is stored in single-precision as 7B.7333, but is expressed more accurately with double-precision as 7B.733333333333—there is no exact hex representation for 123.45.

BASE 16 FLOATING-POINT.   We previously converted 123.45 to X'7B.7333'. Any hex number can be represented by:

$$
\begin{aligned}
N_{16} &= 16^e \times f_{16} \\
7B.7333 &= 16^0 \times 7B.7333 \\
&= 16^1 \times 7.B7333 \\
&= 16^2 \times .7B7333
\end{aligned}
$$

We may therefore store this floating-point number without the base (16) as

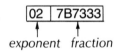

$$
\begin{array}{cc}
\uparrow & \uparrow \\
\textit{exponent} & \textit{fraction}
\end{array}
$$

meaning $16^2 \times$ X'.7B7333'.

Floating-point, like binary data, may be defined in storage or loaded in registers. Either way, floating-point values are represented in three formats:

FORMAT	PRECISION	LENGTH
Short	Single	Fullword
Long	Double	Doubleword
Extended Long	Extended	Two doublewords (larger systems)

The float number consists of a *sign, characteristic (exponent),* and *fraction:*

single-precision	s	char	fraction	
bits	0	1– 7	8–	31

double-precision	s	char	fraction	
bits	0	1– 7	8–	63

SIGN.   The sign, in bit position zero, applies to the *fraction*. A 0-bit means plus, and a 1-bit means minus fraction.

CHARACTERISTIC.   In a value such as 16^3, 16 is the fraction, and 3 is the exponent, and means $16 \times 16 \times 16$, or 4096. The 360 and 370 store the exponent (characteristic) in *excess-64 notation,* by adding 64 (X'40') to the stored exponent, as follows:

DECIMAL REPRESENTATION	HEXADECIMAL REPRESENTATION
Exponent + 64 = Characteristic	Exponent + 40 = Characteristic
03 + 64 = 67	03 + 40 = 43
00 + 64 = 64	00 + 40 = 40
−03 + 64 = 61	−03 + 40 = 3D

The exponent is incremented by 64 (X'40), and stored in hex format in bit positions 1–7. The lowest exponent is X'−40'; it is stored as X'−40' + X'40' = X'00'. The highest exponent is X'3F'; it is stored as X'3F' + X'40' = X'7F'. This maximum exponent is stored with all 7 bits on. Although the characteristic has no sign stored, there is an implicit sign. For example, the exponent −2 is stored as X'−02' + X'40' = X'3E'. Under base 16, such an exponent means 16^{-2}.

FRACTION.   The fraction may be represented as single-precision (short), double precision (long), or as extended long. Single-precision processes faster and requires less storage; double-precision provides greater accuracy. Single-precision stores the fraction in hex in bits 8–31, and double-precision in bits 8–63. (Bit zero is the sign.) Negative fractions are stored the same as positive fractions (unlike binary that uses two's complement for negatives). The *radix point* (in base-10 the decimal point) *is immediately to the left of the fraction.*

Following are examples of floating-point values:

Example: positive exponent, positive fraction. The decimal value 128.0 equals X'80', or $16^2 \times$ X'.8'. It is stored in short form as:

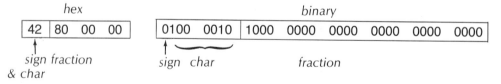

Based on $16^2 \times$ X'.8', the characteristic is calculated as 02 + 40 = X'42'. Because the fraction is positive, the sign bit becomes 0. The fraction with the radix point to the left is represented as X'.8'. We may now compute its value using the exponent 2 and the fraction as $16^2 \times$ X'.8' = 256 × 0.5 = 128.

Example: positive exponent, negative fraction. The decimal value −2816.0 equals X'−B00', or $16^3 \times$ X'−.B'. It is stored in short form as:

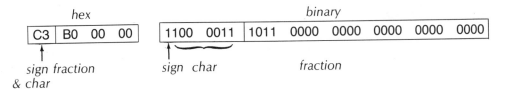

The characteristic is calculated as $03 + 40 = X'43'$. Because the fraction is negative, the characteristic is stored as $X'C3'$. The fraction becomes $X'-.B0'$. We may now compute its value using exponent 3 and the fraction as $16^3 \times X'-.B0' = 16^3 \times -11/16 = 16^2 \times -11 = -2816$.

Example: Negative exponent, positive fraction. Assume a floating-point value stored in short form as:

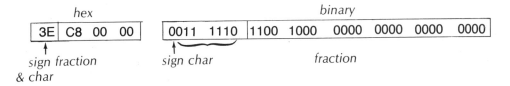

The characteristic is calculated as $X'3E' - X'40' = -02$. We may now compute the value as $16^{-2} \times X'.68' = \dfrac{1}{16^2} \times \left(\dfrac{12}{16} + \dfrac{8}{16^2}\right)$ = approximately 0.0030517.

NORMALIZATION. Precision is maintained more accurately by means of "normalization". The normalization procedure left-adjusts the floating-point fraction until the leftmost hex digit is nonzero, and decrements the characteristic by 1 for each fraction digit shifted. For example, consider the floating-point value:

$$\boxed{43\,00\,88\,00} = 16^3 \times \left(\frac{8}{16^3} + \frac{8}{16^4}\right) = 8 + \frac{8}{16} = 8.5$$

Normalize by shifting the fraction left two digits and decrement the characteristic by 2:

$$\boxed{41\,88\,00\,00} = 16^1 \times \left(\frac{8}{16} + \frac{8}{16^2}\right) = 8 + \frac{8}{16} = 8.5$$

Certain float operations involve prenormalizing (before the operation) and postnormalizing (after the operation). This practice is discussed along with the instructions.

Problems 17-1 through 17-4 should now be attempted.

DECLARATIVES

We define floating-point data in decimal format, which the Assembler converts to float. We may define data as single-precision (E-format), double-precision (D-format), or on some systems extended long (L-format). (D-format was used earlier as a DS to facilitate the CVB and CVD operations.) Also, we may define float constants with or without an *exponent modifier En.*

NAME	OPERATION	OPERAND
[symbol]	DC	dTLn'constant'

Optional: d = duplication factor to signify the number of repetitions of the constant. If it is omitted, the Assembler assumes one constant.

Required: T = type. E defines single-precision (32 bits of which 24 are the fraction). D is double-precision (64 bits of which 56 are the fraction). L defines extended long as two doublewords.

Optional: Ln = length in bytes. This factor is normally omitted because the Assembler aligns E on a fullword and D on a doubleword boundary—the required format for floating-point RX instructions. If Ln is specified, this alignment is not done.

Required: 'constant'. We define the constant as a decimal value, with a preceding minus sign if necessary. We may also code a decimal point; if omitted, it is assumed to be to the right. The Assembler uses the decimal point in the conversion to float. We may further modify the value with an optional exponent En. For example, 3.1416 may be coded as .31416E1 (meaning 0.31416×10^1) or as 3141.6E–3 (meaning 3141.6×10^{-3}). The Assembler rounds and normalizes the constant if necessary. For an *unnormalized* constant, we may use a *scale modifier,* written as Sn. The n tells the Assembler how many hex digits to right-shift the fraction so that there are hex zeros to the left.

Figure 17-1 illustrates various definitions of floating-point constants. Note the alignment and the generated object code in each case. The first group defines single-precision or short form.

FLOATE1 simply defines a 4-byte DS aligned on a fullword boundary.

FLOATE2 and FLOATE3 define the same constant as positive and as negative.

FLOATE4 has a duplication factor of 3, causing definition of three identical constants.

FLOATE5 illustrates a multiple declaration: one statement defines three different constants. The third constant, 0, defines "true zero"—a zero fraction and characteristic.

FLOATE6, FLOATE7, and FLOATE8 depict the exponent modifier. Each case generates the same float constant.

```
                        6 *    --------------------------
                        7 *    DC    E SINGLE-PRECISION
                        8 *    --------------------------
003804                  9 FLOATE1  DS   E                DEFINE FULLWORD AREA
003808 427B7333        10 FLOATE2  DC   E'123.45'        POSITIVE VALUE
00380C C27B7333        11 FLOATE3  DC   E'-123.45'       NEGATIVE VALUE
003810 413243FE413243FE 12 FLOATE4 DC   3E'3.1416'       3 CONSTANTS
003818 413243FE
00381C 4164FDF4BD9D4952 13 FLOATE5 DC   E'6.312,-.00015,0' MULTIPLE DECLARATION
003824 00000000
003828 427B7333        14 FLOATE6  DC   E'123.45E0'      123.45 X 1    = 123.45
00382C 427B7333        15 FLOATE7  DC   E'1.2345E2'      1.2345 X 100 = 123.45
003830 427B7333        16 FLOATE8  DC   E'12345E-2'      12345  X .01 = 123.45
003834 450007B7        17 FLOATE9  DC   ES3'123.45'      UNNORMALIZED, USE OF SCALE
                                                                     MODIFIER
                       19 *    --------------------------
                       20 *    DC    D DOUBLE-PRECISION
                       21 *    --------------------------
003838                 22 FLOATD1  DS   0D               ALIGN ON DOUBLEWORD BOUNDARY
003838 427B733333333333 23 FLOATD2 DC   D'123.45'        POSITIVE DOUBLE-PRECISION
003840 475912BC00000000 24 FLOATD3 DC   D'93.4E6'        93,400,000
003848 450007B733333333 25 FLOATD4 DC   DS3'123.45'      UNNORMALIZED, USE OF SCALE
                                                                     MODIFIER
```

FIGURE 17-1 Floating-point declares in single and double-precision.

FLOATE9 uses a scale modifier to prevent normalization. The S3 causes the assembler to shift the fraction three positions to the right. The generated constant, 450007B7, is interpreted as

$$16^5 \times \left(\frac{7}{16^4} + \frac{11}{16^5} + \frac{7}{16^6} \right)$$

Note that compared to FLOATE6, this constant has lost some precision.

The second group defines double-precision or long form.

FLOATD1 is a DS with a zero duplication factor to force alignment on a doubleword boundary.

FLOATD2 and FLOATD3 define double-precision constants. FLOATD2 gives more precision than the same constant defined as short form in FLOATE2.

FLOATD4 uses a scale modifier and defines the same constant as FLOATE9.

Problems 17-5 and 17-6 should now be attempted.

FLOATING-POINT REGISTERS

From context it should be clear where "register" in this chapter means floating-point and where it means general register. The four floating-point registers (FPR's) numbered 0, 2, 4, and 6, are each a doubleword in length (8 bytes or 64 bits). The only valid references to FPR's are 0, 2, 4, and 6. The type of instruction determines that it is a floating-point and not a general register. For example, AR references two general registers, whereas ADR references two floating-point registers. A float operation may specify the use of the entire 64-bit register (double-precision) or the leftmost 32 bits (single-precision).

FLOATING-POINT INSTRUCTIONS

The floating-point instruction set, although less extensive, is similar to that for binary. The instructions are in RR and RX format, where R references a FPR and X references a storage address subject to the usual base and index register. These instructions permit data manipulation between registers and between registers and storage. Operations include load, store, add, subtract, compare, halve, multiply, and divide. The operations are named to describe their purpose. Consider the following three Load operations:

operation:	LE	LER	LTER
position:	12	123	1 23

Position-1 signifies the type of operation, such as L for load, A for add. Exceptions are LC, LN, LP, LT, and ST which require two letters.

Position-2 defines the length of the operation. E as in LE means single-precision, and D as in LD means double-precision. U as in AUR implies single-precision unnormalized, and W as in AWR implies double-precision unnormalized.

Position-3 for RX format is blank. For RR, the letter R indicates a register, such as LER and LTER.

LOAD INSTRUCTIONS. The Load instructions load floating-point values from storage into a register or between registers, similar to binary L and LR. The most common ones are:

NAME	OPERATION	OPERAND	
[symbol]	LE	R1,X2	or R1,D2(X2,B2)
	LD	R1,X2	or R1,D2(X2,B2)
	LER	R1,R2	
	LDR	R1,R2	

The rules are:

1. The operations load the floating-point number referenced by the operand-2 address (storage or register) into the operand-1 register without normalization.
2. For LE, operand-2 is an aligned fullword in storage; for LD, operand-2 is an aligned doubleword.

3. LE and LER, being single-precision, process only the leftmost 32 bits of the register; the right half is not affected.

4. These loads do not set the condition code.

Refer to Figure 17-2. In LOADE1, LE loads a short form constant called FLOATEP1 into register-2. In LOADE2, LER loads the contents of register-2 into register-4. Only the leftmost 32 bits of both operands engage in these operations—the rightmost 32 bits are undisturbed. In LOADD1, LD loads a long form constant called FLOATDP1 into register-0. In LOADD2, LDR loads the contents of register-0 into register-6. All 64 bits of both operands engage in these operations.

```
                      29 *      ---------------------------------
                      30 *      LE & LER   LOAD SINGLE-PRECISION
                      31 *      ---------------------------------
003850 7820 3066      32 LOADE1 LE    2,FLOATEP1        REG-2: 434D28F6
003854 3842           33 LOADE2 LER   4,2               REG-4: 434D28F6

                      35 *      ---------------------------------
                      36 *      LD & LDR   LOAD DOUBLE PRECISION
                      37 *      ---------------------------------
003856 6800 305E      38 LOADD1 LD    0,FLOATDP1        REG-0: C27B74BC 6A7EF9DB
00385A 2860           39 LOADD2 LDR   6,0               REG-6: C27B74BC 6A7EF9DB

00385C 00000000
003860 C27B74BC6A7EF9DB  41 FLOATDP1 DC   D'-123.456'
003868 434D28F6          42 FLOATEP1 DC   E'1234.56'
```

FIGURE 17-2 Floating-point load operations: LE, LER, LD, LDR.

SPECIAL LOAD INSTRUCTIONS. We may use certain load operations, for example, to reverse the sign or to set the condition code. (The binary correlates are LCR, LNR, LPR, and LTR.)

NAME	OPERATION	OPERAND	NAME	OPERATION	OPERAND
[symbol]	LCER	R1,R2	[symbol]	LPER	R1,R2
	LCDR	R1,R2		LPDR	R1,R2
	LNER	R1,R2		LTER	R1,R2
	LNDR	R1,R2		LTDR	R1,R2

These instructions are similar to the previous load operations. Each in addition sets the condition code: 0—zero fraction, 1—less than zero (except LPER and LPDR), 2—greater than zero (except LNER and LNDR).

LOAD COMPLEMENT—LCER and LCDR load the operand-2 register into operand-1 and reverse the sign bit: 0 becomes 1 and 1 becomes 0.

LOAD NEGATIVE—LNER and LNDR load the operand-2 register into operand-1 and set the sign bit to 1, for minus.

LOAD POSITIVE—LPER and LPDR load the operand-2 register into operand-1 and set the sign bit to 0, for positive.

LOAD AND TEST—LTER and LTDR load the operand-2 register into operand-1. These work the same as LER and LDR but in addition set the condition code.

STORE INSTRUCTIONS. STE and STD store the contents of a floating-point register into a storage address. (The binary correlates are STH and ST.) The rules are: (1) STE and STD store the contents of the operand-1 register in the operand-2 storage address without normalization; (2) STE stores the leftmost 32 bits of the register; the storage address must be an aligned fullword; (3) STD stores the entire 64 bits into an aligned doubleword address.

NAME	OPERATION	OPERAND
[symbol]	STE STD	R1,X2 or R1,D2(X2,B2) R1,X2 or R1,D2(X2,B2)

In Figure 17-3, LD loads a long form value into register-0. STE stores the leftmost 32 bits of register-0 in the fullword area, STORSING. STD stores the entire 64 bits of register-0 in the doubleword area, STORDOUB.

```
                    46  *    ----------------------------------
                    47  *         STE & STD   STORE FLOATING-POINT
                    48  *    ----------------------------------
00386C 6800 3076    49         LD    0,FLTD1          REG-0:      44392800 00000000
003870 7000 3086    50         STE   0,STORSING       STORSING:   44392800
003874 6000 307E    51         STD   0,STORDOUB       STORDOUB:   44392800 00000000

003878 44392800000000000 53 FLTD1   DC    D'146.32E2'  DOUBLEWORD CONSTANT
003880              54 STORDOUB DS    D                DOUBLEWORD AREA
003888              55 STORSING DS    E                FULLWORD  AREA
```

FIGURE 17-3 Floating-point store operations: STE and STD.

ADDITION AND SUBTRACTION. There are instructions for both normalized and unnormalized addition and subtraction. Subtraction inverts the sign of operand-2 and then adds the operands. The first step in add and subtract ensures that the characteristics of both operands are equal. If unequal, the field with the smaller characteristic is adjusted by shifting its fraction to the right and incrementing the characteristic by 1 until the characteristics are equal.

Example: simple addition of short form:

$$
\begin{array}{lll}
41\ 290000 & 41\ 290000 & \\
+40\ 120000 & -\ +41\ 012000 & \textit{shift right and add} \\
\hline
 & 41\ 2A2000 &
\end{array}
$$

Example: fraction overflow. If the fraction overflows because of addition, then the operation shifts the fraction right one hex digit, and increments the characteristic by 1. (If the characteristic overflows a program interrupt occurs.)

```
41     940000
41     760000
41    11A0000      fraction overflows,
42     11A000      shift fraction right, add 1 to characteristic
```

Example: guard digit and normalization. Normalized addition and subtraction normalize the result after the operation (post-normalization). Also, single-precision add and subtract maintain improved precision by means of a *"guard digit"*. When the fraction is shifted right, this guard digit saves the last digit shifted. The digit is restored during postnormalization.

```
42  0B2584        42  0B2584        guard digit
40  114256   =    42  001142(5)     shift right 2 digits
      Add:        42  0B36C6(5)
Normalize:        41  B36C65         shift left 1 digit
```

ADD AND SUBTRACT NORMALIZED.   The normalized add and subtract instructions are:

NAME	OPERATION	OPERAND		
[symbol]	AE	R1,X2	or	R1,D2(X2,B2)
	AD	R1,X2	or	R1,D2(X2,B2)
	AER	R1,R2		
	ADR	R1,R2		

NAME	OPERATION	OPERAND		
[symbol]	SE	R1,X2	or	R1,D2(X2,B2)
	SD	R1,X2	or	R1,D2(X2,B2)
	SER	R1,R2		
	SDR	R1,R2		

Each operation sets the condition code as follows: 0—zero fraction in the result, 1—fraction less than zero, 2—fraction greater than zero, 3—exponent overflow in the result.

ADD NORMALIZED.   AE, AD, AER, and ADR add the contents of operand-2 to operand-1, and normalize the result. The short form operations—AE and AER—process only the leftmost 32 bits of the register; the rightmost 32 bits are unaffected.

SUBTRACT NORMALIZED. SE, SD, SER, and SDR subtract the contents of operand-2 from operand-1 and normalize the result. The short form operations—SE and SER— process only the leftmost 32 bits of a register; the rightmost 32 bits are unaffected.

In Figure 17-4 ADDFLTE depicts single-precision add. A doubleword is loaded into register-2, and AE adds the left half of a doubleword to register-2. A third doubleword is loaded into register-4, and AER adds the left half of register-2 to register-4. The right half contents of the registers are undisturbed.

ADDFLTD is similar to ADDFLTE except that it uses double-precision. All 64 bits engage in the operations and the results (shown in comments) are more precise.

SUBFLTE is similar to ADDFLTE except that it performs single-precision subtraction. SUBFLTD is similar to SUBFLTE, but uses double-precision subtraction with more precise answers.

```
                          59  *      ------------------------------------------
                          60  *      AE & AER   ADD SINGLE-PRECISION NORMALIZED
                          61  *      ------------------------------------------
00388C  6820 30C6         62  ADDFLTE  LD   2,AMTFLT1      REG-2:  427B7333 33333333
003890  7A20 30CE         63           AE   2,AMTFLT2      REG-2:  429AB603 33333333
003894  6840 30D6         64           LD   4,AMTFLT3      REG-4:  435C0999 9999999A
003898  3A42              65           AER  4,2            REG-4:  4365B4F9 9999999A

                          67  *      ------------------------------------------
                          68  *      AD & ADR   ADD DOUBLE-PRECISION NORMALIZED
                          69  *      ------------------------------------------
00389A  6820 30C6         70  ADDFLTD  LD   2,AMTFLT1      REG-2:  427B7333 33333333
00389E  6A20 30CF         71           AD   2,AMTFLT2      REG-2:  429AB604 189374BC
0038A2  6840 30D6         72           LD   4,AMTFLT3      REG-4:  435C0999 9999999A
0038A6  2A42              73           ADR  4,2            REG-4:  4365B4F9 DB22D0E5

                          75  *      ------------------------------------------
                          76  *      SE & SER   SUBTRACT SINGLE-PRECISION NORMALIZED
                          77  *      ------------------------------------------
0038A8  6820 30C6         78  SUBFLTE  LD   2,AMTFLT1      REG-2:  427B7333 33333333
0038AC  7B20 30CF         79           SE   2,AMTFLT2      REG-2:  425C3063 33333333
0038B0  6840 30D6         80           LD   4,AMTFLT3      REG-4:  435C0999 9999999A
0038B4  3B42              81           SER  4,2            REG-4:  43564692 9999999A

                          83  *      ------------------------------------------
                          84  *      SD & SDR   SUBTRACT DOUBLE-PRECISION NORMALIZED
                          85  *      ------------------------------------------
0038B6  6820 30C6         86  SUBFLTD  LD   2,AMTFLT1      REG-2:  427B7333 33333333
0038BA  6B20 30CF         87           SD   2,AMTFLT2      REG-2:  425C3062 4DD2F1AA
0038BE  6840 30D6         88           LD   4,AMTFLT3      REG-4:  435C0999 9999999A
0038C2  2B42              89           SDR  4,2            REG-4:  43564693 74BC6A7F

0038C4  00000000
0038C8  427B733333333333  91  AMTFLT1  DC   D'123.45'      DOUBLEWORD
0038D0  421F42D0E5604189  92  AMTFLT2  DC   D'31.261'      DOUBLEWORD
0038D8  435C09999999999A  93  AMTFLT3  DC   D'1472.6'      DOUBLEWORD
```

FIGURE 17-4 Floating-point normalized add and subtract.

ADD AND SUBTRACT UNNORMALIZED. We may want to control precision by preventing normalization. Unnormalized operations are desirable, for example, in converting between floating-point and binary formats (illustrated in a later section). Unnormalized add and subtract set the condition code, but omit use of the guard digit and the postnormalization step.

NAME	OPER'N	OPERAND		
[symbol]	AU	R1,X2	or	R1,D2(X2,B2)
	AW	R1,X2	or	R1,D2(X2,B2)
	AUR	R1,R2		
	AWR	R1,R2		

NAME	OPER'N	OPERAND		
[symbol]	SU	R1,X2	or	R1,D2(X2,B2)
	SW	R1,X2	or	R1,D2(X2,B2)
	SUR	R1,R2		
	SWR	R1,R2		

In these operations, U stands for single-precision unnormalized and W (double-U) for double-precision. Examples in Figure 17-5 are similar to those just given for normalized add and subtract and should be compared.

ADDFLTU illustrates single-precision unnormalized addition. A doubleword is loaded into register-2. AU adds a short unnormalized constant to register-2. Another doubleword is loaded into register-4, and AUR adds the left half of register-2 to register-4. The right half of the registers are undisturbed and results are unnormalized. ADDFLTW is similar to ADDFLTU except that it uses double-precision and all 64 bits engage in the addition.

SUBFLTU is also similar to ADDFLTU except that short unnormalized subtract is performed. SUBFLTW is similar to SUBFLTU, with double-precision used. In this example, however, SWR shows a convenient way to clear a register to true zero—the characteristic and fraction are both set to zero.

COMPARE. The following operations compare two floating-point fields:

NAME	OPERATION	OPERAND		
[symbol]	CE	R1,X2	or	R1,D2(X2,B2)
	CD	R1,X2	or	R1,D2(X2,B2)
	CER	R1,R2		
	CDR	R1,R2		

```
                      97 *    -----------------------------------------------
                      98 *    AU & AUR   ADD SINGLE-PRECISION UNNORMALIZED
                      99 *    -----------------------------------------------
0038E0 6820 3116     100 ADDFLTU  LD    2,AMTFLU1           REG-2: 427B7333 33333333
0038E4 7E20 311F     101          AU    2,AMTFLU2           REG-2: 44009AB6 33333333
0038E8 6840 3126     102          LD    4,AMTFLU3           REG-4: 435C0999 9999999A
0038EC 3E42          103          AUR   4,2                 REG-4: 44065B4F 9999999A

                     105 *    -----------------------------------------------
                     106 *    AW & AWR   ADD DOUBLE-PRECISION UNNORMALIZED
                     107 *    -----------------------------------------------
0038EE 6820 3116     108 ADDFLTW  LD    2,AMTFLU1           REG 2: 427B7333 33333333
0038F2 6E20 311F     109          AW    2,AMTFLU2           REG-2: 44009AB6 04189375
0038F6 6840 3126     110          LD    4,AMTFLU3           REG-4: 435C0999 9999999A
0038FA 2E42          111          AWR   4,2                 REG-4: 44065B4F 9DB22D0E

                     113 *    -----------------------------------------------
                     114 *    SU & SUR   SUBTRACT SINGLE-PRECISION UNNORMALIZED
                     115 *    -----------------------------------------------
0038FC 6820 3116     116 SUBFLTU  LD    2,AMTFLU1           REG-2: 427B7333 33333333
003900 7F20 311F     117          SU    2,AMTFLU2           REG-2: 44005C30 33333333
003904 6840 3126     118          LD    4,AMTFLU3           REG-4: 435C0999 9999999A
003908 3F42          119          SUR   4,2                 REG-4: 44056469 9999999A

                     121 *    -----------------------------------------------
                     122 *    SW & SWR   SUBTRACT DOUBLE-PRECISION UNNORMALIZED
                     123 *    -----------------------------------------------
00390A 6820 3116     124 SUBFLTW  LD    2,AMTFLU1           REG-2: 427B7333 33333333
00390E 6F20 311F     125          SW    2,AMTFLU2           REG-2: 44005C30 624DD2F1
003912 2F44          126          SWR   4,4                 REG-4: 00000000 00000000

003914 00000000
003918 427B733333333333 128 AMTFLU1 DC  D'123.45'          DOUBLEWORD NORMALIZED
003920 44001F42D0E56042 129 AMTFLU2 DC  DS2'31.261'        DOUBLEWORD UNNORMALIZED
003928 435C099999999999A 130 AMTFLU3 DC D'1472.6'          DOUBLEWORD NORMALIZED
```

FIGURE 17-5   Floating-point unnormalized add and subtract.

The rules are:

1. The characteristics of the two operands are checked. The shorter one is incremented and its fraction shifted right, as for normalized subtract.
2. Operand-1 is compared algebraically to operand-2, including the sign, exponent, and fraction. However, if both fractions are zero, the result is equal regardless of sign and exponent.
3. CE and CER compare only the leftmost 32 bits.
4. For CE, operand-2 is an aligned fullword in storage. For CD, operand-2 is an aligned doubleword.
5. The condition is set for 0 (equal), 1 (low), and 2 (high).

In Figure 17-6 COMPE compares single-precision and COMPD compares double-precision.

HALVE.   The Halve instructions permit convenient division of an operand by two.

```
                    134 *    ------------------------------------
                    135 *    CE & CER   COMPARE SINGLE-PRECISION
                    136 *    ------------------------------------
003930 7820 314E    137 COMPE    LE   2,COMP1
003934 7920 3156    138          CE   2,COMP2            42787333 > 421F42D0
003938 7840 315E    139          LE   4,COMP3
00393C 3924         140          CER  2,4                42787333 < 435C0999

                    142 *    ------------------------------------
                    143 *    CD & CDR   COMPARE DOUBLE-PRECISION
                    144 *    ------------------------------------
00393E 6820 314F    145 COMPD    LD   2,COMP1
003942 6920 3156    146          CD   2,COMP2            42787333 33333333 >
003946 6840 315F    147          LD   4,COMP3                     421F42D0 E5604189
00394A 2924         148          CDR  2,4                42787333 33333333 <
                                                                  435C0999 9999999A
00394C 00000000
003950 42787333333333333 150 COMP1   DC   D'123.45'      DOUBLEWORD
003958 421F42D0E5604189  151 COMP2   DC   D'31.261'      DOUBLEWORD
003960 435C099999999999A 152 COMP3   DC   D'1472.6'      DOUBLEWORD
```

FIGURE 17-6   Floating-point compare operations.

NAME	OPERATION	OPERAND
[symbol]	HER HDR	R1,R2 R1,R2

The rules are:

1. Operand-2 references a register containing the dividend which is to be divided by two.
2. The operations move operand-2 to operand-1 and the fraction one bit to the right. The sign and characteristic are unaffected. Operand-2 is not changed.
3. HER references only the leftmost 32 bits.
4. The condition code is not set.
5. There is no normalization or test for zero fraction.

In Figure 17-7 a doubleword is loaded in register-6. HER shifts only the left 8 hex digits one bit to the right, and HDR shifts all 16 hex digits.

```
                    156 *    -------------------
                    157 *    HER & HDR   HALVE
                    158 *    -------------------
003968 6860 316F    159 HALVE    LD   6,AMTHALF      REG-6: 434D28F5 C28F5C29
00396C 3446         160          HER  4,6            REG-4: 4326947A

00396E 2426         162          HDR  2,6            REG-2: 4326947A E147AE14

003970 434D28F5C28F5C29  164 AMTHALF  DC   D'1234.56'      DOUBLEWORD
```

FIGURE 17-7   Floating-point halve operation.

MULTIPLICATION.   The following instructions multiply floating-point fields.

NAME	OPERATION	OPERAND
[symbol]	ME MD MER MDR	R1,X2 or R1,D2(X2,B2) R1,X2 or R1,D2(X2,B2) R1,R2 R1,R2

The multiply operation prenormalizes the field if necessary. Then it adds the characteristics and multiplies the fractions. The rules are:

1. The operand-1 register specifies the multiplicand.
2. Operand-2 references the multiplier, either a storage address (ME and MD) or a register (MER and MDR).
3. The operation normalizes the product, which replaces the multiplicand. Regardless of the operation, the product is a *double-precision value*.

    In Figure 17-8 MULTE depicts single-precision. A fullword multiplicand is loaded into register-2. Then ME multiplies the left half of register-2 by the fullword multiplier in storage. Although the fields are defined as doublewords, only the left half engages in the operations. Next, another fullword is loaded into register-4, and MER multiplies the contents of register-4 by register-2. The final product is in register-4. MULTD uses double-precision. All 16 hex digits participate and we gain a slightly more precise product.

```
                            168  *      ----------------------------------------
                            169  *      ME & MER   MULTIPLY SINGLE-PRECISION
                            170  *      ----------------------------------------
003978 7820 3196            171  MULTE    LE    2,MULTCAN1        REG-2: 4326D666
00397C 7C20 319E            172           ME    2,MULTPLER        REG-2: 445CB979
003980 7840 31A6            173           LE    4,MULTCAN2        REG-4: 441205B8
003984 3C42                 174           MER   4,2               REG-4: 476871CC

                            176  *      ----------------------------------------
                            177  *      MD & MDR   MULTIPLY DOUBLE-PRECISION
                            178  *      ----------------------------------------
003986 6820 3196            179  MULTD    LD    2,MULTCAN1        REG-2: 4326D666 66666666
00398A 6C20 319E            180           MD    2,MULTPLER        REG-2: 445CB97A E147AE13
00398E 6840 31A6            181           LD    4,MULTCAN2        REG-4: 441205B8 51EB851F
003992 2C42                 182           MDR   4,2               REG-4: 476871D0 639C0EBE

003994 00000000
003998 4326D66666666666     184  MULTCAN1 DC    D'621.4'          DOUBLEWORD
0039A0 4226333333333333     185  MULTPLER DC    D'38.2'           DOUBLEWORD
0039A8 441205B851EB851F     186  MULTCAN2 DC    D'4613.72'        DOUBLEWORD
```

FIGURE 17-8   Floating-point multiplication.

DIVISION.   The following instructions divide floating-point fields:

NAME	OPERATION	OPERAND	
[symbol]	DE	R1,X2	or R1,D2(X2,B2)
	DD	R1,X2	or R1,D2(X2,B2)
	DER	R1,R2	
	DDR	R1,R2	

The divide operation prenormalizes the fields if necessary. The rules are:

1. The operand-1 register specifies the dividend.
2. Operand-2 references the divisor, either a storage address (DE and DD) or a register (DER and DDR).
3. The operation normalizes the quotient, which replaces the dividend. For DE and DER the quotient is single-precision; for DD and DDR the quotient is double-precision.
4. There is no remainder.
5. A divisor containing a zero fraction causes a program interrupt.

In Figure 17-9, DIVIDE depicts single-precision. A fullword dividend is loaded into register-2. Then DE divides the left half of register-2 by the fullword divisor in storage. Next, another fullword is loaded into register-4, and DER divides the contents of register-4 by register-2. The final quotient is in register-4. DIVIDD uses double-precision. All 16 hex digits participate and we gain a slightly more precise quotient.

```
                        190 *       -----------------------------------
                        191 *       DE & DER   DIVIDE SINGLE-PRECISION
                        192 *       -----------------------------------
0039B0 7820 31CE        193 DIVIDE  LE    2,DIVIDND1         REG-2: 4326D666
0039B4 7D20 31D6        194         DE    2,DIVSOR           REG-2: 4210445B
0039B8 7840 31DF        195         LE    4,DIVIDND2         REG-4: 441205B8
0039BC 3D42             196         DER   4,2                REG-4: 4311B9FC

                        198 *       -----------------------------------
                        199 *       DD & DDR   DIVIDE DOUBLE-PRECISION
                        200 *       -----------------------------------
0039BE 6820 31CE        201 DIVIDD  LD    2,DIVIDND1         REG-2: 4326D666 66666666
0039C2 6D20 31D6        202         DD    2,DIVSOR           REG-2: 4210445B 24304055
0039C6 6840 31DF        203         LD    4,DIVIDND2         REG-4: 441205B8 51EB851F
0039CA 2D42             204         DDR   4,2                REG-4: 4311B9FC E537151B

0039CC 00000000
0039D0 4326D66666666666 206 DIVIDND1 DC   D'621.4'          DOUBLEWORD
0039D8 4226333333333333 207 DIVSOR   DC   D'38.2'           DOUBLEWORD
0039E0 441205B851EB851F 208 DIVIDND2 DC   D'4613.72'        DOUBLEWORD
```

FIGURE 17-9 Floating-point division.

CONVERSION FROM PACKED TO FLOAT

Although it is simple to define data in floating-point format, it is somewhat difficult to convert packed or binary data into float. The standard practice is to use CVB to convert packed to binary in a general register, and there create the floating-point number. Consider the decimal number 268,002. Converted to binary it is X'000416E2'. With the fraction to the right, the double-precision float value is 4E000000 000416E2. We may load this number into an FPR and normalize the fraction with a float operation.

Because negative binary numbers are in two's complement form, we must convert them to positive. For the packed number −268,002 the correct float value is CE000000 000416E2. Figure 17-10 gives the programming steps to convert −268,002 to normalized single-precision floating-point. When converted into binary in general register-8, −268,002 appears in two's complement as X'FFFBE91E'. But a floating-point fraction is stored in absolute form. Therefore we use LPR to adjust the binary number to its absolute value in register-10: X'000416E2'. Next, we load the characteristic X'4E' into register-9 and algebraically shift it left 32 bits into register-8. Now the sign bit of the original binary shift is left 32 bits into register-8. Now the sign bit of the original binary number is the leftmost bit of the characteristic, X'CE' or binary 1100 1110. With the characteristic loaded into register-9 and the fraction in register-10, the two registers are stored in a doubleword.

In order to normalize the floating-point field, we first clear the floating-point register and then add the double-precision value. The floating-point number now contains the correct characteristic and normalized fraction in single-precision: C5416E20.

```
003A30 7840 3262        233 FLOTPACK LE    4,FLOAT              FLT REG-4: C5416E20
003A34 3064             234          LPER  6,4                  FLT REG-6: 45416F20
003A36 7960 325F        235          CE    6,MAXVAL             IF EXCEEDS MAXIMUM,
003A3A 47B0 3266        236          BNL   B10PASS              THEN BYPASS
003A3E 6E40 3256        237          AW    4,ADJUST             FLT REG-4: 4E000000 FFFBE91E
003A42 6040 324F        238          STD   4,DOUBLE             STORE FLOAT DOUBLEWORD
003A46 5890 3252        239          L     9,DOUBLE+4           GEN REG-9: FFFBE91E BINARY
003A4A 4E90 324F        240          CVD   9,DOUBLE             DOUBLE:    -268,002 PACKED


003A50                  242 DOUBLE   DS    D                    DOUBLEWORD AREA
003A58 4E00000100000000 243 ADJUST   DC    X'4E00000100000000'  ADJUSTMENT FACTOR
003A60 48800000         244 MAXVAL   DC    E'2147483648'        MAXIMUM VALUE
003A64 C5416E20         245 FLOAT    DC    E'-268002'           FLOAT VALUE TO BE CONVERTED
```

FIGURE 17-10   Conversion of packed to floating-point format.

CONVERSION FROM FLOAT TO PACKED

Because of the great magnitude of floating-point numbers, we must be careful in converting to packed format. If the absolute floating-point value is greater than $2^{31}-1$ (or 2,147,483,647), then its binary equivalent will exceed the capacity of a 32-bit general register. We may make use of an unique short cut in the conversion. Consider a normalized float value, 45416E20. Its correct unnormalized hexadecimal value is X'416E2', or decimal 268,002. We can use an unnormalized add operation, AW, with an operand containing a characteristic of 4E to shift the radix point from the left to the right as follows:

$$
\begin{array}{r}
4E000000\ 00000000 = 4E000000\ 00000000 \\
+\ 45416E20\ 00000000 = \underline{4E000000\ 000416E2} \\
4E000000\ 000416E2
\end{array}
$$

The rightmost 8 hex digits now contain the correct binary value, which we can next convert to packed. If the float number had contained any significant digits to the right, the operation would have shifted them out.

If the float value is negative, we must convert it to two's complement in binary. A minor adjustment to the preceding routine gives correct results for either positive or negative values. The AW operation adds X'4E00000100000000'. The '1' in the fraction has no effect on positive numbers, but forces two's complement on negative. Assume a float value of C5416E20:

$$
\begin{array}{r}
4E000001\ 00000000 = 4E000001\ 00000000 \\
+\ C5416E20\ 00000000 = \underline{CE000000\ 000416E2} \\
CE000001\ FFFBE91E
\end{array}
$$

The rightmost 8 hex digits now contain the correct two's complement value which we can now translate to packed.

Figure 17-11 converts normalized single-precision float to packed format. The float value is the one just discussed, C5416E20, and is loaded into floating-point register-4. The first step checks that the value does not exceed $2^{31}-1$. Next, AW

			212	*			GENERAL REGISTERS:		
							8:	9:	10:
0039E8	F875	3216 320A	213	PACKFLOT	ZAP	DBLWD,AMTPK			
0039EE	4F80	3216	214		CVB	8,DBLWD	FFFBE91E		
0039F2	10A8		215		LPR	10,8	FFFBE91E		000416E2
0039F4	5890	322A	216		L	9,CHAR	FFFBE91E	4E000000	000416E2
0039F8	8F80	0020	217		SLDA	8,32	CE000000	00000000	000416E2
0039FC	1898		218		LR	9,8	CE000000	CE000000	000416E2
0039FE	909A	321E	219		STM	9,10,SAVEUNOR			
			220	*			FLOATING-POINT REG-4:		
003A02	2F44		221		SWR	4,4	00000000	00000000	
003A04	6A40	321E	222		AD	4,SAVEUNOR	C5416E20	00000000	
003A08	7040	3226	223		STE	4,SAVENORM			
003A0C	00000268002D		225	AMTPK	DC	PL6'-268002'	PACKED FIELD		
003A18			226	DBLWD	DS	D	DOUBLEWORD AREA		
003A20			227	SAVEUNOR	DS	D	DOUBLEWORD AREA		
003A28			228	SAVENORM	DS	F	FULLWORD AREA		
003A2C	4E000000		229	CHAR	DC	X'4E000000'	CHARACTERISTIC		

FIGURE 17-11   Conversion of floating-point to packed format.

unnormalizes the number. STD stores the entire 64-bit register in DOUBLE. Finally, the rightmost four bytes of DOUBLE are converted into packed.

Conversion rules can be much more complicated. The examples given processed only single-precision with integers—that is, the implicit decimal point for the number is to the right. The binary or decimal number may be mixed, that is with a binary or decimal point not to the right, such as 123.45. If so, then the integer portion must be separated from the fraction portion.

The remaining problems should now be attempted.

PROBLEMS

17-1. Under what circumstances should we consider the use of floating-point?

17-2. Why is the characteristic represented in excess-64 notation?

17-3. Convert the binary numbers (represented in hex) to normalized single-precision float: (a) X'1520'; (b) X'9A.312'; (c) X'6B3.F2'.

17-4. Convert the following decimal numbers to normalized single-precision float: (a) 32,768; (b) 79.396; (c) 244. 2166.

17-5. Code the decimal values in problem 17-4 as DC's and assemble them. Compare the assembler object code to your own calculations (remember the USING).

17-6. Code the decimal value 412.673 as below. Assemble and check the results: (a) Normalized single-precision; (b) Normalized double-precision; (c) With an exponent modifier E2 and double-precision; (d) Unnormalized double-precision with three hex digits preceding the first significant digit.

17-7. The slope m of a line joining two points (x_1, y_1) and (x_2, y_2) is $m = (y_2 - y_1)/(x_2 - x_1)$. Define four fields X1, Y1, X2, and Y2 containing single precision constants. Calculate and store the slope as float in M. Code, assemble, and take a storage dump of the results. *Warning:* What if $X2 = X1$?

17-8. Convert m in Problem 17-7 to character format so that it may be printed normally.

17-9. Figure 9-14 calculated finance charge rebates in binary format. Rewrite the routine using float declares and instructions. Take a dump of the registers and storage to check the answers.

APPENDIX A

HEXADECIMAL AND DECIMAL CONVERSION*

Hexadecimal and Decimal Integer Conversion Table

HALFWORD								HALFWORD							
BYTE				BYTE				BYTE				BYTE			
BITS: 0123		4567		0123		4567		0123		4567		0123		4567	
Hex	Decimal	Hex	Decimal	Hex	Decimal	Hex	Decimal	Hex	Decimal	Hex	Decimal	Hex	Decimal	Hex	Decimal
0	0	0	0	0	0	0	0	0	0	0	0	0	0	0	0
1	268,435,456	1	16,777,216	1	1,048,576	1	65,536	1	4,096	1	256	1	16	1	1
2	536,870,912	2	33,554,432	2	2,097,152	2	131,072	2	8,192	2	512	2	32	2	2
3	805,306,368	3	50,331,648	3	3,145,728	3	196,608	3	12,288	3	768	3	48	3	3
4	1,073,741,824	4	67,108,864	4	4,194,304	4	262,144	4	16,384	4	1,024	4	64	4	4
5	1,342,177,280	5	83,886,080	5	5,242,880	5	327,680	5	20,480	5	1,280	5	80	5	5
6	1,610,612,736	6	100,663,296	6	6,291,456	6	393,216	6	24,576	6	1,536	6	96	6	6
7	1,879,048,192	7	117,440,512	7	7,340,032	7	458,752	7	28,672	7	1,792	7	112	7	7
8	2,147,483,648	8	134,217,728	8	8,388,608	8	524,288	8	32,768	8	2,048	8	128	8	8
9	2,415,919,104	9	150,994,944	9	9,437,184	9	589,824	9	36,864	9	2,304	9	144	9	9
A	2,684,354,560	A	167,772,160	A	10,485,760	A	655,360	A	40,960	A	2,560	A	160	A	10
B	2,952,790,016	B	184,549,376	B	11,534,336	B	720,896	B	45,056	B	2,816	B	176	B	11
C	3,221,225,472	C	201,326,592	C	12,582,912	C	786,432	C	49,152	C	3,072	C	192	C	12
D	3,489,660,928	D	218,103,808	D	13,631,488	D	851,968	D	53,248	D	3,328	D	208	D	13
E	3,758,096,384	E	234,881,024	E	14,680,064	E	917,504	E	57,344	E	3,584	E	224	E	14
F	4,026,531,840	F	251,658,240	F	15,728,640	F	983,040	F	61,440	F	3,840	F	240	F	15
8		7		6		5		4		3		2		1	

*Reprinted by permission from *Introduction to IBM Data Processing Systems*, © 1960, 1967, by International Business Machines Corporation.

TO CONVERT HEXADECIMAL TO DECIMAL

1. Locate the column of decimal numbers corresponding to the left-most digit or letter of the hexadecimal; select from this column and record the number that corresponds to the position of the hexadecimal digit or letter.

2. Repeat step 1 for the next (second from the left) position.

3. Repeat step 1 for the units (third from the left) position.

4. Add the numbers selected from the table to form the decimal number.

EXAMPLE

Conversion of
Hexadecimal Value   D34

1. D	3328
2. 3	48
3. 4	4
4. Decimal	3380

TO CONVERT DECIMAL TO HEXADECIMAL

1. (a) Select from the table the highest decimal number that is equal to or less than the number to be converted.
   (b) Record the hexadecimal of the column containing the selected number.
   (c) Subtract the selected decimal from the number to be converted.

2. Using the remainder from step 1(c) repeat all of step 1 to develop the second position of the hexadecimal (and a remainder).

3. Using the remainder from step 2 repeat all of step 1 to develop the units position of the hexadecimal.

4. Combine terms to form the hexadecimal number.

EXAMPLE

Conversion of
Decimal Value   3380

1. D	−3328
	52
2. 3	−48
	4
3. 4	−4
4. Hexadecimal	D34

To convert integer numbers greater than the capacity of table, use the techniques below:

HEXADECIMAL TO DECIMAL

Successive cumulative multiplication from left to right, adding units position.

Example: $D34_{16} = 3380_{10}$

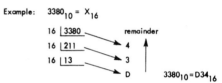

$$
\begin{array}{rl}
D = & 13 \\
 & \underline{\times 16} \\
 & 208 \\
3 = & \underline{+\ 3} \\
 & 211 \\
 & \underline{\times 16} \\
 & 3376 \\
4 = & \underline{+4} \\
 & 3380
\end{array}
$$

DECIMAL TO HEXADECIMAL

Divide and collect the remainder in reverse order.

Example: $3380_{10} = X_{16}$

$$
\begin{array}{rl}
16\ \underline{|\ 3380} & \text{remainder} \\
16\ \underline{|\ 211} & 4 \\
16\ \underline{|\ 13} & 3 \\
 & D
\end{array}
$$

$3380_{10} = D34_{16}$

POWERS OF 16 TABLE

Example: $268,435,456_{10} = (2.68435456 \times 10^8)_{10} = 1000\ 0000_{16} = (10^7)_{16}$

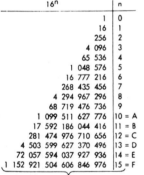

16^n	n
1	0
16	1
256	2
4 096	3
65 536	4
1 048 576	5
16 777 216	6
268 435 456	7
4 294 967 296	8
68 719 476 736	9
1 099 511 627 776	10 = A
17 592 186 044 416	11 = B
281 474 976 710 656	12 = C
4 503 599 627 370 496	13 = D
72 057 594 037 927 936	14 = E
1 152 921 504 606 846 976	15 = F

Decimal Values

APPENDIX B

PROGRAM INTERRUPTS BY CODE

A program interrupt occurs when the program attempts an operation that the CPU cannot execute. The following lists the various program interrupts, by code.

1. *Operation Exception.* The CPU has attempted to execute an invalid machine operation, such as hexadecimal zeros. Possible cause: (1) missing branch instruction—the program has entered a declarative area; (2) the instruction, such as a floating-point operation, is not installed on the computer; (3) during assembly, an invalid instruction has caused the Assembler to generate hexadecimal zeros in place of the machine code. For a 6-byte instruction such as MVC, the computer generates six bytes of hex zeros. At execute-time, the computer tries to execute the zero operation code, causing an operation exception. (Since the computer will attempt to execute two bytes at a time, some systems may generate three consecutive operation exceptions.); (4) see also the causes for an addressing exception.

2. *Privileged-Operation Exception.* An attempt has been made to execute a "privileged instruction" that only the Supervisor is permitted to execute. Possible causes: see Addressing and Operation exceptions. There are many possible causes, and it may be necessary to take a hexadecimal dump of the program to determine the contents of I/O areas and other declaratives to discover at what point during execution the error occurred.

3. *Execute Exception.* An attempt has been made to use the EX instruction on another EX instruction.

4. *Protection Exception.* Some computer models have a useful "storage protection" device that prevents the program from erroneously moving data into the Supervisor area (or into the areas of other programs under multiprogramming). Such attempts (for example, by MVC and ZAP) cause the computer to signal the error. Possible cause: (1) the program has erroneously loaded data into one of the program's base registers; (2) improper explicit use of a base register.

5. *Addressing Exception.* The program is attempting to reference an address that is outside available storage. Possible causes: (1) a branch to an address in a register containing an invalid value; (2) an instruction, such as MVC, has erroneously moved a data field into program instructions; (3) improper use of a base register, for example, loaded with a wrong value.

6. *Specification Exception.* There are many causes. (1) An attempt has been made to execute an instruction that does not begin in an even storage address (possibly an incorrect base register). (2) For packed operations, a multiplier or divisor exceeds eight bytes, or the length of the operand-1 field is less than or equal to that of operand-2. (3) For binary operations, the instruction violates the rule of integral boundaries—halfword, fullword, or doubleword (e.g., operand-2 of binary multiply (M) should align on a fullword location, and that of CVB should align on a doubleword location). Also, operand-1 of the operation (such as M or D) must specify an even-numbered register. (4) For floating-point, there may be a reference to a register other than 0, 2, 4, or 6, or failure to address on the proper single- or double-precision boundary.

7. *Data Exception.* An attempt has been made to perform arithmetic on an invalid packed field. Possible causes: (1) an input field contained blanks or other non-digits that pack invalidly; (2) failure to pack, or an improper pack; (3) improper use of relative addressing; (4) an MVC has erroneously destroyed a packed field; (5) the multiplicand field for an MP is too short; (6) improper explicit use of a base register.

8. *Fixed-Point-Overflow Exception.* A binary operation (add, subtract, shift) has caused the contents of a register to overflow, losing a leftmost significant digit. The maximum value in a register is, in decimal notation, +2,147,483,647.

9. *Fixed-Point-Divide Exception.* A binary divide (D or DR) or a CVB has generated a value that has exceeded the capacity of a register. Common cause for divide operations: dividing by a zero value. Remember that the maximum value that a register can contain, in decimal notation, is +2,147,483,647.

A. *Decimal-Overflow Exception.* The result of a decimal (packed) operation is too large for the receiving field. Solution: redefine the receiving field so that it can contain the largest possible value, or use another available, larger declarative.

B. *Decimal-Divide Exception.* The generated quotient/remainder for a DP is too large for the defined area. Possible cause: (1) failure to follow the rules of DP; (2) the divisor contains a zero value.

C. *Exponent-Overflow Exception.* A floating-point arithmetic operation has caused the exponent to overflow (exceed +63).

D. *Exponent-Underflow Exception.* A floating-point arithmetic operation has caused the exponent to underflow (less than −64).

E. *Significance Exception.* A floating-point add or subtract has caused a zero fraction. All significant digits are lost, and subsequent computations may be meaningless.

F. *Floating-Point-Divide Exception.* An attempt has been made to divide in floating-point using a zero divisor.

In each case, the system issues an error message, giving the type of program interrupt and the address where the interrupt occurred. Sometimes the programming error causes the program to enter a declarative area or some other invalid area outside the program. (The computer may even find some valid machine operation, such as X'3C', Multiply Float!) In debugging, we must determine *how* the program arrived at the invalid address. In many cases, a dump of the program's registers and storage area will be essential in tracing the cause of the error.

INVALID STATEMENT.   Another common error, although not a program interrupt, is one that the operating system generates: INVALID STATEMENT. The reason: the system is trying to read a job control statement that is invalid. Usually, this is a program data card—the program has gone to its end-of-file routine before all the data was read. Possible causes: (1) missing branch instruction causing the program to enter the EOF routine; (2) branching to the EOF routine, such as on an error condition, without flushing remaining input data.

APPENDIX C

360/370 INSTRUCTION SET

MACHINE INSTRUCTIONS

NAME	MNEMONIC	OP CODE	FORMAT	OPERANDS
Add (c)	AR	1A	RR	R1,R2
Add (c)	A	5A	RX	R1,D2(X2,B2)
Add Decimal (c)	AP	FA	SS	D1(L1,B1),D2(L2,B2)
Add Halfword (c)	AH	4A	RX	R1,D2(X2,B2)
Add Logical (c)	ALR	1E	RR	R1,R2
Add Logical (c)	AL	5E	RX	R1,D2(X2,B2)
AND (c)	NR	14	RR	R1,R2
AND (c)	N	54	RX	R1,D2(X2,B2)
AND (c)	NI	94	SI	D1(B1),I2
AND (c)	NC	D4	SS	D1(L,B1),D2(B2)
Branch and Link	BALR	05	RR	R1,R2
Branch and Link	BAL	45	RX	R1,D2(X2,B2)
Branch on Condition	BCR	07	RR	M1,R2
Branch on Condition	BC	47	RX	M1,D2(X2,B2)
Branch on Count	BCTR	06	RR	R1,R2
Branch on Count	BCT	46	RX	R1,D2(X2,B2)
Branch on Index High	BXH	86	RS	R1,R3,D2(B2)
Branch on Index Low or Equal	BXLE	87	RS	R1,R3,D2(B2)
Clear I/O (c,p)	CLRIO	9D01	S	D2(B2)
Compare (c)	CR	19	RR	R1,R2
Compare (c)	C	59	RX	R1,D2(X2,B2)
Compare and Swap (c)	CS	BA	RS	R1,R3,D2(B2)
Compare Decimal (c)	CP	F9	SS	D1(L1,B1),D2(L2,B2)
Compare Double and Swap (c)	CDS	BB	RS	R1,R3,D2(B2)
Compare Halfword (c)	CH	49	RX	R1,D2(X2,B2)
Compare Logical (c)	CLR	15	RR	R1,R2
Compare Logical (c)	CL	55	RX	R1,D2(X2,B2)
Compare Logical (c)	CLC	D5	SS	D1(L,B1),D2(B2)
Compare Logical (c)	CLI	95	SI	D1(B1),I2
Compare Logical Characters under Mask (c)	CLM	BD	RS	R1,M3,D2(B2)

MACHINE INSTRUCTIONS (Contd)

NAME	MNEMONIC	OP CODE	FORMAT	OPERANDS
Compare Logical Long (c)	CLCL	0F	RR	R1,R2
Convert to Binary	CVB	4F	RX	R1,D2(X2,B2)
Convert to Decimal	CVD	4E	RX	R1,D2(X2,B2)
Diagnose (p)		83		Model-dependent
Divide	DR	1D	RR	R1,R2
Divide	D	5D	RX	R1,D2(X2,B2)
Divide Decimal	DP	FD	SS	D1(L1,B1),D2(L2,B2)
Edit (c)	ED	DE	SS	D1(L,B1),D2(B2)
Edit and Mark (c)	EDMK	DF	SS	D1(L,B1),D2(B2)
Exclusive OR (c)	XR	17	RR	R1,R2
Exclusive OR (c)	X	57	RX	R1,D2(X2,B2)
Exclusive OR (c)	XI	97	SI	D1(B1),I2
Exclusive OR (c)	XC	D7	SS	D1(L,B1),D2(B2)
Execute	EX	44	RX	R1,D2(X2,B2)
Halt I/O (c,p)	HIO	9E00	S	D2(B2)
Halt Device (c,p)	HDV	9E01	S	D2(B2)
Insert Character	IC	43	RX	R1,D2(X2,B2)
Insert Characters under Mask (c)	ICM	BF	RS	R1,M3,D2(B2)
Insert PSW Key (p)	IPK	B20B	S	
Insert Storage Key (p)	ISK	09	RR	R1,R2
Load	LR	18	RR	R1,R2
Load	L	58	RX	R1,D2(X2,B2)
Load Address	LA	41	RX	R1,D2(X2,B2)
Load and Test (c)	LTR	12	RR	R1,R2
Load Complement (c)	LCR	13	RR	R1,R2
Load Control (p)	LCTL	B7	RS	R1,R3,D2(B2)
Load Halfword	LH	48	RX	R1,D2(X2,B2)
Load Multiple	LM	98	RS	R1,R3,D2(B2)
Load Negative (e)	LNR	11	RR	R1,R2
Load Positive (c)	LPR	10	RR	R1,R2
Load PSW (n,p)	LPSW	82	S	D2(B2)

MACHINE INSTRUCTIONS

NAME	MNEMONIC	OP CODE	FORMAT	OPERANDS
Load Real Address (c,p)	LRA	B1	RX	R1,D2(X2,B2)
Monitor Call	MC	AF	SI	D1(B1),I2
Move	MVI	92	SI	D1(B1),I2
Move	MVC	D2	SS	D1(L,B1),D2(B2)
Move Long (c)	MVCL	0E	RR	R1,R2
Move Numerics	MVN	D1	SS	D1(L,B1),D2(B2)
Move with Offset	MVO	F1	SS	D1(L1,B1),D2(L2,B2)
Move Zones	MVZ	D3	SS	D1(L,B1),D2(B2)
Multiply	MR	1C	RR	R1,R2
Multiply	M	5C	RX	R1,D2(X2,B2)
Multiply Decimal	MP	FC	SS	D1(L1,B1),D2(L2,B2)
Multiply Halfword	MH	4C	RX	R1,D2(X2,B2)
OR (c)	OR	16	RR	R1,R2
OR (c)	O	56	RX	R1,D2(X2,B2)
OR (c)	OI	96	SI	D1(B1),I2
OR (c)	OC	D6	SS	D1(L,B1),D2(B2)
Pack	PACK	F2	SS	D1(L1,B1),D2(L2,B2
Purge TLB (p)	PTLB	B20D	S	
Read Direct (p)	RDD	85	SI	D1(B1),I2
Reset Reference Bit (c,p)	RRB	B213	S	D2(B2)
Set Clock (c,p)	SCK	B204	S	D2(B2)
Set Clock Comparator (p)	SCKC	B206	S	D2(B2)
Set CPU Timer (p)	SPT	B208	S	D2(B2)
Set Prefix (p)	SPX	B210	S	D2(B2)
Set Program Mask (n)	SPM	04	RR	R1
Set PSW Key from Address (p)	SPKA	B20A	S	D2(B2)
Set Storage Key (p)	SSK	08	RR	R1,R2
Set System Mask (p)	SSM	80	S	D2(B2)
Shift and Round Decimal (c)	SRP	F0	SS	D1(L1,B1),D2(B2),I3
Shift Left Double (c)	SLDA	8F	RS	R1,D2(B2)
Shift Left Double Logical	SLDL	8D	RS	R1,D2(B2)
Shift Left Single (c)	SLA	8B	RS	R1,D2(B2)
Shift Left Single Logical	SLL	89	RS	R1,D2(B2)
Shift Right Double (c)	SRDA	8E	RS	R1,D2(B2)
Shift Right Double Logical	SRDL	8C	RS	R1,D2(B2)
Shift Right Single (c)	SRA	8A	RS	R1,D2(B2)
Shift Right Single Logical	SRL	88	RS	R1,D2(B2)
Signal Processor (c,p)	SIGP	AE	RS	R1,R3,D2(B2)
Start I/O (c,p)	SIO	9C00	S	D2(B2)
Start I/O Fast Release (c,p)	SIOF	9C01	S	D2(B2)
Store	ST	50	RX	R1,D2(X2,B2)
Store Channel ID (c,p)	STIDC	B203	S	D2(B2)
Store Character	STC	42	RX	R1,D2(X2,B2)
Store Characters under Mask	STCM	BE	RS	R1,M3,D2(B2)

MACHINE INSTRUCTIONS (Contd)

NAME	MNEMONIC	OP CODE	FORMAT	OPERANDS
Store Clock (c)	STCK	B205	S	D2(B2)
Store Clock Comparator (p)	STCKC	B207	S	D2(B2)
Store Control (p)	STCTL	B6	RS	R1,R3,D2(B2)
Store CPU Address (p)	STAP	B212	S	D2(B2)
Store CPU ID (p)	STIDP	B202	S	D2(B2)
Store CPU Timer (p)	STPT	B209	S	D2(B2)
Store Halfword	STH	40	RX	R1,D2(X2,B2)
Store Multiple	STM	90	RS	R1,R3,D2(B2)
Store Prefix (p)	STPX	B211	S	D2(B2)
Store Then AND System Mask (p)	STNSM	AC	SI	D1(B1),I2
Store Then OR System Mask (p)	STOSM	AD	SI	D1(B1),I2
Subtract (c)	SR	1B	RR	R1,R2
Subtract (c)	S	5B	RX	R1,D2(X2,B2)
Subtract Decimal (c)	SP	FB	SS	D1(L1,B1),D2(L2,B2)
Subtract Halfword (c)	SH	4B	RX	R1,D2(X2,B2)
Subtract Logical (c)	SLR	1F	RR	R1,R2
Subtract Logical (c)	SL	5F	RX	R1,D2(X2,B2)
Supervisor Call	SVC	0A	RR	I
Test and Set (c)	TS	93	S	D2(B2)
Test Channel (c,p)	TCH	9F00	S	D2(B2)
Test I/O (c,p)	TIO	9D00	S	D2(B2)
Test under Mask (c)	TM	91	SI	D1(B1),I2
Translate	TR	DC	SS	D1(L,B1),D2(B2)
Translate and Test (c)	TRT	DD	SS	D1(L,B1),D2(B2)
Unpack	UNPK	F3	SS	D1(L1,B1),D2(L2,B2)
Write Direct (p)	WRD	84	SI	D1(B1),I2
Zero and Add Decimal (c)	ZAP	F8	SS	D1(L1,B1),D2(L2,B2)

Floating-Point Instructions

NAME	MNEMONIC	OP CODE	FORMAT	OPERANDS
Add Normalized, Extended (c,x)	AXR	36	RR	R1,R2
Add Normalized, Long (c)	ADR	2A	RR	R1,R2
Add Normalized, Long (c)	AD	6A	RX	R1,D2(X2,B2)
Add Normalized, Short (c)	AER	3A	RR	R1,R2
Add Normalized, Short (c)	AE	7A	RX	R1,D2(X2,B2)
Add Unnormalized, Long (c)	AWR	2E	RR	R1,R2
Add Unnormalized, Long (c)	AW	6E	RX	R1,D2(X2,B2)
Add Unnormalized, Short (c)	AUR	3E	RR	R1,R2
Add Unnormalized, Short (c)	AU	7E	RX	R1,D2(X2,B2)

c. Condition code is set.
n. New condition code is loaded.
p. Privileged instruction.
x. Extended precision floating-point.

EXTENDED MNEMONIC INSTRUCTIONS†

Use	Extended Code* (RX or RR)	Meaning	Machine Instr. (RX or RR)
General	B or BR	Unconditional Branch	BC or BCR 15,
	NOP or NOPR	No Operation	BC or BCR 0,
After	BH or *BHR*	Branch on A High	BC or BCR 2,
Compare	BL or *BLR*	Branch on A Low	BC or BCR 4,
Instructions	BE or *BER*	Branch on A Equal B	BC or BCR 8,
(A:B)	BNH or *BNHR*	Branch on A Not High	BC or BCR 13,
	BNL or *BNLR*	Branch on A Not Low	BC or BCR 11,
	BNE or *BNER*	Branch on A Not Equal B	BC or BCR 7,
After	BO or *BOR*	Branch on Overflow	BC or BCR 1,
Arithmetic	BP or *BPR*	Branch on Plus	BC or BCR 2,
Instructions	BM or *BMR*	Branch on Minus	BC or BCR 4,
	BNP or *BNPR*	Branch on Not Plus	BC or BCR 13,
	BNM or *BNMR*	Branch on Not Minus	BC or BCR 11,
	BNZ or *BNZR*	Branch on Not Zero	BC or BCR 7,
	BZ or *BZR*	Branch on Zero	BC or BCR 8,
After Test	BO or *BOR*	Branch if Ones	BC or BCR 1,
under Mask	BM or *BMR*	Branch if Mixed	BC or BCR 4,
Instruction	BZ or *BZR*	Branch if Zeros	BC or BCR 8,
	BNO or *BNOR*	Branch if Not Ones	BC or BCR 14,

*Second operand not shown; in all cases it is D2(X2,B2) for RX format or R2 for RR format.

†For OS/VS and DOS/VS; source: GC33-4010.

APPENDIX D

DOS AND OS JOB CONTROL

DOS JOB CONTROL

Figure D-1 illustrates an example of conventional job control to assemble and execute a program under the Disk Operating System.

```
// JOB        job-name                 Job-name may be 1–8 characters.
// OPTION DECK,DUMP,LIST,LOG,XREF      DECK: Punch an assembled object deck (or NODECK).
                                       DUMP: Print contents of storage on abnormal
                                              execute error (or NODUMP).
                                       LIST: List the assembled program (or NOLIST).
                                       LOG: Print the job control cards (or NOLOG).
                                       XREF: Print a cross-reference of symbolic names
                                              after the assembly (or NOXREF).
   ACTION MAP                          Print a map of the "link-edited" program (NOMAP).
// EXEC ASSEMBLY                       Load Assembler program into storage, begin assembly.
     ·
     ·    (source program here)
     ·
/*                                     Denotes end of assembly.
// EXEC LNKEDT                         Perform "link-edit" — include input/output routines.
// EXEC                                Load assembled program into storage, begin execution.
     ·
     ·    (test data here)
/*                                     Denotes end of data.
/&                                     Denotes end of job, return control to Supervisor.
```

FIGURE D-1   Conventional DOS job control.

384

Larger DOS systems provide for cataloguing commonly-used job control on disk, in the "Procedure Library". The preceding example of job control could be catalogued, for example, to provide for automatic assembly, link-edit and execute, through the use of only a few job statements, as in Figure D-2.

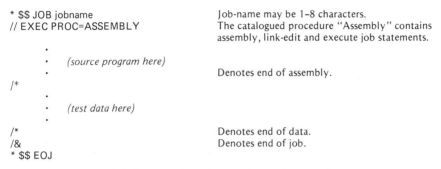

```
* $$ JOB jobname              Job-name may be 1–8 characters.
// EXEC PROC=ASSEMBLY         The catalogued procedure "Assembly" contains
                              assembly, link-edit and execute job statements.
      .
      .   (source program here)
      .                       Denotes end of assembly.
/*
      .
      .   (test data here)
      .
/*                            Denotes end of data.
/&                            Denotes end of job.
* $$ EOJ
```

FIGURE D-2   DOS job control under catalogued procedure.

DOS JOB CONTROL FOR MAGNETIC TAPE

We use the same job control cards for magnetic tape as for card and printer programs. However, tape files require additional information to provide greater control over the file. Under DOS, two additional job cards are LBLTYP and TLBL.

// LBLTYP TAPE precedes // EXEC LNKEDT, and informs the Linkage Editor to reserve 80 bytes ahead of our program for processing tape file labels. If our program normally loads in location X'3800', with LBLTYP it will load in X'3850'. TLBL follows // EXEC LNKEDT and provides details of our file to IOCS.

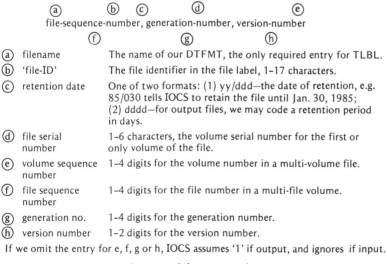

// TLBL filename, 'file-ID', date, file-serial-number, volume-sequence-number,
        (a)   (b) (c)   (d)   (e)
        file-sequence-number, generation-number, version-number
                (f)   (g)   (h)

(a)	filename	The name of our DTFMT, the only required entry for TLBL.
(b)	'file-ID'	The file identifier in the file label, 1–17 characters.
(c)	retention date	One of two formats: (1) yy/ddd—the date of retention, e.g. 85/030 tells IOCS to retain the file until Jan. 30, 1985; (2) dddd—for output files, we may code a retention period in days.
(d)	file serial number	1–6 characters, the volume serial number for the first or only volume of the file.
(e)	volume sequence number	1–4 digits for the volume number in a multi-volume file.
(f)	file sequence number	1–4 digits for the file number in a multi-file volume.
(g)	generation no.	1–4 digits for the generation number.
(h)	version number	1–2 digits for the version number.

If we omit the entry for e, f, g or h, IOCS assumes '1' if output, and ignores if input.

FIGURE D-3   DOS job control for magnetic tape.

DOS JOB CONTROL FOR DIRECT ACCESS STORAGE DEVICES

Each extent for the file requires two job control cards, DLBL and EXTENT, equivalent to the magnetic tape TLBL card (a file may be stored on more than one extent).

// DLBL filename, 'file-ID', date, codes
       ⓐ   ⓑ   ⓒ   ⓓ

ⓐ	filename	The name of our DTFSD, 1–7 characters.
ⓑ	'file-ID'	Our file-ID (within apostrophes), 1–44 characters. This is the first field of the format-1 label. We can code file-ID and optionally generation and version number. If we omit this entry, IOCS uses the filename.
ⓒ	retention date	One of two formats: (1) dddd = retention period in days; and (2) yy/ddd = the date of retention, e.g., 85/030 means retain file until January 30, 1985. If we omit this entry, IOCS assumes 7 days.
ⓓ	codes	The type of file label: SD—Sequential Disk; ISC—Index Sequential Create; ISE—Index Sequential Extend; DA—Direct Access. If we omit this entry, IOCS assumes SD.

// EXTENT symbolic-unit, serial-no., type, sequence-no., relative-track,
             ⓐ   ⓑ   ⓒ   ⓓ   ⓔ

       number of tracks, split-cylinder track
             ⓕ   ⓖ

ⓐ	symbolic unit	The symbolic unit SYSnnn for the file. If we omit this entry, IOCS assumes the unit from the preceding EXTENT, if any.
ⓑ	serial number	The volume serial number for the volume. If we omit this entry, IOCS uses the number from the preceding EXTENT, if any.
ⓒ	type	The type of extent. If omitted, IOCS assumes type 1. 1—Data area with no split cylinder; 2—Independent overflow area for IS; 4—Index area for IS; 8—Data area, split cylinder.
ⓓ	sequence number	The sequence number (0–255) of this extent in a multi-extent file. Not required for SD and DA, but if used the extent begins with 0. For IS with a master index, the number begins with 0; otherwise IS files begin with extent 1.
ⓔ	relative track	1–5 digits to indicate the sequential track number, relative to 0, where the extent begins. The formula to calculate the relative track is: RT = tracks per cylinder × cyl. no + track no. Example for a 2311 (10 tracks/cylinder), on cylinder-3, track-4: RT = (10 × 3) + 4 = 34.
ⓕ	number of tracks	1–5 digits to indicate the number of tracks allocated for the file on this extent.
ⓖ	split cylinder track	Digits 0–19 to signify the upper track number for split cylinders in SD files. (There may be more than one SD file within a cylinder.)

Note: the LBLTYP job control entry used for tape is also required for *non-sequential* disk. For example, if there are two non-sequential disk files in the program, the entry is // LBLTYP NSD(2).

FIGURE D-4   DOS job control for DASD.

OS JOB CONTROL

There are different versions of OS job control language. The following illustrates one version, providing for assembly, link-edit, and execution of test data. The program uses a card and a printer file, both of which require a DD (Data Definition) job card.

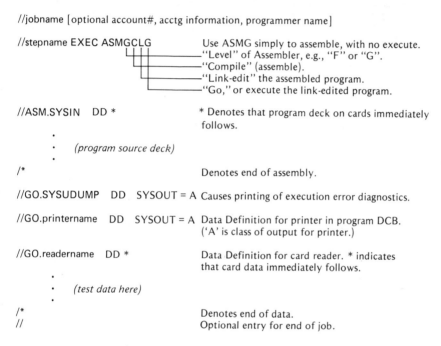

//jobname [optional account#, acctg information, programmer name]

//stepname EXEC ASMGCLG   Use ASMG simply to assemble, with no execute.
                                 "Level" of Assembler, e.g., "F" or "G".
                                 "Compile" (assemble).
                                 "Link-edit" the assembled program.
                                 "Go," or execute the link-edited program.

//ASM.SYSIN   DD *   * Denotes that program deck on cards immediately
                                 follows.

   .
   .   (program source deck)
   .

/*   Denotes end of assembly.

//GO.SYSUDUMP   DD   SYSOUT = A Causes printing of execution error diagnostics.

//GO.printername   DD   SYSOUT = A Data Definition for printer in program DCB.
                                 ('A' is class of output for printer.)

//GO.readername   DD *   Data Definition for card reader. * indicates
                                 that card data immediately follows.

   .
   .   (test data here)
   .

/*   Denotes end of data.
//   Optional entry for end of job.

FIGURE D-5   Simple OS job control.

The use of OS job control for magnetic tape and disk is explained along with the program examples.

APPENDIX E

SPECIAL MACROS: INIT, PUTPR, DEFCD, DEFPR, EOJ

Included in this appendix are the special macros used at the beginning of this text: INIT, PUTPR, DEFCD, and DEFPR. The macros are simple to implement and to use, and anyone is free to catalogue them. Beginners often have trouble coding the regular full macros, making punctuation and spelling errors and omitting entries. The use of macros such as the ones in this appendix can avert a lot of initial coding mistakes and can free the beginner to concentrate on programming logic.

The INIT macro (used to establish base register addressability) requires versions for both DOS and OS (Figure E-1 and E-2). A further refinement (recommended) could include the DOS STXIT or OS SPIE macro for error recovery.

PUTPR (Figure E-3) generates two instructions, of the form:

```
MVI   PRINT,X'nn'     Insert control character
PUT   PRTR,PRINT      Print line
```

If the control character supplied is invalid, the macro-instruction generates write/ space one line.

```
          MACRO
&INITZE   INIT
&INITZE   START  X'DA078'
          BALR   3,0                       LOAD BASE REGISTER 3
          USING  *,3,4,5                   ASSIGN BASE REGS 3,4 & 5
          LA     5,2048                    LOAD X'800' (1/2 OF X'1000')
          LA     4,2048(3,5)               LOAD BASE REG 4
          LA     5,2048(4,5)               LOAD BASE REG 5
          MEND
```

FIGURE E-1

```
          MACRO
&INITZE   INIT
&INITZE   CSECT
          SAVE   (14,12)                   SAVE REGISTERS FOR SUPERVISOR
          BALR   3,0                       LOAD BASE REGISTER 3
          USING  *,3,4,5                   ASSIGN BASE REGS 3,4 & 5
          ST     13,SAVEAREA+4             SAVE ADDRESSES FOR RETURN
          LA     13,SAVEAREA               *    TO SUPERVISOR
          LA     5,2048                    LOAD X'800' (1/2 OF X'1000')
          LA     4,2048(3,5)               LOAD BASE REG 4
          LA     5,2048(4,5)               LOAD BASE REG 5
          B      SAVEAREA+18*4
          SPACE
SAVEAREA  DC     18F'0'                    REG. SAVEAREA FOR INTERRUPTS
          MEND
```

FIGURE E-2

```
          MACRO
&WRITE    PUTPR  &FILE,&PRAREA,&CTLCHR
          LCLC   &CTL
.*
.VALAREA  AIF    ('&CTLCHR' NE 'WSP1').NEXT1     PRINT & SPACE 1?
&CTL      SETC   'X''09'''
          AGO    .NEXT9
.*
.NEXT1    AIF    ('&CTLCHR' NE 'WSP2').NEXT2     PRINT & SPACE 2?
&CTL      SETC   'X''11'''
          AGO    .NEXT9
.*
.NEXT2    AIF    ('&CTLCHR' NE 'WSP3').NEXT3     PRINT & SPACE 3?
&CTL      SETC   'X''19'''
          AGO    .NEXT9
.*
.NEXT3    AIF    ('&CTLCHR' NE 'SP1').NEXT4      SPACE 1, NO PRINT?
&CTL      SETC   'X''0B'''
          AGO    .NEXT9
.*
.NEXT4    AIF    ('&CTLCHR' NE 'SP2').NEXT5      SPACE 2, NO PRINT?
&CTL      SETC   'X''13'''
          AGO    .NEXT9
.*
.NEXT5    AIF    ('&CTLCHR' NE 'SP3').NEXT6      SPACE 3, NO PRINT?
&CTL      SETC   'X''1B'''
          AGO    .NEXT9
.*
.NEXT6    AIF    ('&CTLCHR' NE 'SK1').NEXT7      SKIP TO NEW PAGE?
&CTL      SETC   'X''8B'''
          AGO    .NEXT9
.*
.NEXT7    AIF    ('&CTLCHR' NE 'WSP0').NEXT8     PRINT & SPACE 0?
&CTL      SETC   'X''01'''
          AGO    .NEXT9
.*
.NEXT8    MNOTE  1,'INVALID PRINT CONTROL - DEFAULT TO WSP1'
&CTL      SETC   'X''09'''
.*
.NEXT9    ANOP
&WRITE    MVI    &PRAREA,&CTL              MOVE CTL CHAR TO PRINT
          PUT    &FILE,&PRAREA            *    & PRINT
.NEXT10   ANOP
          MEND
```

FIGURE E-3

389

DEFCD and DEFPR define the card reader and the printer respectively, and assume a workarea for PUT and use of IBM machine code rather than the ASA control characters. DEFCD checks the validity of the supplied end-of-file address, a useful test. The DOS versions (Figure E-4 and E-5) generate DTFCD and DTFPR, and the OS versions (Figure E-6 and E-7) generate DCB's. The particular entries may vary slightly by installation.

```
                MACRO
      &CDFILE   DEFCD &ECF
                AIF   (T'&EOF EQ 'I' OR T'&EOF EQ 'M').A10  EOF ADDRESS VALID?
                MNOTE 1,'EOF ADDRESS NOT DEFINED'   NO -
      &EOF      CLOSE &CDFILE                 *     GENERATE EOF ROUTINE
                EOJ
      .A10      ANOP
      &CDFILE   DTFCD BLKSIZE=80,                   DEFINE CARD FILE         +
                      DEVADDR=SYSIPT,                                        +
                      DEVICE=1442,                                           +
                      EOFADDR=&EOF,                                          +
                      IOAREA1=CDBUFF1,                                       +
                      IOAREA2=CDBUFF2,                                       +
                      TYPEFLE=INPUT,                                         +
                      WORKA=YES
                SPACE
      CDBUFF1   DC    CL80' '                       CARD BUFFER-1
      CDBUFF2   DC    CL80' '                       CARD BUFFER-2
                MEND
```

FIGURE E-4

```
                MACRO
      &PRFILE   DEFPR
      &PRFILE   DTFPR BLKSIZE=133,                  DEFINE PRINTER FILE      +
                      CTLCHR=YES,                                            +
                      DEVADDR=SYSLST,                                        +
                      DEVICE=1403,                                           +
                      IOAREA1=PRBUFF1,                                       +
                      IOAREA2=PRBUFF2,                                       +
                      WORKA=YES
                SPACE
      PRBUFF1   DC    CL133' '                      PRINT BUFFER-1
      PRBUFF2   DC    CL133' '                      PRINT BUFFER-2
                SPACE
                MEND
```

FIGURE E-5

```
                MACRO
      &CDFILE   DEFCD &EOF
                AIF   (T'&EOF EQ 'I' OR T'&EOF EQ 'M').A10  EOF ADDRESS VALID?
                MNOTE 1,'EOF ADDRESS NOT DEFINED'   NO -
      &EOF      CLOSE &CDFILE                 *     GENERATE EOF ROUTINE
                EOJ
      .A10      ANOP
      &CDFILE   DCB   DDNAME=SYSIN,                 DEFINE CARD FILE         +
                      DEVD=CA,                                               +
                      DSORG=PS,                                              +
                      EODAD=&EOF,                                            +
                      MACRF=(GM)
                MEND
```

FIGURE E-6

```
            MACRO
 &PRFILE   DEFPR
 &PRFILE   DCB    DDNAME=SYSPRINT,                                    +
                  DEVD=DA,                                            +
                  DSORG=PS,                                           +
                  RECFM=FBSM,                                         +
                  MACRF=(PM)
 SYSPRINT EQU   &PRFILE
           ENTRY SYSPRINT
           MEND
```

FIGURE E-7

DOS already has a simple EOJ macro. The one included here (Figure E-8) is for OS, to generate the load savearea and return, to tie in with the OS INIT macro.

```
            MACRO
 &LABEL    EOJ
 *         DOS COMPATIBLE EXIT ROUTINE FOR OS      G. KIDD
 &LABEL    L      13,SAVEAREA+4             END-OF-JOB,  RETURN
           RETURN (14,12)                   *     TO SUPERVISOR
           MEND
```

FIGURE E-8

INDEX